Understanding GCSE Geography

Ann Bowen

John Pallister

Heinemann Educational Publishers
Halley Court, Jordan Hill, Oxford OX2 8EJ
A division of Reed Educational and Professional
Publishing Ltd

Heinemann is a registered trade mark of
Reed Educational and Professional Publishing Ltd

OXFORD   MELBOURNE   AUCKLAND
JOHANNESBURG   BLANTYRE   GABORONE
IBADAN   PORTSMOUTH NH (USA)   CHICAGO

Text © Ann Bowen, John Pallister

First published 1999

02 01 00 99
10 9 8 7 6 5 4 3 2 1

British Library Cataloguing in Publication Data

A catalogue record for this book is available from the British Library

ISBN 0 435 35178 8

Typeset and designed by Oxford Designers & Illustrators, Oxford

Printed and bound in Spain by Mateu Cromo, Spain

Acknowledgements
The publishers would like to thank the following for permission to reproduce copyright material.

Photographs
A.P.S. (UK) (Fig. 2, p. 73); Ace Photo Agency (p. 137 [middle]); Aerofilms (Fig. 1, p. 26), (Figs 3 and 4, p. 70), (p. 123), (Fig. 2, p. 186); Apex Photo Agency (Fig. 3, p. 62); Ardea (Fig. 1, p. 92), (Fig. 5, p. 149); Associated Press (p. 5), (Fig. 2, p. 14); Collections/Paul Watts (Fig. 2, p. 20), Collections/Iain McGowan (Fig. 2, p. 26), Collections/Robin Weaver (Fig. 5, p. 29), Collections/Michael Allen (Fig. 2, p. 68), Collections (Fig. 4, p. 85), Collections/Hamish Williamson (Fig. 5, p. 135), Collections (Fig. 4, p. 147), Collections/John D Beldon (Fig. 4, p. 153), Collections/Mike Kipling (Fig. 5, p. 169), Collections (Fig. 1, p. 170); Colorific/Ray Nelson (Fig. 5, p. 79); EOSAT (Fig. 1, p. 96); FLPA/Tony Wharton (Fig. 4, p. 9), (Fig. 6, p. 18), FLPA (Fig. 5, p. 111), (Fig. 2, p. 157); G.S.F. (Fig. 3, p. 93); Ian Hay (Fig. 6, p. 135); Jim Gibson (Fig. 2, p. 43); Middle East Pictures/Christine Osborne (Fig. 4, p. 143); Network Photographers/Peter Jordan (Fig. 3, p. 207), (Fig. , p. 208); Oxfam/Badal (Fig. 4, p. 227); PA News/John Giles (p. 61); Panos/Chris Towers (p. 101 [bottom left]), Panos/Jeremy Horner (p. 101 [top right]), Panos/Jean Leo Dugust (Fig. 4, p. 115), Panos/Howard Davies (Fig. 2, p. 116), Panos (Fig. 5, p. 119), Panos/Daniel O'Leary (Fig. 6, p. 163), Panos (Fig. 1, p. 166), Panos/Jeremy Hartley (Fig. 3, p. 227); Philip Wolmuth (Fig. 2, p. 224); Planet Earth/Andre Bartschi (Fig. 2, p. 36); Popperfoto (Fig. 4, p .17), (Fig. 1, p. 46); Robert Harding (Fig. 1, p. 20), Robert Harding/M Black (Fig. 3, p. 23), (Fig. 2, p. 34), Robert Harding/Roy Rainford (Fig. 3, p. 35), Robert Harding (Fig. 2 [left], p. 38), Robert Harding/Adam Woolfit (Fig. 1, p. 132), Robert Harding (Fig. 4, p. 149), Robert Harding/JHC Wilson (Fig. 3, p. 162); Roger D Smith (p. 165); Roger Scruton (Fig. 1, p. 68), (Fig. 2, p. 70), (p. 136 [right]); Science Photo Library (Fig. 2 [right], p. 38); South American Pictures (Fig. 3, p. 97), South American Pictures/Tony Morrison (Fig. 1, p. 140), (Fig. 2, p. 142); Still Pictures (p89), Still Pictures/Tantyo Bangun (Fig. 1, p. 98), Still Pictures/Mark Edwards (Fig 4, p. 105), (Fig. 2, p. 114), (Fig. 2, p. 159) Still Pictures/Gerard and Margi Moss (Fig. 5, p. 105), Still Pictures/Hartmut Schwarzbah (Fig. 2, p. 122), Still Pictures/Martin Wright (Fig. 6, p. 144), Still Pictures/Ron Giling (Fig. 1, p. 160), Still Pictures/Jorgen Schytte (Figs 2 and 3, p. 164); Sylvia Pitcher (Fig. 3, p. 47); Tony Stone/James Balog (p. 7); Trip/ H Rogers (Fig. 6, p. 153); University of Dundee (Fig. 2, p. 83), (Fig. 2, p. 85); All other photographs are the copyright of the authors, Ann Bowen and John Pallister

Maps, diagrams and extracts
BP Statistical Review of World Energy 1996, (Fig. 1, p. 190); Bruce V (ed), Longman Geography for GCSE, (Fig1, p. 102), (Fig. 4, p. 162); Carr, Patterns, Process and Change in Human Geography, Macmillan, (Fig. 1, p. 120); Dobson & Virgo, Elements of Geography, Hodder & Stoughton, (Fig. 1, p. 8); Financial Times, (Fig. 1, p. 184), (Fig. 5, p. 223); Galbraith & Wigand, An Introduction to Geomorphology, OUP, (Fig. 4, p. 13); GeoActive, Stanley Thornes Ltd, (Unit 68: Fig. 5, p. 155), (Unit 164: Fig. 4, p. 161); Kidron & Segal, The State of the World Atlas, Myriad Editions Ltd, (Fig. 1, p. 106), (Figs 2 and 3, p. 118); Knapp, Ross & McRae, Challenge of the Human Environment, Longman, (Fig. 1, p. 114); LDNP, GCSE Resource Guide 3, (Fig. 6, p. 156); Longman Atlas for Secondary Schools, (Fig. 3, p115); Marsden, World in Change, Oliver & Boyd (Fig. 2, p. 6), Fig. 4, p. 103), (Fig. 1, p. 158); Nelson Atlas, (Fig. 3, p. 143); New Internationalist, (Fig. 2, p194), (Fig. 2, p196), (Figs. 1, 2 and 3, pp206/7); Nixon B, British Isles, Bell & Hyman, (Figs. 1 and 2, p81); Ordnance Survey, Crown Copyright, (Fig.4, p. 27); (Fig. 4, p. 29), (Fig. 2, p. 40), (Fig. 1, p. 42), (Fig. 5, pp. 52/53), (Figs. 2 and 3, p. 74), (Fig. 1, p. 100), (Figs. 4 and 5, p. 125), (Fig. 6, p. 131), (Fig. 2, p. 173), (Fig. 1, p. 175), (Fig. 1, p. 198); Philip's Foundation Atlas, (Fig. 1, p. 148); Philip's Geographical Digest, (Fig. 4, p. 120); Philip's Heinemann School Atlas, (Fig. 3, P. 235); Randle TW, Western Europe, (Fig. 5, p. 18), (Fig. 1, p. 157); Raw & Atkins, Agriculture and Food, Collins (Fig. 2, p. 152), (Fig. 5, p. 153), (Fig. 2, p. 160); Raw & Shaw, Geography in Place 1, (Fig. 1, p. 157); Ross S (ed), Longman Co-ordinated Geography, ëPeople and physical environments', (Figs. 3 and 4, p. 7); Teesside Development Corporation, (p. 43); The Daily Telegraph, (Fig. 2, p. 110), (Fig. 3, p. 112), (Fig. 6, p. 135), (Fig. 3, p. 139); The Guardian, (Fig. 3, p. 62), (Fig. 3, p. 86), (Fig. 4, p. 87), (Fig. 3, p. 109), (Fig. 4, p. 193), (Fig. 3, p. 205); Time International Magazine, (Fig. 2, p. 190), (p. 204); UN Demographic Yearbook, (Fig. 1, p. 108); Waugh, Geography - An Integrated Approach, Nelson, (Fig. 2, p. 22); Waugh, UK and Europe, (Fig. 3, p. 151); Waugh, Wider World, Nelson, (Fig. 2, p. 106), (Fig. 4, p. 107), (Fig. 3, p. 111), (Fig. 4, p. 117), (Fig. 6, p. 121), (Fig. 3, p. 146), (Fig. 1, p. 162); Williams J, The Weather Book, Vintage Books (p. 88); WWF, Data Support Sheet for Education 24, (Fig. 1, p. 194); Yorkshire Life, (Fig. 4, p. 201); Young & Lowry, The British Isles, (Fig. 1, p. 150);

The publishers have made every effort to trace the copyright holders, but if they have inadvertently overlooked any, they will be pleased to make the necessary arrangements at the first opportunity.

Contents

1 Tectonic activity 5
2 Rocks and landscape 19
3 River processes and features 31
4 Ice 49
5 Coasts 61
6 Weather and climate 75
7 Ecosystems 89
8 Population 101
9 Settlement 123
10 Agriculture 145
11 Industry 165
12 Managing resources and tourism 185
13 Development and interdependence 209
14 Examination technique 232
   Glossary 237
   Index 240

Features of the book:	
Activities	Differentiated tasks catering for the need of both foundation and higher tier students
Test questions	Exam style questions familiarising students with exam vocabulary and giving further practice in exam technique
i	A panel giving extra information on a particular topic or theme
There are Case Studies in each chapter both integrated within the text and as separate pages providing further real examples of the topic.	

Chapter 1
Tectonic activity

The great power of natural forces – the Soufrière Hills volcano on the island of Montserrat in the Caribbean erupted in 1997 causing massive damage to a large part of the island. Why do volcanoes occur in certain parts of the world?

Key Ideas

The Earth's crust is unstable:
- the tectonic plates may move together or move apart
- at plate boundaries, earthquakes, volcanoes and fold mountains occur
- there are different types of volcano – composite, acid lava or shield (basic lava).

Tectonic activity influences human activity:
- human activities in fold mountain areas are a result of the physical conditions
- there are advantages and disadvantages for settlement in areas of tectonic activity
- tectonic activity has different effects in rural or urban areas and in rich and poor countries.

The Earth's tectonic plates

Figure 1 shows the structure of the Earth. At the centre there is the **core** surrounded by a large mass of molten rock called the **mantle**. At the surface there is a thin **crust** 'floating' on the mantle below. There are two main types of crust: oceanic crust which is denser and about 5km thick and continental crust which is lighter but about 30km thick.

The Earth's crust is not one continuous layer but is made up of seven large continental **plates** and many smaller ones. Figure 2 shows the distribution of the Earth's continental plates. The Earth's crust is unstable because the plates are moving in response to rising hot currents called **convection currents** within the mantle. The movement of the plates has greatest impact at the plate boundaries, where two tectonic plates meet. The centres of the plates, away from the boundaries, tend to be stable.

The movement of the tectonic plates

The plates move in relation to one another. They may move apart, move closer together or slide past each other. As the plates move, fold mountains, earthquakes, volcanoes, rift valleys and deep ocean trenches may all be formed.

Compressional plate boundaries

Plates that move together form a **compressional** (destructive) plate boundary. Figure 3 shows what happens when two plates are moving together. The Nazca plate is made of oceanic crust which is denser than the continental crust of the South American plate. The Nazca plate is forced to sink below the South American plate. The oceanic crust sinks into the mantle where it melts in the **subduction zone**. Energy builds up in the subduction zone – at certain times this may be

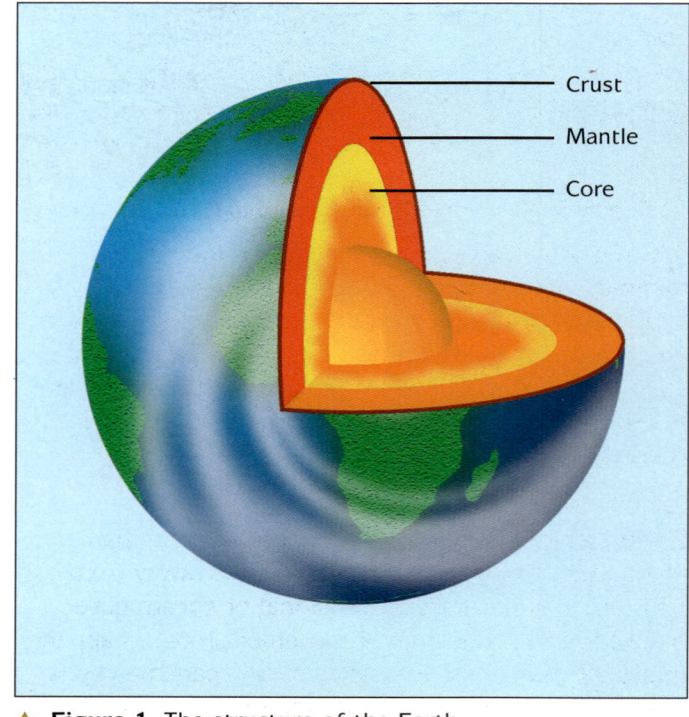

▲ **Figure 1** The structure of the Earth.

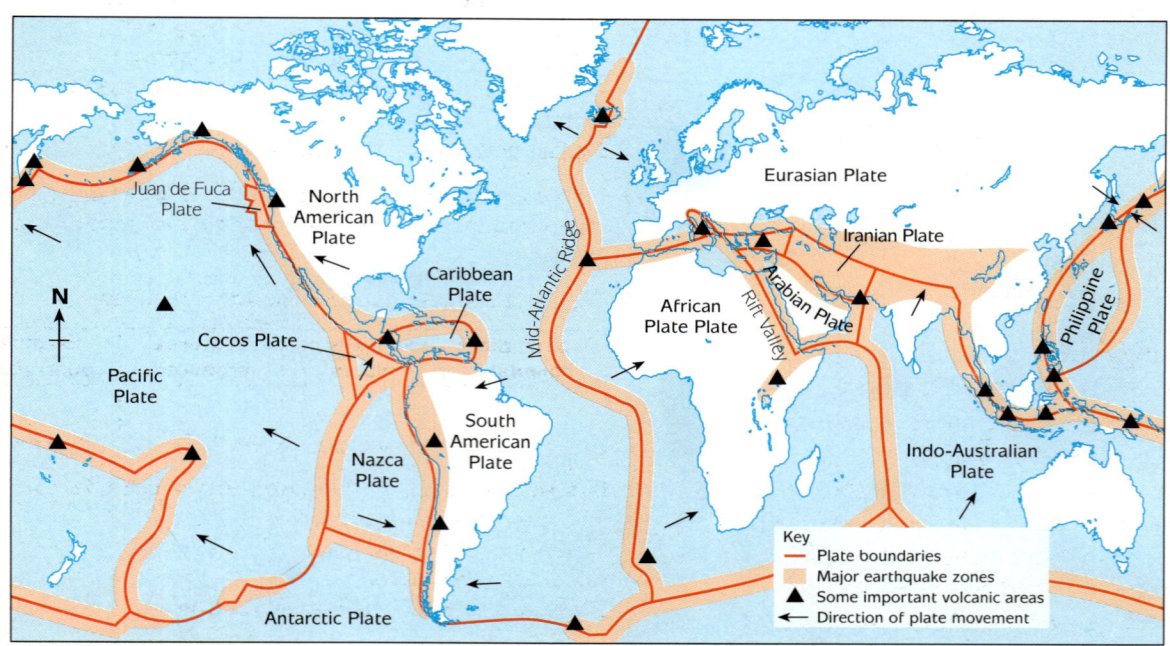

◄ **Figure 2** The Earth's continental plates.

Chapter 1 Tectonic activity

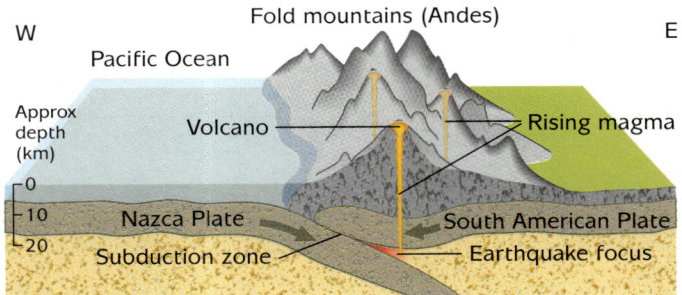

▲ **Figure 3** A compressional plate boundary.

released as an earthquake. The molten rock, called **magma**, may rise upwards, causing volcanic eruptions and leading to the creation of **composite volcanoes**. The lighter continental crust stays at the surface but becomes crumpled into fold mountains. The Andes are the fold mountains that have formed along the west coast of South America.

Tensional plate boundaries

Some plates, like the North American and Eurasian plates, are moving in opposite directions, away from each other. This is called a **tensional** or constructive plate boundary. This type of movement mostly happens under the oceans. As the plates move apart the gap is filled by magma rising up from the mantle below. The rising magma creates **shield volcanoes** which, if they become high enough, form volcanic islands, such as Iceland and the Hawaiian Islands. The edges of the plates also buckle to form ridges like the Mid-Atlantic ridge shown in **Figure 4**.

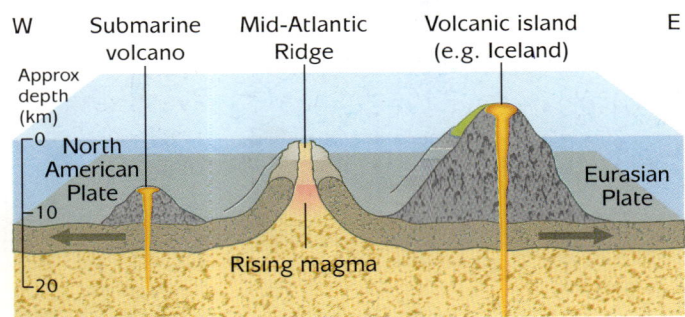

▲ **Figure 4** A tensional plate boundary.

Passive plate boundaries

At the San Andreas fault in California, the North American plate and the Pacific plate are sliding past each other. They are moving in the same direction but the North American plate is moving slightly faster. Pressure builds up along the fault until one plate jerks past the other causing an earthquake. The movement has also caused the land to become ridged and crumpled, as shown in **Figure 5**. This type of plate boundary is called a **passive** or conservative boundary.

▲ **Figure 5** The San Andreas fault.

Activities

1. **a** Draw a labelled diagram to show the structure of the Earth.
   b Describe how the Earth is like an apple – mention the core, the 'fleshy' part and the skin.

2. Use an atlas to place the following countries in two lists – countries that are liable to suffer tectonic activity and countries not liable to suffer tectonic activity.
   - Japan
   - Britain
   - Canada
   - Brazil
   - Morocco
   - Finland
   - Australia
   - Chile
   - Alaska (USA)
   - Italy

   Explain how you made your choices.

3. On a copy of **Figure 2** mark and label the main tectonic plates and indicate the direction of movement of the plates.

4. Copy and complete a table like the one below:

Type of plate boundary	Examples of plates	Features produced	Example country/area

5. Describe and explain the movements which take place at:
   a a compressional boundary
   b a tensional boundary
   c a passive boundary.
   Draw diagrams to illustrate your answers.

Fold mountains

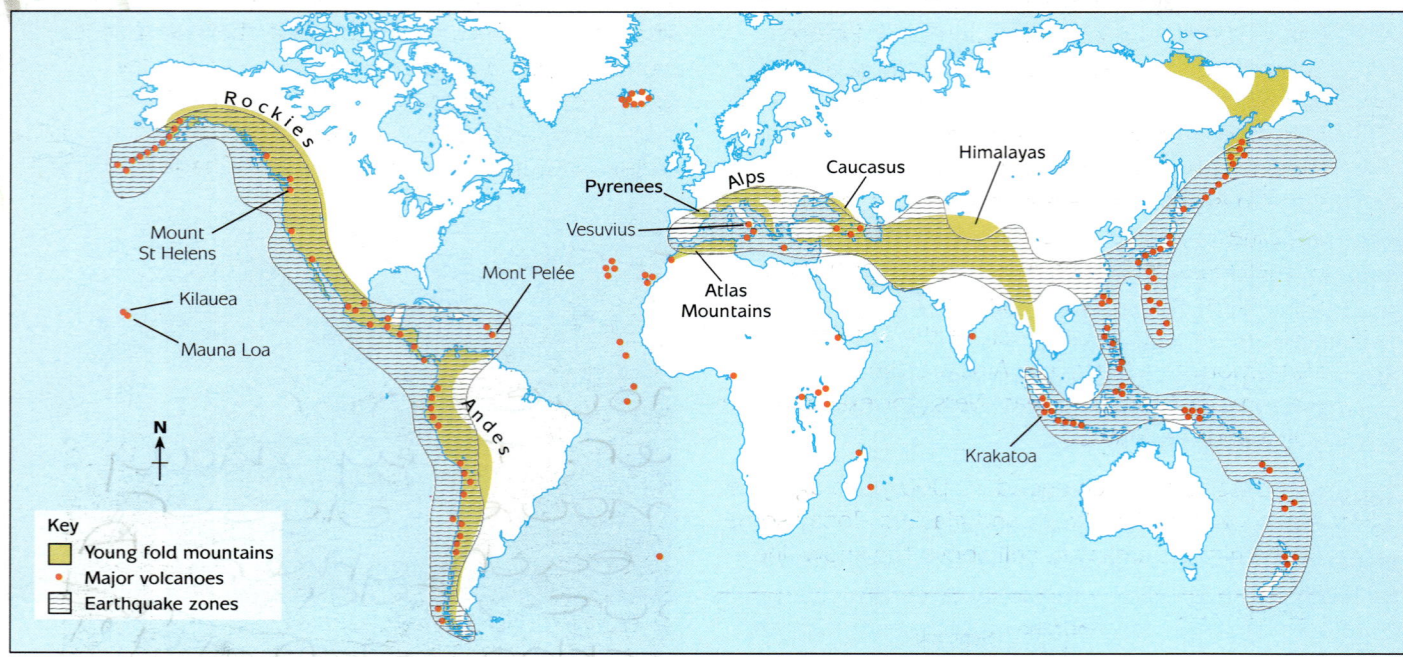

▲ **Figure 1** The world distribution of young fold mountains, active volcanoes and earthquake zones.

Fold mountains are found in many parts of the world (see **Figure 1**) and a glance back at **Figure 2** on page 6 shows that they form along the plate boundaries where great Earth movements have taken place.

Figure 2 shows the formation of fold mountains. There were long periods of quiet between Earth movements during which sedimentary rocks, thousands of metres thick, formed in huge depressions called **geosynclines**. Rivers carried sediments and deposited them into the depressions. Over millions of years the sediments were compressed into **sedimentary rocks** such as sandstone and limestone. These sedimentary rocks were then forced upwards into a series of folds by the movement of the tectonic plates. Sometimes the folds were simple upfolds (**anticlines**) and downfolds (**synclines**), as in the Jura mountains in France. In some places the folds were pushed over on one side giving overfolds, while in some of the highest fold mountains, like the Alps, the rocks have been severely folded and faulted into **nappes** (Figure 3).

Fold mountains have been formed at times in the Earth's geological history called mountain-building periods. Recent mountain-building movements have created the Alps, the Himalayas, the Rockies and the Andes, some of which are still rising. For this reason many of these ranges are called young fold mountains.

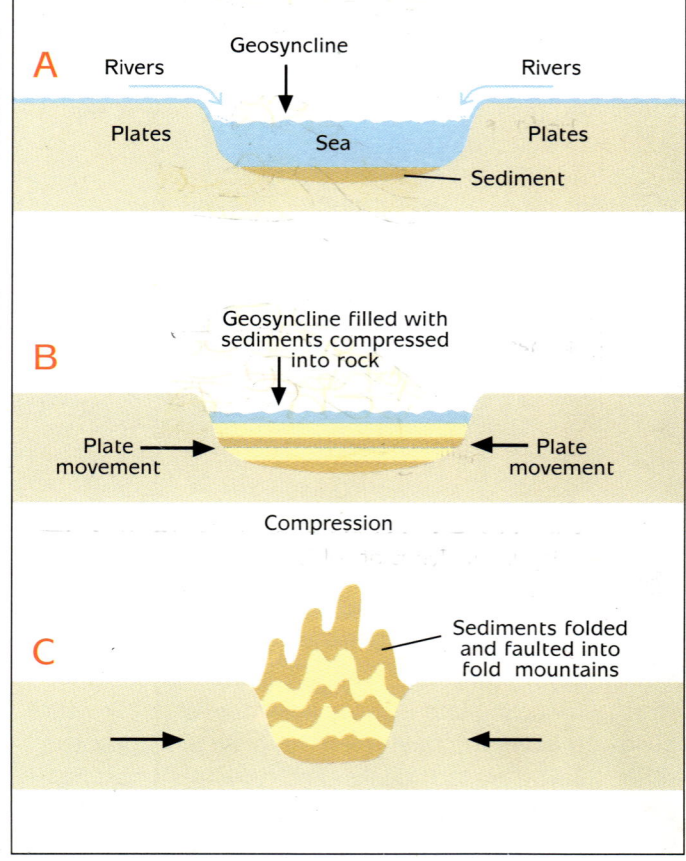

▲ **Figure 2** The formation of fold mountains.

The Alps

The Alps are young fold mountains formed 30–40 million years ago. They form the border between Italy and the neighbouring countries of France, Switzerland and Germany. The Alps lie at a compressional margin where the sedimentary rocks have been heavily folded into parallel ranges running south-west to north-east across northern Italy. These ranges were so severely folded that anticlines, synclines, overfolds and nappes were all formed (**Figure 3**). The Alps reach great heights – the highest peak is Mont Blanc in France at 4810m; other tall peaks include the Jungfrau, Matterhorn and Eiger. The Alps are the source area for some of Europe's great rivers, for example, the Rhine and the Rhône.

In the Ice Age, which ended 10 000 years ago, the Alps had many ice sheets and glaciers. Today some of the highest areas are still above the snow line and have glaciers and snowfields (**Figure 4**). The Alps have many features of glaciation; for example, the Matterhorn is a pyramidal peak, the River Rhône flows through a huge U-shaped glaciated valley, the numerous ribbon lakes include Lakes Como and Garda, and corries and arêtes can be seen. These landforms will be explained in Chapter 4.

▲ **Figure 3** Types of folds.

▲ **Figure 4** Alpine view – the Lauterbrunnen Valley.

Human activity in the Alps

In the Alps land uses and vegetation are zoned because as the altitude increases the climate becomes colder. The main human activities in the Alps are connected with tourism, dairy farming, forestry, HEP and industry (see **Figure 1**).

Farming

The valley floor is the ideal location for farming. It is sheltered, the land is flatter and the soils are deeper and more fertile. The valley floor also has better access and communications.

Traditional farming was dairying, using a system called **transhumance**, the seasonal movement of animals. The cattle were taken up to the saeter or High Alp in the summer to graze on the Alpine pastures once the snow had melted. They returned to the valley floor in the autumn and were stall-fed in large barns over the winter. This allowed hay and other crops to be grown on the valley floor in the summer for use as winter fodder. The milk was made into butter and cheese on the saeter, as these keep better than fresh milk. Cable cars and specially built plastic pipes now transport the milk down the hillsides to cooperative dairies in the villages. Today, there is very little transhumance. The farmers use artificial feeds and prefer to stay at home all year. New roads, quad bikes and cable cars also give easier access to the upland pastures. Most of the farms are on the south-facing or adrêt slope which is warmer and drier. The main crops grown are hay and cereals, with some sugar beet, vines and fruits in the warmer areas.

Tourism

There are many important tourist centres in the Alps, such as Chamonix and St Moritz. Many new resorts have developed since the 1950s as tourism, especially skiing, has expanded. The tourist industry is so important that large amounts of money have been spent on roads, railways, tunnels, avalanche shelters, cable cars, hotels and restaurants. Some of these developments have also benefited the farmers and other local people.

The area attracts skiers, climbers and walkers, as well as people who simply want to admire the spectacular scenery. Alpine features attractive to visitors include:

- beautiful winter scenery with glaciated mountains, snow-capped peaks and forests
- lakeside summer resorts, such as Lucerne and Garda
- extensive winter sports facilities, both indoor and outdoor, such as ski slopes, ice rinks and toboggan runs
- good communications, close to international road and rail routes using Alpine passes such as the Simplon and St Gotthard, as well as international airports at Geneva and Zurich
- close to affluent parts of Europe, such as Germany and France
- the Alpine climate, with good snowfall but also crisp, clear days for winter sports, and summers that are warm with showers.

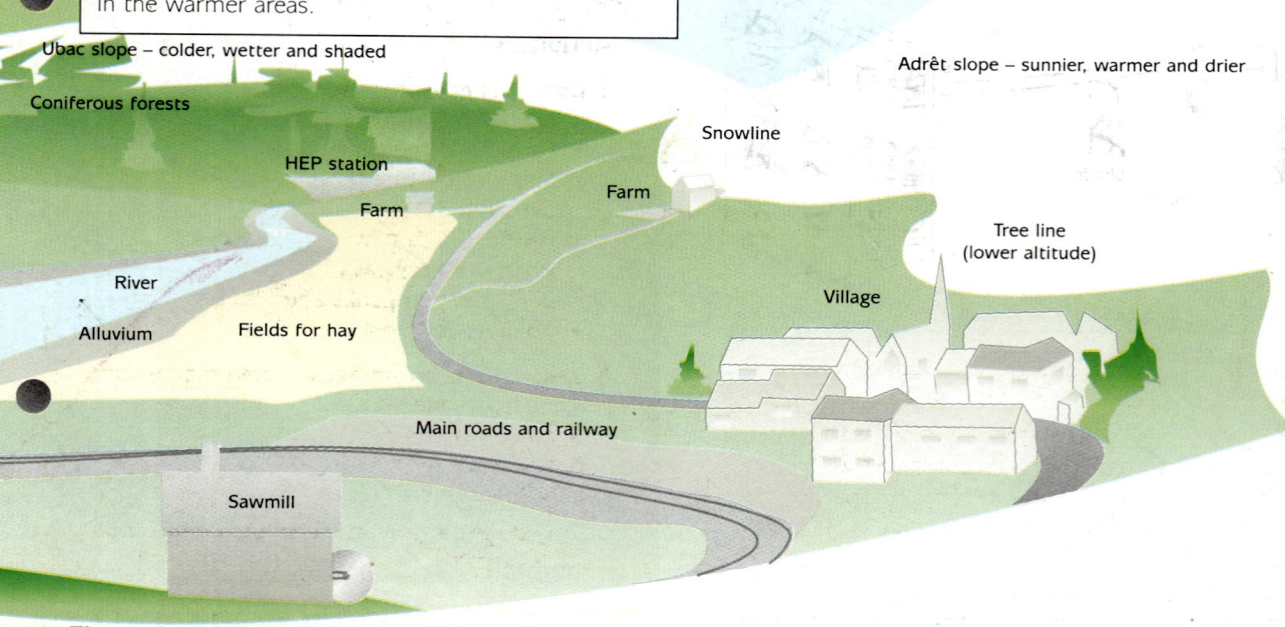

▲ **Figure 1** Human activity in an Alpine valley.

Hydroelectric power (HEP) and industry

The steep slopes, high precipitation and summer melting of the glaciers produce fast-flowing rivers that are ideal for generating HEP. The narrow valleys are easy to dam and there are lakes in which to store water. Some of the cheap HEP is used by industries which require a high input of electricity, such as sawmills, electrochemicals, fertilizer manufacture and aluminium smelting. Some of the electricity is also exported to other regions to supply towns and cities. Traditional industries in the Alps include papermaking, textiles, leatherworking, furniture and cuckoo clocks.

Problems of fold mountain areas

Fold mountains like the Alps tend to have low population densities. The high altitude and steep slopes make it difficult to build houses and communication links, and to locate industries. Roads and railways need expensive tunnels, passes, avalanche shelters and hairpin bends. There is little flat land for farming and the use of machinery is difficult. The climate is also cold and wet with heavy snowfall and strong winds, especially at high altitudes. The growing season is therefore short and travel can be difficult, especially in the winter. Avalanches and rock falls can block roads, and some settlements and roads need avalanche protection measures, e.g. shelters, wooden fencing, wire cages. However, the population density in the Alps is higher than in many fold mountain areas because the soil in the valley floors is reasonably fertile and the region is attractive to tourists from nearby wealthy countries.

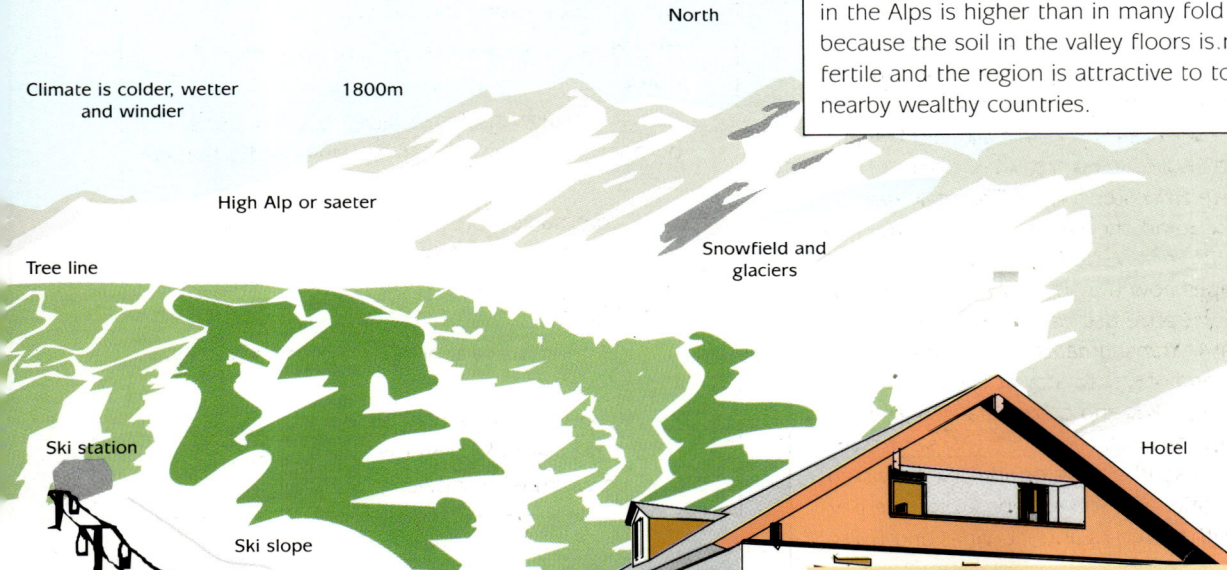

Forestry

Up to a height of about 1800m the slopes are covered in coniferous forests, giving rise to a timber industry. The soft wood is felled for use as fuel, for building and in the manufacture of wood pulp and paper. In Switzerland, small craft industries use the timber in woodcarving and to manufacture the famous cuckoo clocks.

Activities

1 Draw a simple cross-section of an Alpine valley. Add the following labels:
   - Farming in the valley floor
   - Summer pasture on the High Alp
   - Ski stations
   - HEP and industry
   - Roads and railways
   - Snow-capped peaks and glaciers
   - Coniferous forests.

2 Describe the advantages of fold mountains such as the Alps for:
   a dairy farming
   b tourism
   c HEP and industry.

3 Why do the Alps have such low population densities?

Volcanoes

Etna, Vesuvius, Pinatubo, Mount St Helens and Kilauea are all well-known volcanoes formed from many eruptions of magma. Each time an eruption takes place a new layer of lava is added to the volcano, building up the volcano and creating the familiar cone shape. The magma that reaches the surface in an eruption is called **lava**, and is one of many different products that may be thrown out, including ash, cinders, lava bombs, pumice, dust, gases and steam. Violent eruptions throw out **acid lava** and solid material such as ash and cinders. Acid lava has a high silica content and because it is viscous it only travels short distances before cooling. Non-violent eruptions emit **basic lava** which has a low silica content. Basic lava is fluid and may flow long distances before cooling.

How are volcanoes formed?

Volcanoes form where magma escapes through a **vent**, which is a fracture or crack in the Earth's crust. This often happens at plate boundaries, as shown by the distribution of the major volcanoes on **Figure 1** on page 8. **Figures 1** and **2** show how volcanoes are formed at the compressional and tensional plate boundaries.

Different types of volcanoes

Volcanoes are divided into three main types depending upon the material thrown out in an eruption. **Figure 3** shows the three types and their characteristics.

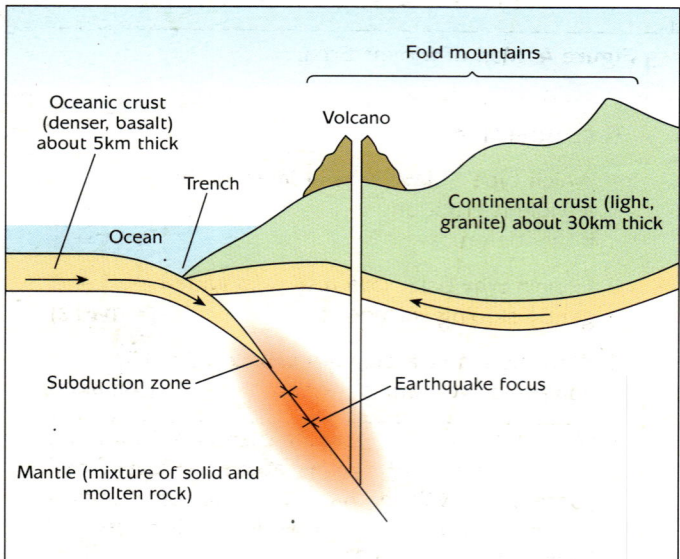

When the plates collide, the denser oceanic plate is pushed down into the mantle. Here the plate melts and is destroyed in the subduction zone. This is a compressional or destructive boundary. In the subduction zone the plate melts to form a pool of magma. The great heat and pressure may force the magma along a crack where it erupts at the surface to build up a volcano.

▲ **Figure 1** The compressional plate boundary.

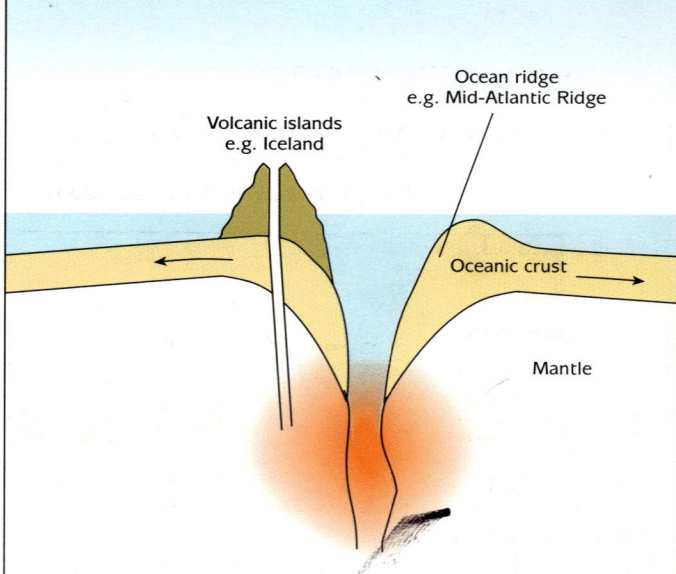

The plates are moving apart at a tensional boundary. As the plates move apart magma rises upwards from the mantle to "plug" the gap. This adds new rock to the spreading plates. Some of the magma may also be forced along a crack or vent and erupt at the surface. A submarine volcano will form which may eventually grow high enough to form a volcanic island e.g. Iceland, Hawaii.

▲ **Figure 2** The tensional plate boundary.

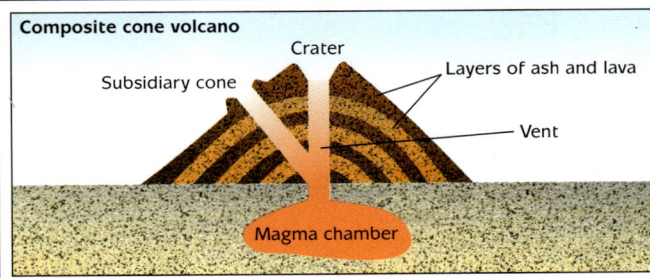

Composite cone volcano
Examples: Mount Etna, Vesuvius, Mount St Helens
Characteristics:
- Steep-sided symmetrical cone shape
- High with narrow base
- Alternate layers of acid lava and ash
- Lava may cool inside the vent – the next eruption is very explosive to remove the plug
- Subsidiary cones and vents form.

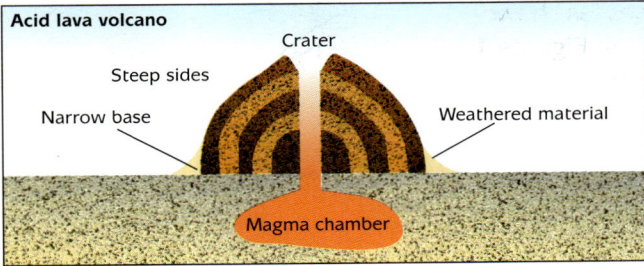

Acid lava volcano
Example: Mont Pelée, in Martinique
Characteristics:
- Very steep cone or spine with narrow base
- Composed of acid lava which does not flow easily
- Very explosive eruptions: Mont Pelée erupted very violently in 1902. The clouds of ash and lava engulfed the town of St Pierre in two minutes, killing 30 000 people.

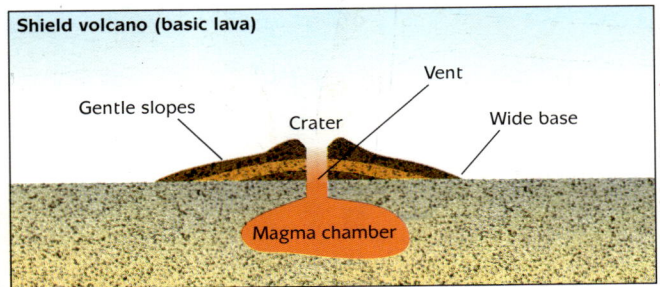

Shield volcano (basic lava)
Examples: Mauna Loa and Kilauea, both on the Hawaiian Islands
Characteristics:
- Gentle slopes and wide base
- Frequent eruptions of basic lava
- Lava flows more easily, travels longer distances before cooling
- Usually non-violent.

▲ **Figure 3** Different types of volcano.

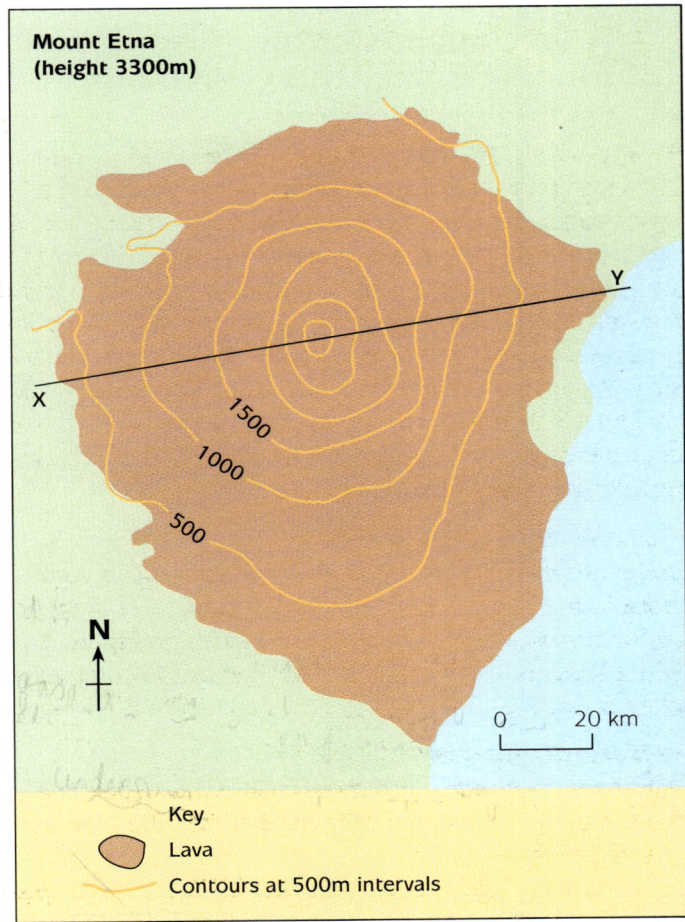

▲ **Figure 4** Map of Mount Etna.

Test questions

1. Which type of lava is associated with:
   a violent eruptions
   b gentle eruptions? (2 marks)

2. Explain why basic lava results in wide-based and gently sloping volcanoes. (3 marks)

3. With the aid of a diagram explain how a composite volcano is formed. (6 marks)

4. Mauna Loa in the Hawaiian islands is 10 000m high, of which 4000m are above sea level. The base of the volcano has a diameter of 400km. In an eruption lava can flow 50km down its gentle slopes (2°–10°).

   a Draw a cross-section through Mauna Loa. (Horizontal scale 1cm : 20km; vertical scale 1cm : 8000m.) (2 marks)
   b Using **Figure 4**, draw a cross-section through Mount Etna from X to Y. (2 marks)
   c Describe and explain the differences between the two cross-sections. (5 marks)

A volcanic eruption – The Soufrière Hills volcano on the island of Montserrat in the Caribbean

▲ Figure 1 The location of Montserrat.

▲ Figure 2 Plymouth, a ghost town.

Montserrat (**Figure 1**) is a small island in the Caribbean which is still a British colony. The island is mountainous and wooded, earning it the name 'Emerald Island of the Caribbean'. It has been popular with many wealthy British people including Paul McCartney and Sting – exclusive villas and hotels line the coast. However, many of the residents of Montserrat are quite poor, living in small villages and practising subsistence farming. Before the eruption the population was 12 000, 50 per cent of whom lived in the capital city, Plymouth, in the south of the island.

In July 1995 the Soufrière Hills volcano erupted for the first time in 350 years. One month later 50 per cent of the population were evacuated to the north of the island away from the danger zone. In April 1996, as the eruptions continued, Plymouth became a ghost town (**Figure 2**) as more and more people were evacuated. The eruptions became more explosive and the lava and ash caused great damage to the island. In June 1997 another eruption destroyed villages in the centre of the island, killing 23 people. Of the island's 40 square miles only 15 square miles in the north of the island were considered safe. Over 5000 people left the island, most to settle on nearby islands such as Antigua or to move to Britain. Study **Figure 3** which shows the impact of the eruptions.

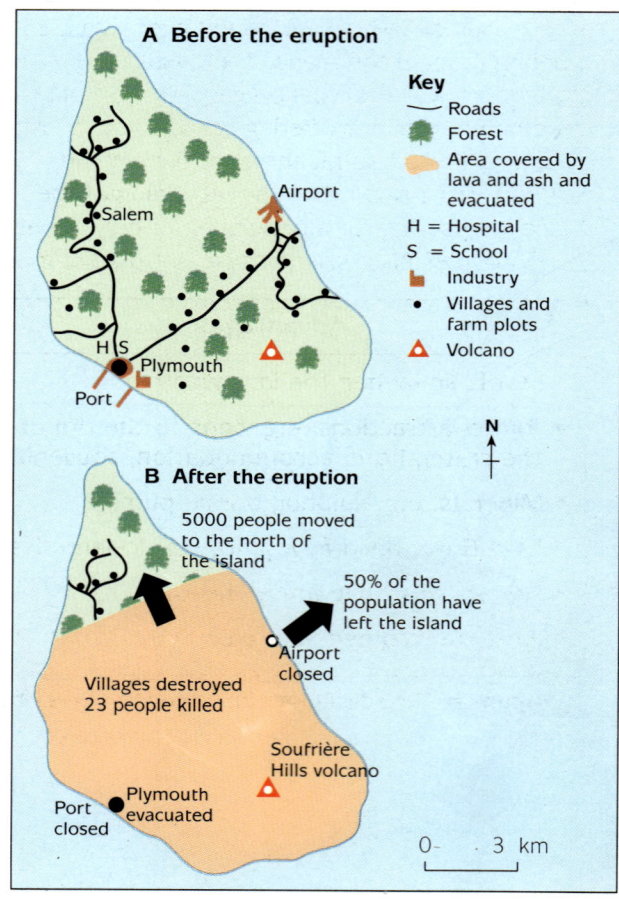

▲ Figure 3 The impact of the eruptions on Montserrat.

Those people who have stayed on the island are suffering very harsh conditions. The south of the island was the most developed, with the main towns, communications and services. In the north there were few roads and settlements. Many of the evacuees are forced to live in makeshift shelters with inadequate sanitation; there are few schools and no proper hospital, and living conditions are very poor. The country's tourist industry has stopped with the closure of the airport, and other industries are suffering with the restricted port activities. The processing of imported rice and the assembly of electronics products have both declined. The country now relies upon aid from London.

After the eruptions which forced the evacuation of most of the island, the people called for the British government to pay compensation and to rebuild the island. Aid totalling £41 million has been offered to redevelop the north of the island and £10.5 million to relocate refugees. In 1997, £2400 was offered to each adult over eighteen wanting to leave the island. There was rioting on the island when the local people felt the British government was not offering enough help to the people. The Montserratians were demanding £20 000 per person. Can the rebuilding of the island be justified for a population of only about 4000 people? Also, scientists cannot predict if and when the volcano may erupt again. Money may be invested in rebuilding the island only to be wiped out by another eruption which destroys the whole island.

Volcanoes: hazard or blessing?

Why do people choose to live near volcanoes when an eruption could happen at any time? Study **Figure 4**, which shows that living near a volcano can be both a hazard and a blessing.

> **Activities**
>
> 1 Draw a sketch map to show the location of Montserrat.
>
> 2 Explain with the aid of diagrams why the volcanic eruption occurred. (Pages 12 and 13 may help.)
>
> 3 a Describe the short-term effects of the eruption.
>   b Describe the long-term effects.
>
> 4 Some of the islanders want the British government to pay huge compensation for evacuation while others would like the island rebuilt. The British government finds it difficult to decide what approach to take. Explain these different points of view.

Advantages	Disadvantages

• Fertile soil when the lava weathers
• Tourist attractions, e.g. trips to the rim of the crater, hotel accommodation, souvenir shops
• Minerals, e.g. sulphur, borax, pumice
• Lava flows build new land, e.g. Iceland, Hawaii
• Hot springs for bathing, heating
• Heat used to generate electricity
	• Explosions and eruptions leading to:
	  – dangerous gases
	  – loss of life
	  – loss of homes, animals and crops
	  – disease and fires
	  – avalanches, mudflows and floods
	  – loss of wildlife, trees and plants

▲ **Figure 4** The advantages and disadvantages of living near volcanoes.

The earthquake hazard

Earthquakes are vibrations in the Earth's crust. They are sudden and, because they happen without warning, often lethal – 1.5 million people have died as a result of earthquakes since 1900. The magnitude of an earthquake is measured using an instrument called a **seismograph** and given a value of between 1 and 10 on the **Richter scale**. The scale is logarithmic: an earthquake measuring 6 is ten times more powerful than one measuring 5.

There are over 6000 earthquakes every year but most movements are too small for people to notice. About fifteen earthquakes every year are large enough to have devastating effects on life and property (**Figure 1**).

Why do earthquakes happen?

Most earthquakes are caused by movement along a fault. They can occur anywhere, but they are most common and most serious along plate boundaries. Over 90 per cent of earthquakes occur where the plates are colliding at a compressional plate boundary. These earthquakes are also more violent.

At the plate boundaries there is movement of the rocks due to convection currents building up heat and pressure, but these movements are not steady or smooth. The plates tend to become jammed together. The pressure then builds up until friction is overcome and one plate jerks past the other. It is these sudden movements that cause the earthquake. The point at which the earthquake happens below the ground surface is called the **focus** (**Figure 2**). The **epicentre** is the point on the ground surface directly above the focus. If the epicentre is in, or close to, large urban areas then the effects can be devastating, as in Kobe in Japan in 1995.

Year	Magnitude on the Richter scale	Location	Approximate number of deaths
1556	8.3	Shansi, China	830 000
1755	9.0	Lisbon, Portugal	100 000
1857	8.3	Fort Tejon, California, USA	1
1906	8.25	San Francisco, USA	700
1920	8.6	Kansu, China	200 000
1923	8.3	Tokyo, Japan	143 000
1960	9.5	Chile	5 700
1964	8.4	Anchorage, Alaska	131
1970	7.8	Ancash, Peru	66 000
1988	7.1	Armenia	25 000
1995	7.2	Kobe, Japan	5 500
1997	7.1	Eastern Iran	1 560

▲ **Figure 1** Some important earthquakes.

The effects of earthquakes

The destructive effects of an earthquake can be classified into **primary** and **secondary** effects.

Primary effects are the immediate damage caused by the quake, such as collapsing buildings, roads and bridges, which may kill many people. Those lucky enough to survive can suffer badly from shock and panic.

Secondary effects are the after-effects of the earthquake, such as fires, tidal waves, landslides and disease.

- **Fire** – earthquakes destroy gas pipes and electric cables, causing fires to spread. Broken water mains prevent the fires being extinguished. Fires spread very quickly in cities, especially in poor-quality housing areas where wooden buildings are common. Fires killed about 25 per cent of the victims in Tokyo in 1923 after the Kanto earthquake.

- **Tsunamis** (tidal waves) – an earthquake on the sea floor or close to the coast may cause huge tidal waves. The Great Chilean earthquake in 1960 created three tsunamis which reached Japan, 16 000km away, three days later. The tidal waves destroyed 3000 houses and 250 bridges; 2500 ships were damaged and 165 people killed.

- **Landslides** – earthquakes often cause landslides, especially in steep river valleys and areas of weak

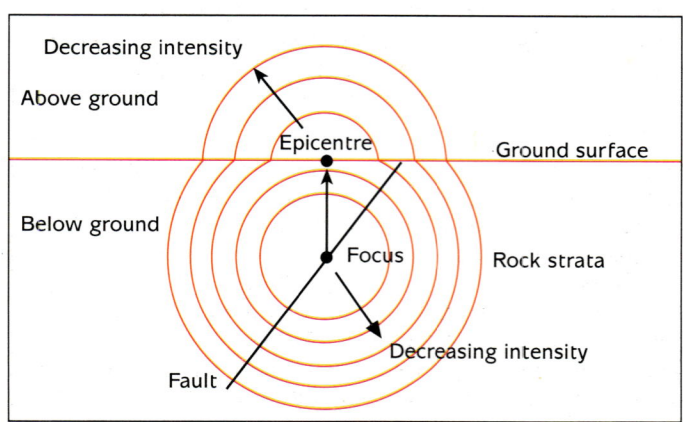

▲ **Figure 2** The features of an earthquake.

sands and clays. In 1970 an earthquake of magnitude 7.8 in Peru caused a huge landslide high in the Andes mountains which killed 20 000 people.

- **Disease and famine** – fresh water supplies are often cut off due to burst water pipes. Typhoid and cholera can spread easily, especially in large cities cut off from medical supplies by damaged communications.

The impact of tectonic activity (earthquakes and volcanoes) is often much more severe in Less Economically Developed Countries (LEDCs) than in More Economically Developed Countries (MEDCs). Many LEDCs cannot afford early warning systems or evacuation plans. Housing is often overcrowded and poorly constructed so that it collapses or catches fire easily. Communications are frequently poor so that emergency services take a long time to reach a disaster area.

An earthquake or volcano usually has less impact in the countryside than in towns and cities, where there are higher population densities. The urban infrastructure means there is very much more damage to property, industry and services. Collapsed power lines and fractured gas mains add to the casualties and increase the chance of fires and explosions. Disease may also spread more quickly in more populated areas.

Kobe, 17 January 1995 – disaster strikes

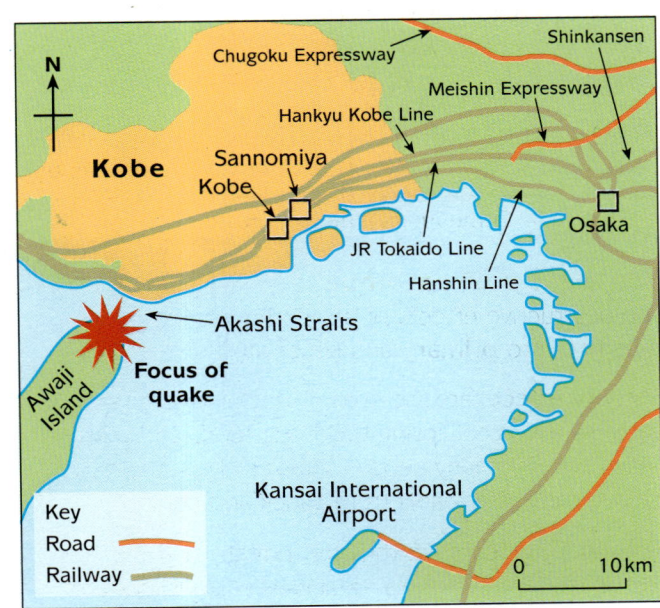

▲ **Figure 3** Kobe and the surrounding area.

▲ **Figure 4** The devastation in Kobe.

Kobe (**Figure 3**) lies on the main island of Honshu in Japan, close to a fairly short fault line between the Philippine and southern Japan plates, which are sliding past each other. In January 1995 about 50km of the fault moved, causing the Great Hanshin earthquake. The focus of the earthquake was about 19km below the sea with the epicentre between Kobe and Awaji Island.

The earthquake and aftershocks caused landslides, and areas of soil liquefied especially in the sands along the coast and in areas of reclaimed land. The port of Kobe was destroyed and over 100 000 houses collapsed. Ten per cent of the city's infrastructure was lost, including roads, railways, electricity, gas and sewerage systems. Ten per cent of schools were destroyed, together with 5 per cent of housing, 12 per cent of industry and 14 per cent of services. About 5500 people were killed, and nearly 30 000 injured. Over three hundred thousand people were left homeless and became refugees just after the earthquake.

No emergency services were available and the electricity supply was cut off, leaving two million homes without power. Over one million homes were without water for ten days.

One week after the earthquake fires were still burning, and the death toll continued to rise. Bulldozers began to clear streets and to knock down unsafe buildings. The electricity supply was restored and telephones began to work again. Some shops and schools reopened.

Two weeks later more highways and railways were reopened. Overcrowding in the makeshift shelters became a health hazard and the cold weather led to a flu epidemic. Many people needed help to cope with the stress and shock of the quake.

After three years parts of Kobe were still being rebuilt. Following the earthquake the Government of Japan was criticized for its slow response and the lack of an emergency action plan. However, Japan has some of the most sophisticated monitoring equipment in the world. Today the whole area is criss-crossed with monitoring equipment in the hope that a few days' warning can be given of any future significant earthquake. However, as yet no one can predict when an earthquake will happen or how strong it will be.

Vesuvius and the the Plain of Campania

Campania is a region in southern Italy (**Figure 1**). It includes the major city of Naples and the famous volcano, Mount Vesuvius (1198m).

Vesuvius (**Figure 6**) is a composite cone volcano which is dormant at present but has been very destructive in the past. Its most notable eruption was in AD79 when the towns of Pompeii and Herculaneum were destroyed. Thousands of people were killed by the poisonous gases and the area was buried under metres of ash. So why do so many people choose to live close by?

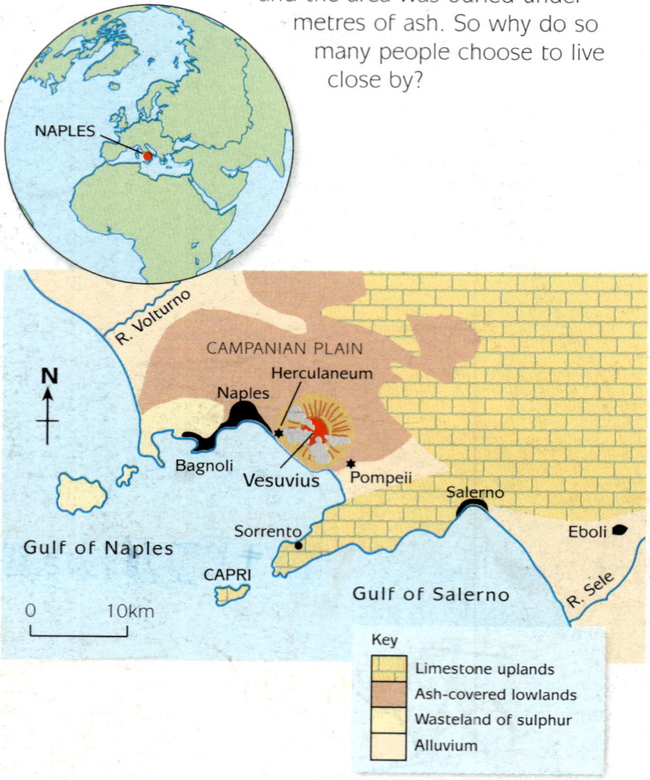

Excavations at Pompeii and Herculaneum, trips to the crater on Vesuvius and visits to hot springs have brought a thriving tourist industry employing many local people. Others farm the very fertile soils. The fine ash with the long growing season and adequate winter rainfall make farming very productive. Wheat, maize, peaches, almonds, vines and especially tomatoes are all grown intensively. Yields are five times higher than the national average and many of the products are exported.

The fertile plain contrasts sharply with the rest of the region where mountains and hills occupy 80 per cent of the land and the rock is mostly limestone. The limestone is dry with thin, infertile soils. To the west of Naples there is an area called the Phlegraean Fields. This is a wasteland with hot springs, geysers and sulphur domes. It is useless for farming and settlement but sulphur is extracted for use in industry.

Despite the threat of another eruption in the future – and scientists have recorded the highest number of earthquakes in the area for 50 years – people continue to live and work in Campania. Perhaps most believe, or want to believe, that an eruption will not happen in their lifetime...

▲ **Figure 5** Map of Campania.

▲ **Figure 6** Naples and Mount Vesuvius.

Test questions

1. **a** (i) Name the features shown by letters A–E on the diagram. (5 marks)
   (ii) Describe and explain the differences between a composite and a shield volcano. (5 marks)
   (iii) Explain the formation of a volcano. (4 marks)
   b Using an example, describe the advantages and disadvantages of living near a volcano. (6 marks)

2. **a** Name two fold mountain ranges. (2 marks)
   b Explain with the aid of diagrams how fold mountains are formed. (6 marks)
   c Give three examples of human activities in fold mountain areas. (3 marks)
   d Explain the disadvantages of fold mountains for settlement, transport and farming. (4 marks)

3. Explain why earthquakes, volcanoes and fold mountains form at plate boundaries. (2 marks)

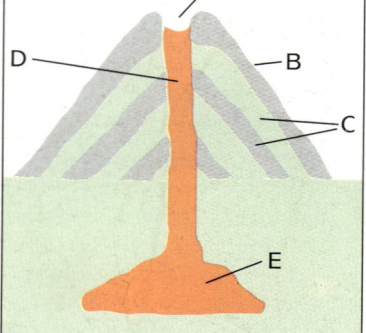

▲ **Figure 7**

Chapter 2
Rocks and landscape

Limestone pavement near Malham in the Yorkshire Dales National Park. This landscape feature forms only in areas of Carboniferous limestone rocks.

Key Ideas

The Earth's crust is composed of different rock types:
- the three rock groups are igneous, sedimentary and metamorphic
- rock types such as granite, Carboniferous limestone, chalk and clay form distinctive landscapes
- each rock type has economic uses, although quarrying rocks is often a local issue.

The Earth's crust is modified by weathering:
- physical weathering processes include freeze–thaw and exfoliation
- chemical weathering leads to limestone solution and distinctive landscape features.

Types of rocks and their distribution within the UK

Types of rocks

Although there are many different types of rock on the Earth's surface, there are only three groups of rocks. Rocks are either igneous, sedimentary or metamorphic.

Igneous rocks are formed by 'fire'; they begin as magma in the interior of the Earth. Some are formed by lava cooling on the Earth's surface after being thrown out by a volcanic eruption. For example, the basic lava that flows from constructive margins and forms shield volcanoes cools to form *basalt* rock. This has been eroded into hexagonal blocks at the Giant's Causeway in Northern Ireland (**Figure 1**). Others are formed by magma cooling underground after having been intruded into other rocks without reaching the surface. *Granite* is an example of this type of igneous rock. It is often intruded during the building of fold mountains along destructive plate boundaries. Granite outcrops on the surface after erosion of the rocks above it over millions of years. Today it is exposed in many places within Scotland (**Figure 4**) and forms most of the moorlands of Devon and Cornwall as well the dramatic cliffs at Land's End (**Figure 2**).

Sediments are small particles of rock transported by water, ice and wind. Most eventually reach the sea bed where over the years successive layers of sediments accumulate. The weight of materials above compresses the sediments below into **sedimentary rocks**. These rocks are laid down in layers, or beds, with lines of weakness, or bedding planes, between layers (**Figure 3**). When sand is compressed, *sandstone* rock is formed. *Clay* forms from the accumulation and compression of deposits of mud. *Limestone* and *chalk* consist of calcium carbonate which comes from the remains of plants and animals. For example, the shells of sea creatures are made of calcium carbonate; when these animals die, masses of shells accumulate on the sea floor, building up layers of limestone rock. A lot of limestone was formed during the Carboniferous period (280–345 million years ago) because at that time much of Britain was a warm shallow sea, rich in plant and animal life.

Metamorphic rocks are those which have been changed in shape or form. They begin as either igneous or sedimentary rocks but are later altered by heat or pressure. This happens, for example, along destructive plate boundaries and fault lines. Heat and pressure change limestone into *marble* and clay into *slate*. Both marble and slate are harder forms of the original rocks, and have greater economic value. Marble is widely used in building and for floors in Mediterranean countries such as Italy. Slate splits easily into sheets and, until recent times, was the main roofing material used in the UK.

◄ **Figure 1** The Giant's Causeway is built of basalt.

▼ **Figure 2** Land's End is built of granite. Notice the many vertical joints.

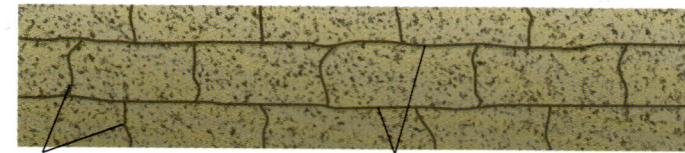

joints – vertical weaknesses within the layers of rock

bedding planes – horizontal weaknesses between the layers of rock

fault – earth movements have broken up the beds of rock

▲ **Figure 3** Rock weaknesses. These are important because they are the first points to be attacked by processes of weathering and erosion.

Distribution of rock types within the UK

The distribution of rocks reflects the geological history of the UK. It is customary to divide the country into two parts using a line running from the mouth of the River Tees to the mouth of the River Exe, separating Highland from Lowland Britain (**Figure 4**).

The geology of Highland Britain to the north and west of the Tees–Exe line is dominated by old and hard rocks. The majority are igneous and metamorphic rocks which have resisted erosion and therefore form the upland and mountainous parts of the country.

In Lowland Britain, to the south and east of the Tees–Exe line, the geology is dominated by younger sedimentary rocks. There is much low-lying and flat land, such as in the clay vales. Chalk, however, is more resistant to erosion than many of the other sedimentary rocks which surround it. This is why chalk ridges and scarps, such as the North and South Downs, appear to be high and steep, but they form lower, gentler and more rounded landscapes than the rocks in the uplands of Highland Britain.

Activities

1. Use **Figure 4** and a map of the British Isles.
    a. On an outline map of the British Isles, shade and name two areas covered by each of the following rock types:
        - granite
        - Carboniferous limestone
        - chalk
        - clay.
    b. Describe the differences between Highland and Lowland Britain using these headings.
        (i) Rocks
        (ii) Relief (height and shape of the land).
2. Draw a larger version of the table and fill it in using information from pages 20–21.

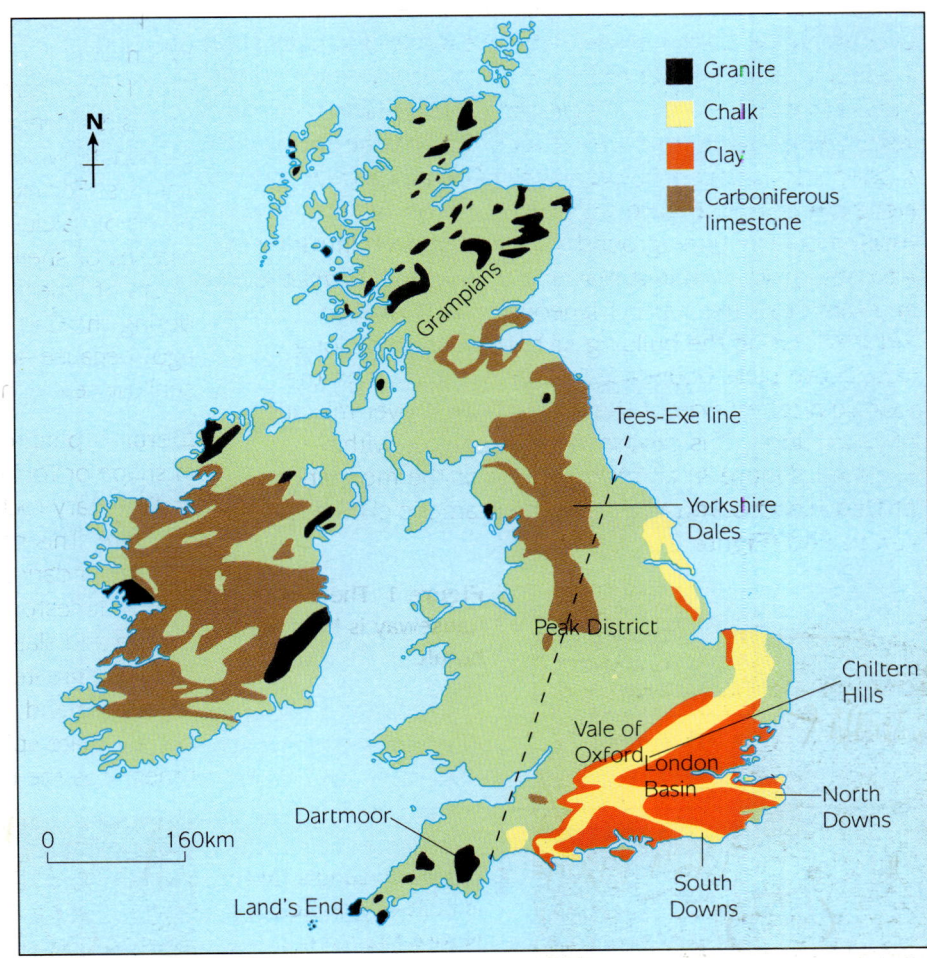

▲ **Figure 4** The distribution of some of the rocks found in the British Isles.

	Igneous	Sedimentary	Metamorphic
Brief definition			
Where they were formed			
How they were formed			
Rock types found in the UK			
Main UK areas where rock outcrops occur			

Granite

All the granite rocks in the UK are found to the north and west of the Tees–Exe line (see **Figure 4** on page 21).

Landscape features

In south-west England granite gives relatively flat-topped moorland plateaus with frequent rock outcrops, which from time to time form rock blocks called **tors** (**Figure 3**). Tors are some five to ten metres high and are surrounded by weathered materials of all sizes from boulders to sand. On the higher parts of the moorlands there are many areas of standing surface water forming marshes and bogs. The many surface streams have cut deeply into the upland block of Dartmoor to form deep and steep V-shaped valleys, especially where rivers such as the Dart go over the edge of the plateau.

Dramatic coastal scenery occurs where granite and Atlantic breakers meet, as at Land's End (see **Figure 2** on page 20). In Scotland the granite peaks in the Grampians and on Goat Fell in Arran are rocky and frost-shattered, although where the land is relatively flat, such as on Rannoch Moor, extensive bogs occur.

Granite is a hard rock, resistant to erosion, which is why it forms areas of high relief inland and cliffs along the coast. It is an impermeable rock, which explains why there is so much surface water. Another reason for the presence of so many bogs is the high precipitation in western upland areas.

Formation of tors

The rock which forms tors is that which remains after the surrounding rocks have been weathered and carried away. Where tors occur, the joints in the granite are wider apart than in the rock around them. Freeze–thaw weathering (**Figure 1**) can operate more effectively and blocks of rock break off more quickly where the joints are close together, because there are more cracks in the rock for the water to fill (**Figure 2**). Each time the water freezes and expands within a joint, more pressure is put on the surrounding rock and the crack widens. Where there are fewer joints, it takes longer for the blocks of rock to be broken off and the blocks are left upstanding as tors.

Land use and economic uses

On the higher areas, bog, marsh and moorland produce some of the least useful land in the UK. In some places there may be opportunities for water storage. At lower levels there may still be nothing better than poor grazing land suitable only for sheep and cattle, and on Dartmoor, also for ponies. Soils are acidic and infertile; it is only around the edges of the uplands that the pastures improve sufficiently to allow grazing by dairy cattle.

Granite is a fine building stone. Aberdeen is known as 'the granite city' since so much use was made by builders of locally available supplies of stone. It is also often used for headstones in graveyards.

Granite rock is susceptible to attack by chemical weathering and in some places it has decomposed. This resulted in the feldspar in the granite being converted into clay minerals, such as china clay (kaolin). China clay is best known as the raw material for the pottery and porcelain industries, and much is sent to the Potteries region around Stoke-on-Trent. It is also used in the manufacture of paper and is an ingredient in paint, toothpaste, skin creams and many other products.

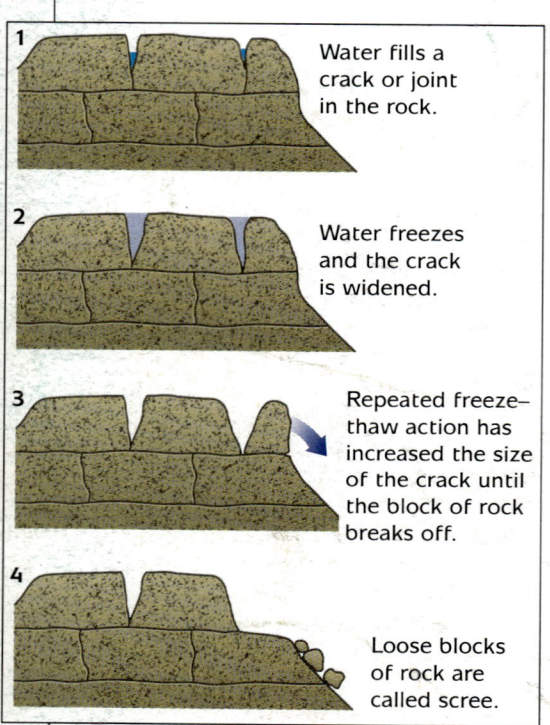

▲ **Figure 1** How freeze–thaw weathering operates.

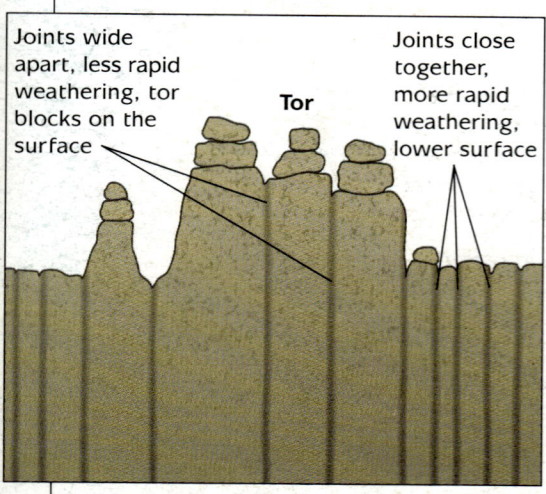

▲ **Figure 2** Effects of joints upon tor formation.

Case Study of a granite landscape – Dartmoor

Figure 3 Bowerman's Nose, a tor on Dartmoor.

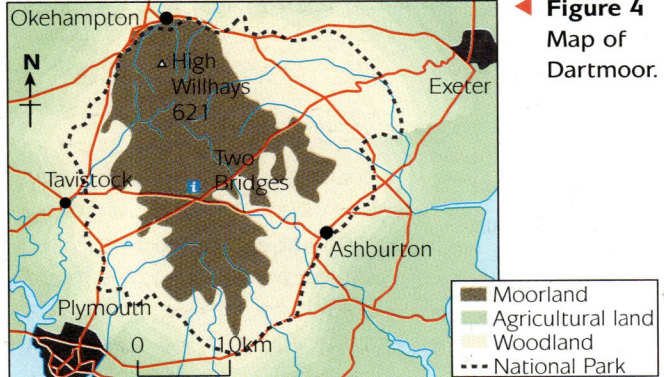

Figure 4 Map of Dartmoor.

Dartmoor

- Dartmoor has a high rainfall and is known for its mists and fogs.
- Much of the land is covered by heather.
- The many boggy areas contain a rich variety of plant life.
- The central upland block was enclosed within a National Park in 1951.
- The Park covers almost 100 000 hectares and over 30 000 people live inside it.
- Up to eight million people visit or pass through the Park each year.
- Most of the towns, such as Tavistock, Okehampton and Ashburton, are located around the edges of the central block.
- Places popular with visitors include Buckfast Abbey, Haytor, Becky Falls and Lydford Gorge.
- Some of the remains of old woodlands have been preserved as natural nature reserves.

Activities

1. Draw a frame the same size as **Figure 3**. Draw a sketch from the photograph and label the landscape features and land uses shown.

2. The tor is the most distinctive granite landform.
   a. Name and locate an example of a tor.
   b. With the aid of a diagram, describe the features of a tor.
   c. Explain how a tor is formed.

3. Answer the questions below using information from **Figure 4**.
   a. *Relief and drainage*
      (i) Name and give the height of the highest point on Dartmoor.
      (ii) Describe where the highest land (above 600m) is located.
      (iii) In which directions do most of the rivers flow?
   b. *Land uses*
      (i) Describe and explain the pattern of land use shown in Figure 4.
      (ii) Suggest as many reasons as you can why the tourist information centre has been located in Two Bridges.

4. Use the information provided and do some research of your own. Produce a short case study on one side of A4 paper with the title 'Tourism on Dartmoor'. Make it interesting and informative; try to use a mixture of maps, sketches, diagrams and written information.

Carboniferous limestone

Although outcrops of Carboniferous limestone occur widely in the uplands of England and Wales, the greatest number and variety of distinctive landforms can be seen in two of the English National Parks – the Yorkshire Dales around Malham and Ingleton, and the Peak District near Castleton. Outcrops of Carboniferous limestone cover much more extensive areas around the Mediterranean – you may have visited caves and caverns while on holiday in places such as Majorca.

Landscape features

Carboniferous limestone weathers to produce distinctive landforms both above and below ground. **Limestone pavements** (see page 19) are flat surfaces of bare rock broken up into separate blocks. The flat surfaces of the blocks are **clints** and the gaps are **grykes**. Rivers disappear underground either through small holes in the rock, called **sink holes**, or down larger holes with a funnel shape above, called **swallow holes** (Figure 1). Underground the limestone is full of holes: small passageways, or **cave** systems, which from time to time open out into large chambers, or **caverns**. **Stalactites** made of lime hang down from the roofs like long icicles, whilst **stalagmites** are the thicker columns built up from the floor. In places the two meet to form a **pillar** of limestone. Rivers reappear on the surface once they have passed through the limestone outcrops and reach impermeable rocks. In a few places there are surface rivers across the limestone flowing at the bottom of a **gorge**. When many limestone landforms like those described above occur together in an area, they form **karst scenery** (Figure 2).

▲ **Figure 1** The swallow hole at Gaping Gill.
Fell Beck is the surface stream seen disappearing underground. It drops 110m as a waterfall into a giant chamber more than 150m long and 30m high (i.e. large enough to fit a cathedral into). The stream flows several kilometres underground through a complex system of caves before it reappears on the surface through Ingleton Cave and forms Clapham Beck.

Chemical weathering, by **limestone solution**, is the process most responsible for producing these distinctive landforms. Limestone is little affected by pure water, but rain water is slightly acidic and contains some carbon dioxide. Rain water and carbon dioxide in the atmosphere combine to form carbonic acid, in which calcium carbonate (of which the limestone is made) slowly dissolves. Limestone is changed into calcium bicarbonate, which is removed. The limestone is very vulnerable to attack from chemical weathering because of its many lines of weakness, both horizontal (bedding planes) and vertical (joints). The joints are widened by limestone solution to form grykes within the limestone pavement.

Streams also disappear underground down joints widened by limestone solution. The surface opening is gradually enlarged until the funnel-shaped hollow of the swallow hole is formed. Underground streams follow the lines of joints and bedding planes. Fresh supplies of acidic water continue the work of solution until a labyrinth of caves is dissolved out of the limestone. Loosened blocks of rock fall from roofs which have been weakened by solution, turning caves into caverns. There is a slow seepage of water charged with lime into the roofs and walls of caves. Lime (calcium carbonate) is deposited when water evaporates or loses its carbon dioxide. The lime builds up to form the stalactites, stalagmites and pillars.

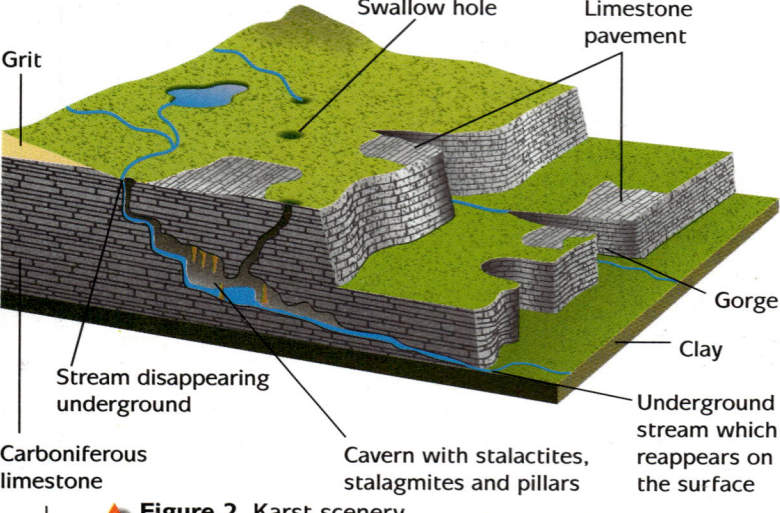

▲ **Figure 2** Karst scenery.

Occasionally the holes that are formed by solution become so large that the roof collapses. When the roof of a long underground passageway falls in, a deep steep-sided valley, or limestone gorge, forms with the river flowing at the bottom of it. A possible example is Gordale where the blocks which may have formed the cavern roof can be seen as debris on the floor (**Figure 3**).

Land use and economic uses

Carboniferous limestone lies on or close to the ground surface, so the soil is too thin to be used for cultivation, and also dry. However, a turf-like grass covers the surface. This is good for sheep farming because they graze short grass. Population density in limestone areas is low, but the limestone landforms are attractive to visitors. Service sector employment has been boosted in the villages and small towns, while some farmers earn a supplementary income from camping and caravan sites and bed and breakfast.

Limestone is of great economic importance. It is widely used as building stone. It is more easily worked than a hard rock such as granite. Limestone has been used in well-known buildings such as St Paul's Cathedral, the Houses of Parliament and the front of Buckingham Palace. When crushed up it is used for chippings for drives or for making concrete and cement. Farmers spread lime on their fields as fertilizer. Limestone is also used as a cleanser in many industries such as smelting steel, to absorb harmful sulphur dioxide from coal-fired power stations, and to purify water. With so many and varied uses there are many quarries in limestone areas, and some visitors feel that these ruin their scenic beauty (pages 28–29).

▲ **Figure 3** The gorge at Gordale, a possible collapsed cavern.

Carboniferous limestone scenery near Malham

The stream which disappears underground at A1 on **Figure 4** reappears at A2 at the bottom of Malham Cove. The stream which disappears underground at B1 on **Figure 4** is shown on the photograph (**Figure 5**). It reappears on the surface as a spring at B2 on **Figure 4**.

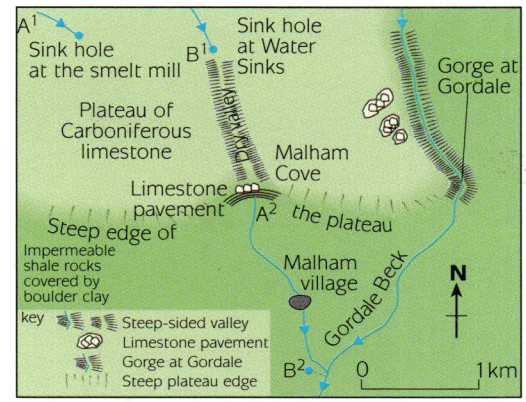

▲ **Figure 4** Location of Carboniferous limestone features near Malham.

▲ **Figure 5** Sink hole at Water Sinks.

The water is gradually sinking underground through sink holes in the stream bed so that little water is left in the stream in the foreground of the photograph.

Activities

1. Describe the physical features of each of the following on a labelled sketch. Explain how it was formed.
   a The sink hole at Water Sinks.
   b The limestone pavement above Malham Cove.
   c The gorge at Gordale.

2. What underground features are likely to be present between Water Sinks and the bottom of Malham Cove? Explain your answer with the help of diagrams.

Chalk and clay

Figure 1 Chalk and clay meet at the foot of the South Downs near Fulking.
In many places in England chalk (on the right) and clay (on the left) outcrop next to one another; together they form a distinctive but contrasting landscape of chalk escarpment and clay vale. Chalk and clay are both sedimentary rocks and only outcrop in Lowland Britain; they have little else in common.

Landscape features

The **chalk escarpment** (also known as a cuesta) is the most distinctive feature of chalk scenery in England. It consists of two parts – the **scarp** slope, which is steep, and the **dip** slope, on which the land falls away more gently. The top of the escarpment has gently rolling hills with rounded summits. There is little surface drainage and rivers are few and far between; however, in places the dip slope has been cut by deep, steep-sided, V-shaped **dry valleys**, which are marked landscape features (**Figure 2**). After spells of wet weather temporary streams may flow in the valleys; these are known as **bournes**, and this term is used in place names such as Bournemouth and Eastbourne.

▲ Figure 2 Devil's Dyke dry valley east of Fulking.

Chalk outcrops along the coast often lead to high cliffs such as the famous 'white cliffs of Dover', and to prominent headlands, such as Beachy Head in Sussex and Flamborough Head in Yorkshire. Erosion around headlands can lead to the formation of caves, arches and stacks. The Needles off the north-west corner of the Isle of Wight are examples of stacks (Chapter 5). In contrast, the **clay vale** is a wide and often totally flat area of land. Surface drainage is abundant and the vale is crossed by meandering streams. At the coast, clay forms weak cliffs which slide and collapse.

Formation of the chalk escarpment

There are two requirements before an escarpment can be formed (**Figure 3A**):

1. Alternate outcrops of different types of rocks. One rock needs to be soft and the other needs to be more resistant to erosion.
2. Beds of rock dip at an angle to the ground surface. Instead of being horizontal, the beds were tilted by earth movements so that they lie at an angle to the surface.

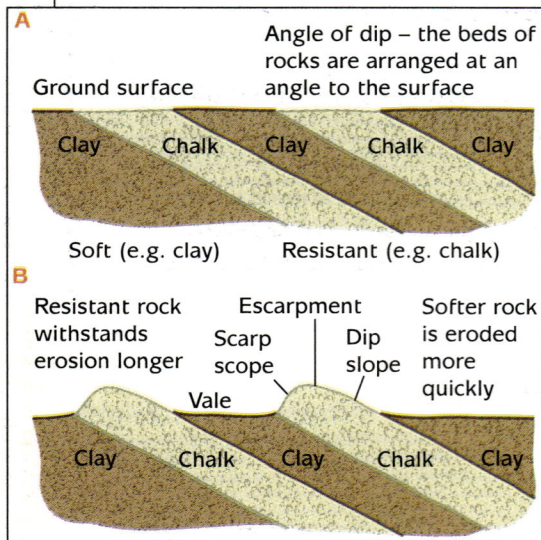

▲ Figure 3 (A) Rock arrangement needed for the formation of an escarpment. (B) Formation of an escarpment.

These two needs are commonly met in eastern and southern England. The clay is eroded more quickly than the chalk. As the clay is eroded down into a vale, the chalk is left standing up because of its greater resistance. The scarp slope forms a prominent feature where the layer of chalk reaches the surface. The dip slope is more gentle following the tilt of the beds of rock.

Land use and economic uses

There are great differences in settlement and other land uses between areas of chalk and clay.

Settlement
Some of the earliest human arrivals to the British Isles settled on chalk escarpments. Above the village of Fulking on **Figure 4** there are signs of burial mounds (tumulus) and old defences (fort and motte and bailey). The chalk escarpments were drier than the wet clay vales and contained flint which could be used for tools and weapons by the early settlers. The main problem for settlement in areas of chalk was shortage of water. **Springs** form at the junction of the chalk and clay; water seeping down through the spaces in the porous chalk meets the impermeable clay and reappears on the surface as a flow of water. Settlements grew along the spring line and Fulking is a classic example.

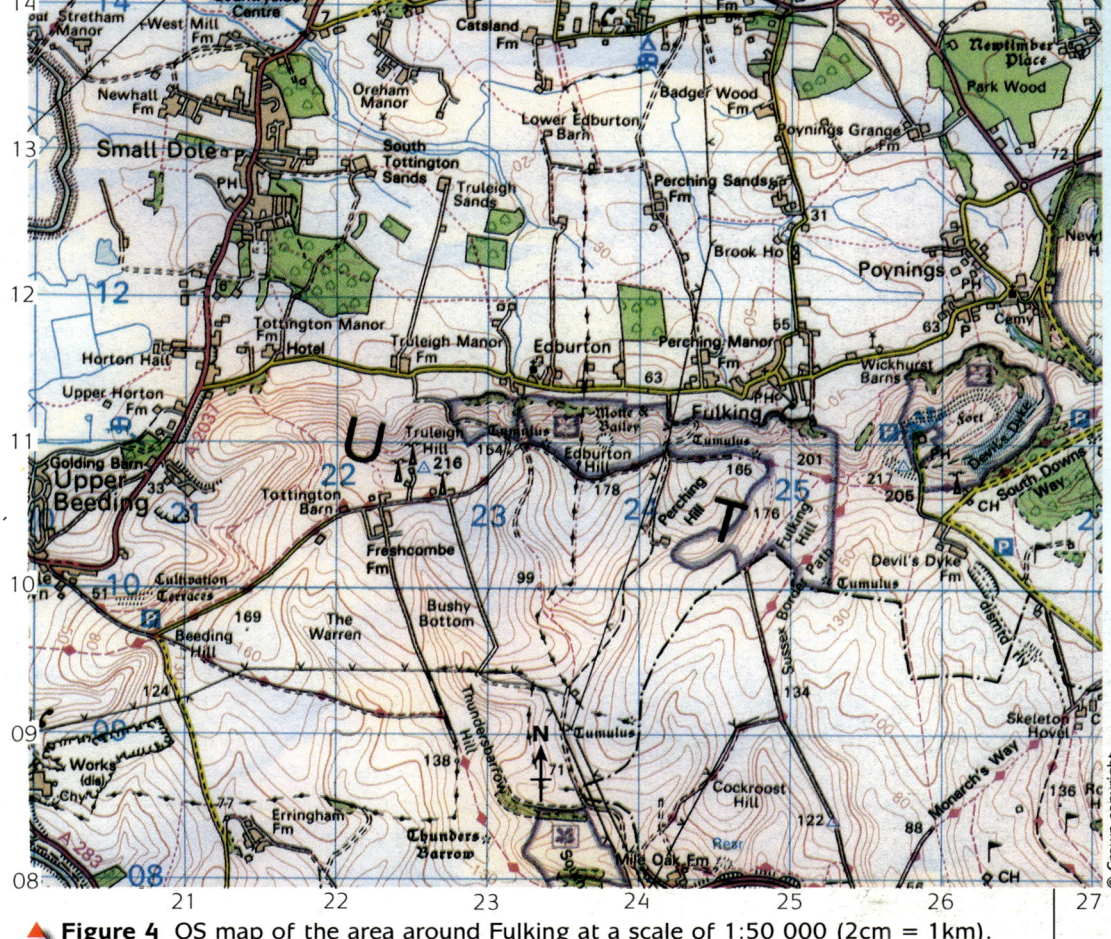

▲ **Figure 4** OS map of the area around Fulking at a scale of 1:50 000 (2cm = 1km).

Land uses
The main land use on chalk is pasture. The short but rich turf is good for grazing sheep and training racehorses. Famous racecourses such as Epsom are situated on the Downs. High cereal prices and intensification of farming have led some farmers to plough up gentler and lower slopes for wheat and barley, despite the dry and stony nature of the chalk soils. The main land use on clay is also pasture. In general the soils are too wet and heavy to plough. The grass grows longer than that on the chalk and is more likely to be grazed by dairy cattle.

Economic uses
Chalk with flint provides a strong and attractive building material. Chalk has many of the same economic uses as limestone, such as in the manufacture of cement. The underground stores of water, known as **aquifers**, are widely used for water supply in south-east England. Clay, taken from pits, is a raw material for making bricks.

Activities

1 Describe the differences between the areas north and south of Fulking using these headings.
   a Relief (height and shape of the land)
   b Drainage (number and density of surface streams)
   c Land uses and economic activities (woodlands, farms, settlement, quarrying, etc.).

2 Using **Figure 4**, draw a sketch cross-section from grid reference 226140 in the north (height 10m) to 226080 in the south (height 100m). Add labels for the clay vale, scarp slope and dip slope.

3 a In which direction was the camera pointing when the photograph for **Figure 1** was taken?
   b Describe the additional information about land uses given on the photograph compared with the OS map.

Quarrying

Quarrying and mining are almost as old as settlement itself in the British Isles. Early settlers used stone for building shelters, defensive works and burial mounds. Metals were needed for making implements, weapons and armour. As populations grew over the centuries and economic development occurred, the demand for stone and metals increased as well. For example, the numerous dry-stone walls, which are such a distinctive feature of the human landscape in many parts of the Pennines, testify to the importance of limestone quarrying over many centuries (**Figure 1**). Until quite recently lead mining was also a widespread and important activity in the Pennines.

What happens in quarrying?
There are several stages, from preparing the site to the eventual cleaning up of the site and reclamation of the land after quarrying has finished.

A **Preparing the site.** Once planning permission to quarry the site has been obtained, giant earth-moving equipment is brought in. All the vegetation and topsoil are scraped off and piled up.

B **Extracting the rock.** Explosives are placed in holes drilled into the rock face. Powerful blasts can bring thousands of tonnes of rock crashing down, which are cleared by giant diggers.

C **Treating the rock.** Giant crushers break down the rock into smaller pieces. Rocks are screened, or sorted into pieces of different sizes, before being used or sent to market. In some quarries the rock is processed into a manufactured product on site; for example, chalk and limestone are often made into cement to avoid costs of transporting a bulky raw material. Waste materials are dumped.

D **Transporting the rock.** For most quarry owners, the favoured method of transport is by road.

E **Cleaning up the site.** After quarrying has finished there are various options, depending upon factors such as the size and location of the quarry. A quarry may be infilled with rubbish from urban areas; landfill sites are reclaimed once they have been fully filled in. Other quarries are left much as they are, but are cleaned up and landscaped as much as possible, perhaps for recreational uses.

Some of the advantages associated with quarrying rocks are given in **Figure 2**.

▲ **Figure 1** Dry-stone walls, made of limestone, around the farm and between the fields are part of the traditional Yorkshire Dales way of life. The camp site reflects new opportunities from tourism.

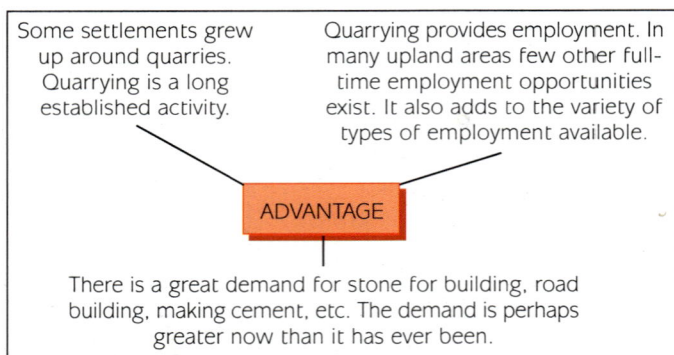

▲ **Figure 2** Positive impacts of quarrying.

Problems caused by quarrying
Planners and Local Authorities have an important role to play in preventing the commercial companies that operate the quarries from thinking only of how to make the largest profits.

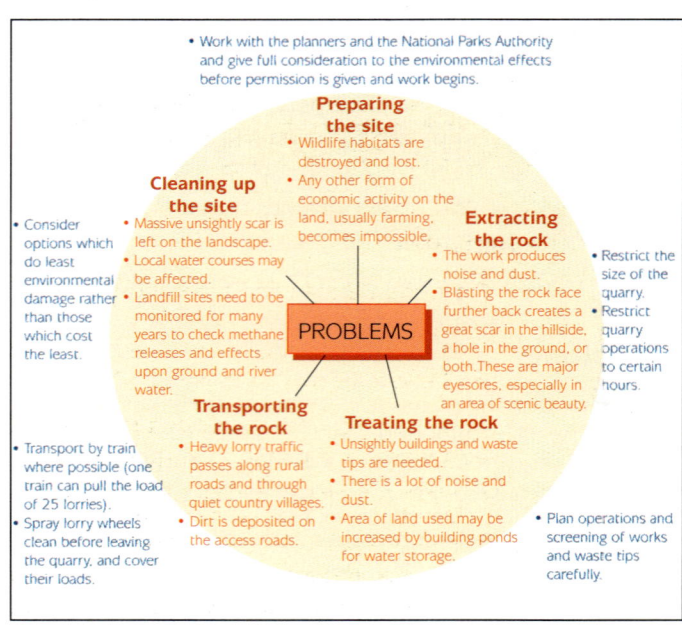

▲ **Figure 3** Negative impacts of quarrying. Ways of reducing impacts are given in blue.

Chapter 2 Rocks and landscape

Limestone quarrying and Hope cement works in the Peak District

The village of Castleton (**Figure 4**) grew due to its closeness to lead mines. Some of the limestone caves and caverns in the region that now attract thousands of visitors each year, such as Blue John and Speedwell Caverns, previously had been used by miners. The railway line, which gives access with a station in Hope, was also part of Britain's mining history because it was built to transport salt from Cheshire to Sheffield just before the end of the nineteenth century. Tourists first arrived in the area by train, but road access is now much more important. Although there are still several farms in the area, many people make at least a part-time living from tourism, in hotels, B&Bs, camp sites, cafés, pubs and shops. The Hope quarry and cement works, however, is the largest single employer in this area (**Figure 5**). Some 300 people are employed, nearly all of whom live locally. Without the works, many more people would be forced to commute by road to towns and cities outside the Park, particularly Manchester and Sheffield.

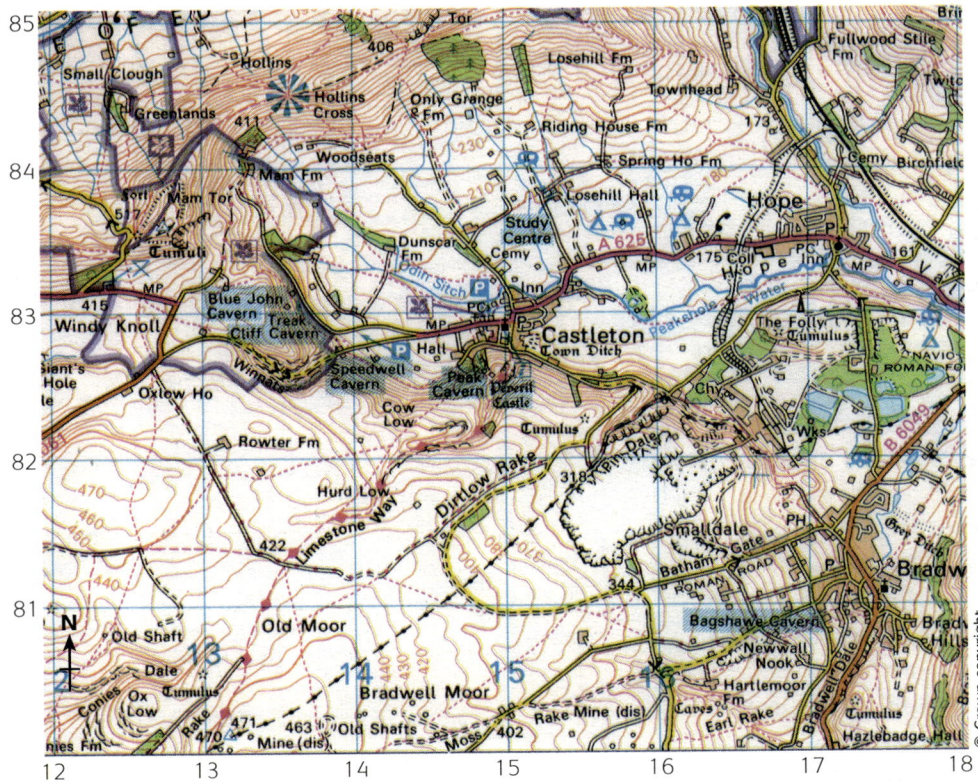

▲ **Figure 5** Hope quarry and cement works.

◀ **Figure 4** OS map of Castleton at a scale of 1:50 000 (2cm = 1km).

Case Study – Peak District National Park near Castleton

Activities

1. From the OS map and other information, state the evidence for:
   a. settlement for many centuries in the area
   b. the long history of mining in the region.

2. Hope cement works is located in square 1682, north-east of the limestone quarry.
   a. From the OS map measure the length and width of the quarry in metres and state the approximate area covered by it.
   b. From **Figures 4** and **5**, describe the other ways in which the presence of the cement works is affecting the landscape.
   c. Why might transport of the limestone and cement to market be less of a problem here?

3. Castleton is a tourist honeypot – it attracts many tourist visitors. From the OS map:
   a. describe the attractions for visitors in and around Castleton
   b. state the facilities provided for them.

4. Local people in Castleton have differing views about both the quarry and tourist visitors.
   a. Suggest some of the different views that may exist among the villagers.
   b. Explain why they have arisen.

Weathering

Weathering is the breakdown of rock at or near the surface, for which the weather, such as changes in temperature, is mainly responsible. The rocks are broken down 'in situ', which means that no movement is involved (unlike erosion, which is caused by the movement of water, ice and wind). There are two main types of weathering, **physical weathering** and **chemical weathering**.

Physical weathering

This leads to the break-up of the rock without any change in the minerals which form the rock.

In *cold climates* the most widespread type is **freeze–thaw** (**Figure 1** on page 22). The more often the temperature fluctuates above and below freezing point during the year, the more effective freeze–thaw is at breaking off pieces of rock. The sharp-edged (or angular) pieces of rock broken off form **scree**; scree slopes can be seen below rock outcrops in all upland areas (**Figure 1**).

▲ **Figure 1** Scree slopes on the side of Wastwater in the Lake District.

In *hot dry climates*, **exfoliation** is a more important type of physical weathering. The outer layer of the rock is heated greatly by the sun during the day and it expands. At night cooling of the rock leads to contraction. After this expansion and contraction has been repeated many times, the outer 'skin' of the rock peels away like that of an onion. Exfoliation leaves rounded boulders and dome-shaped rocky outcrops, which are features of many desert landscapes.

Chemical weathering

This happens when the minerals of which the rock is composed are changed, leading to the disintegration of the rock. Chemical weathering affects granite rocks when feldspar, one of the minerals which make up granite, is converted into clay minerals such as kaolin (china clay). This product is of great economic importance (see page 22). The distinctive landforms in areas of Carboniferous limestone, both above and below the ground, owe their origins to **limestone solution** (pages 24–25). This type of chemical weathering is also called carbonation because the dissolving of the limestone changes calcium carbonate into calcium bicarbonate.

ℹ️ Information Box

The chemical formula for limestone solution is:

$$\underset{\text{calcium carbonate}}{CaCO_3} + \underset{\underset{\text{carbonic acid}}{\underbrace{}}}{\underset{\text{water}}{H_2O} + \underset{\text{carbon dioxide}}{CO_2}} \rightarrow \underset{\text{calcium bicarbonate}}{Ca(HCO_3)_2}$$

Now that you have worked through Chapters 1 and 2, you are probably aware of the **sediment cycle** (**Figure 2**).

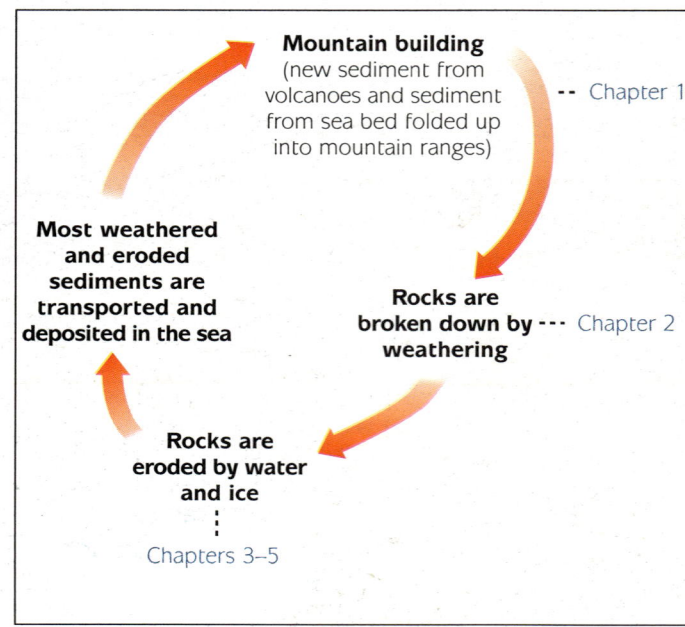

▲ **Figure 2** The Earth's sediment cycle.

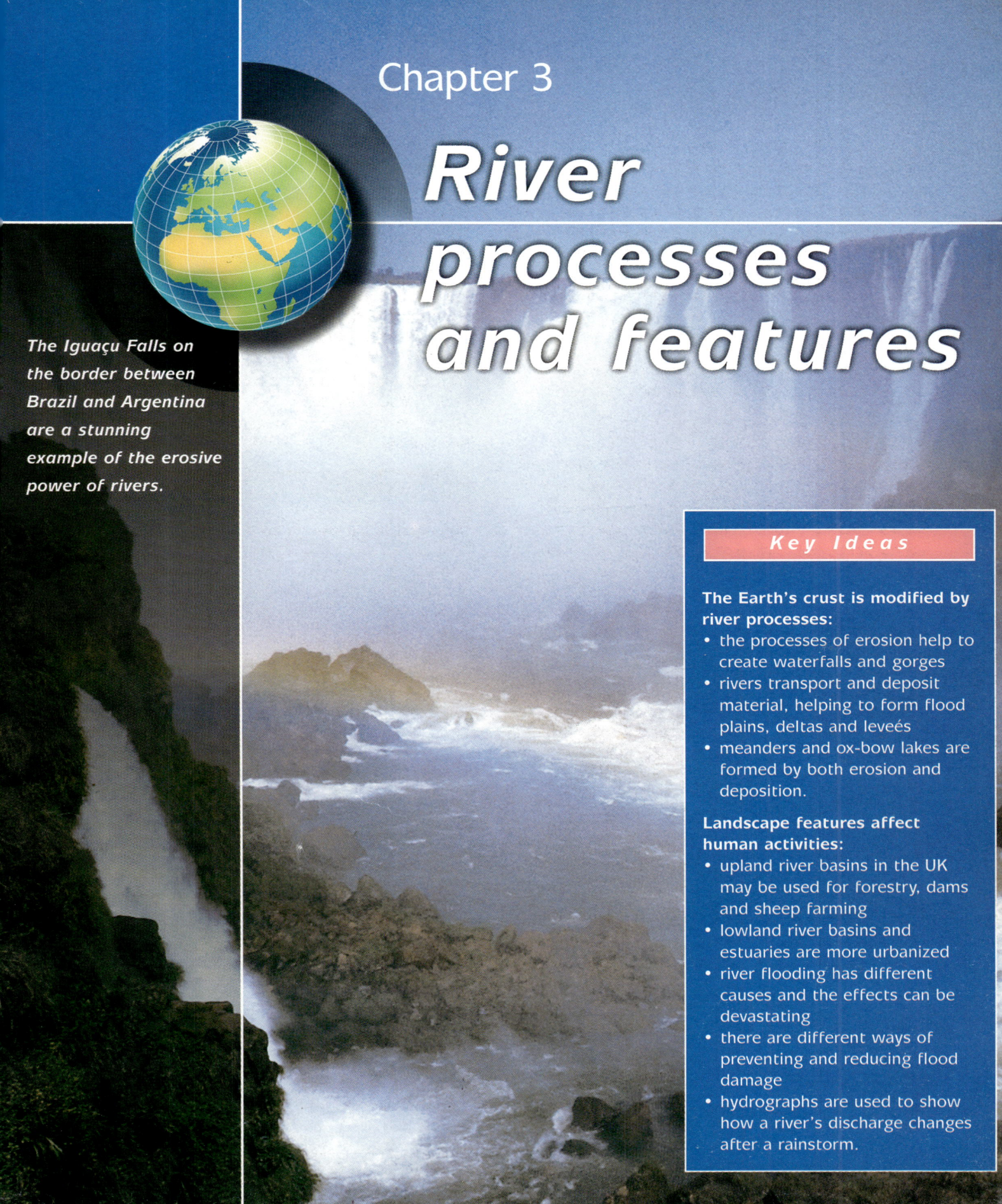

Chapter 3
River processes and features

The Iguaçu Falls on the border between Brazil and Argentina are a stunning example of the erosive power of rivers.

Key Ideas

The Earth's crust is modified by river processes:
- the processes of erosion help to create waterfalls and gorges
- rivers transport and deposit material, helping to form flood plains, deltas and leveés
- meanders and ox-bow lakes are formed by both erosion and deposition.

Landscape features affect human activities:
- upland river basins in the UK may be used for forestry, dams and sheep farming
- lowland river basins and estuaries are more urbanized
- river flooding has different causes and the effects can be devastating
- there are different ways of preventing and reducing flood damage
- hydrographs are used to show how a river's discharge changes after a rainstorm.

River basins

Rivers begin in upland areas and flow downhill, becoming wider and deeper, until they enter the sea. Where a river begins is called the **source** and where it ends is the **mouth**. Along a river's journey to the sea other smaller rivers called **tributaries** may join the main river at a **confluence**. A river and its tributaries obtain their water from the surrounding land. The area drained by a river and its tributaries is called the **drainage basin** (**Figure 1**). The boundary of the drainage basin is called the **watershed** and it is usually a ridge of high land.

A drainage basin is part of the **hydrological cycle** in which water is recycled between the sea, air and land. **Figure 2** shows the basin hydrological cycle.

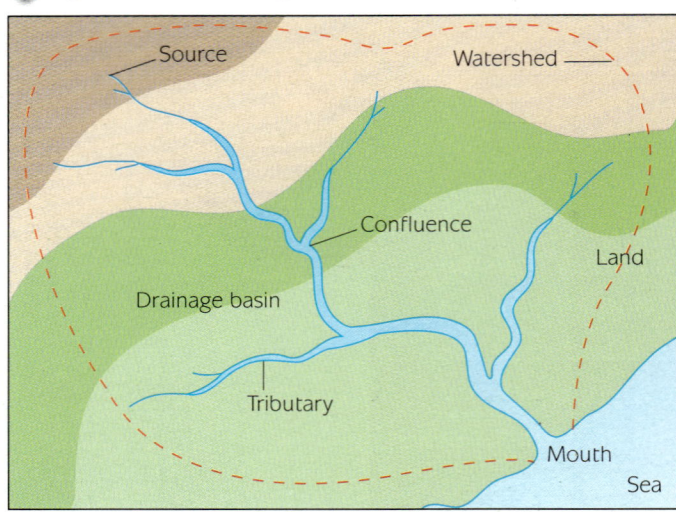

▼ **Figure 1** The drainage basin of a river.

The water in a river flows within a **channel** unless the river floods and spills out onto the surrounding land. The size and shape of the channel changes as the river flows downstream, becoming wider and deeper. A river also flows within a valley; the size and shape of the valley changes downstream from a V-shaped river valley to a broad, flat U-shape. **Figure 3** shows some of the changes which take place downstream in a river valley.

Many of these changes are caused by changes in the river energy. In the uplands, close to the source, the river is high above its base level (usually sea level). This gives the river a lot of potential energy. The river is also trying to reach its base level, therefore the main processes at work are erosional. The river mainly erodes in a downwards direction (vertical erosion) to try to reach its base level. This helps to create V-shaped river valleys in upland areas. As the river moves downstream it uses a lot of energy to transport the material or load it has eroded. Surplus energy is now used to erode sideways (lateral erosion) because the river is much closer to its base level, and so the river valley becomes wider and flatter.

The long profile of a river shows a steep gradient at the source, gradually becoming lower and less steep until the gradient is almost nil near to sea level. The normal profile is smooth and concave. The changes in the river valley and features along the profile allow the river to be sub-divided into three sections – the upper, middle and lower courses. Study **Figure 3** to find out more about how a river and its valley change downstream.

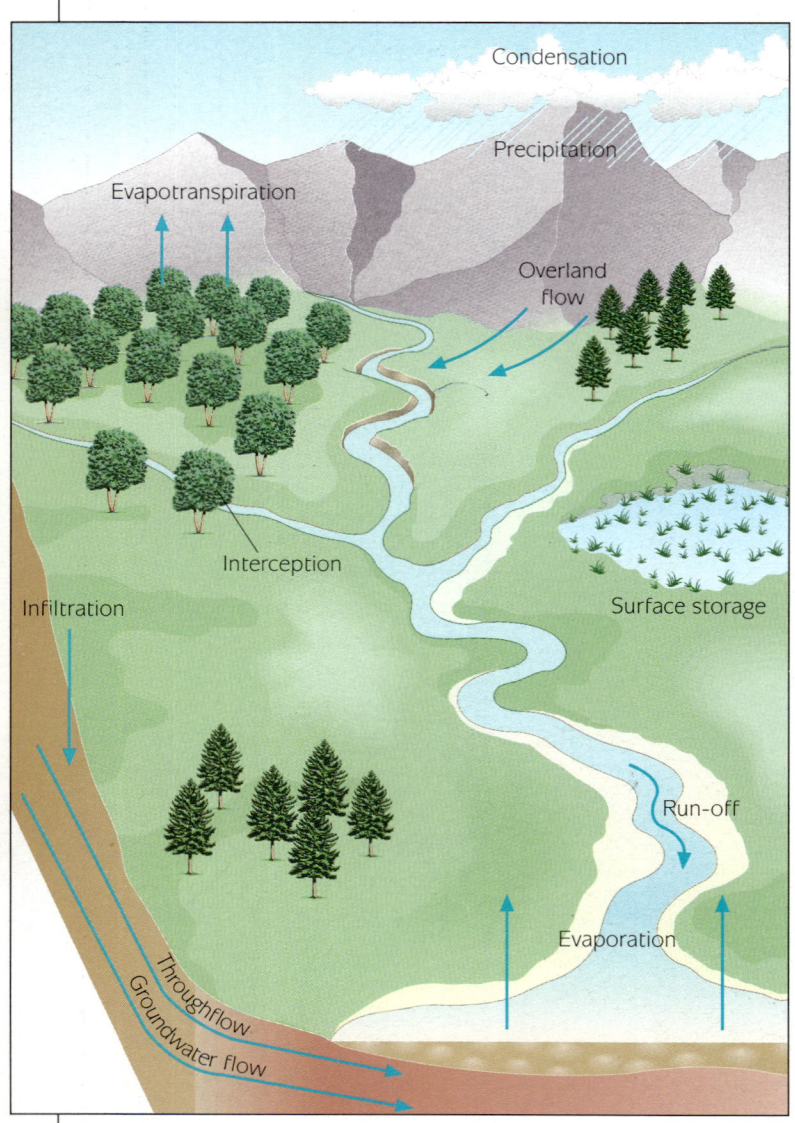

▲ **Figure 2** The basin hydrological cycle.

Chapter 3 River processes and features

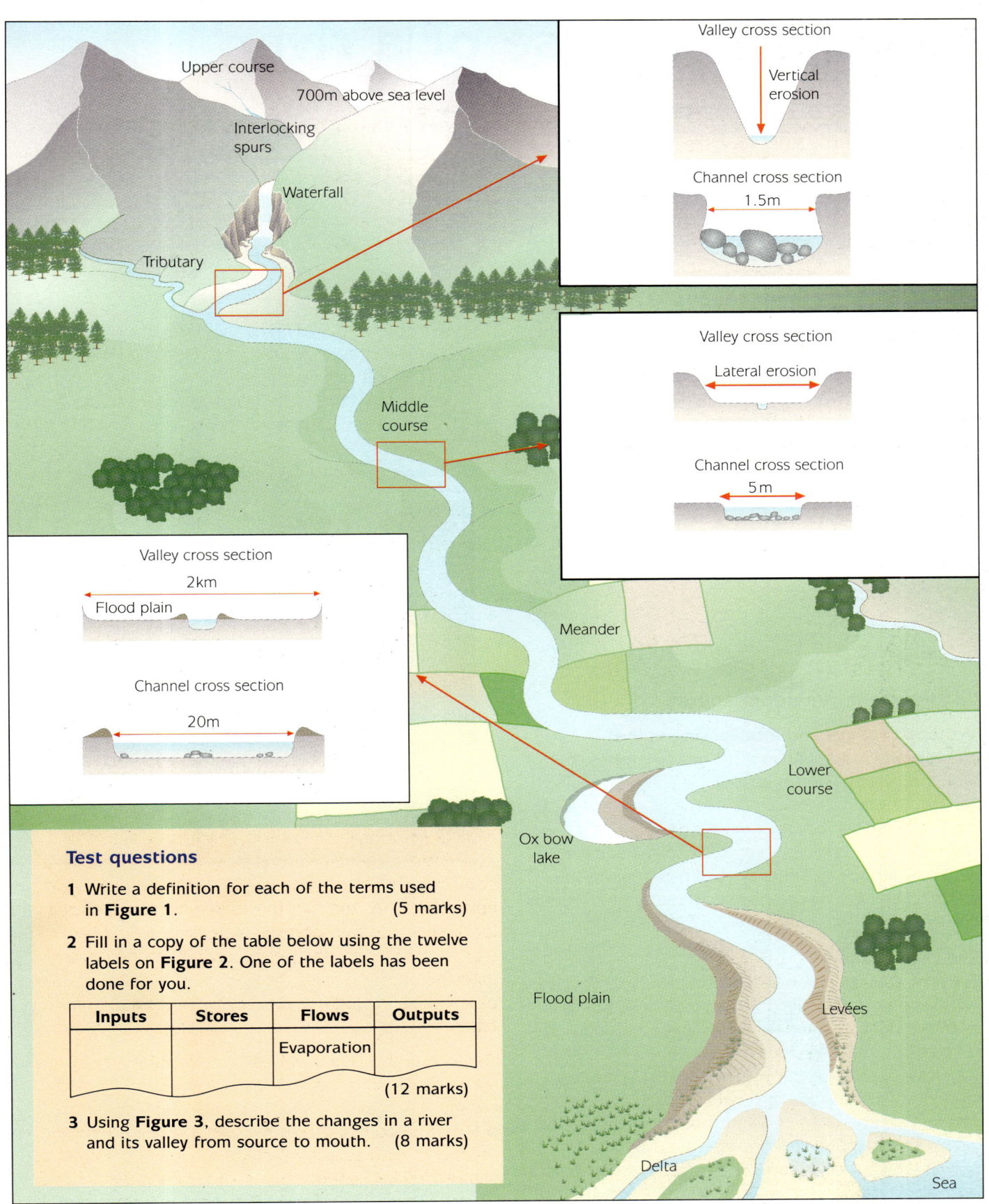

Figure 3 The changes downstream in a river.

Test questions

1. Write a definition for each of the terms used in **Figure 1**. (5 marks)

2. Fill in a copy of the table below using the twelve labels on **Figure 2**. One of the labels has been done for you.

Inputs	Stores	Flows	Outputs
		Evaporation	

(12 marks)

3. Using **Figure 3**, describe the changes in a river and its valley from source to mouth. (8 marks)

The upper course of a river

In the upper course of a river, erosion is the dominant process. A river may erode by one of the four processes shown in **Figure 1**.

▼ **Figure 1** Processes of erosion.

Hydraulic power: This is the force of the water on the bed and banks of the river. It is particularly powerful when the river is in flood. The force of the water removes material from the bed and banks of the river.	**Corrosion:** Some rock minerals, such as calcium carbonate in limestone and chalk, slowly dissolve in river water, which is sometimes slightly acid.
Corrasion: The river carries with it particles of sand and silt and moves pebbles and boulders at times of high flow. This material rubs against the bed and banks of the river and wears them away. This process is also called **abrasion**.	**Attrition:** The load being carried by the river collides and rubs against itself, breaking up into smaller and smaller pieces. The rough edges also become smooth, forming smaller, rounded material. Eventually the particles are reduced to sand and silt-sized particles.

Landforms in the upper course

V-shaped valleys and interlocking spurs

The vertical erosion in the upper course creates the **V-shaped valley** (Figure 2) which is steep-sided and narrow. As the river erodes downwards, soil and loose rock on the valley sides are moved downhill by slopewash or soil creep. The river also winds its way around **interlocking spurs** of hard rock (Figure 2), which should not be confused with meanders! There is no flat valley floor and the valley gradient is steep.

The river channel

The river channel is narrow and shallow; it is often lined with large angular boulders. The gradient of the river may be quite steep and waterfalls and rapids may be found along the river. The velocity of the river is high at waterfalls and rapids but may be quite low in other stretches because so much energy is used in overcoming friction with the rocky bed and banks of the river. The water is often quite clear because the river is not carrying much load in suspension. The river has not had time to grind down the boulders into fine sand and silt-sized particles by abrasion and attrition.

▲ **Figure 2** A V-shaped valley with interlocking spurs.

Waterfalls and gorges

A waterfall (**Figure 3**) is a steep drop in the course of a river. It has a high head of water and a characteristic plunge pool at the base. The rocks at the top of the waterfall are often hard and resistant, forming a cap rock, and softer rocks below are undercut (**Figure 4**). The waterfall may lie within a gorge.

Waterfalls often form when a band of resistant rock lies over softer, less resistant rocks. The softer rock is eroded more quickly, causing undercutting of the hard rock. The hard rock overhangs until it can no longer support its weight. The overhang then collapses, adding large blocks of rock to the base of the waterfall. The great power of the water falling to the base moves the material around, eroding the base into a deep plunge pool. The bed of the river below a waterfall contains boulders eroded by splashback from behind the waterfall, and some blocks of rock from the collapse of the hard cap rock.

Over a very long time the process of undercutting and collapse is repeated many times, causing the waterfall to retreat upstream. The retreat creates a steep-sided **gorge of recession** (**Figure 5**). At the same time chips of the hard cap rock are eroded away, which reduces the height of the waterfall.

▲ **Figure 3** Niagara Falls.

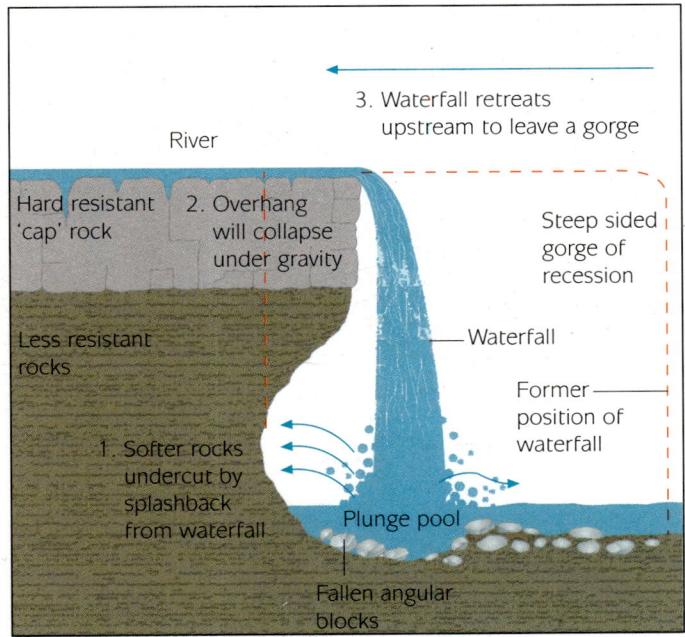

▲ **Figure 4** The formation of a waterfall.

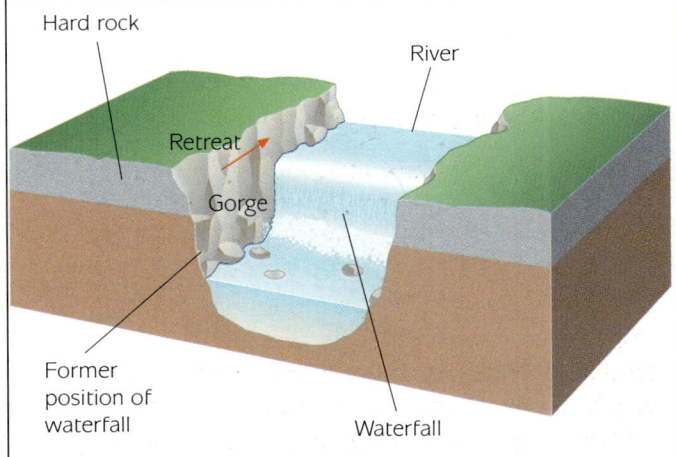

▲ **Figure 5** Formation of a gorge of recession.

Activity

Use the photographs on these pages to draw labelled sketches.

a Draw a frame about the same size as each photograph.
b Sketch in the main features shown.
c Label your diagram as fully as you can.
d Colour in your sketch and give it a title.

The middle course of a river

As the river flows downstream, the gradient over which it flows becomes less steep and the river is not as high above its base level. The river continues to erode vertically, but lateral or sideways erosion becomes more important. When the river emerges from its upland area it begins to **meander** in order to use up surplus energy. The erosion on the outside of meanders removes the ends of the interlocking spurs and the valley becomes wider and has a more recognizable valley floor. Some of the river's energy is also used in transporting the eroded material downstream. The material is transported in one of four ways (**Figure 1**). The amount of load being carried depends on:

- the volume of water – the greater the volume, the more load it can carry
- the velocity – a fast-flowing river has more energy to transport and can move larger particles
- the local rock types – some rocks, e.g. shales, are more easily eroded than others, e.g. granite.

Meanders

Meanders are bends in the river's course (**Figure 2**). On the outside of a meander the water is deeper and the current flows faster. The force of the water erodes and undercuts the outside bend by corrasion, forming a steep bank called a **river cliff**. On the inside bend there is slack water and the current is less strong, which encourages deposition. Sand and small pebbles are deposited creating a gentle **slip-off slope**. An underwater current spirals down the river, carrying the eroded material from the river cliff to the slip-off slope.

Traction—large boulders roll along the river bed

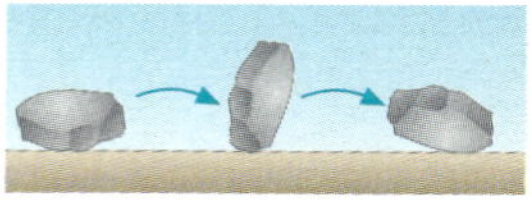

Saltation—smaller pebbles are bounced along the river bed, picked up and then dropped as the flow of the river changes

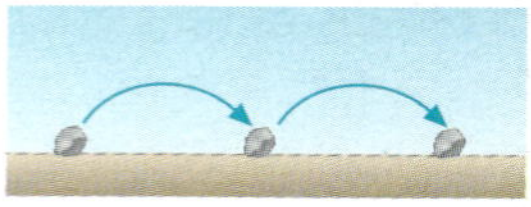

Suspension—the finer sand and silt-sized particles are carried along in the flow, giving the river a brown appearance

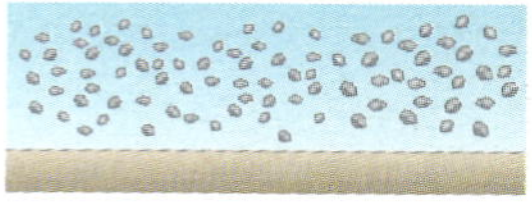

Solution—minerals, such as limestone and chalk, are dissolved in the water and carried along in the flow, although they cannot be seen

▲ **Figure 1** Transporting the river's load.

The lateral erosion on the outside bend of the meander widens the valley floor and erodes away the ends of the interlocking spurs. A more recognizable flat valley floor is created.

Meander migration

As the river flows downstream it becomes deeper and wider. The meanders also become larger and wider and they migrate downstream (**Figure 3**). The erosion on the outside bend of the meander widens the valley. Deposition builds up the deposits of alluvium to create the valley floor. At the same time the erosion and deposition cause the meanders to move gradually downstream. This creates a line of river cliffs along the edge of the valley floor. You can see the former course of the river on **Figure 4**.

▲ **Figure 2** The features of a meander.

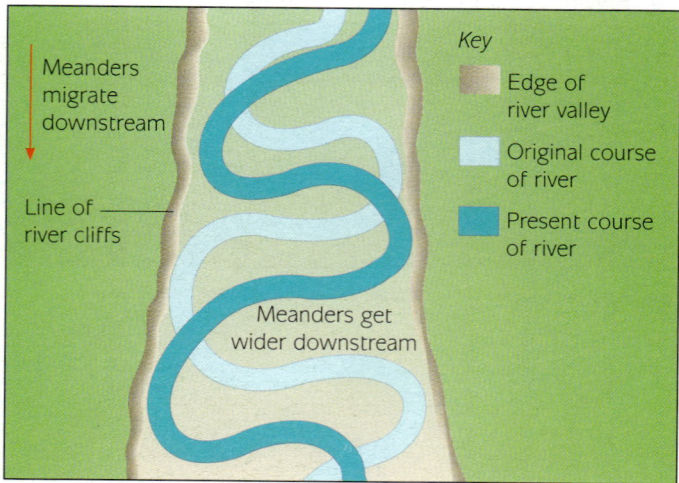

▲ **Figure 3** Meander migration.

The lower course of a river

In the lower course the river channel becomes wider and deeper. The velocity is often greater than in the upper course because the channel is more efficient with less friction. The channel is almost semi-circular and much smoother because of deposits of sand and mud. In the lower course a river flows through a wide, flat valley called the flood plain (**Figure 4**).

The river carries a large load of suspended material. Deposition of the sand and silt, called **alluvium**, becomes the most important process. Alluvium is found in great thicknesses on the flood plain, especially where levées are formed. Deposition is encouraged by several factors:

- a river carrying a large load, providing a great deal of material for deposition
- a reduction in velocity such as at the inside bend in a meander
- an obstruction, e.g. a river enters a lake and velocity falls, or it meets waves and currents, or bridge parapets interrupt flow
- a fall in the volume of river water, e.g. at times of low flow during a period of drought.

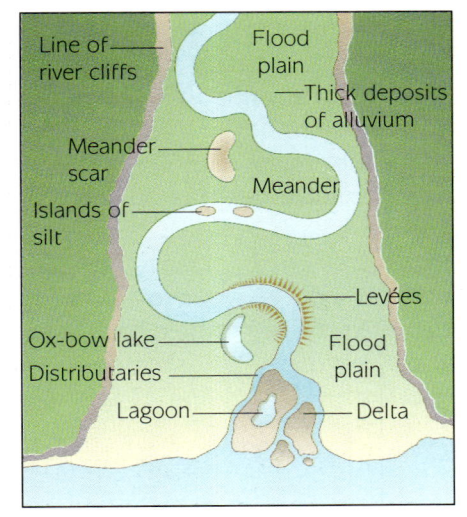

Figure 4 Features of the flood plain.

Ox-bow lakes

The meander bends become even larger in the lower course as the river meanders more vigorously. Continued erosion on the outer bends and deposition on the inside of the bends may eventually lead to the formation of an **ox-bow lake** (Figure 5). The neck of the meander narrows as erosion continues on the outside bends. Eventually the neck is broken through, creating a straight channel. This often happens during a flood when the river is particularly powerful. As the flood waters fall, and at times of low flow, alluvium is deposited which seals off the old meander and forms an ox-bow lake. Gradually the ox-bow lake dries up, forming a **meander scar**.

The flood plain

The flood plain is the wide, flat area of land either side of the river in its lower course. The flood plain is formed by both erosion *and* deposition. Lateral erosion is caused by meanders and the slow migration downstream to widen the flood plain. The deposition on the slip-off slopes provides sediment to build up the valley floor. This is added to during a flood when the river spills over its banks onto the surrounding land. The river carries with it large quantities of suspended load. As the water floods onto the flood plain there is greater friction, the water is shallow and the velocity falls so its load is deposited onto the flood plain as alluvium. Over many thousands of years these deposits build up into great thicknesses of alluvium.

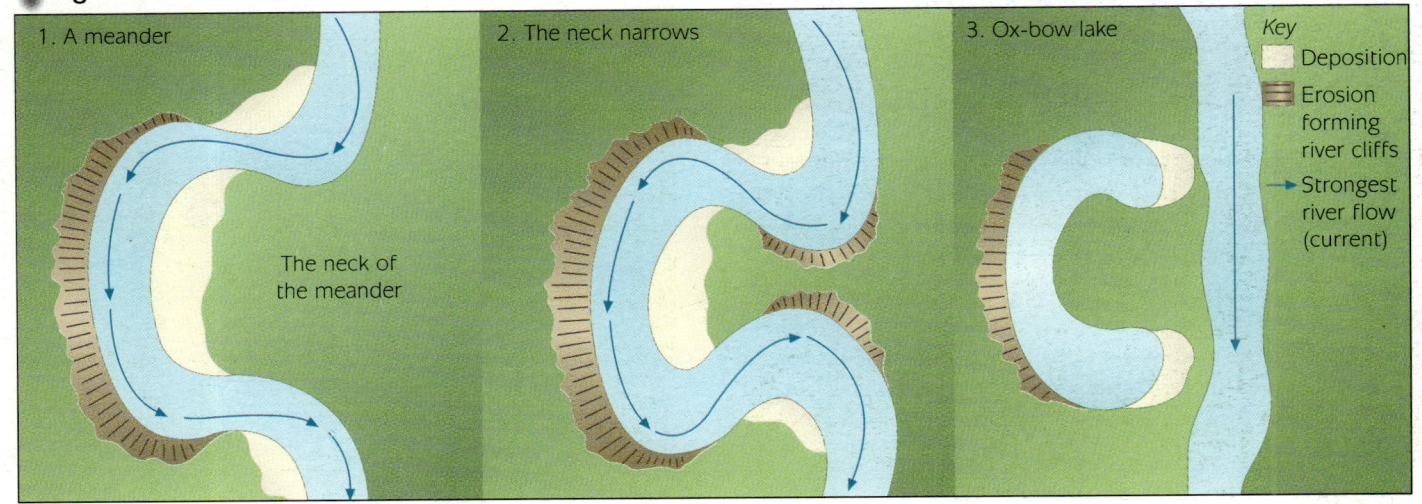

Figure 5 Formation of an ox-bow lake.

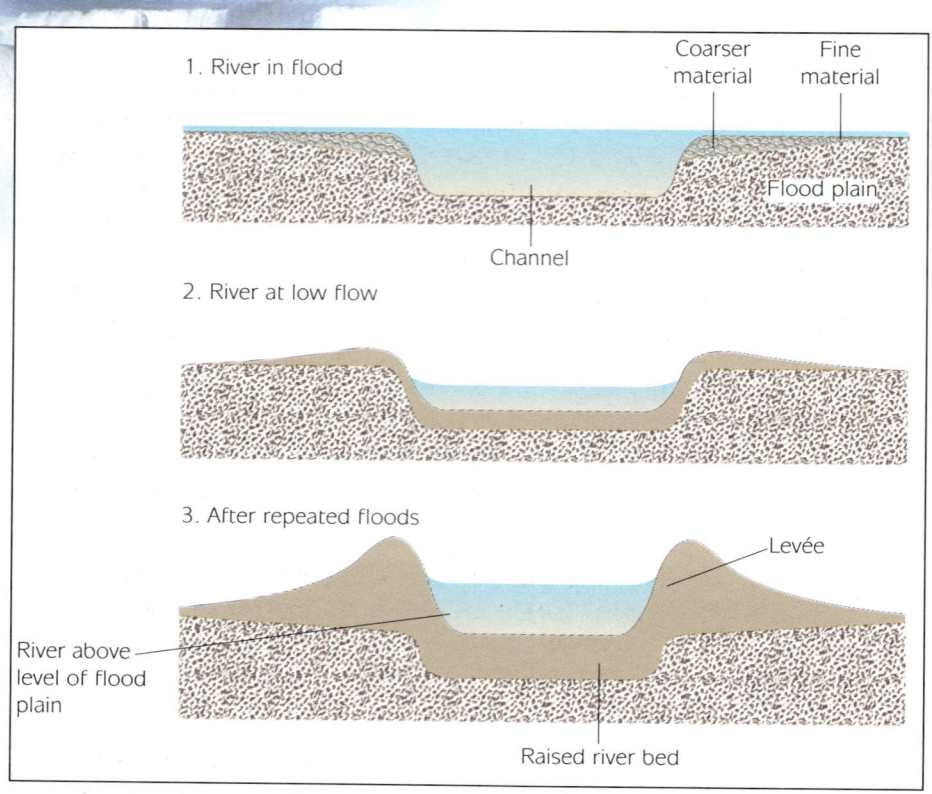

Figure 1 The formation of levées.

Levées

Levées are natural embankments of silt along the banks of a river, often several metres higher than the flood plain. Levées are formed along rivers that flow slowly, carry a large load and periodically flood (**Figure 1**). Large sections of the lower course of the Mississippi River in the USA have natural levées. The US Corps of Engineers have artificially heightened the levées in many areas to help prevent flooding. However, in 1993, the levées could not hold back the water and there was catastrophic flooding.

The mouth of a river

As a river reaches the sea it may flow into a **delta** or an **estuary** (Figure 2).

▲ **An estuary** – the lower course of a river valley which has been drowned by a rise in sea level or fall in the land level. The river channel is very wide with mud flats and salt marshes. The valley is low-lying and relatively flat. Estuaries in Britain include the Thames, the Mersey, the Humber and the Tees.

▶ **A delta** – a flat area of sand and silt built into the sea. It is formed by river deposition. When a river enters the sea carrying a large load of sand, the velocity falls and the load is deposited. In a sheltered sea where there are no strong tides and currents the sand and silt accumulate to form a fan-shaped delta.

Figure 2 The mouth of a river.

Chapter 3 River processes and features

The Rhône delta in southern France

The River Rhône (**Figure 3**) flows into the Mediterranean Sea just to the west of Marseilles in southern France. The river has its source in the Alps, but it has a major confluence at Lyons with the River Saône which starts in northern France. At the mouth of the River Rhône there is a large delta (**Figure 4**). The deposition of sand and silt in the river channel has caused the river to split into two **distributaries**, the Grand Rhône and the Petit Rhône. The channels also have many islands of silt within them. The delta grows as sand deposition builds up levées along the banks of the distributaries. Sea currents form spits and bars which trap lagoons such as the Etang de Bèrre. Over time the lagoons dry up and are colonized by vegetation, so extending the delta even further into the open sea.

There are no large deltas around the coast of the British Isles. Why do deltas only form in the mouths of certain rivers, such as the Nile, the Mississippi, the Ganges and the Rhône? For a delta to form the following conditions are necessary.

- The river carries a large load of sediment, i.e. there is active erosion upstream and the rocks over which the river passes must be relatively easy to erode.
- There are no strong tides or currents which would wash the sediments away faster than they could build up to form the delta.
- The river's flow is slowed down by entering the sea. Sea water is denser and contains salt, which helps the sand particles to bind together, becoming heavier and sinking to the seabed.
- The river's flow is blocked so much by deposition that it is forced to divide up into distributaries.
- Sediment is deposited along the distributaries, and extends out into the sea.

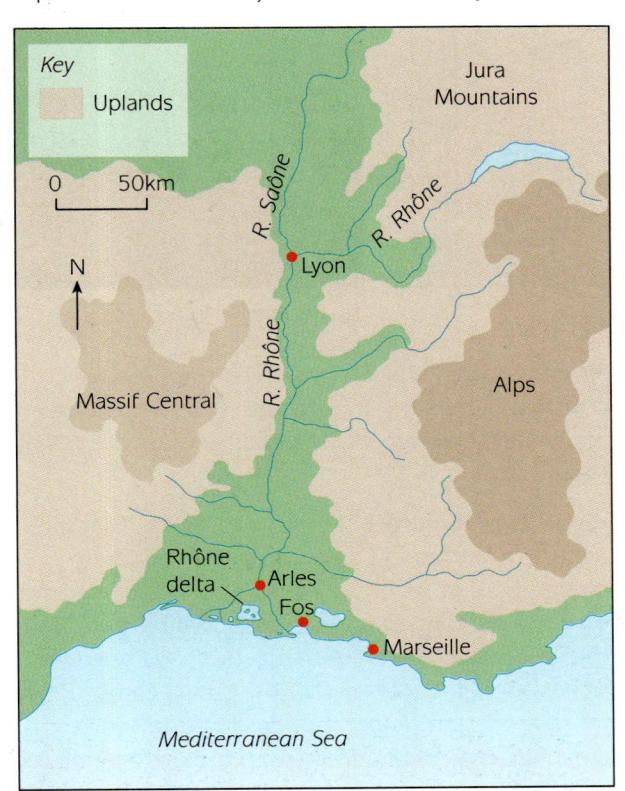

▲ **Figure 3** The River Rhône.

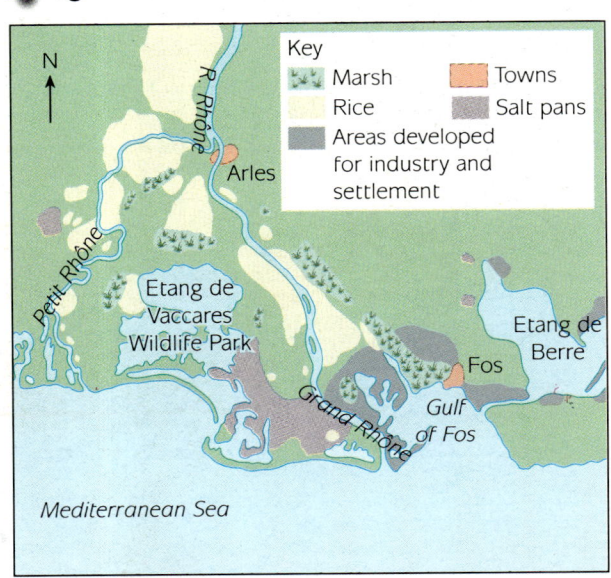

▲ **Figure 4** Physical features and land uses of the Rhône delta.

Activities

1. Suggest why a delta has formed at the mouth of the River Rhône.
2. Describe and explain the natural features of the Rhône delta.
3. What are the traditional land uses on the delta and why might they be threatened in the future?

Case Study – delta formation

Case Study – the River Tees

Land use in the drainage basin of the River Tees

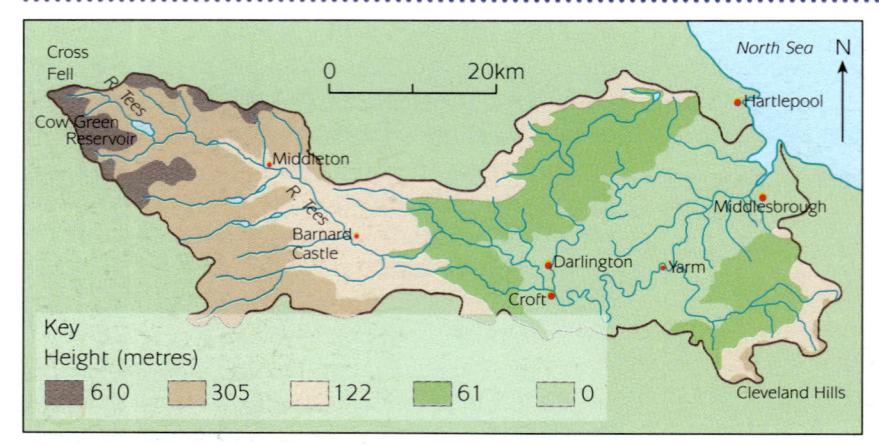

Figure 1 The drainage basin of the River Tees.

Figure 3 High Force.

The River Tees (**Figure 1**) is located in north-east England. Its source area is high in the Pennines in the west and the river flows eastwards into the North Sea.

In the uplands

The source of the River Tees lies on Cross Fell in the Pennines, 893m above sea level, where rainfall is over 2000mm a year. Run-off is high because of the impermeable rocks and the steep slopes. **Figure 2** shows part of the upper course of the River Tees. The valley cross-section is steep-sided and V-shaped and the long profile has a steep gradient. The river occupies the whole of the valley floor. The river is turbulent and clear, although often stained brown by the peat which covers much of the moorlands. The river bed is rocky and there are many rapids and a waterfall at High Force.

High Force (**Figure 3**) in grid square 8828 is the highest waterfall in England, with a very deep plunge pool at its base. The cap rock is made of a very resistant igneous rock called **whinstone**. Below the whinstone there are bands of sandstone and shales as well as some very thin coal seams. These rocks are less resistant and erode more easily, creating an overhang in the cap rock. Over many thousands of years the waterfall at High Force has retreated upstream, creating an impressive gorge of recession.

▼ **Figure 2** OS map of part of the upper course of the River Tees at a scale of 1:50 000 (2cm = 1km).

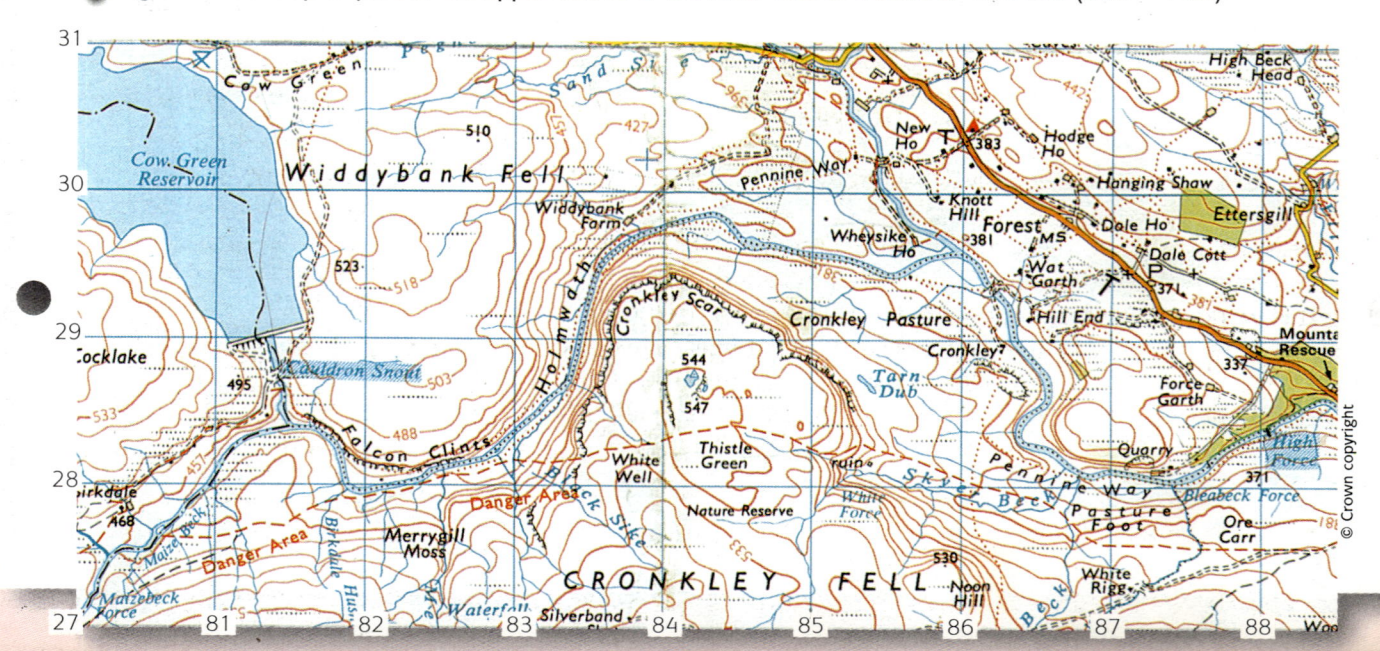

Chapter 3 River processes and features

Human activity in the upper course of the River Tees

Settlement and communications
The steep slopes and lack of flat land in the valley floor make the building of communications and settlements very difficult, and employment opportunities are limited. As a result the population density is very low. On the bleaker moorlands there is no settlement at all, but more farms and small villages are sited along the B6277 road which follows the more sheltered land in the Tees valley.

Water supply
In the Tees Valley the water quality is very high, which makes it suitable for use as a water supply for homes and industry. The high rainfall also gives a reliable water supply. There are several reservoirs in the river basin. **Figure 2** on page 42 shows the highest of these, Cow Green reservoir. The reservoir also helps in flood control. The River Tees is 'flashy', meaning that water levels can rise very quickly following a rain storm. Storing water in the reservoir helps to reduce flooding in the lower course.

▲ **Figure 4** Hill sheep farming in upper Teesdale.

Sheep farming
One of the major land uses in the upper Tees is rough grazing for sheep. The land is too steep to use machinery, the growing season too short and the soils too thin and acidic for growing crops. Above about 400m is found open moorland where the sheep roam freely in the summer. Below 400m there are fields bounded by traditional dry-stone walls. Only where the slopes are less steep is the pasture improved by fertilizers, the occasional crop of hay or barley is grown and a small herd of dairy cattle is grazed.

Tourism
The open moorland, High Force, the nature trail at Widdybank Fell, the shooting estates, the Pennine Way (a long-distance footpath) and the attractive villages and market towns such as Middleton-In-Teesdale, all attract visitors to Upper Teesdale. The visitors provide much-needed employment for local people in the hotels and restaurants, as car park attendants, visitor centre staff and shop assistants. However, tourism also brings traffic congestion, litter and overcrowding.

Industry
Upper Teesdale once had a thriving lead mining industry. Today the disused lead mines are attractive to visitors. There has been little other large-scale industry to replace lead mining. There is some limited employment in forestry, and in various craft industries, e.g. artists and textile workers. Whinstone is quarried at Holwick and used for roadstone because of its great resistance. The first really large employer in the valley is Glaxo-Wellcome, a chemical and pharmaceuticals company located on the outskirts of Barnard Castle.

> **Test questions**
>
> Study **Figure 2**.
> a What is the highest altitude shown on the map? Give the four-figure grid reference for the spot height.
> (2 marks)
> b Name and locate by six-figure grid reference **two** places visitors could stay in this part of Upper Teesdale
> (4 marks)
> c Describe the attractions for visitors to this part of Teesdale
> (4 marks)
> d Describe the shape of the Tees valley at Holmwath named in grid squares 8328 and 8329.
> (2 marks)
> e Describe the land uses in the area of the map extract.
> (8 marks)

Case Study – the River Tees

Case Study – the River Tees

The River Tees in the lowlands

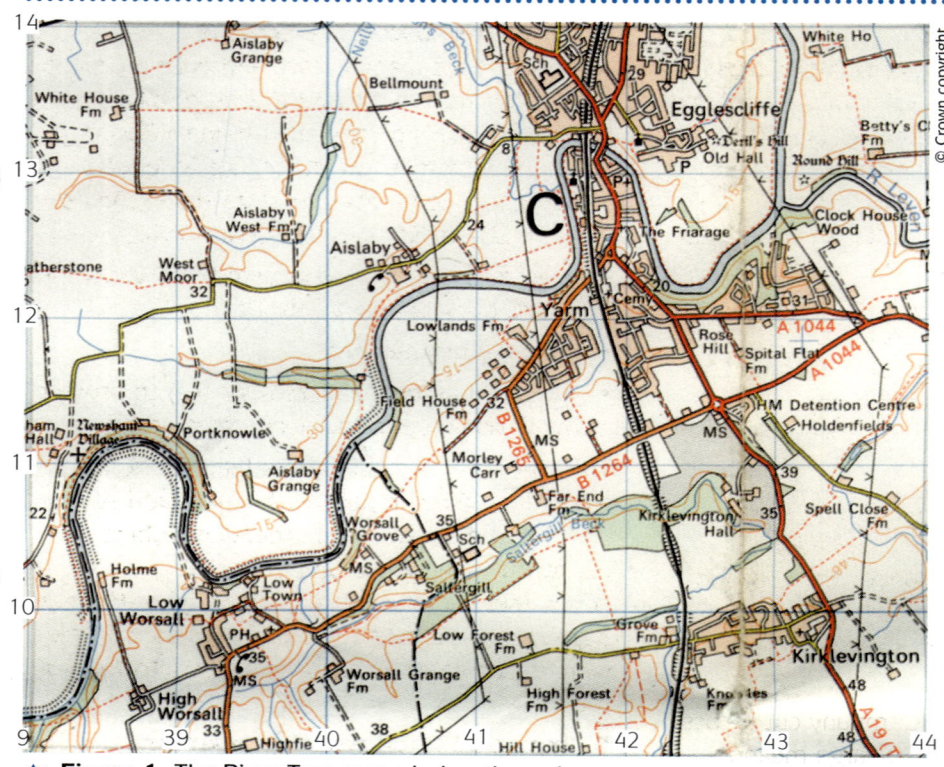

Figure 1 The River Tees meandering through Yarm. Scale: 2cm = 1km.

Moving downstream the valley begins to widen and the river starts to meander (**Figure 1**). There are more bridging points and larger villages and towns, such as Yarm. Nearing the river mouth the river meanders in large loops across its flat flood plain. It is 30km as the crow flies from Darlington to Teesmouth but the river travels 75km. It used to be longer but several of the meanders were cut off in the nineteenth century to shorten the journey for boats navigating the river up to Stockton and Yarm. At Teesmouth the river flows into an estuary where there are huge areas of mud flats such as Seal Sands. These are important wildlife areas for migratory birds and seals.

Human activity in the lower course

The lower course is much more urbanized and industrialized than the upper sections, with large towns such as Stockton and Middlesbrough and the vast port of Teesside. Industries such as chemicals, ships, steel-making and engineering developed during the Industrial Revolution. Today, Teesside is a major centre for the ICI petrochemicals industry based at Billingham and Wilton, and is well placed to receive oil and gas from the fields in the North Sea. Shipbuilding has been replaced by oil platform construction and there is a huge modern integrated steelworks at Redcar. The heavy industries have taken advantage of the flat and relatively cheap expanses of mud flats in the estuary. The land is easily reclaimed and there is a nearby labour supply and good transport networks. The port also provides a sheltered harbour for the import of raw materials and the export of finished goods.

River basin management

The River Tees has a long history of flooding. The first documented flood was at Croft (**Figure 1**, page 40) on the lower Tees in 1356. The Tees valley is also home to a large population and many industries, all requiring a reliable water supply. The river is managed to provide a water supply and to control flooding. In recent years there have also been developments to increase its potential for recreation and tourism.

Cow Green reservoir (**Figure 2**) was built in 1970 to provide water for the growing industries on Teesside. It is a regulating reservoir, storing water in times of plenty and releasing enough for the needs of industry in times of low flow. In times of severe summer drought, water can be added to the River Tees via a tunnel which connects it to the River Tyne and Kielder reservoir.

Figure 2 Cow Green reservoir.

Chapter 3 River processes and features

Management in the lower Tees valley

1 The Tees Barrage
The aim of the Tees Barrage was to improve the water quality and recreational value of 22km of the lower Tees. The barrage was completed in 1995 and cost £54 million. The 22km stretch of river between Yarm and Stockton is now kept permanently at high tide. The water is fresher and cleaner as it does not mix with the tidal, salt water in the lower estuary. The barrage also reduces the risk of flooding at very high tides or during a storm surge. The barrage has acted as a catalyst for £500 million of investment in offices, housing, educational, leisure and shopping facilities.

2 Dredging
The lower stretches of the Tees estuary are dredged periodically to improve navigation by maintaining a deep-water channel. There has also been some dredging in the upper parts of the estuary to reduce the flood risk.

3 Cutting of meanders
In 1810, the Tees Navigation Company cut across the neck of the Mandale Loop, a large meander near Stockton. The new route shortened the river by 4km. Other stretches of the river have been artificially straightened. This allows the water to move faster along the channel, reducing the flood risk.

4 Yarm's flood defence scheme
Yarm, a historic market town and once an inland port, is located on the inside bend of a large meander. Yarm is particularly prone to flooding. The most recent serious flood was in January 1995. Since then a new flood defence scheme costing £2.1 million has been built with:

- reinforced concrete walls with flood gates for access by people and vehicles
- earth embankments
- gabions (baskets filled with stones) to protect the walls and embankments from erosion.

The scheme also incorporates features designed to reduce the visual impact of the walls and to enhance the environment. There are fishing platforms, new street lighting and a comprehensive planting scheme. English Heritage approved all building materials used so that they were in keeping with the existing architecture of the town.

5 Improved flood warning systems
These have better liaison with the Meteorological Office, police and other emergency services.

6 New development discouraged
Building on low-lying and flood-prone land is discouraged.

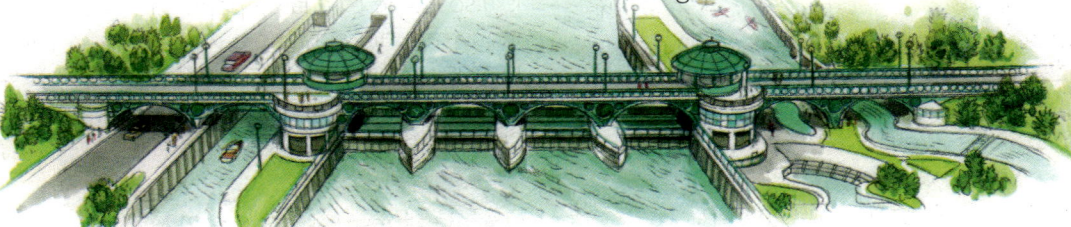

▲ Figure 3 The Tees Barrage.

Case Study – the River Tees

Activities

1 **Figure 2** on page 40 and **Figure 1** on page 42 are maps showing two sections of the River Tees as it flows from source to mouth. Describe the changes which take place along the river. Include details and grid references from the maps. The following ideas may help you to structure your account:

- changes in the river size and features
- changes in the valley size and shape
- changes in land use (including settlement, bridges and communications).

2 a What is river basin management?
  b Give three aims of the management of the Tees river basin.
  c Explain how the management has achieved these aims.

River regimes

The regime of a river is the variation in the **discharge** of water carried by the river at different times of the year. The discharge depends upon the relationship between precipitation (rain, snow, sleet) and run-off, which is summarized in the hydrological cycle (**Figure 2**, page 32).

▼ **Figure 1**

> **Discharge** is the velocity of a river multiplied by its volume, and is thus a measure of the amount of water which passes a particular point at a given time. It is measured in cumecs (cubic metres per second).
>
> **Velocity** is the speed of the river measured in metres per second.
>
> **Volume** is the amount of water in a river measured in square metres. It is calculated by working out the cross-sectional area of the river.

Figure 2 shows three different river regimes. An *even regime*, where the river's discharge varies little over the year, means that the river is in an area where rainfall and run-off remain very similar all year round. A *summer maximum of discharge* is typical in areas of snow melt or where there is a summer maximum of rainfall. Alpine streams have low winter discharge, because most of the precipitation falls as snow and the ground is often frozen, so little water enters the streams. In the summer when the snow melts the streams have a much higher discharge. Rivers with a *winter maximum of discharge* are found in areas with higher precipitation and lower temperatures in winter. In much of Britain the rivers have a winter maximum of discharge. Winter temperatures are lower so there is less evaporation of water and there is more rainfall. At certain times of the year the discharge may increase so much that the river channel cannot hold all of the water, and flooding occurs.

Flooding

Flooding is a normal occurrence in the lower course of a river, and is why a flood plain is created by a river. A flood occurs when the water in a river overtops its banks and leaves the channel (**Figure 3**). Most floods occur because of the weather, for example:

- long, continuous periods of rainfall, as happened in continental Europe in the winter of 1992–93
- a cloudburst in a thunderstorm which causes large amounts of run-off
- a sudden increase in temperature that rapidly melts snow and ice. In winter the water often cannot seep into the ground because it is still frozen.

Sometimes human activities can also make the flooding worse:

- building new towns or increasing an urban area makes surfaces impermeable so that more water runs off the surface
- deforestation reduces interception and increases run-off
- occasional disasters occur, such as a burst dam.

▲ **Figure 3** River in flood.

After a rain storm, the discharge of a river usually increases. However, two drainage basins may react very differently to a rain storm, producing identical amounts of rainfall. The River Tees is a 'flashy' river (page 41). Water levels in it can rise very quickly after a rainfall event and also fall equally fast following a dry spell. The River Tees and other similar rivers are therefore more likely to flood. The discharge in other rivers may be much more even and the flood threat is then much less.

▲ **Figure 2** Three different river regimes.

Chapter 3 River processes and features

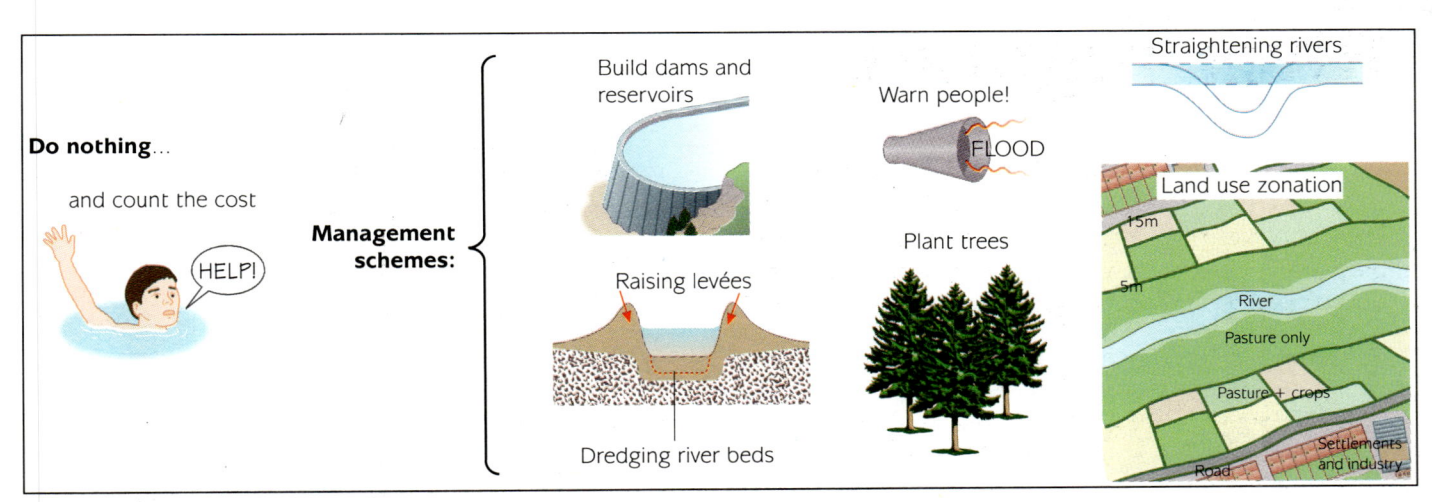

Figure 4 Dealing with floods: what are the options?

Flood hydrographs

A hydrograph is a graph showing the discharge of a river over a period of time. They can be drawn for a day, a month or a year, or even longer.

A flood hydrograph (**Figure 5**) is drawn for one particular period of rainfall. When rain begins to fall in a drainage basin the river's discharge does not increase immediately. Only a very small proportion of rain falls directly into the river. Most falls onto the land, where some may be intercepted by trees, some will soak into the ground and some may run across the ground surface towards the river channel. The discharge of the river increases when the first surface run-off begins to enter the river. Later on, the water that has soaked through the soil (throughflow) will add to the river's discharge. The increase in discharge is shown by the **rising limb** on the hydrograph. The **falling limb** indicates the fall in discharge which occurs after the rainfall has ceased when surface run-off and throughflow reduce. The **lag time** is the time between the peak of the rainfall and the peak discharge. A river with a short lag time and a high peak discharge is more likely to flood than a river with a long lag time and low peak discharge.

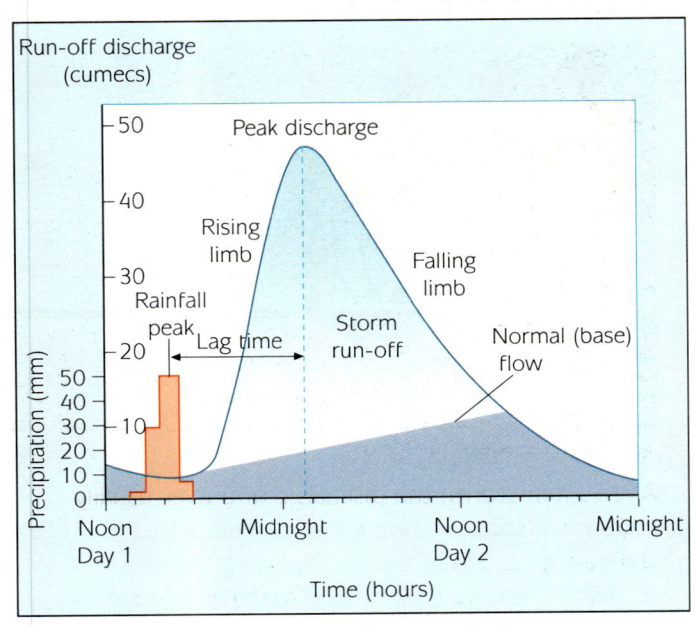

Figure 5 A flood hydrograph

Activity

Make a copy of the table below and complete it for the techniques shown in **Figure 4**. The first one has been done for you.

Option	Impact	Advantages	Disadvantages
Do nothing	None, may discourage people from settling	Cheap River naturally floods Fertile silt/water supply for farming	Floods homes, fields, roads, services, etc. Costly to clean up and repair damage

Case Study – Mississippi River Floods

The Mississippi river floods in spring and summer 1993

The floods in 1993 were the worst since records began (**Figure 1**). At the peak of the flood the Mississippi river was up to 18m deep, 25km wide and flowing at a speed of 96km per hour.

The causes of the flood

The floods began when snow melting in the spring was followed by 50 days of very heavy rain and thunderstorms across the American mid-west. The map in **Figure 2** shows that the area of the USA affected by the flooding was larger than the whole of Britain.

The results of the flood

- Lives lost: 28.
- Homes lost: 36 000 people.
- Many more people were evacuated.
- Roads and railway lines were under water.
- Electricity lines collapsed, leaving towns without power.
- Six million acres of farmland were flooded, ruining maize crops.
- Millions of tonnes of silt and sand were deposited in the flood zone. This needed to be cleared after the flood.
- Estimated US $10 billion were needed to repair the flood damage.

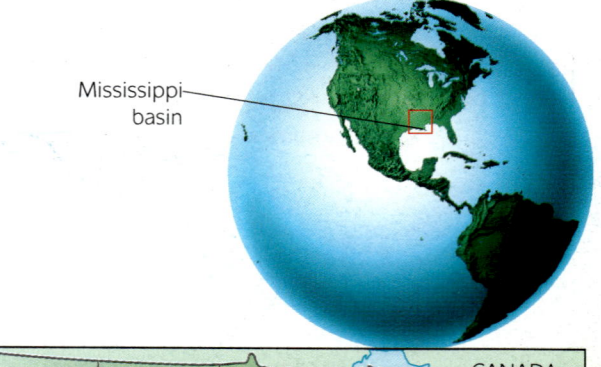

▲ **Figure 2** The extent of the flooding in 1993 in the USA.

Flood protection

For many years the US Corps of Engineers have tried to reduce the flood risk and prevent serious floods affecting land and property. They have raised and strengthened levées, excavated cut-offs to straighten out meanders, dredged the river bed and built revetments (**Figure 3**).

The levées were meant to prevent flood water from spilling out of the river onto the surrounding land. In 1993 the floods were just too great and the water rose over the tops of the levées. Emergency action was taken. In some places, massive quantities of boulders were piled on top of the levées to make them higher, in the hope of keeping the river in its channel. Houses in danger of being flooded were protected by sandbags. In just one town, Sainte Genevieve, 750 000 sandbags were used.

After the floods some people began to question the wisdom of flood prevention schemes such as

▲ **Figure 1** The 1993 Mississippi river floods.

levées. They argued that less damage would have been done if the flood water had been allowed to extend gradually and spill out over farmland rather than the catastrophic flooding which occurred when levées failed. The water would have been absorbed by the land and would have flowed back into the channel once the floods began to recede. Others argue that people have no right to settle on the flood plains and to cover large areas with concrete and tarmac which makes them impermeable. They believe that the function of the flood plain is to be a store for water when the river floods.

▲ **Figure 3** A raised and strengthened levée on the Mississippi.

Activities

1 Produce a newspaper article with illustrations for the 1993 Mississippi floods. Your article should contain the following:
   - an eyecatching headline
   - the dates of the floods
   - the causes of the floods
   - the long-term and short-term effects of the floods
   - the response to the floods.

2 List the effects of the flood.

3 Suggest possible reasons why the Mississippi floods killed relatively few people but the cost of repairs was quite expensive.

4 Describe how you think the US Corps of Engineers should respond to the flood threat – build protection schemes, do nothing, or some other solution? Explain your ideas.

Case Study – Mississippi River Floods

Summary: How a river changes as it flows downstream

How much can you remember? This summary does not describe the characteristics of each landform nor does it explain its formation – you will need to look back into the chapter for this information.

	Upper course	Middle course	Lower course
Valley long profile			
Valley cross-section and features	Shape of valley: V-shaped with inter-locking spurs and a steep gradient	A more open U-shape with a flatter valley floor and sloping valley sides.	The valley is now wide and flat – the flood plain emerges with levées and meander scars.
Valley cross-section			
Processes at work	Mainly vertical erosion, cutting downwards.	Still some vertical erosion but lateral or sideways erosion is becoming more important, widening the valley.	Some lateral erosion on the outside bends of meanders, very limited vertical erosion. Deposition increases in importance on the river bed in times of low flow and on the flood plain when floods occur.
Features of the river	Pools, potholes and boulders in river bed: river narrow and turbulent with rapids and waterfalls; water often clear.	The river begins to meander with river cliffs and slip-off slopes. The river channel is broader and flatter.	Meanders may become cut off to form ox-bow lakes, islands of silt may braid the river and levees may form. At the mouth a delta is a possibility or mud flats and salt marshes in estuaries.
Human land uses	Rough grazing used for sheep farming; some coniferous plantations, dams for water supply and tourism.	The land becomes cultivated with smaller fields for both crops and animals. There are the occasional market towns and many villages, as well as more lines of communication.	The flat fertile flood plains and sheltered river mouths provide ideal sites for intensive farming as well as towns, cities and ports. The land uses are increasingly urban as the sea is approached.

▲ **Figure 1** Summary of the changes along the course of a river.

Test questions

1 Make a copy of the table below. Place the following eight river features into the correct column to show which are formed by processes of erosion, by deposition or by a mixture of the two:
   • ox-bow lake   • levée   • waterfall
   • meander   • delta   • gorge of recession
   • flood plain   • V-shaped valley.   (4 marks)

Erosional features	Depositional features	Formed by both erosion and deposition

2 Explain the differences between the following pairs of terms:
   a Lateral erosion and vertical erosion
   b Slip-off slope and river cliff
   c Corrasion and corrosion.   (6 marks)

3 Describe the features of the river and its valley in the upper course.   (4 marks)

4 Select any two of the following landforms. With the help of labelled diagrams explain their formation.
   a Waterfall   b V-shaped valley
   c Ox-bow lake   d Delta
   e Levée.   (6 marks)

Chapter 4
Ice

The Andes in southern Chile, where the effects of frost shattering, glacial erosion and glacial deposition upon the landscape can be seen.

Key Ideas

The Earth's crust is modified by glacial processes which result in distinctive landforms:
- glacial processes (abrasion and plucking) combine with freeze–thaw weathering to produce landforms of erosion
- in upland areas valley glaciers form landforms of erosion such as corries, glacial troughs and ribbon lakes
- in lowland areas valley glaciers and ice sheets form landforms of deposition such as moraines and drumlins.

Landscape features affect human activities:
- upland areas offer opportunities for farming and tourism, but they need to be managed.

Valley glaciers and ice sheets

Freshly fallen snow is composed of ice crystals and many air spaces. When you make a snowball, you compress the snow and remove the air spaces. The same happens naturally when snow accumulates; the weight of snow above compresses the air out of the snow below and converts snow into ice. As the ice becomes thicker it will move down the slope by its own weight. When ice moves it is called a **glacier**. Glaciers are of two main types.

1. **Valley glacier** – a moving mass of ice in which the movement is confined within a valley. It begins in an upland area and follows the route of a pre-existing river valley (**Figure 1**). Today most valley glaciers are found near the tops of young fold mountain ranges, such as the Alps, Andes, Rockies and Himalayas. Examples include the Mer de Glace near the ski resort of Chamonix in the Mont Blanc region of south-east France and the Rhône glacier in south-east Switzerland, the source for one of Europe's largest rivers.

2. **Ice sheet** – a moving mass of ice which covers the whole of the land surface over a wide area. In some cases the ice is sufficiently thick to blanket the entire area of a continent. In Antarctica, where only the peaks of some high mountains stick through the ice, only a tiny strip of bare rock is exposed along a few parts of the coast in summer (**Figure 2**).

Processes of glacial erosion

There are two main processes (or ways) of glacial erosion.

1. **Abrasion** – rocks and rock particles embedded in the bottom of the glacier wear away the rocks over which the glacier passes. These sharp-edged pieces of rock of all sizes held rigid by the ice above are used as the tools for abrasion. Smaller rock particles have a sandpaper effect on the rocks over which the ice passes, while the sharp edges of the large rocks make deep grooves, called **striations** (**Figure 3**).

2. **Plucking** – this is the tearing away of blocks of rock from the bed rock as the glacier moves. These blocks of rock had been frozen to the bottom of the glacier where water had entered joints in the rock and become frozen. The blocks of rock between the joints are pulled away or plucked.

Glaciers would be less effective at eroding the landscape without the help of freeze–thaw weathering (see page 22). Before the ice advanced, freeze–thaw left many frost-shattered rocks which were easily removed by the glacier and then used as tools for abrasion. Even when the ice is present, freeze–thaw action affects rocks

◀ **Figure 1** A valley glacier reaching the sea in southern Chile.

▼ **Figure 2** Antarctica covered by its ice sheet with just enough bare rock for the location of a base for Chilean scientists.

▲ **Figure 3** Striations on the hard rocks which outcrop in Central Park in New York. They are useful to geologists for working out the direction of ice movement.

Chapter 4 Ice

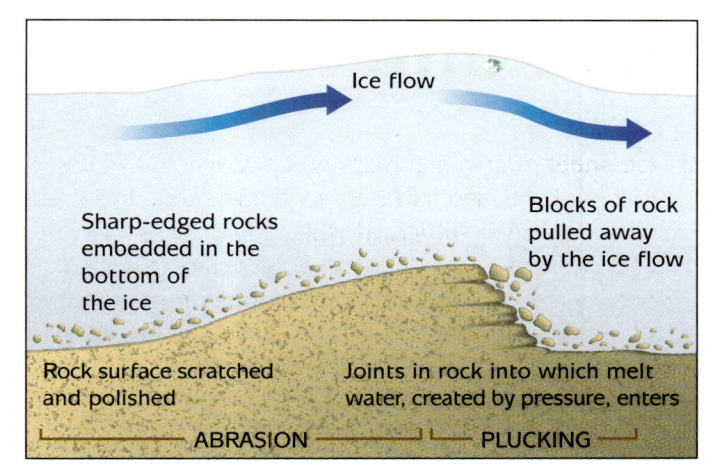

Figure 4 How the rocks below ice are eroded by glacial processes (abrasion and plucking).

which outcrop above the surface of the ice because, in a cold climate, there are likely to be many changes of temperature above and below freezing point.

Of the two types of glacier, valley glaciers are considered to be more effective agents of erosion than ice sheets. Confined in a valley, the ice touches both the floor and the sides so that there is more contact between the ice and the rock and therefore more erosion. Also, valley glaciers flow more quickly, partly because of steeper gradients and partly because more meltwater is present to lubricate their flow. There is a plentiful supply of rock fragments from the frost-shattered peaks above so that these glaciers are well supplied with tools for abrasion. However, ice sheets cover and therefore erode a much greater area, so that, even though they erode more slowly, a large total amount of rock can still be removed by them. As with the other agents of erosion, rocks which are soft or which have weaknesses, such as many joints, are eroded more quickly, irrespective of whether it is a valley glacier or an ice sheet that is present.

Distribution of landforms of glaciation in the British Isles

If you are sitting north of the line from London to Bristol and take a look out of the window, it must be difficult for you to imagine that just 40 000 years ago all the land you can see would have been part of a snow- and ice-covered white wilderness. The British Isles was invaded by ice sheets from Scandinavia during the **Pleistocene Ice Age**, which covered everywhere except for the extreme south of England. In the higher areas, such as the Cairngorms, Lake District and Snowdonia, heavy snowfall led to the accumulation of snow and ice in hollows on the rocky mountain sides. These were the sources for valley glaciers which flowed down valleys previously eroded by rivers. Over the past 10 000 years the world has warmed up. Today no part of the British Isles lies above the **snow line** (the line above which snow and ice remain all year). However, the present-day landscapes of the British Isles show plenty of signs that ice sheets and glaciers once ruled the country (**Figure 5**).

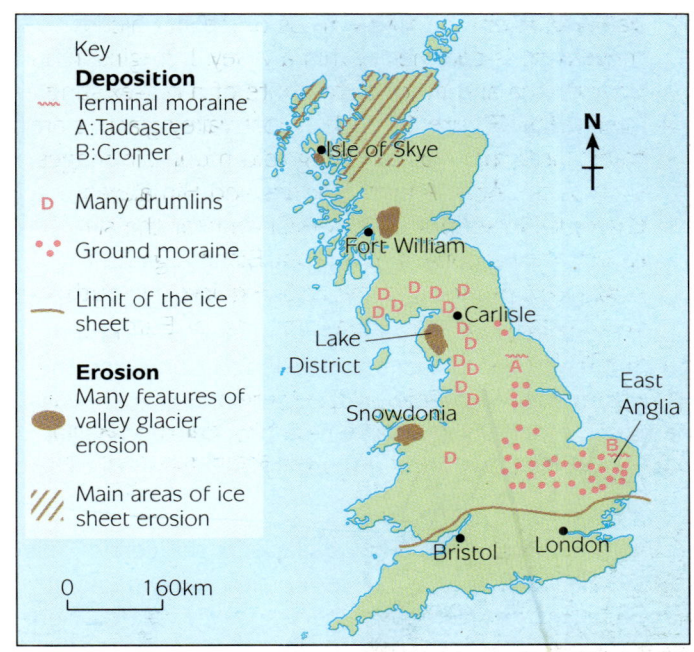

Figure 5 Distribution of glacial landforms from the Ice Age.
The landforms of erosion are explained on pages 52–55 and those of deposition are dealt with on pages 56–57.

i Pleistocene Ice Age
- It began 2 million years ago.
- At its peak 30 per cent of the Earth's surface was covered by ice.
- It ended just 10 000 years ago.

Activities

1. Give the similarities and differences between glaciers and ice sheets.

2. a Draw labelled diagrams to show how each of the following processes operates:
    (i) freeze–thaw weathering
    (ii) plucking
    (iii) abrasion.
   b Explain why the breakdown and removal of rock is quicker when
    (i) all three processes operate in the same area
    (ii) rocks have many lines of weakness.

Glacial erosion: corries and mountain peaks

Figure 1 Panoramic view of part of the Swiss Alps taken from a tourist leaflet for the Jungfrau Region. You should be able to identify the corries, arêtes and pyramidal peaks after studying these two pages. How many visitors to the region can do this?

Glaciers modify and enlarge landscape features which existed before the Ice Age. The effects of glacial erosion upon the landscape are greatest in upland areas where glaciers have been present for the longest time and the ice was deeper. In general, slopes are steeper and peaks narrower, especially in areas where processes of glacial erosion are still operating (**Figure 1**).

Corrie (cirque)

The first landform formed by a glacier is the **corrie**. This is a circular rock hollow (hence the alternative name of **cirque** used by some geographers), usually located high on the mountain side, with a steep and rocky backwall

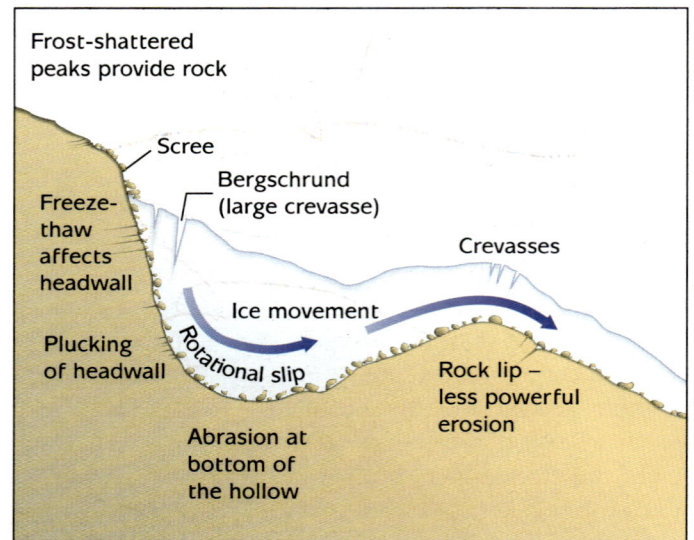

Figure 3 Formation of a corrie.

up to 200 metres high in the UK, but much higher in the Alps. Although most of the corrie is ringed by steep rocks leading to sharp rocky ridges, the front is open with nothing more than a small rock lip on the surface. The hollow is typically filled with a small round lake, called a **tarn**, after the ice has melted. The information above *describes* the corrie; **Figure 2** shows a corrie which matches this general description.

Corries begin where snowfields (called **névés**), which accumulate below the mountain tops, form ice and grow. As with many landforms, it is necessary to refer to several different processes in order to explain the *formation* of the corrie (**Figure 3**).

Figure 2 Corrie hollow occupied by Red Tarn on the side of Helvellyn in the Lake District.

- *Freeze–thaw weathering* plays a part in its formation. Frost action on the mountain tops and slopes above supplies loose rocks (scree). Water seeps down the bergschrund crevasse onto the headwall, increasing the amount of freeze–thaw activity, cutting back the headwall and making it steeper.
- Ice sticking to the headwall pulls away blocks of rock by *plucking* as the glacier moves.
- Loose rocks obtained from freeze–thaw and plucking are embedded in the ice and act as tools for scraping out the bottom of the hollow by *abrasion*.
- As a result of the *rotational slip movement* of the ice, there is greater pressure from the ice at the bottom of the headwall and in the base of the hollow than near to the front where the glacier leaves the corrie hollow to flow down valley; the rock lip forms near the exit as a result of less powerful erosion.

▲ Figure 4 The Matterhorn near Zermatt in Switzerland.

When all the ice has melted the corrie provides an ideal place for a **tarn lake** to form. There is a natural ice-carved hollow in which the water can accumulate. The rock lip acts as a natural dam on the one side that is not surrounded by steep slopes. A location in upland areas means that precipitation is likely to be high and there will be a large amount of run-off down the steep sides of the corrie, because the corrie forms a natural catchment area. A tarn lake fills the floor of most well-developed corries.

Arête and pyramidal peak

Look at a photograph showing the peaks of any of the world's high mountains ranges, not just the Alps, and you will find pointed mountain peaks and long and narrow knife-edged ridges. An **arête** is a two-sided sharp-edged ridge, whereas the **pyramidal peak**, as its name suggests, is a three-sided slab of rock, of which the most famous example is the Matterhorn (**Figure 4**) with its three near-vertical rock faces. Both landforms are formed by the cutting back of the headwalls of corries on the slopes below the peaks by the processes of freeze–thaw weathering and plucking. For an arête, two corries, one on each side of the ridge, cut back until only a narrow piece of rock is left as the ridge top. For a pyramidal peak, three corries cut back. All the peaks continue to be sharpened by frost action.

Activities

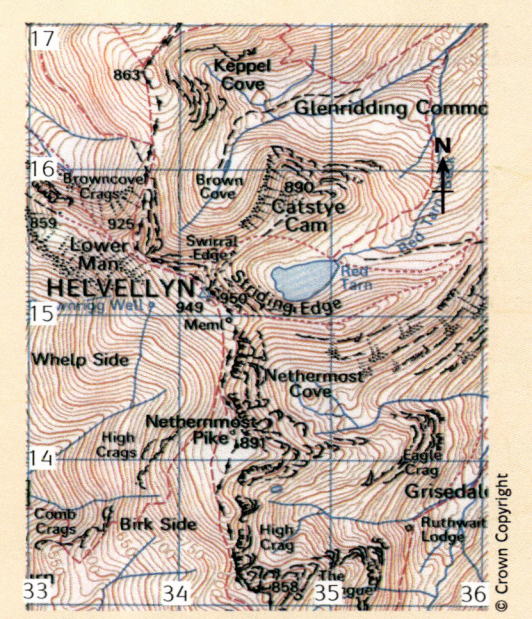

▲ Figure 5 OS map of Helvellyn at a scale of 1:50 000 (2cm = 1km).

1 a Using **Figures 2** and **5**, describe fully the features of the corrie occupied by Red Tarn.
  b Explain how it may have been formed.
2 From **Figure 5**, draw a labelled sketch map to show how corries and arêtes can be recognized on OS maps.

Glacial erosion: valley landforms

Figure 1 The Lauterbrunnen valley in Switzerland, carved out by glacial erosion. It is too large a valley to have been eroded by the small stream which flows in the valley today.

The **glacial trough**, often more simply called a U-shaped valley, is an impressive landscape feature (**Figure 1**). These glaciated valleys can be hundreds of metres deep with vertical rock walls, down which waterfalls cascade from **hanging valleys**. On the top of the valley sides the land often flattens out to form a **high-level bench**, known as an 'alp' in the Alps of Switzerland (the area in the foreground on **Figure 1**). The width and flatness of the floor are in marked contrast to the steepness of the sides. These valleys are drained by **misfit streams** which are dwarfed by the size and scale of the new glaciated valley. In some glacial troughs, lakes fill parts or all of the valley floor; these lakes are **ribbon lakes**, so called because of their shape, which is long and thin. In the lower parts of the valley, examples of landforms of glacial deposition, such as **terminal moraines**, are found. The valley's *long profile* is characterized by its irregular shape (**Figure 2**), providing many hollows for lake formation.

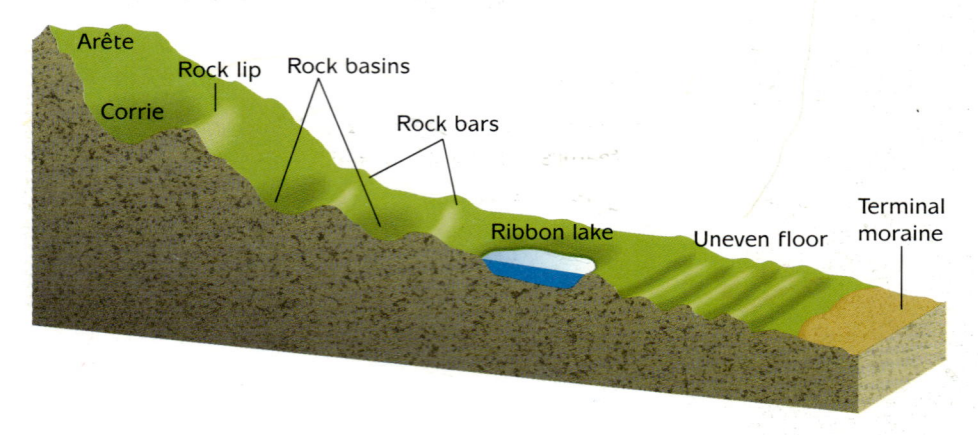

Figure 2 Long profile of a glacial trough.

Formation of valley landforms

Everything about a glacial trough speaks of the power of ice to erode. The former V-shaped river valley is widened, deepened and straightened by the valley glacier into a U-shaped valley. Before the ice, river erosion was confined to the small part of the valley where the river flowed; the glacier, however, fills the whole valley. This means that ice is in contact with all the floor and with both valley sides so that erosion is no longer confined to the centre of the valley. The V-shaped river valley is changed into the U-shaped glacial valley because glacial erosion by abrasion and plucking occurs everywhere in the valley where the ice is in contact with rock. The river moved around obstacles in its path, and its winding course created interlocking spurs. The more powerful glacier cannot flow as freely around corners as a river can, and it pushes straight forward, cutting off the edges of interlocking spurs to form truncated spurs and straight valley sides. The ice is thicker in the main valley because it is fed by all the glaciers from tributary valleys. In each tributary valley there was a smaller glacier with lower powers of erosion than the main glacier. When only the rivers remained after the ice melted, those in tributary valleys were left hanging well above the level of the main valley floor. The streams from these hanging valleys fall as **waterfalls** into the main valley.

As a glacier flows down a valley it is ruthless at picking out weaknesses in rocks, eroding those rocks that are soft and well-jointed more rapidly than those which are hard and resistant. In those places where outcrops of hard and soft rocks alternate, the glacier erodes the soft rock more quickly and more deeply, by abrasion and plucking, forming a **rock basin**. The hard rock is left as a **rock bar**. After the ice melts, the rock basin is left as a hollow on the valley floor between two rock bars, and it is soon filled up by rivers to form a **ribbon lake**.

The map (**Figure 5**) shows that the centre of the rock basin which contains Wast Water is over 70m deep. Note how the submarine contours indicating water depth show the U-shaped cross-profile of the glacial trough. The steep valley sides continue below water until the flat valley floor in the centre of the lake is reached.

◀ **Figure 3** Waterfall from a hanging valley along the side of the Lauterbrunnen valley.

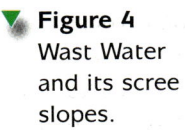

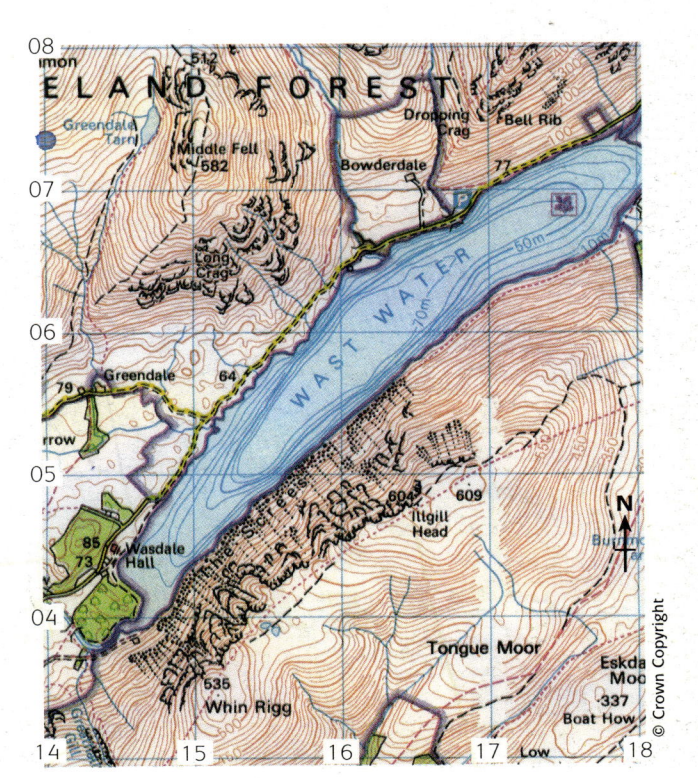

▼ **Figure 4** Wast Water and its scree slopes.

▲ **Figure 5** OS map showing Wast Water, the deepest of the English Lakes, at a scale of 1:50 000 (2cm = 1km).

Activities

1 Make a sketch of **Figure 1**. Name and label the features of glacial erosion shown.

2 a From **Figure 5**, draw a sketch cross-section across Wastwater valley.
  b Explain how the screes have formed.

Landforms of glacial deposition

Ice behaves in the same way as all the other agents of erosion:

- it wears away the land surface – *erosion*.
- It carries away the materials eroded – *transportation*.
- It dumps elsewhere the materials it is carrying – *deposition*.

Valley glaciers erode with so much power, and ice sheets erode such great expanses of land, that large amounts of loose rock are available for transport. Glaciers can transport enormous loads. Look at **Figure 1** which shows an **erratic**, the name given to a boulder dropped by ice in an area where it does not belong. This big grit boulder has been dumped on top of the local white limestone rock. This boulder is just one of hundreds that an ice sheet deposited in the same area. Can you imagine a river having the power to transport one of these boulders, never mind hundreds of them? In a river channel a boulder of this size would need to be broken down by corrasion and attrition into small pieces before it could be transported; the ice simply carries it.

All materials transported by glaciers are called **moraine**. Although most are carried in the glacier's base, some are carried on the surface, which show up as dark lines of moraine (**Figure 2**) on the top of the glacier. Piles of material along the sides are called **lateral moraines**; those somewhere in the middle of the glacier, formed after valley glaciers join together, are called **medial moraines**. Two separate lateral moraines unite to form one medial moraine. The material for these moraines is broken off from the rocky peaks above by freeze–thaw weathering and it falls down the valley sides on to the top of the ice.

▲ **Figure 1** Erratic block of grit perched on limestone in the Yorkshire Dales National Park.

▲ **Figure 2** A glacier with lateral and medial moraines on the ice surface.

◀ **Figure 3** Boulder clay.

However, not even a glacier can keep on growing for ever. It reaches a point where the ice loss is greater than the amount of new ice supplied. For example, most valley glaciers begin to melt when they reach lower ground where temperatures are higher. Only a few reach the sea before they have completely melted (see **Figure 1** page 50). As the ice melts and thins, its carrying capacity is reduced. When the glacier reaches the point of overload (load greater than carrying capacity), it must deposit some or all of its load. Any obstacle along its course encourages deposition.

The general name given to all materials deposited by ice is **boulder clay**. As its name suggests, this is usually clay which contains numerous boulders of many different sizes (**Figure 3**). It is an *unsorted* deposit. This means that large and soft rocks, as well as finer particles, are all mixed together. The boulders it contains are described as *angular*. They have sharp edges, not yet rounded off, as they would have been if they had been transported by rivers. The 'ingredients' of the boulder clay vary greatly according to what the glacier eroded before it reached the area. Sometimes the deposits are more sandy than

Chapter 4 Ice

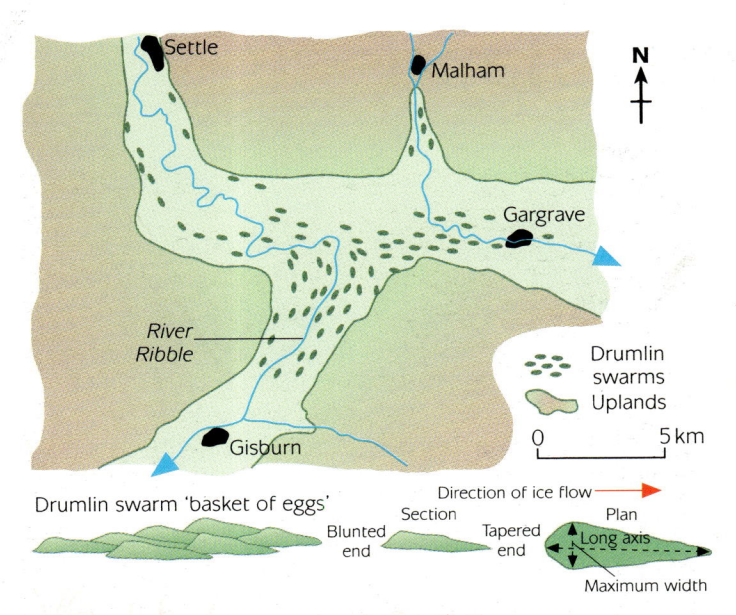

Figure 4 Drumlins in the Ribble Valley.

clayey, which is why some physical geographers prefer to use the term **glacial till** instead of boulder clay to describe all ice-deposited materials. As the glacier continues to push forward, melting more and more all the time, it leaves a trail of boulder clay behind it which forms a hummocky surface of **ground moraine**.

Drumlins

In many of the lowland areas of south-west Scotland and north-west England, glacial deposition has produced a distinctive landscape of many low hills, each one typically about 30–40 metres high and 300–400 metres long. These hills all lie in the same direction and have similar shapes – blunt at one end and tapered at the other; in fact, each hill looks like an egg. Each of these hills is a **drumlin**. Drumlins occur in swarms and are said to form 'basket of eggs' topography, so called because of the appearance of the landscape (**Figure 4**).

Drumlins form when the ice is pushing forward across a lowland area, but it is overloaded and melting. It does not need much to encourage more deposition; any small obstacle, such as a rock outcrop or mound, is sufficient. Most deposition occurs around the upstream end of the obstacle, which forms the drumlin's blunt end. The rest of the boulder clay that is deposited is then moulded into shape around the obstacle by the moving ice to form the tapered end downstream. The drumlin is another landform from which it is possible to detect the direction of ice movement.

Terminal moraine

All the remaining load is dropped and dumped at the glacier's **snout** – the furthest point reached by the ice.

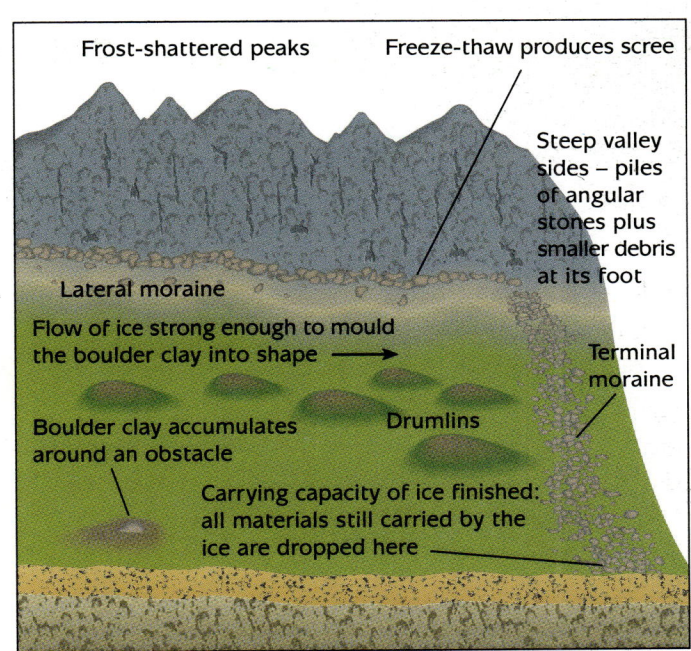

Figure 5 Location and formation of drumlins and terminal moraines.

This point is marked by a ridge of boulder clay across the valley or lowlands, running parallel to the ice front, and is called a **terminal moraine**. Where ice sheets remained stationary for a long time, such as in central Europe during the main ice advances in the Ice Age, sufficient boulder clay was deposited to form ridges more than 200 metres high. More typically, terminal moraines formed by valley glaciers are between 20 and 40 metres high. Terminal moraines which cross valleys form natural dams behind which river water can pile up and form lakes. These lakes are also long and thin and called **ribbon lakes**. This tells you that landforms with the same appearance can have different methods of formation.

Test questions

1. Draw a labelled sketch which shows four types of moraine. (4 marks)
2. a State two distinctive features of boulder clay. (2 marks)
   b Explain why these features show deposition by ice and not by rivers. (2 marks)
   c Where and why do glaciers deposit boulder clay? (4 marks)
3. a Describe the distribution of drumlins in the UK. (3 marks)
   b Explain why drumlins are 'egg-shaped' and are found in 'swarms'. (5 marks)

Human activities in upland glaciated areas

Difficulties

Many upland areas are naturally unattractive for people to settle in, even without considering the effects of ice on the landscape. Climate deteriorates with height. It becomes colder, which reduces the length of the growing season and narrows the possibilities for farming. There is more precipitation, which also means more cloud and less sunshine, and there is more chance of the precipitation falling as snow, which makes farming more difficult. Many of the changes made by glaciers do not help. Glaciers are such powerful agents of erosion that the land can be scraped bare of all its soil. Valley glaciers increase the steepness of the land and the height of the valley sides, making access more difficult, if not impossible.

Possibilities for settlement and use

The information below refers mainly to the UK. In Chapter 1 human activity in the Alps was discussed in detail (pages 10–11). Although this was in the context of fold mountains, it is often difficult to separate out the effects of high mountains and the effects of glaciation upon people and their activities, so much of that material is relevant here as well. For example, Alpine countries such as Switzerland and Austria rely much more heavily upon electricity supplied by hydro-electric power (HEP), which in the UK is only significant in the Highlands of Scotland. All well-watered high mountains offer opportunities for setting up HEP stations, but glacial erosion improves these opportunities. After glaciation, there are more and higher waterfalls, and large ribbon lakes provide areas of natural water storage.

Farming and forestry

In the British Isles the first human activity that comes to mind – because most of these areas are rural – is farming. Valley glaciers widen the valley floors and make them flatter. In upland areas land on the valley floor is precious for farmers, and there is more space and better shelter in a glaciated valley than in a river valley. It is on the valley floor that the melting glacier deposits most of its load, giving a greater thickness of soil. The soils formed by boulder clay vary greatly, but some are quite fertile and the high clay content favours grass growth. Compared with elsewhere in the uplands, the land around the farm on the valley floor is used intensively for growing crops and for making hay and silage, particularly if the *aspect* (the way the valley slope faces) is south-facing for greater warmth from the sun. Further away from the farm, the land can only be used for pastoral farming (keeping livestock). Cattle rearing (dairy if possible, beef otherwise) is more likely to be carried out in the lower parts of the valley, while sheep rearing dominates on the steeper slopes and moorlands where the physical conditions are suitable only for rough grazing. Farming in upland areas is often described as *marginal*, which means that it is difficult for the farmer to make a profit or a good living from farming there. Rocky land around and below the peaks may be useless. In some areas, especially on lower slopes too steep for farming, coniferous trees have been planted. Planting coniferous trees on the steep sides of a glaciated valley is one example of *diversification*; diversification means that farmers are creating new and additional sources of income.

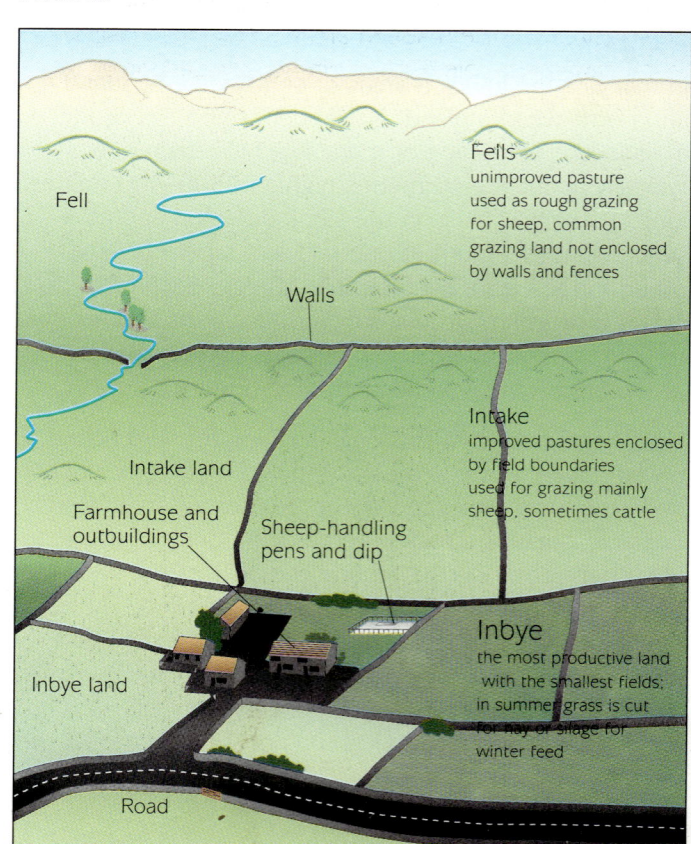

Figure 1 Layout and land uses on a Lake District farm. A typical farm can be split up into three parts.

Figure 2 Lake District farm. Notice how much greener the improved pastures are on the valley floor.

Tourism

Catering for and making money out of tourist visitors is another way many farmers in glaciated upland areas have diversified. Although some money has to be invested in building toilet and shower blocks, much more money can be made in areas with lots of visitors from charging people for camping or for parking a caravan in a field than from using it for grass. Some rooms in the farmhouse may be used for bed and breakfast; B&B boards are frequently seen in areas such as the Lake District and Snowdonia. The farm may be some distance from the nearest shop, giving the farmer a captive market for farm produce such as milk and eggs.

Without the effects of glaciation, the landscape in the Lake District would be much less attractive to visitors. Glaciation sharpened up the landscape; rounded tops were changed into knife-edged peaks and valleys were deepened, making the scenery more spectacular for visitors and fell walkers. Glaciation steepened and increased the size of many rock faces, increasing the area's attractiveness to mountaineers and rock climbers. Glaciers formed the large ribbon lakes, without which it would not be 'The Lake District'. Water always attracts tourists. Some come for the easy walks or rambles around the edges of the lakes, or for picnics or boat trips. Others, who are more active or more sporting, principally come to participate in water-based activities such as water-skiing and sailing. Without the effects of glaciation on its landscape, the Lake District would not be the great magnet for visitors that it is today.

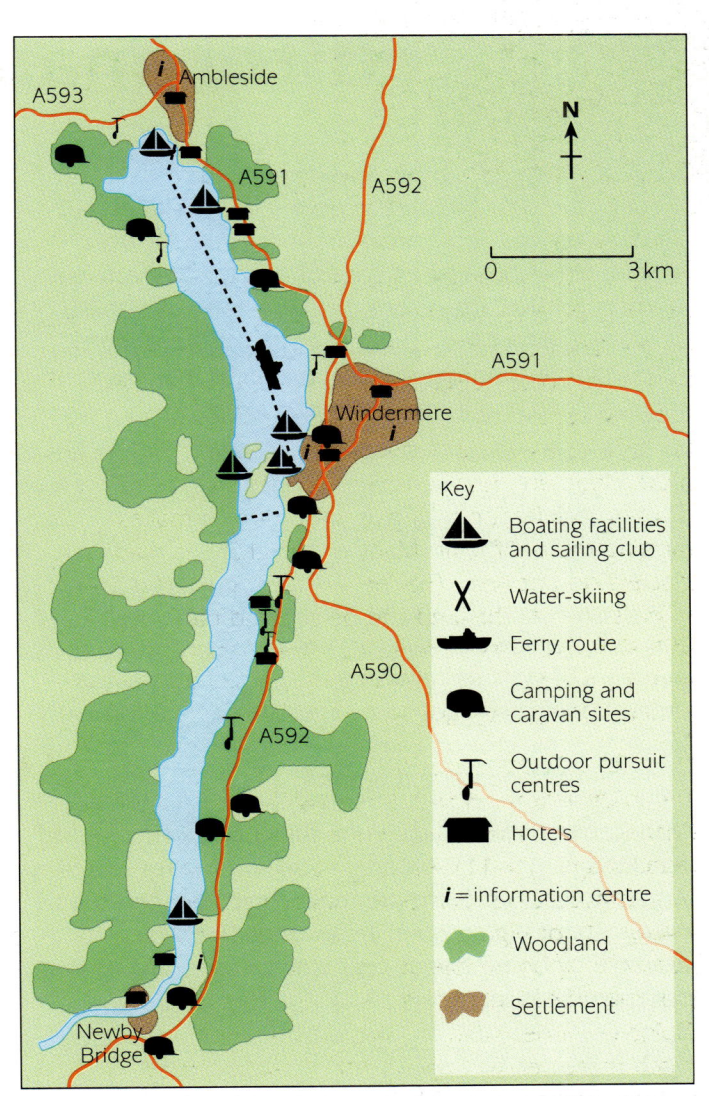

Figure 3 Windermere – places of interest and facilities for visitors.

Activities

Lake Windermere as a case study

1 Windermere fills a rock basin and there is a terminal moraine at its southern end. Explain how the lake has been formed by both glacial erosion and glacial deposition.

2 Describe the tourist uses of Lake Windermere and explain why there are so many visitors to the lake each year. Research other sources of information to support what is given on this page.

3 With the help of information on page 60:
   a explain why management of tourist activities is needed on Lake Windermere
   b describe the management methods used.

The need for management

Large numbers of visitors anywhere need to be managed. Visitor pressure is never equally shared out within a region. Some areas are more popular than others, either because of ease of access, or the presence of more natural attractions, or the greater availability of services and facilities. The most popular areas are referred to as **honeypots**. In these areas management is most needed and it has two broad aims:

1. To lessen damage to the environment
2. To reduce the conflicts which may arise between local residents and visitors, or between different groups of visitors with varied interests.

The glaciers left the upland areas with steep slopes and thin soils, which are vulnerable to people pressure. Large numbers of walkers following the same paths cause erosion, which spreads to a larger area as the footpath is widened. This erosion caused by humans can lead to scars on the landscape (**Figure 1**).

Management involves diverting the course of paths and fencing off the old footpaths to allow time for recovery. Also, artificial footpaths are made which are better able to withstand the constant tread of people's feet, for example by laying stones over soft surfaces and making steps on steep slopes.

Making a living from farming is difficult enough in glaciated upland areas without visitors from the cities making it more difficult. City people, on the other hand, often feel that they have the right to roam freely, which puts them on a collision course with the farmers. Some engage in specialist activities, such as water-skiing, which puts them in conflict with other lake users. Some of these conflicts are summarized in the table below.

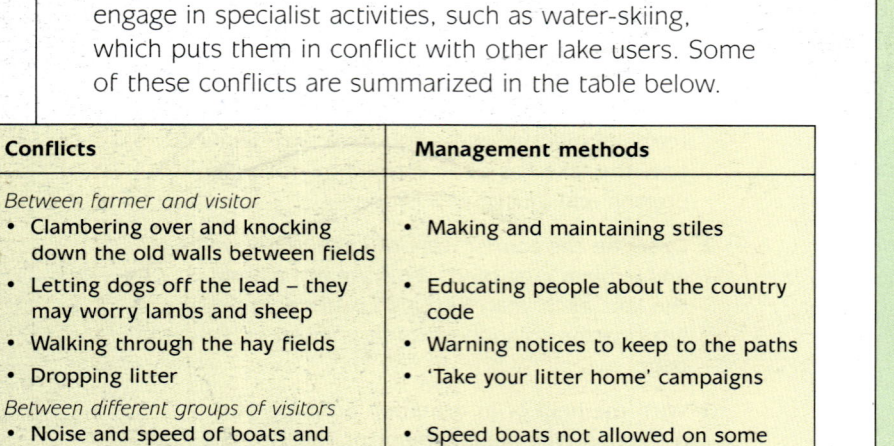

Figure 1 Footpath on Striding Edge on Helvellyn.

This brief survey does not cover all the pressures and conflicts that arise. In some glaciated areas the issue is quarrying, which was referred to in Chapter 2. In other areas it is extending the natural lakes to make reservoirs to supply water to other places, by flooding the only good land for local farmers, which is on the valley floor. In many areas transport is an issue. Should a bypass be built? Should access roads be improved or should visitor numbers be controlled instead? Issues such as these will be explored again in those parts of Chapter 12 relating to tourism.

Conflicts	Management methods
Between farmer and visitor	
• Clambering over and knocking down the old walls between fields	• Making and maintaining stiles
• Letting dogs off the lead – they may worry lambs and sheep	• Educating people about the country code
• Walking through the hay fields	• Warning notices to keep to the paths
• Dropping litter	• 'Take your litter home' campaigns
Between different groups of visitors	
• Noise and speed of boats and water-skiers compared with quiet and peaceful activities such as sailing and fishing	• Speed boats not allowed on some lakes, while large lakes such as Windermere are divided up into zones for different activities

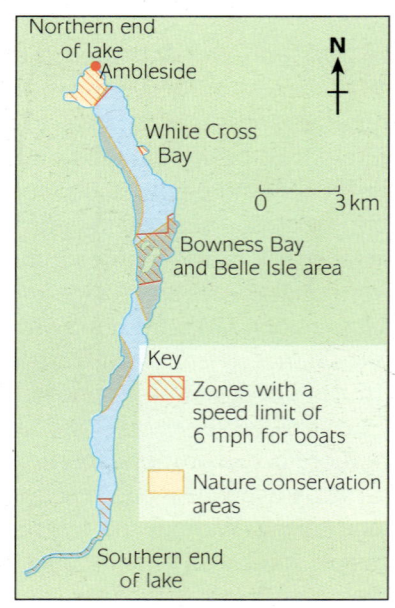

Figure 2 Lake Windermere: attempts at management to conserve areas that are important for wildlife and to keep parts of the lake free from speed boats.

Chapter 5
Coasts

On the brink ... in 1996 a farmer in Holderness (Yorkshire) next to her farmhouse after coastal erosion had already destroyed a garage and dairy unit. Is it still there now?

Key Ideas

The Earth's crust is modified by coastal processes, resulting in distinctive landforms:
- destructive waves are responsible for coastal erosion
- processes of erosion form distinctive landforms such as cliffs, wave cut platforms, caves, stacks and arches
- longshore drift transports eroded materials along the coast which are deposited elsewhere by constructive waves
- beaches and spits are examples of landforms of deposition.

Landscape features affect human activities:
- coastal management is needed for sea defences and tourism.

How is the coast eroded?

Waves are responsible for most of the erosion along coasts. Wind blowing over a smooth sea surface causes small ripples which grow into waves. When a wave approaches the coast its lower part is slowed by friction with the sea bed, but the upper part continues to move forward. As it is left unsupported, it topples over and breaks forward against the cliff face or surges up the beach. The waves which erode most are called **destructive waves** (Figure 1).

The power of destructive waves

Destructive waves have three main features:

1. They are high in proportion to their length.
2. The backwash is much stronger than the swash so that rocks, pebbles and sand are carried back out to sea.
3. They are frequent waves, breaking at an average rate of between eleven and fifteen per minute.

The height and destructiveness of these waves depend upon the distance over which the waves have travelled and the wind speed. If the waves driven by the wind have crossed over a large area of ocean or sea, they have had time to build up and grow to their full height, so that a lot of energy is released when they break against the coastline. The length of water over which the wind has blown is called the **fetch**. The greater the fetch and the stronger the wind, the more powerful is the wave and the greater its potential for erosion. From time to time ideal conditions occur for the formation of huge destructive waves, as they did in Cornwall on 4 January 1998 (Figure 3). There were onshore south-westerly winds, the winds were strong with frequent gusts over 160 kph and the winds had had a long journey over the Atlantic Ocean. Imagine the weight and force of the water crashing against the coastline under these storm conditions.

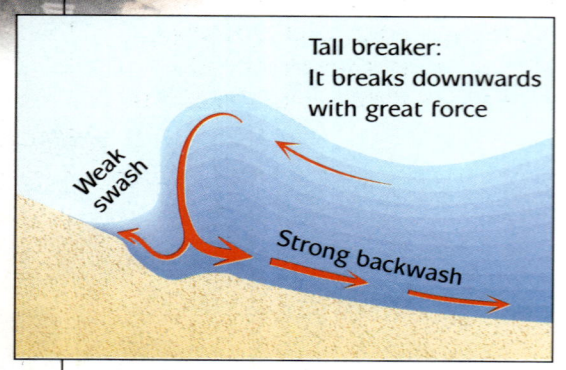

▲ **Figure 1** A destructive wave.

▲ **Figure 2** Chalk cliffs at Beachy Head created by destructive waves.

▲ **Figure 3** 'Waves lash the sea front at Porthleven in west Cornwall' – photograph from *The Guardian*, 5 January 1998. Headlines from other newspapers are shown to the right of the picture.

Insurance companies face £500 million payout for storm damage

We don't like to be beside the quayside

Worst storms since 1987 hurricane

The newspapers were mainly interested in telling their readers about the damage caused. Can you suggest a caption for **Figure 3** that a geographer would be more likely to write?

Processes of coastal erosion

There are many similarities between the ways in which rivers and waves erode, which is why the names used for the processes of erosion are the same.

> **A Hydraulic power:** This is the sheer weight and impact of the water against the coastline. It is greatest under storm conditions when hundreds of tonnes of water may hit the rock face. Also, air trapped in cracks and caves is suddenly compressed by the breaking waves, which increases the pressure on the rock.
>
> **B Corrasion:** Another name for this is abrasion. The breaking waves throw sand and pebbles against the rock face. These break off pieces of rock and cause undercutting. In large storms boulders will also be flung against the cliff face causing even greater damage.
>
> **C Attrition:** Particles carried by the waves are reduced in size as they collide with the rock face and one another. Boulders and pebbles are broken down into sand-sized particles which are easier for the waves to carry away.
>
> **D Corrosion:** This is the chemical action on rocks by sea water and is most effective on limestone rocks, which are carried away in solution.

The speed of erosion

You should refer to one or more of these processes whenever you are explaining the formation of a landform by coastal erosion. Of the four processes, hydraulic power and corrasion are the most significant, especially under storm conditions, which is when the highest rates of erosion are recorded. The type of rock also affects the speed at which a stretch of coastline is eroded. Rock faces which are riddled with joints, bedding planes or faults will be eroded more quickly than those which are in massive blocks, because there are lines of weakness which the waves can exploit. Cliffs built of a hard rock, such as granite in Cornwall and Devon (page 20), resist erosion longer than those made of soft sediments, such as boulder clay in Yorkshire and Norfolk, which the waves find easy to wash away (pages 72, 73).

In some cliffs the arrangement of the rocks increases the rate of erosion. The clay and sand cliffs at Barton on Sea, east of Bournemouth, are an example. Next to the sea is a layer of clay which is too weak a rock to withstand the strong destructive waves in the English Channel with their long Atlantic fetch. However, rain water seeps down through the sand which lies above the clay. This saturates the base of the sand layer along the junction with the clay and causes landslides and slumping. This results in erosion at the top of the cliff as well (**Figure 4**).

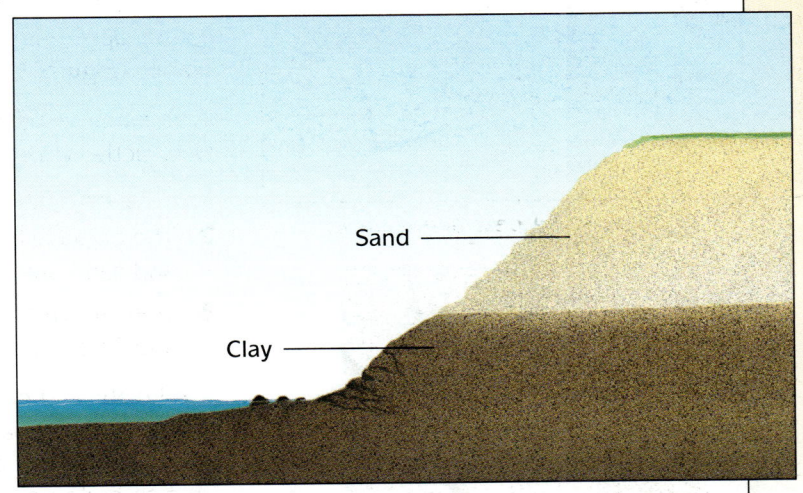

▲ **Figure 4** Cliff erosion at Barton on Sea.

> **Activities**
>
> 1 Show that you understand the differences between
>   a corrosion and corrasion
>   b corrasion and hydraulic action.
>
> 2 a Using an atlas, state which one of the following will have the longest fetch and which one the shortest:
>   • a south-westerly wind to Cornwall and Devon
>   • a north-westerly wind to the north coast of Ireland
>   • a northerly wind to the north coast of Scotland
>   • a south-easterly wind to East Anglia.
>   b Explain your choices.
>
> 3 a Explain why so much coastal erosion takes place during storms.
>   b Why will a storm cause more erosion along some parts of the coastline than others?

Landforms of coastal erosion

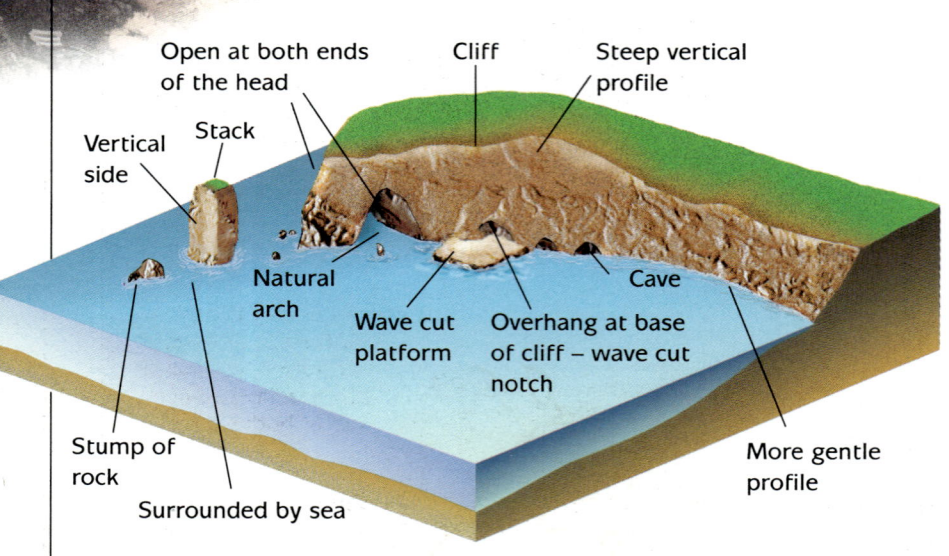

Figure 1 Main features of landforms of coastal erosion.

Labels: Open at both ends of the head; Cliff; Steep vertical profile; Vertical side; Stack; Natural arch; Wave cut platform; Overhang at base of cliff – wave cut notch; Cave; More gentle profile; Stump of rock; Surrounded by sea.

The main landforms of erosion, which can be seen in many places around the British coast, are described in **Figure 1**. Pay particular attention to the labels which are being used to *describe* the landforms. No attempt is being made on Figure 1 to explain their formation.

Cliffs and wave cut platforms

The sea **cliff** is the most widespread landform of coastal erosion. Cliffs begin to form when destructive waves attack the bottom of the rock face between the high and low water marks. By the wave processes described on page 63, such as hydraulic power and corrasion, the waves undercut the face forming a wave-cut notch. The rock above hangs over the notch. With continued wave attack, the notch increases in size until the weight of the overhanging rock is so great that it collapses. Once the waves have removed all the loose rocks and stones from the collapsed cliff, they begin to undercut the new rock face which is now exposed to wave attack. Wave erosion, followed by cliff collapse, happens time and time again so that the cliff face and coastline retreat inland. Impressive cliffs are found where rocks resist erosion, such as the 'White Cliffs of Dover' which are built of chalk.

As the cliff retreats a new landform, the **wave cut platform**, is created at the bottom of the cliff face. This is the gently sloping rocky area between the high and low water marks. It is covered at high tide but exposed as the tide goes out. It is not a smooth platform of rock; rather its surface is broken by ridges and grooves. This is the area of flat rocks that holidaymakers often venture onto when the tide has gone out, looking for crabs, and where they are liable to get trapped as the tide races in! The wave cut platform is formed where the rock above has been cut away by the

Figure 2 Formation of cliff and wave cut platform.

A: New rock face exposed; Area attacked by waves between high and low water marks.
B: Rock face overhangs; Wave cut notch showing undercutting by the waves.
C: Cliff retreats inland; Overhanging rock has collapsed; Wave cut platform is formed.

Figure 3 Marsden Rocks – stacks near Sunderland. Notice in particular the amount of undercutting around the base of the rocks.

waves to form the cliff. Because wave erosion is concentrated where the waves break between the high and low water marks, the rock below is little affected and is left as an area of flat rocks.

Caves, arches and stacks

Waves are particularly good at exploiting any weakness in a rock, such as a joint. By the same processes of erosion, and particularly by hydraulic power and corrasion, any vertical line of weakness may be increased in size into a **cave**. However, the rock needs to be relatively hard or resistant otherwise it will collapse before the cave is formed. Once a cave has formed, when a wave breaks, it blocks off the face of the cave and traps the air within it. This compresses the air trapped inside the cave, which increases the pressure on the roof, back and sides. If the cave forms part of a narrow headland, the pressures from the waves may result in the back of the cave being pushed through to the other side so that it is open at both sides. The cave then becomes a natural **arch**. The base of the arch is attacked by waves, putting more and more pressure on the top of the arch. After continued erosion, and especially if there is a weak point at the top of the arch, the arch collapses and becomes a **stack**. The stack is a piece of rock isolated from the main coastline (**Figure 3**).

You can see that there is a sequence of features formed by wave erosion – notch, cave, arch and stack (**Figure 4**). However, the stack itself is attacked by waves from all sides. It is gradually reduced in size and eventually it collapses so that all the signs of where the coastline used to lie disappear. When you look at a line of cliffs which mark the present-day coastline, as it is shown on maps, you must remember that it may be many kilometres further back than it used to be, as a result of the unceasing energy of destructive waves.

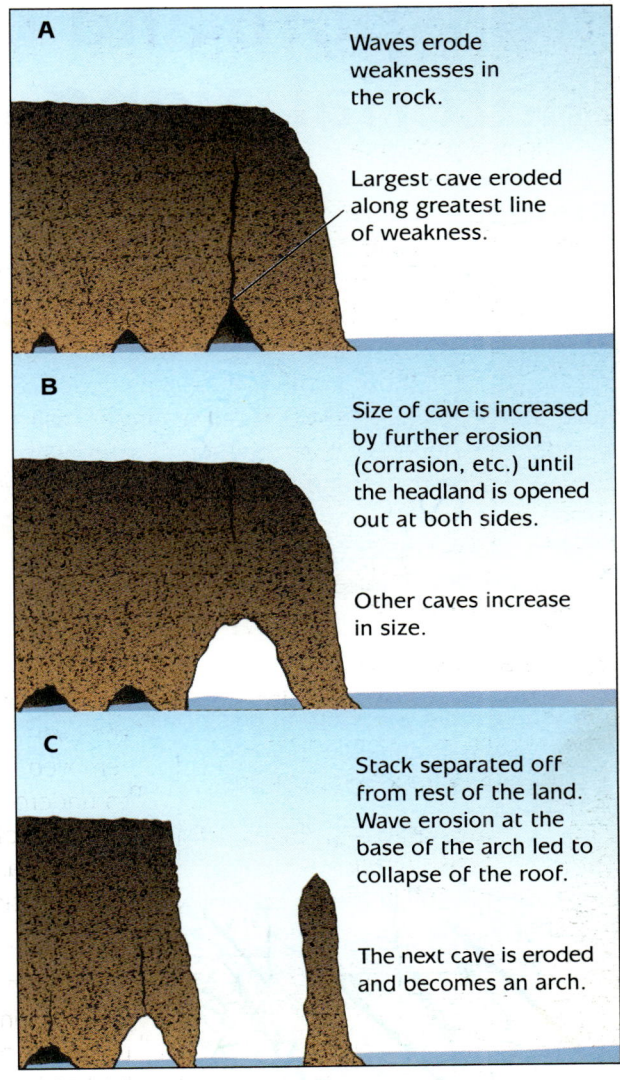

A Waves erode weaknesses in the rock.

Largest cave eroded along greatest line of weakness.

B Size of cave is increased by further erosion (corrasion, etc.) until the headland is opened out at both sides.

Other caves increase in size.

C Stack separated off from rest of the land. Wave erosion at the base of the arch led to collapse of the roof.

The next cave is eroded and becomes an arch.

▲ **Figure 4** Formation of caves, arches and stacks.

▼ **Figure 5** Part of the coastline a few kilometres west of Bournemouth.

Activities

1 a On a sketch show and label the coastal features on **Figure 5**.
  b Explain how they were formed.

2 Why are these cliffs being eroded less quickly than those at Barton on Sea a few kilometres east of Bournemouth (page 63)?

Transport and deposition of material along the coast

Transport

Loose, eroded materials of all sizes are transported by waves and deposited further along the coast. Rivers also carry sediment into the sea, which is picked up and carried away by the waves. The methods of transport are the same as those in the river channel (page 36): large boulders are rolled along the sea bed, smaller boulders are bounced along (saltation), sand grains are carried in suspension, and lime from chalk and limestone rocks dissolves and is carried in solution. The transport of sand and pebbles along the coast by waves is called **longshore drift** (Figure 1). Waves often approach a coastline at an angle, but sand grains and pebbles roll back down the slope at right angles to the coastline because this is the steepest gradient. As **Figure 1** shows, a pebble will keep on being pushed up the beach by the waves at an angle, but every time it rolls back down the beach at right angles to the coastline. In this way the pebble is transported along the coastline.

The general direction of the longshore drift around the coasts of the British Isles is controlled by the direction of the dominant wind (**Figure 1**). Prevailing south-westerly winds cause the drift from west to east along the Channel coast and from south to north along the west coast. The east coast is protected by land from the prevailing south-westerly winds. However, winds from the north cause longshore drift movement from north to south on the east coast. Northerly winds (winds from the north) have crossed a long stretch of open sea so that, although they do not blow as frequently as the westerly winds, they have the greatest influence overall. The longshore drift is important in the formation of all landforms of coastal deposition. Why do Local Authorities need to take the direction of the longshore drift into account when planning to protect tourist beaches and construct sea defences?

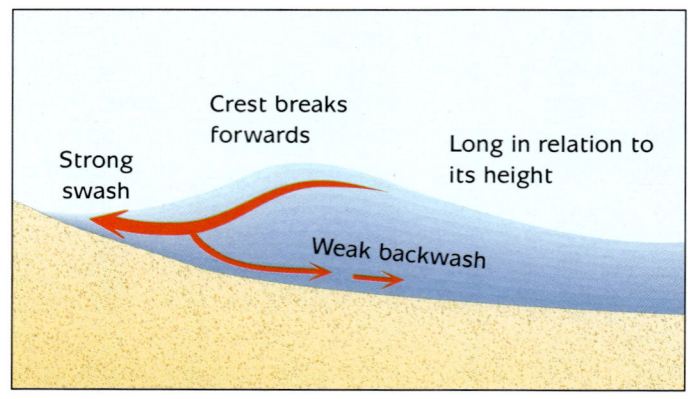

▲ **Figure 2** Features of a constructive wave.

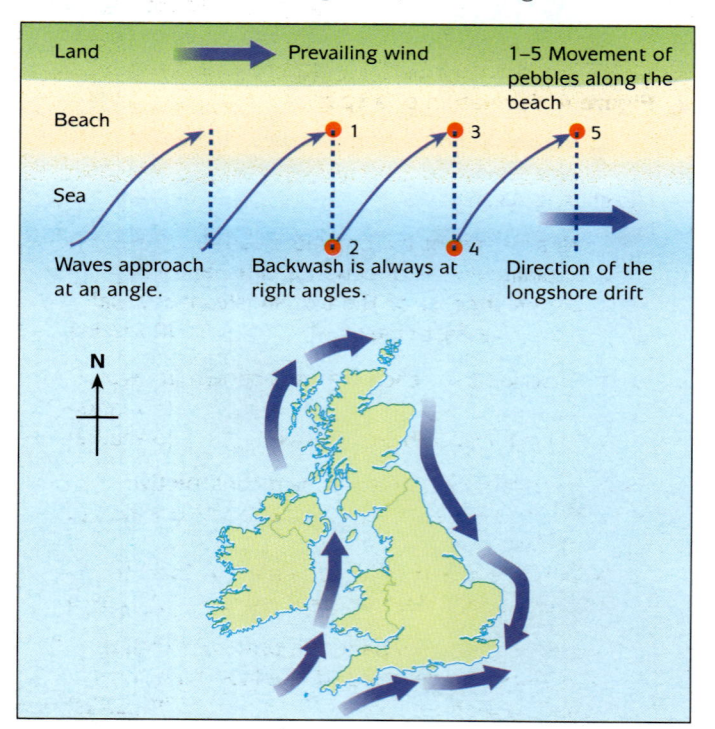

▲ **Figure 1** Direction of longshore drift around the British Isles.

Deposition

The load of the waves – sand, shingle and pebbles – is deposited by constructive waves (**Figure 2**). Such waves add more material than they remove from the coastline. Constructive waves have three main features:

1. They are long in relation to their height.
2. They break gently on the beach so that the **swash** carrying materials up the beach is stronger than the **backwash** carrying them away.
3. They break gently, with between only six and nine waves per minute.

These waves are associated with calm sea conditions when winds are light and are not blowing directly onshore. Therefore they occur more often in summer than in winter. Constructive waves operate most effectively in sheltered coastal locations such as in a bay sheltered by rocky headlands on both sides.

The formation of beaches

Everyone knows what a beach is, but can you describe it in geographical terms? The beach is the gently sloping area of land between the high and low water marks. Most of it is covered by the sea at high tide. Some beaches are straight and may extend for several kilometres. Others, located in bays, are more likely to be curved. The most common beach materials are sand, shingle and pebbles, but you may have seen many other types of materials (both natural and manmade) washed up on beaches. However, most of these stay on the beach for only a short time before being moved on by the longshore drift and the next high tide. The materials from which a beach is formed are carried by the longshore drift. If there is a coastline of weak rocks which has been greatly eroded on the up-drift side, the waves will be heavily laden with material. Where there is a bend in the coastline, deposition by constructive waves is always likely to take place because a more sheltered area has been created. Material accumulates over time and builds up the beach.

How do spits form?

A **spit** is an long and narrow ridge of sand or shingle (Figure 4). One end is attached to the land while the other end lies in the open sea. It is really a beach which, instead of hugging the coastline, extends out into the sea. If the spit is formed of sand, sand dunes are usually found at the back of it. Behind the spit there is an area of standing water, some of which may have been colonized by marsh plants. Some spits, particularly those found along the coast of the English Channel such as Hurst Castle spit near Christchurch, have a hooked end (page 74). Others, particularly those found on the east coast, run parallel to the coast, perhaps for several kilometres. Some of these, such as Spurn Point (pages 70–71), extend across estuaries, while others stretch across river mouths diverting river flow southwards for a time behind the spit.

The formation of a spit begins in the same way as that of a beach. Eroded materials are carried along the coast by longshore drift. Deposition begins at a bend in the coastline. For a spit, however, the deposited materials accumulate away from the coast into the open sea until a long ridge of sand or shingle is built up. Fresh water and sea water are trapped behind this ridge as it forms. As the ridge extends into deeper and more open water, the end of the spit is affected by strong winds. These winds and sea currents help to curve the end of the spit. Do you understand how the direction of the longshore drift along a coastline can be worked out from the form of a spit?

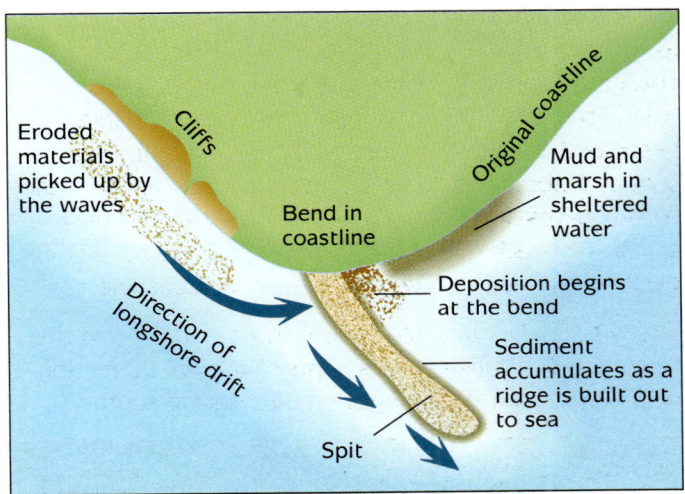

Figure 3
Two different beaches:
A is made of sand;
B is made of shingle.

Figure 4 Formation of a spit.

Test questions

1. a What is meant by longshore drift? (2 marks)
   b Explain why its direction is different along the west coast of the British Isles from that along the east coast. (2 marks)

2. a Describe the beach features shown in Figure 3. (4 marks)
   b Explain how a beach forms. (3 marks)

3. a Describe two ways in which constructive waves are different from destructive waves. (2 marks)
   b Why are constructive waves more likely to deposit than destructive waves? (2 marks)

4. Using Figure 2 on page 74, draw a sketch of the Hurst Castle spit and label its main physical features. (5 marks)

Human activities and coasts

Many people dream of living in a house next to the sea; sea views, plenty of fresh air and places to exercise the dog are just some of its attractions. When people choose to live as close to the sea as possible, coastal erosion and the danger of flooding become problems.

Coastal areas have always attracted settlement, and many stretches are heavily built up. Tourism is of great and increasing importance. In Victorian times, with the coming of the railway, first the rich and then the less well off began to go to the seaside for day trips and holidays. Today's well known coastal resorts, from Brighton in the south to Blackpool in the north, grew in Victorian times. Today, as well as attracting holidaymakers and day-trippers, they house many commuters and retired people, seeking a pleasant place to live. Although concentrated in the coastal resorts, tourism has spread along other parts of the coastline. Many coastal pathways for walkers and hikers have been created. Is there one close to your home? Some paths have proved so popular that they are being worn away by the pressure of visitor numbers. In some cases visitors accidentally contribute to cliff erosion by loosening stones and starting rock slides.

How are coasts managed?

The greater the number of people who live near or who visit the coastline, the greater is the need for **coastal management**. In seaside resorts management is usually deemed to be necessary for two reasons:

- to keep the sea out
- to keep the beach there.

▲ **Figure 1** Sea wall at Scarborough.

To keep the sea out, the usual method is to build a sea wall (**Figure 1**). On your visits to the coast you must have noticed the vertical walls at the back of the beach on the sea-ward side of the promenade. Did you notice their shape? The curved lip at the top is to deflect the force of the wave and to direct any sediment it may be carrying away from the sea front. Such walls are expensive to build and costly to maintain. They require a lot of maintenance because they absorb the concentrated energy of the waves, and we have seen how great that can be (page 62). They can only be justified economically if there are many people and much property to defend.

To keep the beach, without which resorts would lose much of their attraction for visitors, groynes and breakwaters are built out into the sea at right angles to the shore line (**Figure 2**). These trap the sediment as it is transported along the coast by longshore drift. They also reduce the energy of the waves, making erosion of the beach and cliffs less likely.

▲ **Figure 2** Groynes at Bournemouth.

In most seaside resorts the Local Authority has only been interested in managing its own stretch of coastline. Usually it has not considered the consequences further along the coast. Groynes are a simple and generally effective way of keeping a beach, but their construction can have disastrous consequences for the beaches on the down drift side. Deprived by the groynes of their load of sediment, the waves remove material from the beaches, and the cliffs, further along the coast with renewed vigour. The same groynes which do a good job of protecting the beach and soft cliffs at

Chapter 5 Coasts

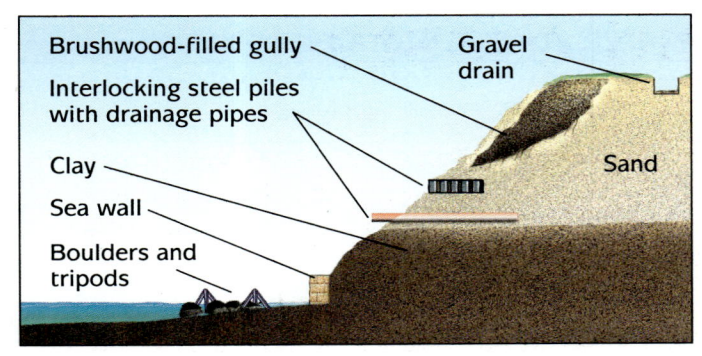

Figure 3 Protection for the cliffs at Barton on Sea.

Bournemouth are speeding up the already rapid erosion of the cliffs at Barton on Sea (page 63). Despite spending more than £1 million and using a variety of methods, the cliffs are still retreating at Barton on Sea, threatening holiday villages and housing estates.

Natural beaches are dynamic landforms – the sand is constantly deposited and washed away by the waves. Beaches rely upon new supplies of sediment for their survival. Any interruption in supply caused by human features such as groynes, breakwaters, harbour walls and jetties threatens their existence. Management which considers all the relevant factors is needed. A full cost–benefit analysis needs to be done before any money is spent.

Costs	Benefits
• What will it cost to complete?	• What are the advantages which justify the cost?
• How much will it cost to maintain?	• For how long will the benefits last?
• Who will be badly affected by it?	• Who will gain from it?
• Which areas will be badly affected by it?	• How large an area will gain from it?
• Will there be environmental damage?	• Will it improve the environment?

Activities

1. Name three methods of coastal protection.
2. For each one:
   a. describe how it works
   b. name and locate an area where it is used
   c. explain its advantages and disadvantages for coastal management.
3. Explain why the national policy for coastal management used in the Netherlands may be better than Local Authority policies in the UK.

Coastal management in the Netherlands

Some people have reached the conclusion that it is not cost-effective to protect parts of the British coastline and that it would be cheaper to pay compensation to those affected by erosion and flooding. The Dutch, however, have had to take another view. In the Netherlands, the large cities, most of the industries and the best farmland are all located in the western half of the country (in Holland), which lies up to 8m below the present sea level. Coastal protection is essential, irrespective of cost. Sand dunes line much of the west coast; these are the one natural defence against the sea and it is vital that they remain. As a result the coastline is lined with groynes to save the sand and in some places trees have been planted to fix the sand. Across inlets of the sea, enclosing dams were built; the Great Dyke across the entrance to the Zuider Zee is over 20km long. In the Delta region in the south, where very serious flooding occurred in 1953, four great dams, and many more supporting small dams, have been built to seal off the large inlets. The enormous costs of construction and maintenance have to be paid for by money raised from taxes, so that in the Netherlands everyone is paying for coastal protection, which is seen as a national problem rather than as a local one, as in the UK.

Figure 4 Coastal protection in the Netherlands.

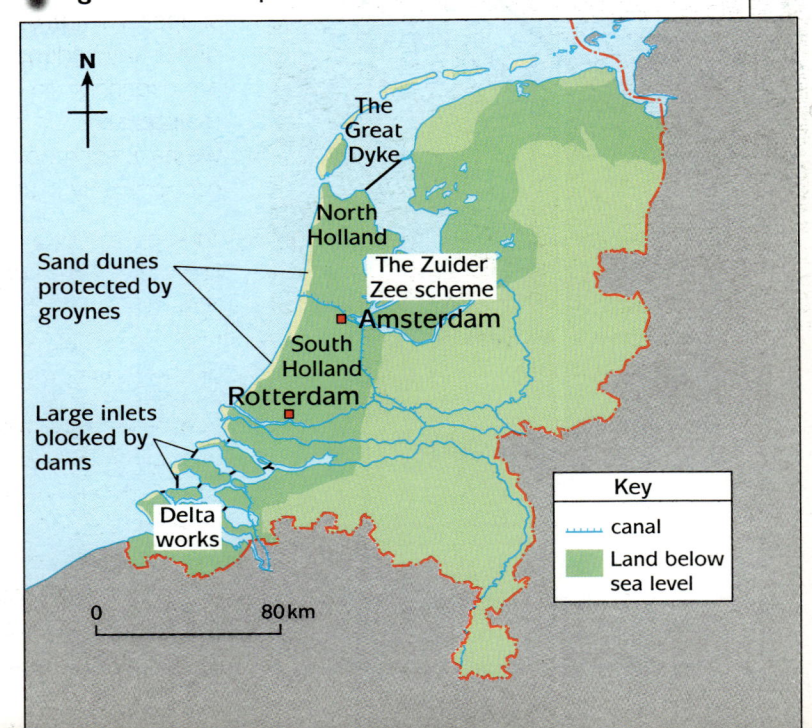

Case Study – a stretch of coastline

The Yorkshire coastline from Scarborough to the Humber estuary

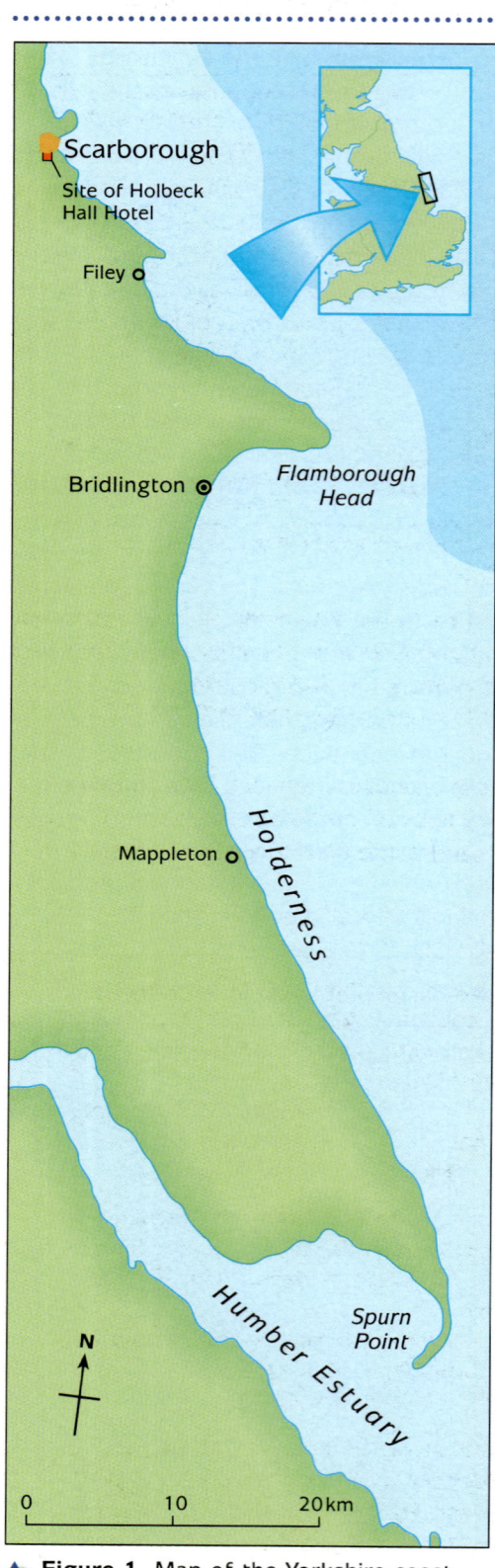

Figure 1 Map of the Yorkshire coast from Scarborough to the Humber estuary.

Figure 2 The beach at Scarborough.

Figure 3 The cliffs, caves, arches and stacks at Flamborough Head.

Figure 4 The spit at Spurn Point.

Case Study – a stretch of coastline

Scarborough – the number one resort of the Yorkshire coast

Sandy beaches are found on both sides of the castle headland. Most tourists visit the beach on the South Bay which is nearer to the town centre. On a hot summer's day the narrow strip of sandy beach is packed with adults sitting in deckchairs, children playing on the beach and people of all ages bathing in the North Sea (despite water temperatures below 14°C). Behind the beach, on the other side of the promenade and coast road, is a line of amusement arcades, gift shops and cafés, catering almost exclusively for tourists. One street runs up the steep hillside behind the South Bay linking the beach area with the town centre shops and stores. A sea wall runs the full length of the bay.

However, the collapse of the cliff under the five-star Holbeck Hall hotel in 1993, located on the southern side of the bay in what was thought to be a safe position on the cliff top, highlighted the serious problem of coastal erosion along the Yorkshire coast. It has led Local Authorities to think again about what needs to be done for coastal protection.

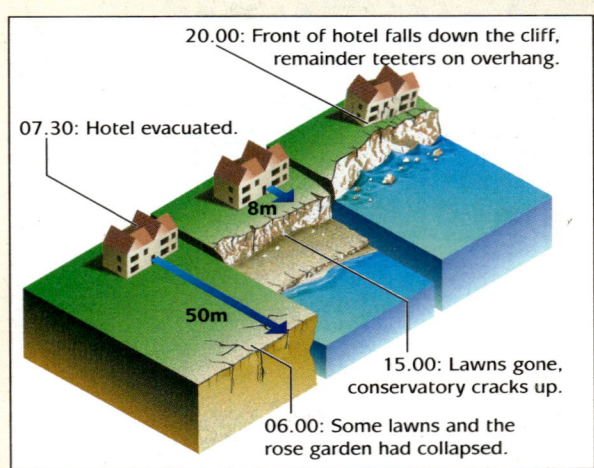

How the Holbeck Hall hotel fell over a cliff on 4 June 1993.

- 20.00: Front of hotel falls down the cliff, remainder teeters on overhang.
- 07.30: Hotel evacuated.
- 15.00: Lawns gone, conservatory cracks up.
- 06.00: Some lawns and the rose garden had collapsed.

Flamborough Head

A thick band of resistant chalk rock outcrops here. The chalk is a much harder rock than the boulder clay which covers Filey Bay to the north and Holderness to the south and has produced impressive cliffs (**Figure 3**). These are highest along the northern side where they form some of the highest cliffs in England with vertical faces more than 200 metres high. In front of many of the cliffs, rocks are exposed at low tide. The chalk which outcrops on the edge of the headland is well jointed. Wave erosion has been concentrated in the joints and along any other lines of weakness. The bottom of the cliffs is full of caves. Where vertical joints or faults are present, some of the caves have grown and have been cut through to form arches. Small stacks have been left and have names such as the King and Queen rocks or the Adam and Eve pinnacles.

Spurn Point

This spit is a major feature of coastal deposition (**Figure 4**). The longshore drift of material is from north to south. There is plenty of sand and clay for the waves to collect because of the rapid erosion of the boulder clay cliffs along the coast of Holderness from Bridlington southwards. At the bend in the coastline formed by the Humber estuary, deposition begins. In the past 150 years a ridge of sand some 8km long has been built up.

Activities

1 Trace or draw an outline of this stretch of coastline. Mark and name on it one example of each of the following coastal landforms:
   - cliff
   - cave
   - stack
   - wave cut platform
   - natural arch
   - beach and spit.

2 Choose one landform of coastal erosion from along this stretch of coastline and one landform of deposition. For each one:
   a on a sketch or diagram, show and label its main features
   b explain its formation.

3 Individually or in small groups, put together a leaflet, suitable for issue to visitors by the local tourist office, with the title 'The geographical attractions of the Yorkshire Coast'.

Holderness – problems of coastal management

Being number one in Europe for coastal erosion does not bring much pleasure to the people who live along the coast of Holderness. On average the waves remove between seven and ten metres of land each year – this may not sound very much, but it adds up. The coastline is today some three to four kilometres further west than it was in Roman times. Twenty-nine villages have been lost to the sea in the past thousand years. All along the Holderness coast farmers keep losing some of their land. Farmhouses are threatened (page 61); caravan sites and holiday homes have already been lost to the sea. The rate of erosion is unlikely to be reduced because of a combination of land sinking on the eastern side of the British Isles and possible sea level rising as a result of global warming. Sea levels in Holderness are estimated to be rising by 4mm a year.

Why is the coastline being eroded so quickly? After all, the east coast does not receive as regular a battering from destructive waves as do the west coast and exposed parts of the Channel coast. The main factor is rock type. The boulder clay is made up of soft clay and sands which are not consolidated (cemented together).

The waves can wash away the clay and sands from between the boulders to leave them unsupported. Also, when it rains, water enters cracks and spaces in the rock; after heavy rains this makes the cliff top unstable and liable to slumping. Most erosion occurs when winds blow from the north or north-east along this coast because the waves cross a long stretch of open sea (a long fetch), which increases wave energy for erosion. There are problems protecting a coastline which stretches for more than 50km.

Coastal defences at Mappleton

Mappleton is a small village which by 1990 was under real threat of becoming lost village number 30 along the coast of Holderness. The B1242 is the vital road link along this coast and it would have been expensive to find a new route for it. This helped to justify spending almost £2m upon a coastal protection scheme for a village of about 100 people. Blocks of granite were imported from Norway for sea defences at the bottom of the cliff and for the two rock groynes. The purpose of the two rock groynes is to trap beach material, which will protect the sea wall from wave attack.

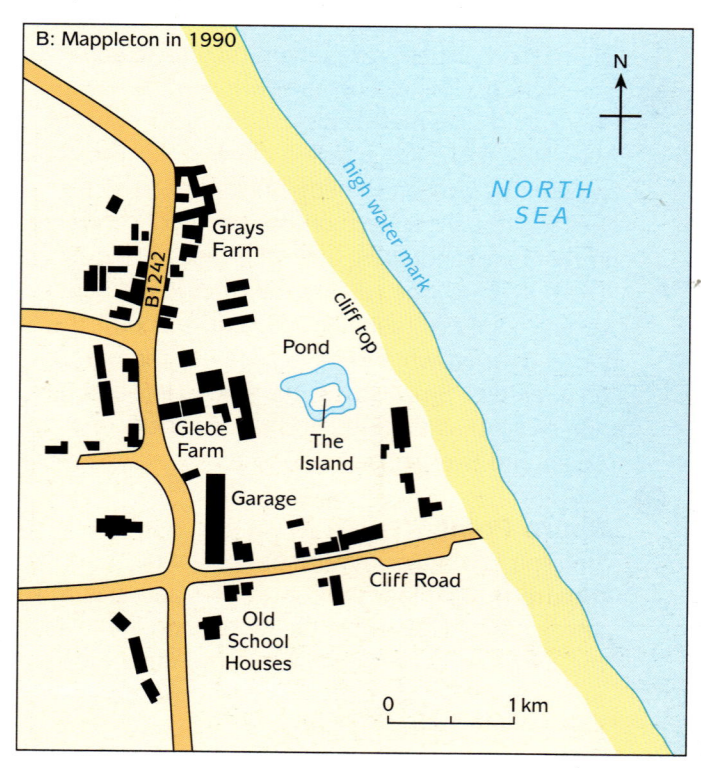

▲ **Figure 1** Mappleton in 1910 and 1990.

▲ **Figure 2** Mappleton and its sea defences.

Some views about coastal protection in Holderness

Holderness Council
We are a small authority with a total annual budget of only £4m. Spending a large amount of money to protect a village is hard to justify. Many people agree that the village should be allowed to disappear ... but it is terribly difficult to say this.

Ministry of Agriculture
We are moving towards a policy of 'managed retreat'. Although towns, villages and roads would be protected, farmland and even isolated houses would be regarded as dispensable and allowed to disappear. There are food surpluses in the EU so that every bit of farmland is no longer needed.

Dr John Pethick – a top scientist at the University of Hull
Low-lying farmland should be abandoned and cliffs allowed to collapse because they are the main sources of sand and silt that build up to protect other parts of the coast, including towns and cities.

Farmer living just south of Mappleton
My farm is at greater risk from the sea than ever because of the coastal protection works at Mappleton.

Activities

1 Describe the physical features of the coastline of Holderness as shown on **Figure 2** on this page and on page 61.

2 a State three pieces of evidence from this page for rapid erosion along the coast of Holderness.
  b Give the physical reasons for this rapid erosion.
  c Why is the natural rate of erosion not expected to decrease in the future?

3 a From **Figure 1** state:
    (i) by how many metres the sea has invaded inland between 1910 and 1990
    (ii) the distance between the B1242 road and the top of the cliffs in 1990.
  b With the help of Figure 2, describe the methods used to protect Mappleton.
  c Explain why the farmer who owns the land south of the cliff road, which can be seen on Figure 2, is complaining about the coastal protection works at Mappleton.

4 a Make two columns and list the arguments for and against protecting the coastline of Holderness.
  b What do you think would be the best policy? Explain and justify your own view.

Case Study – Barton on Sea

The Channel coastline near Bournemouth

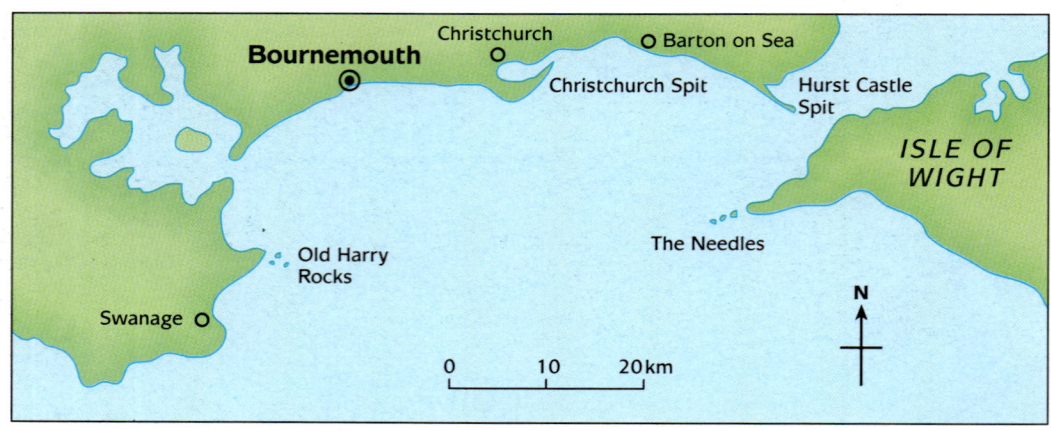

▲ **Figure 1** Map of coastline.

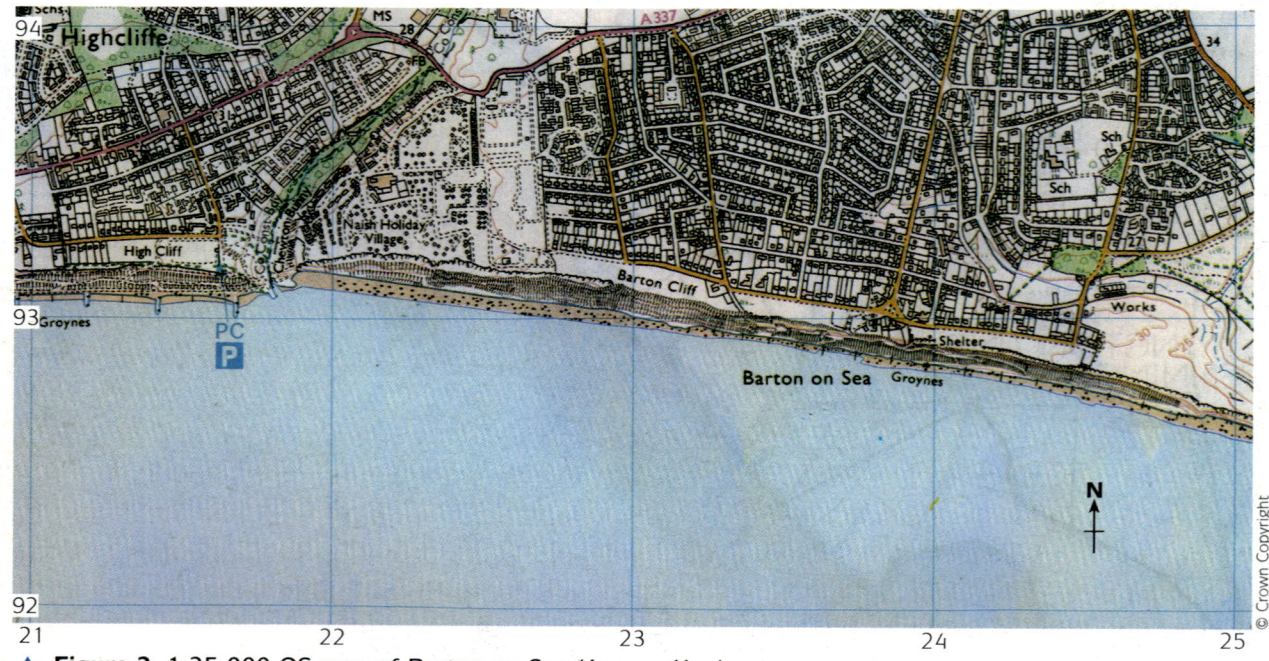

▲ **Figure 2** 1:25 000 OS map of Barton on Sea (4cm = 1km).

Activities

1 Briefly describe the location of Barton on Sea.

2 From the OS map, draw a labelled sketch map to show the physical features of the coastline at Barton.

3 From the OS map and page 63, describe the features of the cliffs at Barton which have led to their rapid erosion.

4 a Explain why coastal protection is needed at Barton.
  b Describe the methods used for coastal protection at Barton (page 69).
  c How successful has coastal protection been here?

Chapter 6

Weather and climate

Winter weather in the Lake District under anticyclonic conditions. Under the settled and calm weather conditions created by an area of high pressure, radiation fog forms in the valleys and frost lingers longer on the shaded slopes.

Key Ideas

Weather and climate are influenced by location:
- the global (world) distribution of climates is affected by factors such as latitude, distance from the sea and prevailing winds
- there are regional differences in climate in the UK based upon factors such as temperature and precipitation
- depressions and anticyclones lead to different and varied weather conditions in the UK.

Weather and climate influence human activity:
- drought, tropical storms, strong winds and fog affect human activities in different ways
- people respond to these weather hazards in different ways.

Global distribution of climates

What is meant by the climate of a place?

If someone asked you to describe the climate of the UK, what would you say? Wet? Cold? Unpredictable? Unless you had researched the answer, you would be unlikely to give the description used by many geographers, which summarizes the UK's climate as mild (or cool), wet winters and warm, wet summers. This is called a **temperate maritime climate**. Temperate means that the UK experiences neither the heat of the tropics nor the coldness of the poles. Maritime indicates that the UK feels the influence of the sea. One effect of the sea is to reduce the temperature differences between winter and summer. Another effect is increased precipitation.

Climate is a summary of a place's weather conditions, such as temperature and precipitation, averaged out over a long period of time (usually at least 30 years). It shows the conditions that can normally be expected at a place month by month during the year. If you are going on holiday, for example to Majorca, a study of the climate of its capital city, Palma, would tell you how hot it is likely to be and how much rain you can expect to fall while you are there (**Figure 1**). Note that in **Figure 1** a line graph is used to show average monthly temperatures and a bar graph is used to show precipitation; this is the usual way to show these features.

Figure 1
Distribution and characteristics of five of the world's major types of climate.

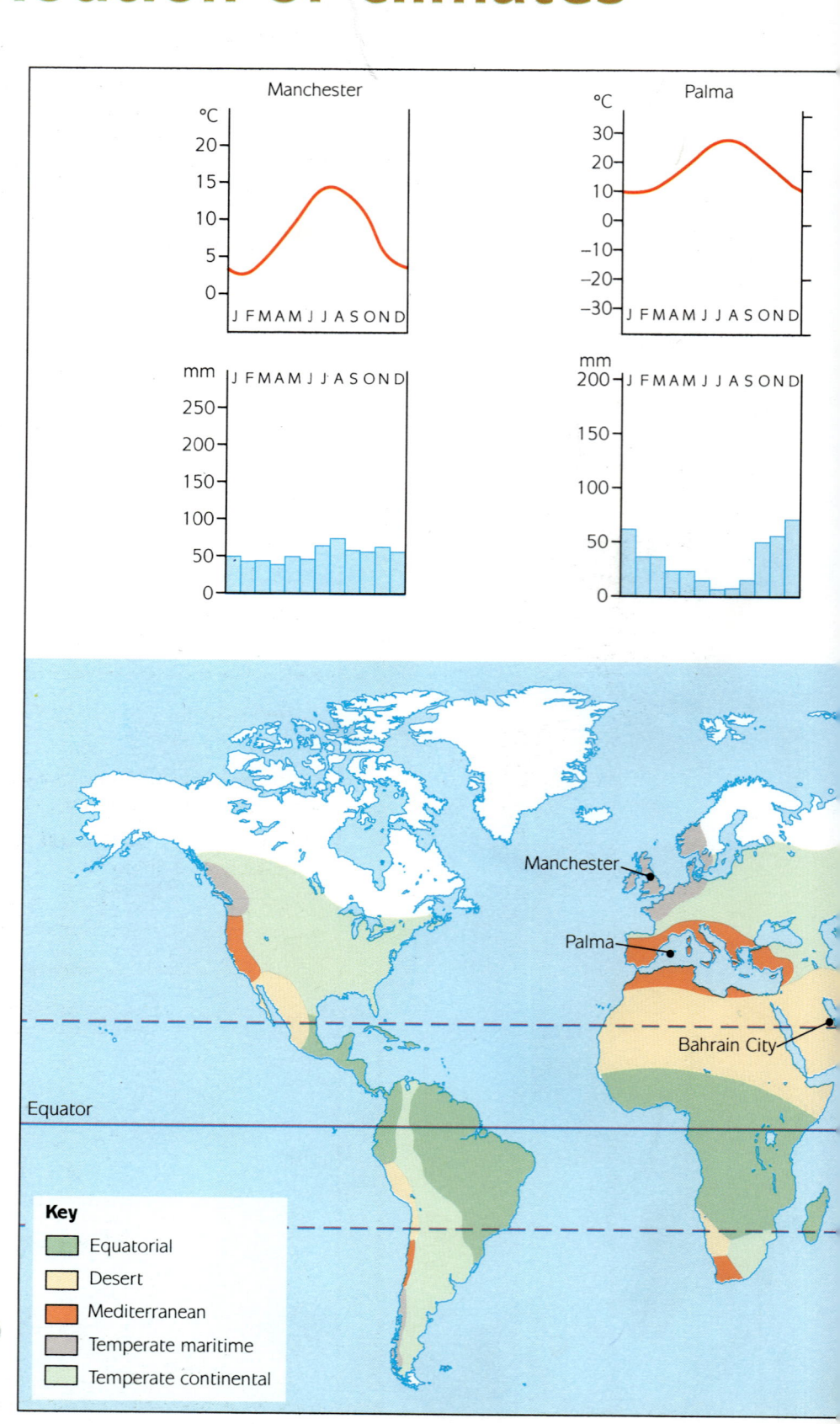

Key
- Equatorial
- Desert
- Mediterranean
- Temperate maritime
- Temperate continental

Chapter 6 Weather and climate

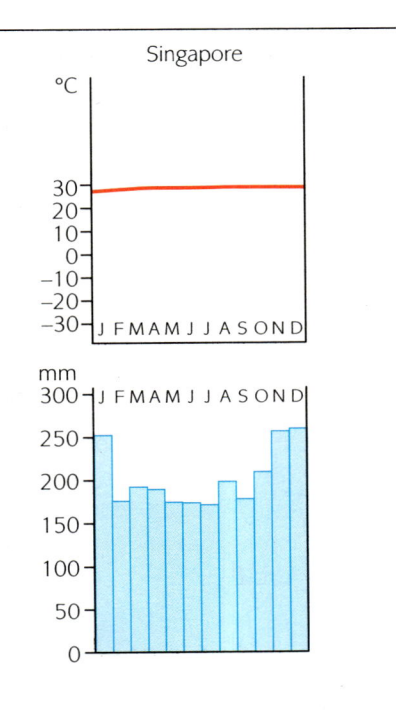

ℹ How to describe and use climatic graphs

A Temperature graph
1. State the highest (maximum) temperature and name the month.
2. State the lowest (minimum) temperature and name the month.
3. Work out the annual range of temperature by subtracting the lowest from the highest and stating the difference.
4. Describe the shape (gradient) of the temperature line.
5. Check that you have quoted the temperature unit and that your answers are accurate.

B Precipitation graph
1. Name the month with the highest amount of precipitation and state the amount.
2. Name the season or seasons in which most precipitation falls. (Note that in some places the answer could be 'all year'.)
3. Name the month with the lowest amount of precipitation and state the amount.
4. Name the season or seasons in which little precipitation falls.
5. Give some idea of the total amount of precipitation for the year. (Occasionally you may need to calculate the exact total; usually it is sufficient to use descriptions such as 'little' or 'very low' for under 250mm per year and 'high' for over 1500mm per year).
6. Check that you have quoted the precipitation unit and that your answers are accurate.

C Both graphs
Suggest the name for the type of climate shown (if it has not been given).

Activities

1. Following the instructions in parts A and B of the Information Box above, describe Manchester's climate.
2. Describe the main ways in which Manchester's climate is different from those of **a** Singapore, **b** Bahrain City, **c** Palma and **d** Ulan Bator.
3. From **Figure 1**, describe the distributions of **a** equatorial and **b** temperate continental climates.

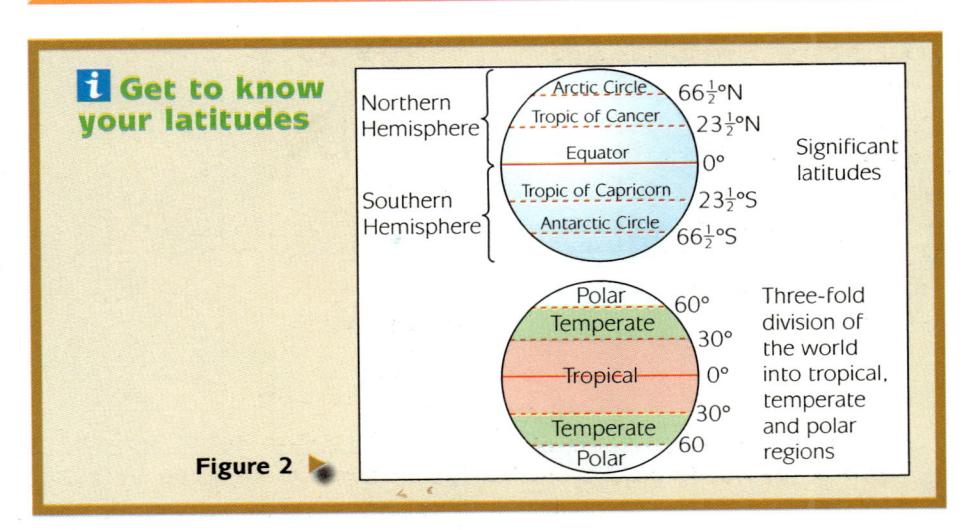

ℹ Get to know your latitudes

Northern Hemisphere:
- Arctic Circle — $66\frac{1}{2}°N$
- Tropic of Cancer — $23\frac{1}{2}°N$
- Equator — $0°$

Southern Hemisphere:
- Tropic of Capricorn — $23\frac{1}{2}°S$
- Antarctic Circle — $66\frac{1}{2}°S$

Significant latitudes

Polar 60°
Temperate 30°
Tropical 0°
Temperate 30°
Polar 60°

Three-fold division of the world into tropical, temperate and polar regions

Figure 2

Factors that affect the global (world) distribution of climates

Temperature and precipitation are the measurements used most frequently for describing the characteristics of a particular climate. So what causes temperature and precipitation to vary from one part of the Earth's surface to another?

Factors affecting temperature

A Latitude

On a global scale the effects of **latitude** are of greatest importance. The highest temperatures are recorded in low latitudes in the tropics between 0° and $23\frac{1}{2}°$ north and south of the Equator. Lowest temperatures are recorded in polar latitudes north and south of $66\frac{1}{2}°$. There is a gradual decrease in temperature between the Equator and the Poles because of reduced **insolation** (Figure 1). The Sun shines from a high angle in the sky in the tropics all year. As a result, the Sun's light travels directly through the Earth's atmosphere so that less is lost by reflection. Also, because the Sun's rays are (almost) vertical, there is a smaller area of the Earth's surface for each ray to heat up. In contrast, near the Poles the Sun's rays approach the Earth's surface at an oblique angle, which means that each ray has a larger area of surface to heat up. Having had a longer journey through the atmosphere where more of the light was reflected, less sunlight remains to be absorbed by the Earth's surface and used for heating it up.

B Distance from the sea

Particularly in temperate latitudes, **distance from the sea** influences temperature. During *summer*, when rates of insolation are highest, the sea heats up less quickly than the land. The Sun's light penetrates below the water surface so that the Sun's rays have more than just the surface to heat up, and constant movement mixes up warm and cool water. If you swim in the Mediterranean Sea in summer the temperature of the water will be up to about 20°C, whereas on land, even in the shade, temperatures between 25°C and 30°C are common. During *winter* months the opposite happens. The sea retains its store of summer heat longer than the land; on many winter days the temperature of the sea water will be higher than that of the air temperature on land. The result is that places close to the sea have summers that are less hot and winters that are less cold than those a long way inland (Figure 2).

C Prevailing winds

The British Isles and Western Europe have a much warmer *winter* climate than might be expected for their latitude. This is because the **prevailing winds** (the winds that blow most often) are south-westerly and have had a long sea journey across the Atlantic Ocean. The Atlantic Ocean is itself warmer than expected for its latitude because a warm ocean current, the North Atlantic Drift, is present. The south-westerly winds blow over this current and are warmed by it. This shows one way in which the direction of the prevailing winds has an effect on temperatures. Can you understand the two reasons why, if the prevailing winds had blown from the east instead of from the south-west, the winter climate of the British Isles would be much colder?

▲ **Figure 1** The effects of latitude on temperature – insolation.

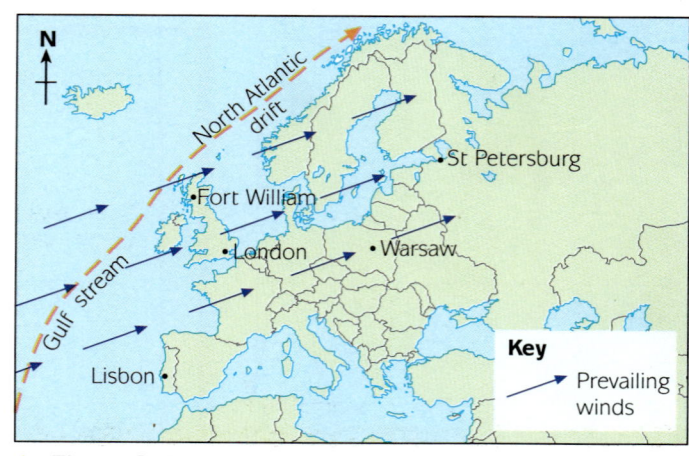

▲ **Figure 2** The effects of distance from the sea and of prevailing winds on temperature.

D Altitude

At the local scale **altitude** (the height of the land) can greatly affect temperature. If you go walking in the hills you will know that it becomes colder the higher up you go. The average rate of temperature loss is about 1°C for every 150m you climb (**Figure 3**). This is because the air becomes thinner so less of the Earth's heat is trapped and more is lost into space. However, when you are in the uplands the loss of temperature may seem greater than the average rate stated above, because the wind chill is higher and cloud is more likely to block out the Sun. However, great variations in temperature occur within upland areas, with sunny south-facing slopes in the northern hemisphere being warmer than slopes that face north and are more often in the shade.

Activity

1 For each of the following statements A–D:
   a Using **Figure 2**, state the evidence that supports the statement.
   b Give reasons for the temperature features stated.

A Average summer temperatures increase with greater distance from the sea.
B Average winter temperatures decrease with greater distance from the sea.
C The British Isles and Western Europe are much warmer than they should be when their latitude is considered.
D Annual range of temperature increases with distance inland.

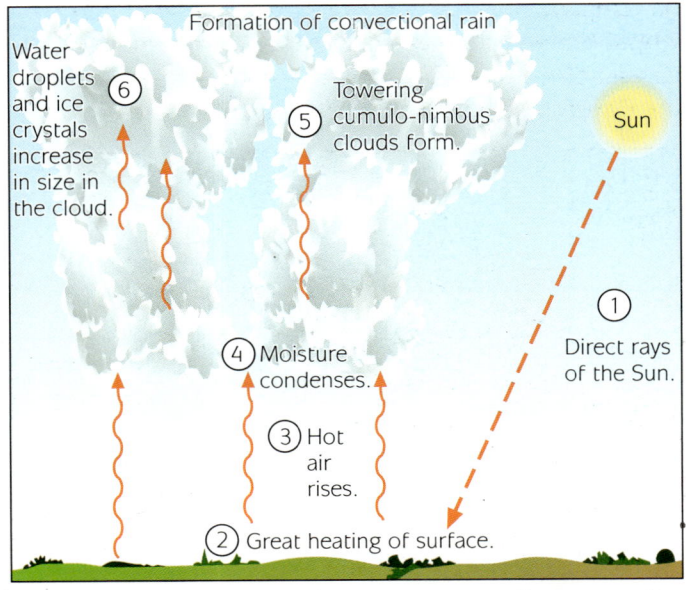

Figure 3 Formation of convectional rain. The stages in the formation of convectional rainfall are numbered 1–6.

Precipitation

Precipitation is the name for all types of moisture from the atmosphere. Usually this means rain (droplets of water), but also other forms such as snow (ice crystals) and hail (bullets of ice). Most precipitation falls after air has been forced to rise to high levels in the atmosphere.

One type of precipitation is **convectional** rainfall (**Figure 3**). The air next to the Earth's surface is heated by contact with the hot surface. This happens all year round near the Equator where rates of insolation are constantly high, and in summer in the middle of the land masses of North America, Europe and Asia. Hot air is lighter and rises up through the atmosphere. As it rises, the air reaches lower air pressure and expands. Expansion causes the air to cool. Continued rising and cooling leads to moisture condensing, forming clouds. The intense heating of the ground drives the hot air (or convection) currents up to such high levels in the atmosphere that tall cumulo-nimbus clouds form. In these clouds water droplets crash against each other and increase in size, until they are too large to be supported by the rising air currents and fall as precipitation (**Figure 3**). Heavy tropical downpours result, often accompanied by thunder and lightning (**Figures 4** and **5**). The other types of rainfall are **relief rainfall** (page 81) and **frontal rainfall** (page 82).

Figure 4 An aeroplane skirting around the edge of a cumulo-nimbus cloud.

Figure 5 Tropical thunderstorm in Malaysia.

The climate of the UK

Mention has already been made of the name of the UK's climate (*temperate maritime*) and of its general characteristics (*mild, or cool, wet winters and warm, wet summers*). However, there are significant differences in average conditions of temperature and precipitation from one part of the country to another. These are important because they have a great influence on human activities.

Temperature

The temperature pattern changes between summer and winter (**Figure 1**).

In *summer* (**Figure 1A**) the south is warmer than the north. The isotherms (lines linking places with the same average temperature) run mainly from west to east. The Sun shines from a higher angle in the sky in the south, which means that rates of insolation are higher here than in the north of Scotland, making for a difference of about 4°C in average temperatures. The built-up area around London, where the effects of the **urban heat island** are felt, is particularly warm. If there was no difference in the effects of sea and land on temperatures, the isotherms would run in a straight line from west to east. However, the lines bend southwards near to and over the sea, showing that the sea has a cooling effect in summer. Where on **Figure 1A** is the cooling effect of the sea on summer temperatures shown to be the greatest?

In *winter* (**Figure 1B**) some of the isotherms run north to south, and the west of the country is in general warmer than the east. North-west Scotland is warmer than many parts of England. At this time of the year the Sun's influence on temperatures is less because it is at a low angle in the sky and there are fewer hours of daylight. The winter warmth of the sea and the North Atlantic Drift is of greater importance; their warmth is transferred onshore by prevailing westerly winds, which warm up the western side of the country first and are cooled as they pass over the land surfaces. Spells of cold weather are brought by northerly winds from the Arctic or easterly winds from the continental interior and Siberia.

Influence of temperature on human activities

Farmers are most directly affected by temperatures. Temperature is the main control for the length of the growing season (**Figure 2**). Grass grows for much of the year in coastal regions in Cornwall and Devon, favouring dairy farming. Flowers and vegetables from the same regions are the first to reach market, fetching higher prices for farmers. Coastal holiday resorts are concentrated along the south coast of England, which has the highest summer temperatures. A study of **Figure 1** should explain why so many people also retire there.

ℹ Urban heat island

Buildings and dark surfaces such as tarmac roads store heat. Further heat comes from car fumes, factories, lights and central heating systems. The larger the built-up area, the greater the effect, which is why it is noticeable in London, where the centre may be 4–5°C warmer than the suburbs.

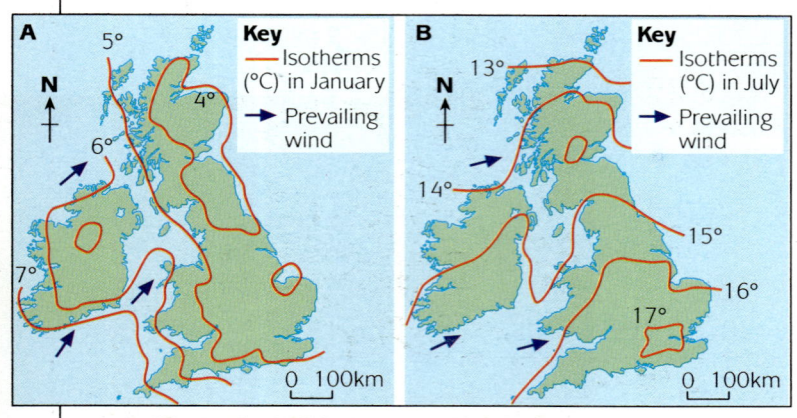

▲ **Figure 1** A: July temperatures; B: January temperatures.

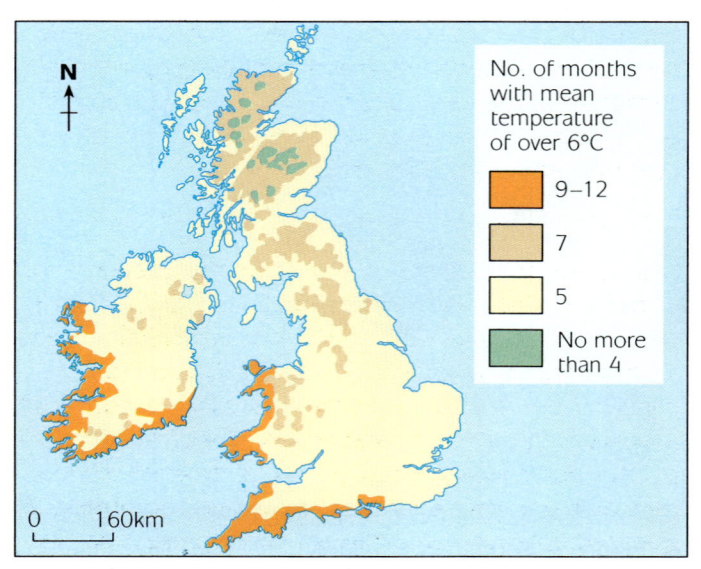

▲ **Figure 2** Length of growing season.

Precipitation

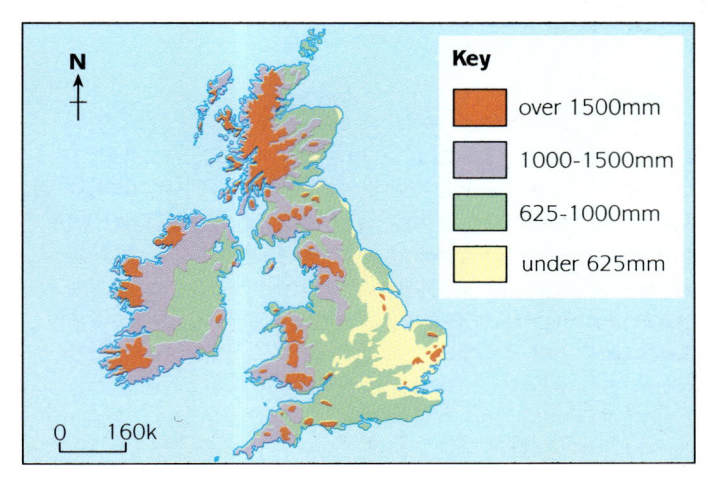

Figure 3 Average annual precipitation.

Precipitation in the UK is generally highest in the west and lowest in the east (**Figure 3**).

The factor most responsible for this is the *direction of the prevailing winds*. The south-westerly winds have had a long sea journey and are laden with moisture when they blow onshore. They release less moisture as they move east. Other factors contribute as well. *Frontal depressions* (areas of low pressure with warm and cold fronts) are also driven from west to east by the westerly circulation and they drop rainfall first in the west. What makes the difference in the amount of precipitation between east and west so large is *relief*. In the west are upland areas; in the highest of these annual precipitation totals exceed 2000mm. The amount of precipitation released increases when winds laden with moisture are cooled even more by being forced to rise over the uplands. In contrast, in some places in eastern England, such as East Anglia, the annual precipitation total barely reaches 500mm. East Anglia is one of the lowest-lying parts of the country; winds and frontal depressions arriving from the west have crossed the widest area of land so that the rain shadow effect is felt more strongly here than elsewhere (**Figure 4**).

Influence of precipitation on human activities

High rainfall washes the minerals (and the goodness) out of the soil. This is called **leaching**. Soils in upland areas become acid and infertile after heavy leaching. In upland areas where the relief is gentle and the rocks are impermeable, such as on many granite moorlands (pages 22–23), the agricultural potential of the land is poor or non-existent. However, the same areas are ideal for water storage even if they are useless for farming. In glaciated uplands, natural lakes may be present or the steep-sided valleys offer suitable sites for creating reservoirs. In western lowlands, where the annual precipitation averages about 1000mm, good grass growth means that dairy farming is the main type of farming, whereas in eastern parts of England and Scotland crop growing is favoured by annual rainfall totals below 750mm. Cereals such as wheat and barley, and root crops such as potatoes and sugar beet, need water for growth but they do not like too much. Also, wet ground makes the use of machinery difficult.

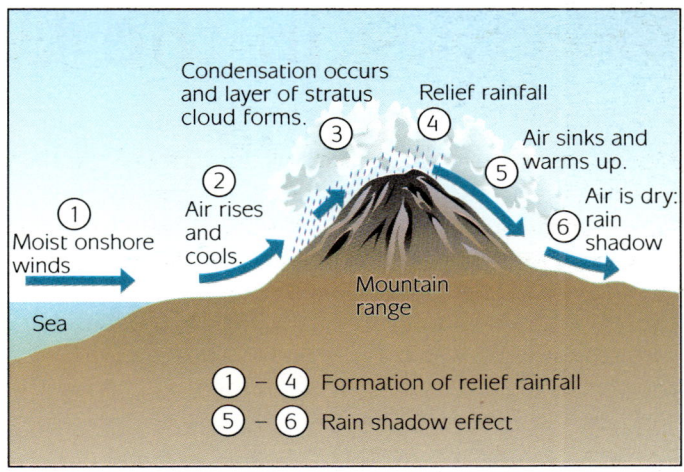

Figure 4 Relief rainfall and the rain shadow effect.

Activities

1. Study the relief map of part of the north of England (**Figure 5**).
   a. Describe the pattern of precipitation shown.
   b. With the help of a labelled diagram, give reasons for the differences in annual precipitation in northern England.

2. Some of the precipitation falls as snow, especially in upland areas. Suggest ways in which snow **a** hinders and **b** gives opportunities for human activities within the UK.

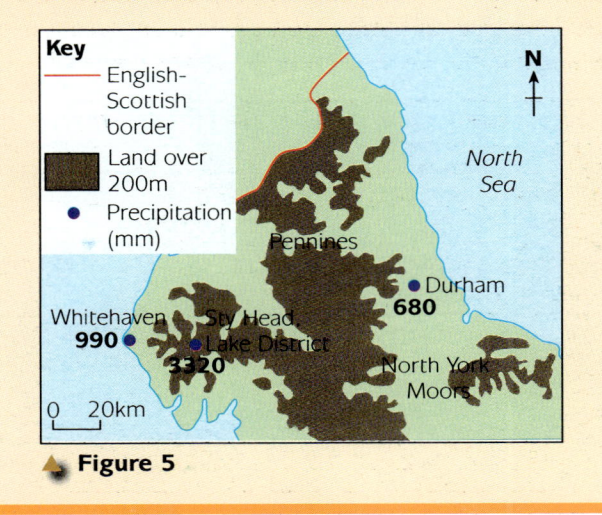

Figure 5

Weather in the UK – frontal depressions

While climate is the long-term average, **weather** is the day-to-day conditions of temperature, precipitation, cloud, sunshine and wind. A typical weather forecast for the UK on a winter's day might be 'Rain in the morning with strong winds will be followed by sunshine and showers in the afternoon; overnight there will be fog and frost'. A cynic might say that the weather forecaster has no idea what the weather is going to be and has mentioned just about every type of weather that can occur in the UK! That would be a harsh judgement – the British weather is notoriously changeable and usually no two days are alike. There has been a tremendous improvement in the accuracy of weather forecasts, which now rely on satellite data and pictures, radar showing precipitation and computer models for the behaviour of depressions and anticyclones.

Frontal depressions

Depressions are areas of **low pressure**. There is relatively low air pressure at the surface because the air is rising. Air, carried by surface winds, is drawn into the centre of the depression to replace the rising air. In the northern hemisphere winds blow in an anti-clockwise direction around a depression, spiralling towards its centre. In general, depressions bring spells of unsettled weather with plenty of wind, cloud and rain. Occasional deep depressions (those with a particularly low pressure below 960 millibars (mb)) are responsible for releasing heavy downpours leading to local flooding, or for bringing severe storm-force winds, which cause extensive damage to trees and buildings, such as the famous 'hurricane' which hit south-east England in October 1987.

Formation

Frontal depressions form where warm air from the tropics meets, and is forced to rise above, cold air from the poles. The rising air creates the centre of low pressure. The line which separates the two air masses is called a **front**. As the depression develops and moves

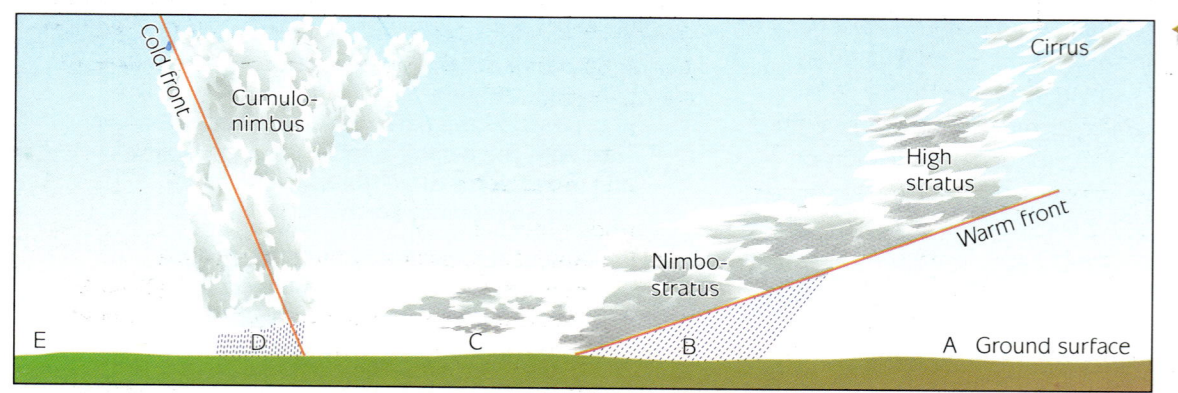

Figure 1 Cross-section of a frontal depression.

Location	Weather	Reasons
A Well ahead of the warm front	Clouds over with high cirrus and stratus cloud.	Moisture in the warm air condenses high in the sky showing that it is being forced to rise.
B Ahead of the warm front	A period of steady rain from a thick sheet of stratus cloud.	Moisture in the rising warm air is now condensing at low levels in the atmosphere.
C Between the warm and cold fronts	The temperature increases and the rain stops.	The warm air touches the ground and it is not being forced up as strongly as along the front.
D At the cold front	A short period of heavy rain from cumulo-nimbus clouds, sometimes accompanied by thunder and lightning.	The warm air is being forced up to high levels in the sky by the powerful push of the cold air.
E Behind the cold front	Temperatures fall. The weather is a mixture of sunshine and showers.	The main belt of rising air along the front moves away. A cold air mass follows. In it there are pockets of rising air giving showers.

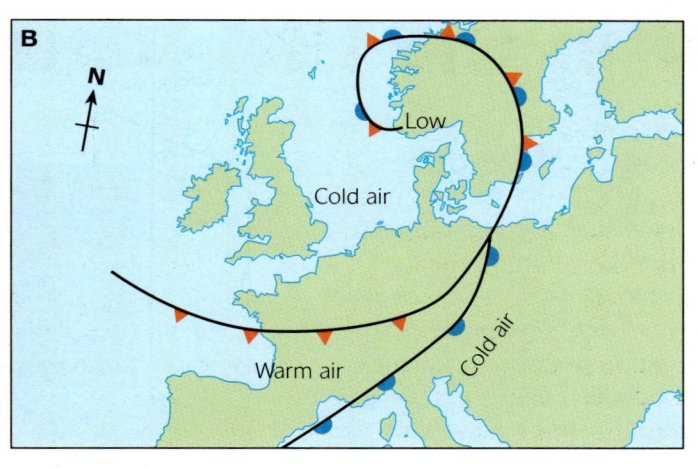

Figure 2 A: Satellite photograph of a frontal depression. B: Position of fronts and air masses.

east driven by the westerly circulation, two fronts can be recognized. The leading front is the **warm front**, so called because once the warm front passes over a place, the warm air of the tropical air mass brings warm weather. The front at the rear of the depression is the **cold front**, so called because after it passes the cold air of the polar air mass brings colder weather.

Typical weather patterns associated with the passage of a depression

Most of the activity takes place along the fronts. It is here that the lighter warm air is being forced to rise most vigorously as the cold air pushes underneath it. Rising air leads to belts of cloud and rain.

On **Figure 2A** the centre of the low pressure can be detected by the swirl of cloud. This is where the wind is being sucked into the centre from surrounding areas of high pressure. The swirl is caused by the rotation of the Earth. The fronts show up as trailing lines of cloud on the southern sides of the depression. It is along the fronts that most activity is occurring as air is being pushed upwards leading to condensation of its moisture into cloud. The white speckles of cloud in the area behind the cold front indicate shower clouds. Cold air is being warmed up by its journey over the sea, encouraging air to rise and to form the cumulo-nimbus shower clouds shown.

On **Figure 2B** the occluded front was formed by the cold front moving more quickly than the warm front. In a well-developed depression such as this the cold front has caught up with the warm front near the centre of the depression.

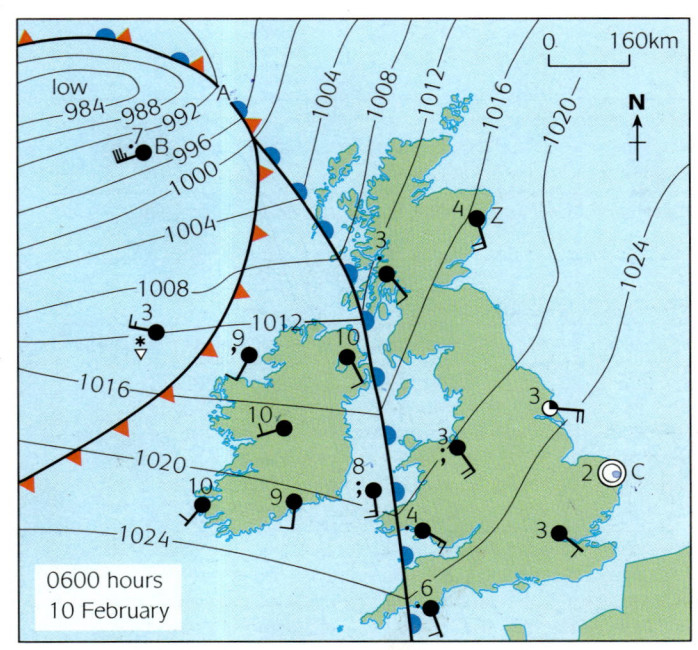

Figure 3 Synoptic chart dominated by a frontal depression.

Test questions

Study **Figure 3**.

1 a State the pressure in the centre of the depression. (1 mark)
  b Name the type of front marked A. (1 mark)

2 a State the wind direction and wind speed at station B. (2 marks)
  b Explain why its wind speed is the highest on the chart. (2 marks)

3 a Describe the differences in temperatures shown between England and Ireland. (3 marks)
  b Give reasons for these differences. (3 marks)

4 Explain why the western areas of Scotland, Wales and England are being affected by a belt of rain. (5 marks)

5 The weather system is moving eastwards. Describe three ways in which the weather at station C is likely to change during the rest of the day. (3 marks)

Weather in the UK – anticyclones

These are areas of **high pressure** in which the air is descending to the Earth's surface. The air 'piles up' near the surface to create a higher than average air pressure. The air drifts outwards from the centre of the anticyclone and the winds blow in a clockwise direction around the centre in the northern hemisphere. Only light winds are caused by the **gentle pressure gradient** (small differences in pressure over wide areas, which are shown by wide spacing of the isobars on synoptic charts).

A strong anticyclone, above 1030mb, may establish itself over the British Isles and stay for several days, or even weeks, blocking out the frontal depressions. At *any time of year*, dry and settled weather with little wind is expected when an anticyclone is dominant. In *summer*, temperatures are likely to be higher than average as strong sunshine from clear cloudless skies heats up the land. This leads to a *heatwave* if the anticyclone does not move and release its grip on the weather. In *winter*, temperatures are lower than average. Sunny but cool days are followed by long cold nights with frost and fog, both of which are most likely on valley floors (page 75). The intensity of the frost can build up night after night leading to a *big freeze*, which brings problems such as burst pipes.

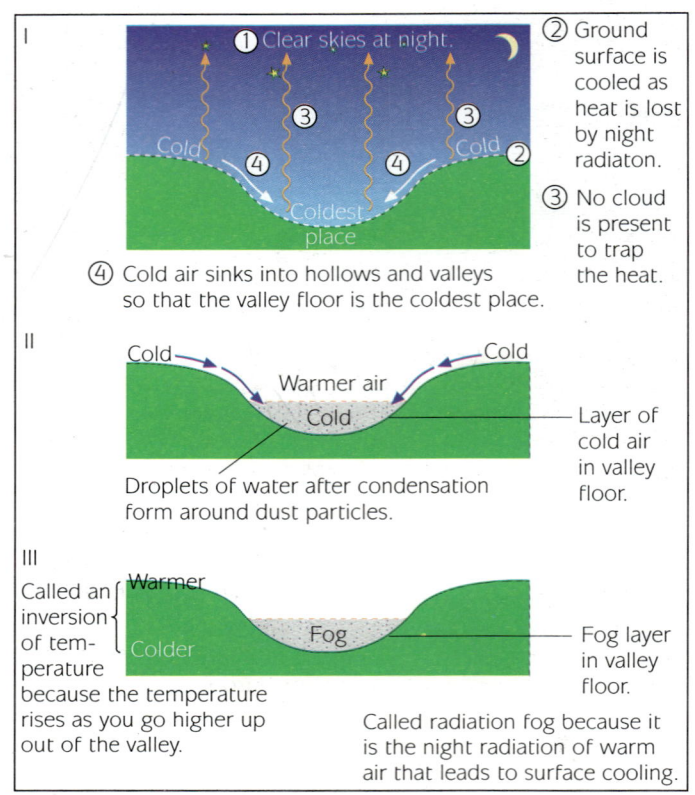

Figure 1 Formation of radiation fog. This type of fog is shown on page 75.

Diagram I: ① Clear skies at night. ② Ground surface is cooled as heat is lost by night radiation. ③ No cloud is present to trap the heat. ④ Cold air sinks into hollows and valleys so that the valley floor is the coldest place.

Diagram II: Warmer air; Cold; Droplets of water after condensation form around dust particles. Layer of cold air in valley floor.

Diagram III: Called an inversion of temperature because the temperature rises as you go higher up out of the valley. Warmer/Colder. Fog. Fog layer in valley floor. Called radiation fog because it is the night radiation of warm air that leads to surface cooling.

Anticyclonic weather and the reasons for it

Weather	When and where in the UK it is most likely to occur	Why it occurs
Dry	Any time of the year; everywhere	Descending air is warmed up because air pressure increases near the surface. Warm air can more comfortably hold its moisture (i.e. the opposite of what is needed for condensation and precipitation).
Little wind	Any time of the year; everywhere	Low-pressure gradient showing that there is little difference in pressure over a wide area.
Hot and sunny	In summer, especially in areas away from the sea	Long hours of daylight during which the sun shines from cloudless skies. The Sun is at a high angle in the sky for greater insolation.
Cold days	In winter; everywhere, but especially in areas away from the sea	Short hours of daylight from the weak winter sun. The Sun shines from a low angle in the sky and insolation rates are low.
Frost	On winter nights, particularly in low-lying and inland areas	Clear skies allow heat loss from the ground surface at night; moisture in contact with the cold ground surface condenses into ice when the temperature falls below freezing point. The coldest places are inland away from the warming influence of the sea and on valley floors into which cold air, being denser, sinks. Wind speeds are too low to stop this happening.
Fog	Mainly in winter; it is likely to be mist rather than fog in summer. Low-lying areas and valley floors are more prone to fog.	Clear skies allow heat loss from the ground surface at night; moisture in the air in contact with the cold ground surface condenses; droplets of water form around tiny dust particles in the air which reduce visibility to less than 1km (this is fog). A slight breeze may stir up the coldness from the ground surface and thicken the fog; if a strong breeze develops this will lift the fog and clear it.

Chapter 6 Weather and climate

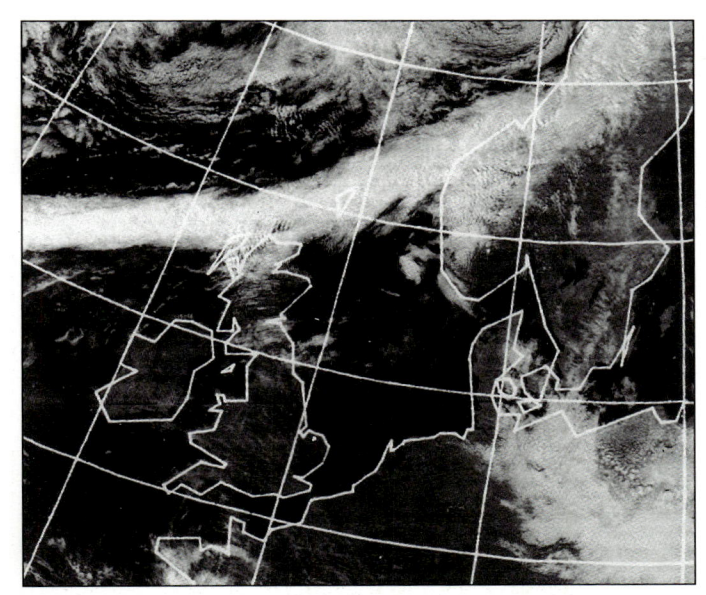

Figure 2 Satellite photograph taken when an anticyclone is dominating the weather over most of the British Isles. Cloud associated with the fronts of the depression centred off the coast of Norway can be seen touching the north of Scotland. Its progress southwards over the rest of the UK has been blocked by the anticyclone, which has given largely cloudless skies to the rest of the UK and much of central Europe.

The effects of fog upon human activities

Fog is the most common hazard of anticyclonic weather in the UK. People on the move are most affected. Thick fog, especially if it occurs in patches, can cause road accidents and motorway pile-ups (**Figure 4**). Motorists who suddenly meet a patch of thick fog, most probably in a hollow or low-lying stretch of road, do not reduce their speed. Motorway warning signs and the addition of lights along those sections of motorway known to be most prone to fog have helped to reduce the numbers of accidents.

Many jet planes are fitted with automatic landing systems, although there are always delays; sometimes the fog is so thick that the pilots cannot see to taxi to the terminal and all aircraft movements have to stop. Flights are cancelled or planes diverted to other airports. Lighthouses have foghorns to warn ships of dangers to navigation, such as rocks, when the light cannot be seen.

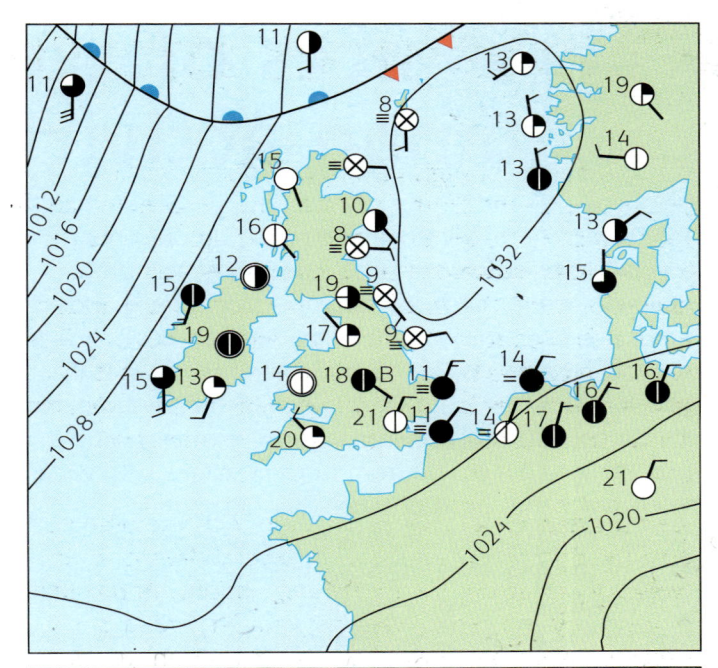

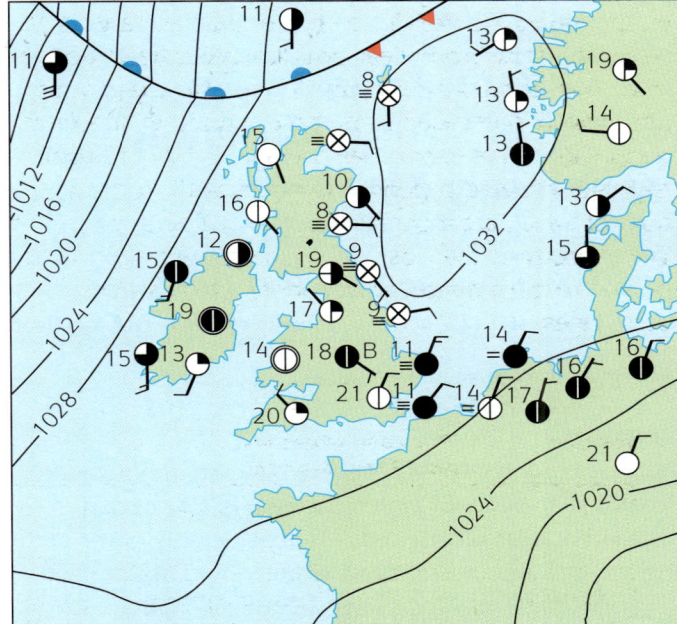

Figure 3 Synoptic charts for summer and winter.

Figure 4 A motorway in fog.

The effects of weather and climate on human activity

The temperate maritime climate of the UK does not generally give extreme weather conditions. The UK weather cannot match the torrential tropical downpours which are an everyday event in the Amazon Basin. It is not dry day after day for ten months of the year as in most of the world's hot deserts. Unlike the West Indies, the UK has no hurricane season for four months of the year, bringing a high risk from tropical storms with winds nearly twice the speed of those that did so much damage in the English 'hurricane' of October 1987. For most of the time the British weather can be described as unexciting. However, from time to time the UK weather hits the headlines (**Figure 1**).

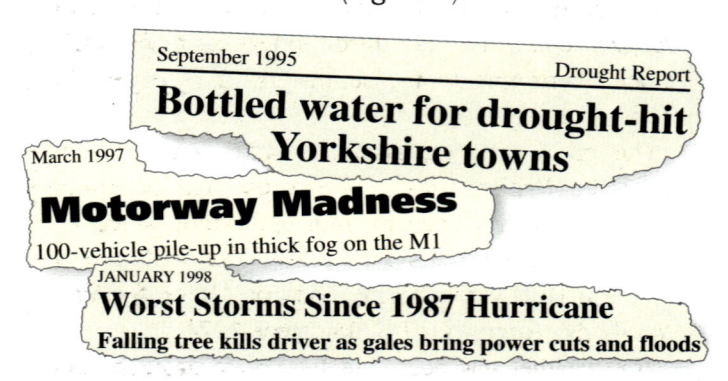

September 1995 — Drought Report
Bottled water for drought-hit Yorkshire towns

March 1997
Motorway Madness
100-vehicle pile-up in thick fog on the M1

JANUARY 1998
Worst Storms Since 1987 Hurricane
Falling tree kills driver as gales bring power cuts and floods

▲ **Figure 1** Newspaper headlines.

Drought

Water is essential for life. People only live in hot deserts if there is a source of water. Drought is a hazard in populated areas when rainfall is considerably lower than the average amount that was planned for. The droughts in various parts of Africa since 1970 have had devastating effects. It is a continent where most people subsist on the food they produce for themselves; when crops fail or animals die because pastures are burnt off by the heat, people starve. The most vulnerable groups of people – the young, the sick and the elderly – die first. When the drought in Ethiopia was at its worst in 1983, thousands died. Survivors in remote regions not reached by food aid migrated long distances on foot to refugee camps in Sudan. The droughts in southern Africa in the early 1990s received less attention from the media, but the failure of the maize crop, upon which rural people depend, led to malnutrition and death. The shortage of crops for export badly hit the economies of countries such as Zimbabwe.

Drought in the UK

Even England, normally wet, suffered from a drought in the 1990s (**Figure 2**). Farmers faced some extra economic costs for water supply and some reductions in crop yields, but, for most people, measures such as a ban on the use of hosepipes were inconvenient, rather than a matter of life and death as in Africa.

▲ **Figure 2** Haweswater in the Lake District, August 1995. Instead of a reservoir full of water to supply Manchester, it became a tourist attraction.

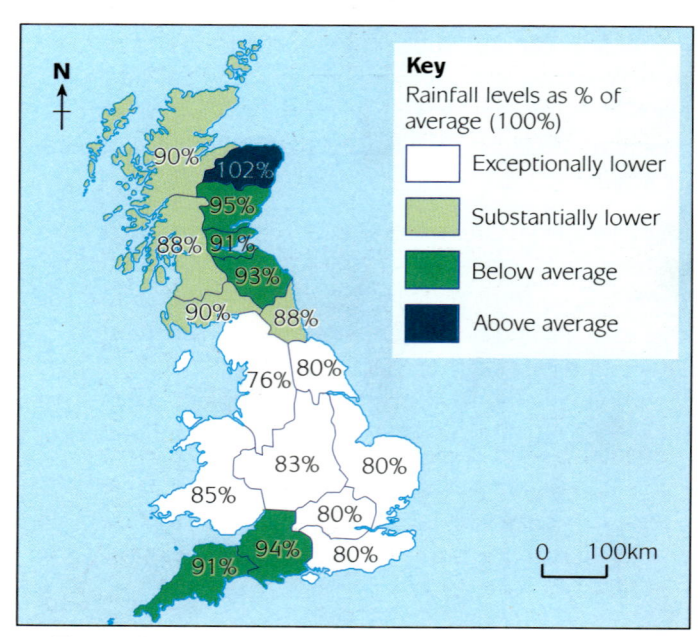

▲ **Figure 3** April 1995 to September 1997 was the driest period since records began.

Chapter 6 Weather and climate

Summer of '95 blazes its way to a new record

Heat wave

Cool is hot
Block of high pressure moving across the British Isles is actually relatively cool and heavy. It is this weight which pushes down, 'squeezing' clouds away and giving clear skies.

Rotating anticyclone

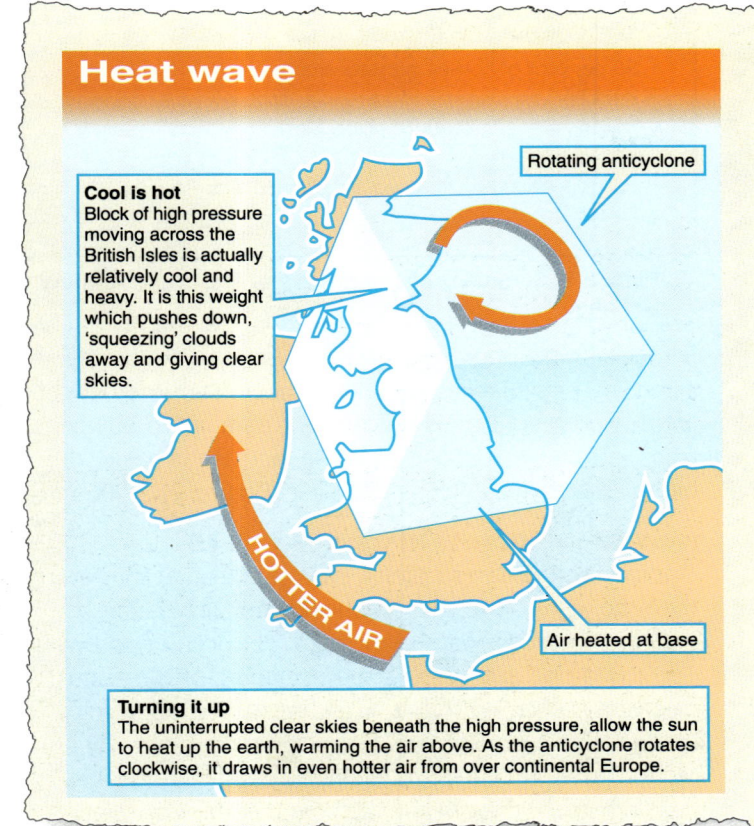

HOTTER AIR

Air heated at base

Turning it up
The uninterrupted clear skies beneath the high pressure, allow the sun to heat up the earth, warming the air above. As the anticyclone rotates clockwise, it draws in even hotter air from over continental Europe.

▲ **Figure 4** Adapted from *The Guardian*, 17 August 1995.

Another water authority stepped in last night to ban hosepipes, as weather forecasters confirmed that the summer of 1995 looks set to become the driest since records began in 1727.

North West Water introduced hosepipe bans, and standpipes have been installed in Bradford in case of emergency.

Forecasters also confirmed that June, July and August could be the third hottest summer spell since thermometer measurements first began in 1659.

The problem – the stubborn anticyclone system over the British Isles – shows no sign of going away. There has been no rain in London since 26 July nor in Sheffield since 27 July. The bookmakers William Hill were offering odds of 4/1 on the first totally dry August for London since 1924.

The weather has been bad for potato growers and some dairy farmers are reported to be using winter feed because of dry pastures. But the hot weather has helped cereal growers to an early harvest.

A

The sun and heat have come as a welcome fillip to British seaside resorts, with hotels full and seafront stalls doing a roaring trade. Spending in Kent, Surrey and Sussex reached a record £1.5 billion last month, the South East England Tourist Board reported.

By contrast, halfway through the busiest tourist period of the year, more than a million foreign holidays worth £350 million remained unsold this weekend.

B

Supermarkets announced record sales of soft drinks and ice-cream so far this month. A spokesperson for one of the big chains said 'We listen to the weather forecasts and change or move our stock around accordingly. Hot weather usually means good sales for salad produce and for any kind of drinks, so we extend our shelf space for these items. On the meat counter, people just aren't interested in joints of meat for roasts, but chops, burgers and sausages are selling as soon as we put them out. Everyone must be having barbecues!'

▲ **Figure 5** Cuttings from other newspapers in August 1995.

Activities

1 Use **Figure 3**.
 a Describe which parts of Britain were most and least affected by drought between 1995 and 1997.
 b On a sketch or outline map of England, shade the areas where the rainfall from 1995 to 1997 was 15 per cent or more below average.

2 a From **Figure 4** describe the pressure pattern in mid-summer 1995.
 b Explain why it led to (i) little rainfall and (ii) great heat.

3 In two columns, make a list of winners and losers in the hot dry summers of 1995 and 1996.

Tropical storms

These are areas of low pressure which are much deeper and more intense than the depressions which bring strong winds and rain to the British Isles. They have much more energy because they form over warm tropical oceans, at the time of the year when water temperatures are at their highest; their energy is gained from having a continuous source of heat and moisture.

Tropical storms are greatly feared by people living in coastal areas in the tropics. There are *high winds*, between 150 and 300km per hour, capable of flattening everything in their path. There are *torrential downpours* dropping up to 500mm of rain in 24 hours – the same amount that Cambridge receives in a whole year! *Storm surges* whipped up by the waves can cause a wall of water up to 10m high crashing down on coastal areas. This amount of water leads to extensive flooding of coastal and low-lying areas and sets off landslides of soil, stones and rock on slopes. Devastation can be almost total.

For these reasons, rich countries like the USA, where tropical storms are called **hurricanes**, spend millions of dollars monitoring and trying to predict a hurricane's course, issuing warnings, setting up and alerting the emergency services, and ensuring that people board up their homes and move inland to places where the threat is much lower. Improved forecasting has undoubtedly saved lives by enabling people to move from the danger areas. However, it does not prevent damage to buildings, transport and crops, and as these increase in value, the bill for the damage keeps on rising (**Figure 2**).

- 58 people killed
- US $27 billion damage
- 50 000 homeless in the southern suburbs of Miami
- 90 per cent of houses in estate around the Homestead Air Base hit
- Route 1 highway south of Miami blocked by broken power lines and debris
- Roadsides lined by smashed and flooded shops and businesses

Figure 1 Summary of the effects of Hurricane Andrew in 1992.

Hurricane Andrew in Florida in 1992

Tropical storms can suddenly change track, so that even the Americans, with their sophisticated forecasting systems, do not always get it right. Hurricane Andrew in 1992 was one example. At the beginning of the August weekend it seemed that it would head north and miss Florida, and everyone began to relax their guard. By Monday the hurricane had changed course and was heading straight for Miami. Although some last-minute preparations were possible, the loss of life was higher than usual during a hurricane in the USA.

Imagine how much greater are the effects of tropical storms in poor, low-lying and densely populated countries such as Bangladesh and the Philippines.

Activities

1. What is meant by a tropical storm?
2. For one named tropical storm:
   a describe the damage
   b explain how and why the tropical storm caused the damage.
3. Explain why some tropical storms cause more loss of life than others.
4. Do your own research. Give details of the effects of one tropical storm on a less economically developed country such as Bangladesh or the Philippines.

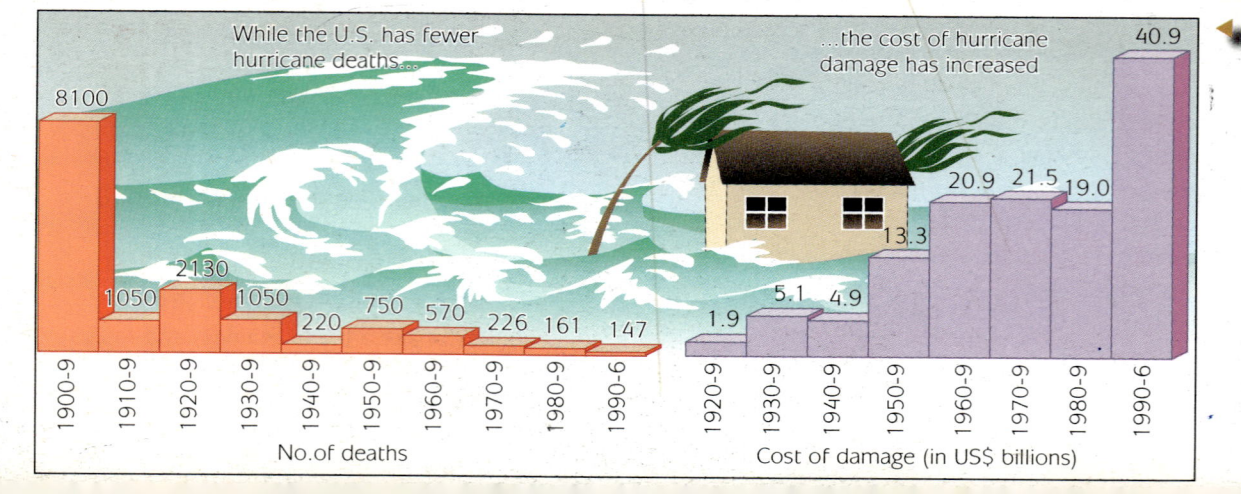

Figure 2

No. of deaths (While the U.S. has fewer hurricane deaths...):
- 1900-9: 8100
- 1910-9: 1050
- 1920-9: 2130
- 1930-9: 1050
- 1940-9: 220
- 1950-9: 750
- 1960-9: 570
- 1970-9: 226
- 1980-9: 161
- 1990-6: 147

Cost of damage in US$ billions (...the cost of hurricane damage has increased):
- 1920-9: 1.9
- 1930-9: 5.1
- 1940-9: 4.9
- 1950-9: 13.3
- 1960-9: 20.9
- 1970-9: 21.5
- 1980-9: 19.0
- 1990-6: 40.9

Chapter 7
Ecosystems

A young boy in Nigeria takes the measure of an old and once mighty ironwood tree, which has just been felled by clearance of the tropical rain forest.

Key Ideas

Globally different ecosystems can be recognized:
- the main factor controlling the world distribution of ecosystems is climate
- two ecosystems which extend over great areas are coniferous woodlands and tropical rain forests
- the nature of the soils associated with these ecosystems is influenced by both climate and vegetation.

Human activity has an impact on natural ecosystems:
- tropical rain forests are under pressure as human uses increase
- there is need for management of the world's natural forests.

Global distribution of ecosystems

An **ecosystem** is a living community of plants and animals which also includes elements of the natural environment, such as climate and soil. Each element in the system, whether living or natural, depends upon, and influences, others. This is why the diagram summarizing the ecosystem (**Figure 1**) shows some two-way relationships.

On a world scale, *climate* is the main factor which determines the nature and extent of the natural vegetation cover. **Figure 2** shows the distribution of five of the world's main ecosystems. Look back at **Figure 1** on pages 76–77 which showed five of the world's main climatic regions. Is the distribution of the ecosystems similar to that of the climatic regions?

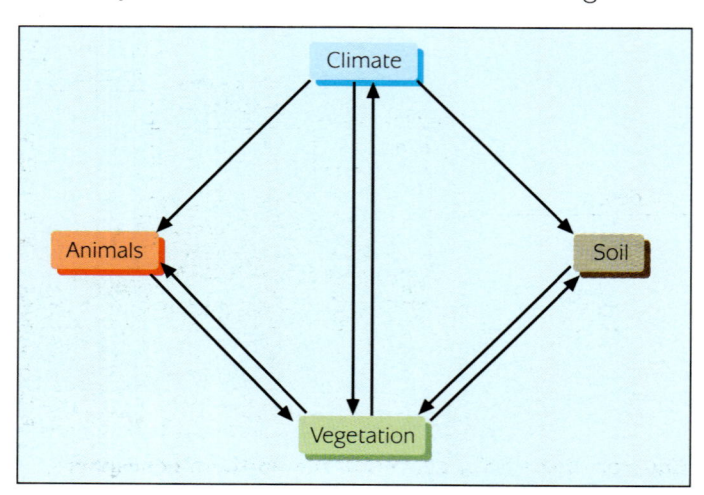

Figure 1 Ecosystem – systems diagram.

Figure 2 Distribution of five ecosystems.

Tropical rain forest
Climatic summary. Hot all year – average temperature 27–30°C. Wet all year – annual precipitation 2000–3000mm

Hot desert
Climatic summary. Very hot most of the year – above 30°C. Low annual rainfall – below 250mm

Mediterranean vegetation
Climatic summary. Hot summers – about 25°C. Mild/warm winters – about 10°C. Dry in summer, wet in winter. Annual rainfall total – about 750mm

Deciduous woodland
Climatic summary. Warm summers – about 18°C. Mild/cool winters – about 5°C. Precipitation all year – about 1000mm

Coniferous woodland
Climatic summary. Warm summers – 16–20°C. Very cold winters – well below freezing point. Precipitation mainly in summer – low annual total – less than 500mm

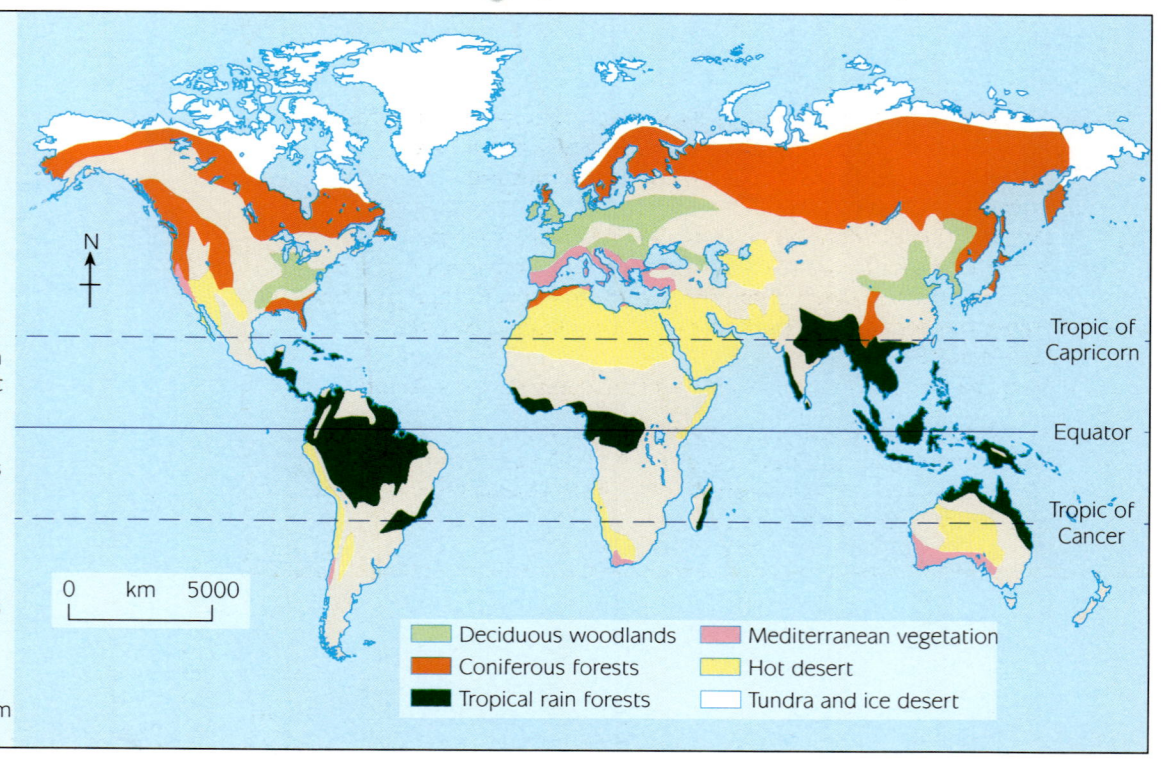

Within the tropics, areas covered by tropical rain forest closely coincide with areas experiencing the hot and wet Equatorial climate. These areas are close to the Equator and down the wet eastern sides of the continents. Also largely within the tropics are the areas with a hot desert climate. In these areas there is plenty of sunlight and heat for plant growth, but water is in short supply. The effects of lack of water on vegetation are shown in **Figure 3**. In hot deserts there are large areas of bare ground between the plants; plant roots below the surface are often 20 times or more longer than the height of the plant above the surface, which reflects the desperate need to search for underground supplies of water.

In temperate latitudes, temperature becomes a more important factor for controlling the nature of the vegetation cover. With increasing distance from the Equator, lack of warmth and shortness of the growing season restrict plant size and variety (**Figure 3**).

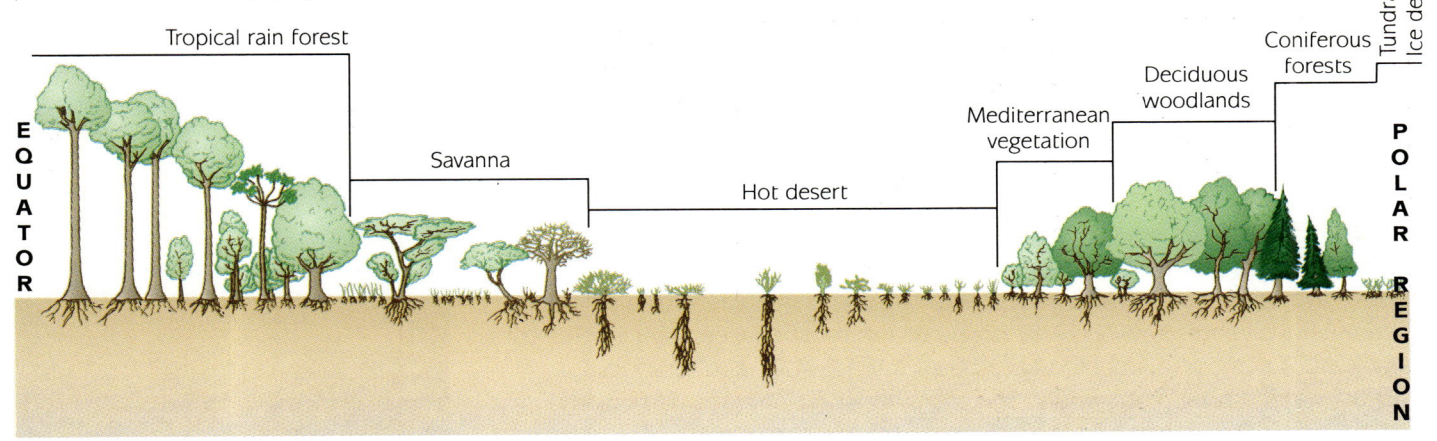

▲ **Figure 3** The changing pattern of vegetation cover from the Equator to the Polar regions in the northern hemisphere.

Activities

1 Use an atlas and **Figure 2**.
   a Name one country covered by large areas of tropical rain forest in each of these continents: South America, Africa and Asia.
   b Name the continent with the largest continuous area covered by tropical rain forest.
   c Describe the distribution of tropical rain forest in Africa.
   d Name one country covered by large areas of coniferous forest in each of the following continents: North America, Europe and Asia.
   e Name the continent with the largest continuous area covered by coniferous forest.
   f Describe the distribution of coniferous forests in North America.

2 a From **Figure 3**, describe the ways in which vegetation changes within the tropics as the distance from the Equator increases.
   b Name the main factor responsible for these changes. Explain why this factor is important.

Coniferous woodlands

Characteristic features

The *woodlands* are evergreen. The coniferous trees of which they are composed, such as fir, pine and spruce, are remarkably uniform in shape, height and size. There may be only two or three species of tree in a square kilometre of woodland, which increases the uniform appearance of the woodlands over wide areas of land. There tends to be only one layer of vegetation – the tree layer. In the forest gloom, caused by the trees growing so closely together, little else grows. The forest floor is covered by a thick mat of dead needles (**Figure 1**). The dark woods do not attract bird life. Little food is provided and only a few animals, such as deer, can feed by browsing the trees.

The *trees* reproduce from cones, which protect their seeds. The trees have a conical shape with branches sloping downwards along the whole length of the trunk. They are softwoods. Their leaves are small needles which give the trees their evergreen appearance. They have thick bark which contains resin. Tree roots are shallow, spreading out only small distances near the surface.

Adaptations to climate

Each of the vegetation characteristics mentioned above has a purpose. The trees have adaptations which allow them to survive in areas with a cold continental climate. In winter this is one of the most challenging climates for any kind of plant or animal life because of intense cold, snow-covered surfaces and strong, cold winds. Summers are short and not particularly warm, and water is often only readily available in early summer. The climate of Irkutsk is an example (page 76). Some of the adaptations of trees to climate are explained in **Figure 2**.

▲ **Figure 1** Coniferous woodlands.

Soils

A very distinctive soil – the **podsol** – forms under coniferous woodlands (**Figure 3**).

Look carefully at the colours of the different layers of soil on **Figure 3**. Working downwards from the surface you should be able to recognize the following layers.

1. A narrow layer near the surface which is dark, almost black. This is the humus layer next to the surface; the humus gives it the dark colour.

2. A wider layer, of a much lighter colour, almost grey. This is called the **A horizon**; minerals and organic material, which give soils a dark colour, have been washed out from this layer, which is why it is so light in colour.

Tree characteristic	Adaptation to the climate
Conical shape	They are flexible and bend in the strong winds.
Downward sloping branches	Snow slides off them more quickly.
Evergreen	Leaves are always present so that trees can begin to grow as soon as it is warm enough in spring/early summer; necessary because of the shortness of the growing season.
Needle leaves	They reduce water loss by transpiration; necessary when water is not available (e.g. when ground is frozen in winter and when little rain falls in summer).
Thick bark	This protects trunk from extreme winter cold.

▲ **Figure 2** Adaptations of trees to climate.

Chapter 7 Ecosystems

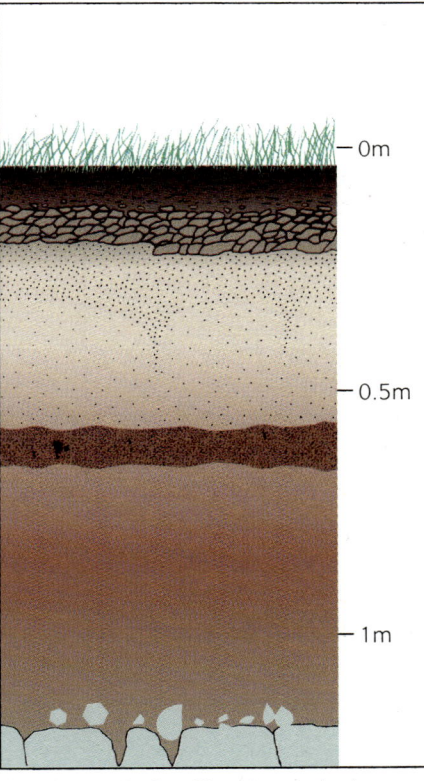

▲ **Figure 3** Profile of a podsol soil.

▲ **Figure 4** Profile of a podsol.

3 A reddish-brown layer that looks quite different from the layer above it. This is the top of the **B horizon**; the dark-coloured organic material and the dark red oxides of iron washed out from the A horizon are re-deposited here. They are compressed together which forms a **hard pan** just over half a metre below the surface.

4 A wider layer that is orange-brown or orange-yellow in colour. This is the lower B horizon which gets its colour from deposited clays.

5 Small pieces of rock in the soil show the beginning of the **C horizon**; below this is the parent rock.

This is what you would expect to find if you were to dig a pit below a coniferous woodland. Figure 4 shows a **soil profile** – the soil features between the ground surface and the solid rock below (the parent rock).

Soil is the name for the loose material above the solid rock. Although rock weathering provides the soil materials, climate and vegetation are important factors affecting the formation of podsol soils to create the distinctive layers. The most significant feature of the *climate* is that precipitation is greater than evapo-transpiration. This means that water drains downwards through the soil carrying organic material and minerals such as iron and clay with it; these are washed out of the A horizon, a process called **leaching**. They are re-deposited lower down the soil profile in the B horizon. At the top of the B horizon minerals such as iron are compressed to form a **hard pan**. The most significant feature of the *vegetation* is that the pine needles decay slowly and what little humus they produce is acidic. There is little in the soil to hold on to the minerals and to stop them being washed out by leaching. Also, the soil is too acidic for much earthworm activity, which is why there is little mixing up of the different layers.

ℹ Soil

Soil has four constituents:
1 Mineral matter – mainly from weathering of the parent rock
2 Organic matter – humus is formed from the decomposition of plant remains by organisms in the soil
3 Air
4 Water.

Activities

1 From the graph for Irkutsk on page 77, describe the main features of the cold continental climate.

2 a Draw a coniferous tree and add labels to describe its characteristic features.
   b Choose **three** of the features labelled in (a) and explain how each is an adaptation to the climate.

3 Make a copy of the podsol profile in **Figure 4**.
   a Colour it in or clearly label the different colours.
   b Label the positions of the humus layer and the A, B and C horizons.
   c Mark L for leaching and W for rock weathering in places where they occur.

4 a Define *leaching*.
   b Explain why it occurs.
   c Explain how leaching has influenced the characteristics of a podsol soil.

Tropical rain forests

A Discontinuous canopy of tree crowns of the tallest trees (called emergents)

B Continuous layer of the main canopy formed by the crowns of the many tall trees

C Discontinuous under-canopy of trees between 10m and 20m high

D Layer of shrubs and young trees

E Herb layer with ferns 6m or more high

▲ **Figure 1** The five layers in a tropical rain forest.

Characteristic features

Tropical rain forest is distinguished from the vegetation of all other ecosystems by its **biodiversity**. This is the term used to describe the immense number and great variety of living organisms found there. A 100-hectare block of coniferous woodland may contain only two or three different types of tree; in the same area in a tropical rain forest there may be over 500 species of tree, and double this number of species of flowering plants.

Despite the sheer quantity of vegetation present and the way in which climbing plants and creepers run from tree to tree in a chaotic manner, it is possible to recognize five distinctive forest layers (**Figure 1**). The canopy provides a habitat for monkeys and numerous birds such as macaws; on the ground floor are some larger animals such as tapirs and anteaters. There are countless insects everywhere. However, it is the plant life that is really abundant.

These are evergreen forests. The tall trees are deciduous, but they shed their leaves at different times and for only six to eight weeks each year, so that the forests always look green. The tallest trees, by reaching up to 50m high, stand head and shoulders above the forest canopy; these are hardwoods and include types such as mahogany and ironwood. They have long trunks without any branches until their rounded crowns extend out over the canopy. Their leaves are oval in shape with extended points known as drip tips, and they have dark green and leathery upper surfaces. The smooth bark is thin. Their shallow roots, which mainly extend sideways below the ground surface, extend above the ground as buttress roots.

▲ **Figure 2** Some characteristic features of the tropical rain forest ecosystem.

Adaptations to climate

The tropical rain forest's biodiversity is a response to *climate*. There are constant high temperatures, with a mean monthly average above 27°C, accompanied by high solar light intensity. Rainfall is regular and high, with above 2000mm falling during the year, which creates humid conditions. There is no more favourable climate on Earth than this for plant growth.

Plant communities are fiercely competitive. There is survival of the tallest as the tall trees are drawn upwards by the heat and light, which is why leaf growth is concentrated in the canopy. The leathery upper surfaces of the trees' leaves are necessary to withstand the great power of the sun's rays. The drip tips help the leaves to shed water during the heavy rains.

In the lower layers of the forest, sunlight is in short supply. Ferns are adapted to life on the forest floor by having leaves which intercept a high proportion of the light that reaches there. The shrub layer is sparse because of lack of light, although shrubs quickly take advantage of any gap in the forest canopy.

Soils

Figure 3 shows a **latosol**, which is the name given to soils which form under tropical rain forest. They are red or yellowish-red in colour throughout and they do not have the distinct horizons of the podsol (page 93). The red colour comes from the oxides of iron and aluminium which remain in the soil. They are deep soils, often 20–30m deep, whereas podsols are 1–2m deep.

Looking at the density and diversity of the vegetation cover you might think that it is growing from the world's most fertile soil. Nothing could be further from the truth. Precipitation is much greater than evapo-transpiration; even with the protection given by the forest canopy, there is the downward movement of rain water through the soil. Leaching washes organic material and silica downwards and then out of the soil. The most important activity is concentrated at the top of the soil profile. This is where the rapid recycling of forest nutrients upon which the life of the forest depends takes place (**Figure 4**). Leaf fall and falling branches provide a continuous supply of litter to the forest floor. The high temperatures and rainfall encourage intensive biotic activity which leads to rapid decomposition of the organic material.

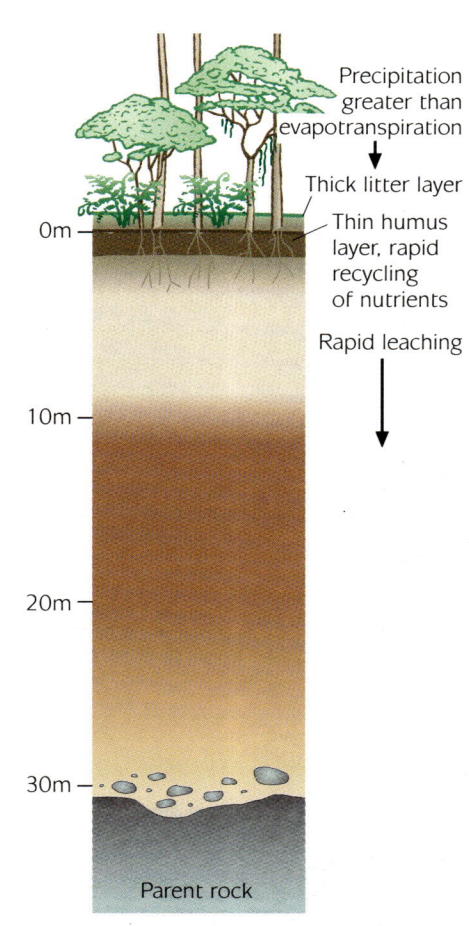

▲ **Figure 3** Profile of a latosol.

▲ **Figure 4** Systems diagram for nutrient recycling in a tropical rain forest ecosystem.

Human use of tropical rain forests

While the natural deciduous forests of Europe and North America have been cleared almost to extinction, large areas of tropical rain forests remain. This suggests that people have not found it easy to make a living in the rain forest environment. Despite all the losses from clearances, rain forests comprise 50 per cent of the world's growing wood. Even in that part of Brazil's Amazon Basin close to Manaus, the largest town in the Amazon Basin with over 2 million people, there are still large areas of untouched forest (**Figure 1**).

Some human uses of the forest are long established. Groups of Indians in the Amazon Basin either collected and hunted to use the food provided in the forest, or practised slash and burn and grew crops such as manioc, or did both. With slash and burn, the clearing was small and the Indian group cultivated only for as long as the soil retained its fertility, probably two or three years. They then moved to another part of the forest. These indigenous (native) peoples with their low levels of technology hardly left a mark on the forest, which re-invaded within a few years as if there had been no human activity. This is an example of **sustainable** use of the forests. Rubber tapping can also be described as a sustainable activity, provided that the tappers allow sufficient time for trees to recover between each collection.

Recent human activity, however, has in nearly all cases been destructive, as governments, companies and wealthy individuals have realized that rain forest regions such as the Amazon Basin are rich in resources. The first forest clearances are usually for building roads; soon the forest along the roadsides is cleared for farming and settlement, as is happening north of Manaus (**Figure 1**). In Brazil the construction and surfacing of the Marshal Rondon Highway from Brasília, the capital, to Porto Velho, on the edge of the untouched western fringes of Brazil's Amazon Basin, opened up the forest to farmers, loggers and miners (**Figure 4**).

▲ **Figure 1** Satellite photograph of part of the Amazon Basin near Manaus. Below Manaus the Negro River joins up with the main channel of the Amazon.

▲ **Figure 2** Forest clearance for cattle ranching in Brazil.

ℹ Development of the Amazon Basin

Some reasons why the Brazilian government encouraged development in the Amazon region in the 1960s.

1 **Economic:**
   - export minerals, gain foreign exchange and pay off international debts
   - use the minerals and other raw materials in its growing industries
   - become a more economically developed country.

2 **Social:**
   - relieve population pressure along the coast
   - give landless peasants the opportunity to own land.

3 **Political:**
   - gain international prestige from its big new schemes
   - take people's minds off problems such as poverty and landlessness.

The farming is no longer slash and burn. Cattle ranching is dominant in many parts of the Amazon Basin. The ranchers want all the forest cleared so that it can be replaced by pastures. Many are not even interested in saving and selling the timber, and most of it is just burned (**Figure 3**).

The logging companies are only interested in certain types of tree, but in the rain forests individual species of tree are widely dispersed. To reach the limited numbers of trees considered to be commercially useful, all the other trees are felled and cleared.

Brazil's Amazon Basin is rich in minerals. The largest concentration of mineral resources is at Carajas, which includes the world's largest iron ore reserves and major deposits of bauxite, gold, nickel, copper and manganese. These are mined by big companies. Discovery of gold creates gold rush fever and thousands of individuals flock in, almost overnight, wherever gold is found (**Figure 3**).

Figure 3 Gold rush at Serra Pelada; at its peak 40 000 *garimpeiros* (miners) were working here.

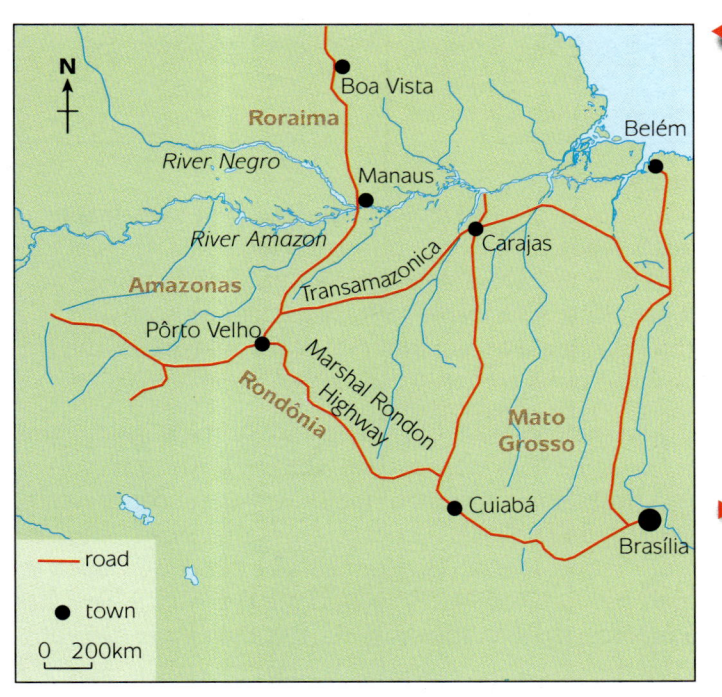

Figure 4 The Amazon Basin in Brazil.

Figure 5 Nutrient recycling before and after clearance of tropical rain forest.

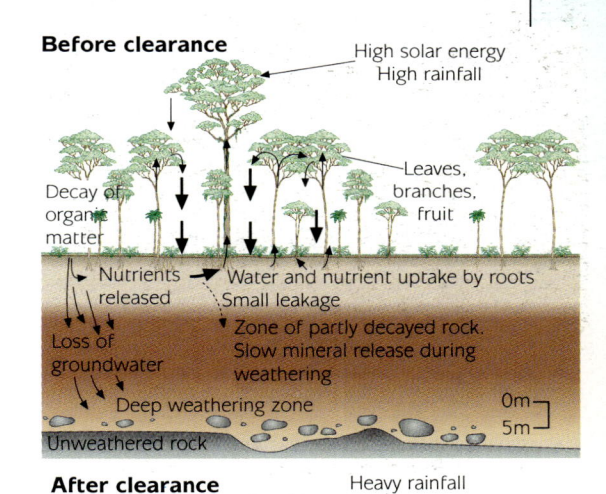

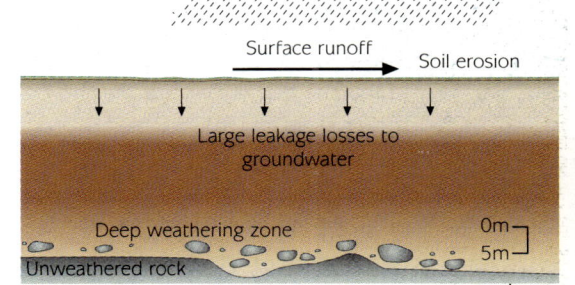

The effects of forest clearance upon the local environment

The natural forest is a closed system from which little leakage of nutrients occurs. However, once the forest is cleared the rich nutrient cycle is broken and the nutrients are soon washed out with nothing to replace them (**Figure 5**).

Effects on soils
After a large area is cleared, the surface is exposed to the full force of the often daily, and always heavy, tropical downpours. These erode the topsoil and wash it away into rivers. There is less organic matter in the soil to hold back the water as it seeps downwards, so leaching increases. Most of the soil's minerals are quickly removed.

Effects on hydrology
Without trees and the dense cover of the forest canopy, there is nothing to intercept the rain. More water now reaches the ground surface, which increases runoff. Because of greater overland flow, rivers flood more frequently. More soil and sediment are carried, some of which accumulates in river channels, which in turn increases the frequency and seriousness of the flooding. In parts of the Amazon Basin gold miners are creating a potential hydrological catastrophe; an estimated 1000 tonnes of mercury, used to amalgamate gold, has entered the Amazon river system with unknown consequences for human and animal health. Little treatment of waste takes place from any of Amazonia's many mining operations before it is fed into the rivers.

The need for management of forests

Clearance of natural forests and woodlands continues. The fires from clearances in Indonesia, both legal and illegal, in 1997 caused massive air pollution and affected people over a wide area (**Figure 1**).

Forest clearances are not restricted to the tropics. Many formerly untouched natural forests in Russia have been opened up to foreign logging companies because of the government's desperate need for hard currency. The trees are cut down without any management or re-planting. One estimate is that Siberia may be losing up to 4 million hectares of forest a year, twice as much as Amazonia. The need for management of existing forests is now more urgent.

Some advantages of keeping the forests
Reasons for keeping the world's forests.
- Trees use the sun's energy and provide food; they offer habitats for most land-based plants and animals.
- They provide a wealth of foods and medicines essential to human health.
- They intercept rain water, delaying run-off and reducing the risks of flooding and soil erosion.
- They absorb carbon dioxide, one of the greenhouse gases responsible for global warming.
- They regulate local temperature and rainfall.

Can the forests be saved?
Much depends upon the ability of governments to implement **sustainable management of forests**. They can still use forest products, but so as not to destroy the forests and their resources. Management involves planning, training workers and practising sustainable forestry techniques such as selective logging and re-planting. Policing the forests and monitoring the work to make sure that the plans are being carried out are essential.

So far the records of governments have not been good. At the Earth Summit in Rio in 1992 no formal agreement was reached. Governments in the MEDCs, which have no tropical rain forests of their own, are under pressure from environmental groups and political parties, such as the Green Party, to stop the destruction of the rain forests. Governments of the LEDCs, such as Brazil, resent being dictated to by countries such as the USA which have little natural forest left to protect. (Natural forests cover less than 2 per cent of the land area of the USA.)

Government attitude is important. The democratically elected governments in Brazil in the 1990s have been much more conservation-minded than the previous military governments. In 1997 the Brazilian government suspended the issue of licences to harvest mahogany.

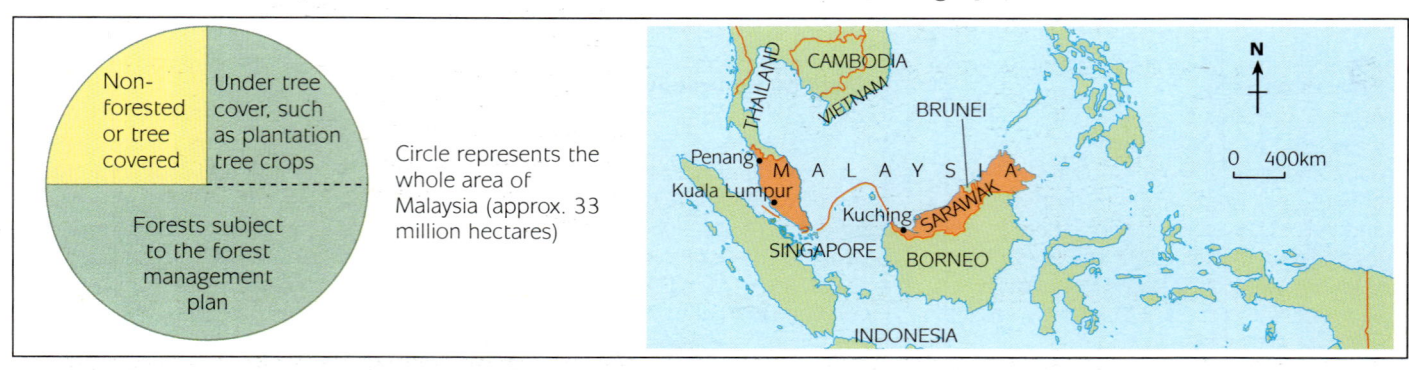

Figure 1 Effects of Indonesian forest fires in 1997.

Figure 2 Information about forested areas in Malaysia.

Sustainable forestry

A Divide the forests into two groups:
- Protection and Conservation Forests: these include National Parks, Wildlife and Bird Sanctuaries.
- Production Forests: in these forests logging takes place but it is carefully planned and controlled.

B Make a *survey* of the area to be logged and its resources.

C Use *selective logging*. Only between seven and twelve mature and fully grown trees per hectare are cut down in each logging cycle. This allows the logged area to regain full maturity after 30 to 50 years. The forest recovers because the younger trees and saplings are given more space and sunlight to grow.

D *Monitor* what happens. At all stages it is necessary to check that the work being done conforms to the plan. Illegal activities and clearances are easier to detect now that aerial photography and remote sensing are available. They still occur, which is why the number of staff enforcing the rules has increased, as have the size of the fines and length of prison sentences.

Forest management is supported by heavy investment in research and development. One of the aims is to find alternatives which are faster growing and higher yielding than the natural species but which are still renewable. One example is rubberwood, now used by the local furniture industry, which accounted for 80 per cent of total furniture exports in 1994. Another is to improve methods of logging. Heli-logging (using helicopters to haul out the logs) is used in parts of Sarawak because less damage is done to the surrounding forest.

Development and conservation can go hand in hand. Malaysia is one of the economically better developed countries of Asia, having had high rates of economic growth in the 1980s and early 1990s.

About 75 per cent of Malaysia's land area is under forest and tree cover (**Figure 2**). Some of this area is covered by plantation tree crops such as rubber, oil palm and cocoa, along with other land uses. This leaves about half the land area under forest, for which Malaysia developed its Forest Management Plan.

Activities

1 Natural rain forests (pages 94–95):
  a By means of a labelled diagram, describe the vegetation features of the rain forest.
  b (i) State the main features of the Equatorial climate.
    (ii) Explain why it leads to the densest vegetation cover on the Earth's surface.
    (iii) Why does the Equatorial climate lead to the formation of latosol soils?
  c (i) What is meant by 'nutrient recycling'?
    (ii) Why is it vital to the growth and survival of tropical rain forests?

2 Removal of rain forests (pages 96–97):
  a (i) From **Figure 1** on page 96, describe the distribution of areas of forest clearance.
    (ii) Suggest reasons why more of the forest has been cleared in some areas than in others.
  b (i) Explain why a large area of rain forest has been cleared in Brazil.
    (ii) On a sketch map, show some of the areas which have been cleared and label the land uses.
  c Explain why many of the rivers flowing through the Amazon Basin
    (i) now carry more sediment than they previously did
    (ii) are being polluted.

3 Preservation of the rain forests (pages 98–99):
  a Say what is meant by sustainable use of rain forests.
  b Describe how Malaysia is trying to make sure that its remaining forests are used in a sustainable way for logging.
  c Give examples of types of farming which can be described as sustainable. Explain your answer.

Case Study – Forest management in Malaysia

Human use of coniferous forests

Usefulness to people

Softwood coniferous trees are the world's main source of commercial timber. Their use has many advantages.

1 Except in very cold areas, they grow quickly; replanted trees can be cut again after 40 to 50 years.
2 Many trees of the same type grow together.
3 Frozen ground in winter makes access easier for heavy machinery and means of transport.
4 The softwood has many different uses – from lengths of timber used for construction to pulp used for making paper.

On the other hand the soils are almost worthless for farming once the woodland has been cleared. The goodness – organic material and minerals – has been leached out beyond the reach of crop roots. The soils are too acidic for most crops. The iron pan forms an impermeable layer which may cause surface waterlogging.

Therefore coniferous woodlands have been planted in many of the upland areas of the UK, where farming is far from easy. The trees are a profitable way of using land which may be too high, steep and infertile for farming; the forests can also be used by visitors for recreation. Kielder Forest near the Scottish border in northern Northumberland is one example.

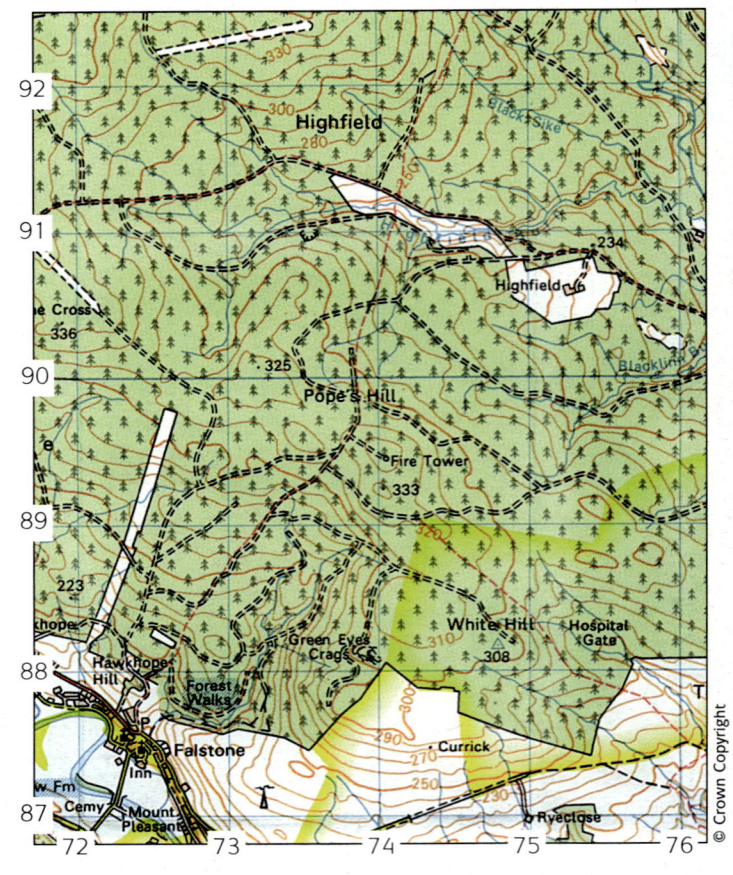

▲ **Figure 1** OS map of a small part of Kielder Forest at a scale of 1:50 000; 2cm = 1km.

ℹ️ Kielder Forest

- The forest covers 100 000 hectares.
- Over 1 million coniferous trees have been planted.
- Sitka spruce covers the largest area – planted because it is fast growing.
- Timber is used for construction purposes and paper-making.
- There are 300 000 visitors to the forest each year.
- Forest tracks, picnic sites, log cabins and camping/caravan sites are provided.
- Visitor activities include walking, horse riding, cycling and orienteering.

Test questions

1 Find the highest point on **Figure 1**.
   a State its height above sea level.
   b Give its six-figure grid reference. (3 marks)

2 Approximately how large an area of forest (in km^2) is shown? (2 marks)

3 State the map evidence which suggests that tourists visit this area. (2 marks)

4 Kielder is a managed coniferous forest.
   a Suggest *two* reasons for the large number of tracks through the forest. (2 marks)
   b Describe *two* ways in which forest managers have tried to deal with the fire risk. (4 marks)

5 Using map evidence and other information about coniferous woodlands and their soils, explain why most of the area covered by the map is used for forestry instead of farming. (7 marks)

Chapter 8
Population

Places where there are many people ... places where there are very few people ... why are some parts of the world crowded with people while others remain empty?

Key Ideas

The global distribution of population is uneven:
- physical factors and human factors are used to explain why some areas are crowded and others have few people.

Population change depends upon birth rate, death rate and migration:
- high birth rates and low death rates have led to rapid world population growth
- there are contrasting population problems between LEDCs and MEDCs
- there are many different types of migration.

Population change presents opportunities and problems:
- some countries need to reduce population growth, others need to encourage an increase
- different strategies are used to feed and house the growing numbers of people in LEDCs and MEDCs.

The world distribution of population

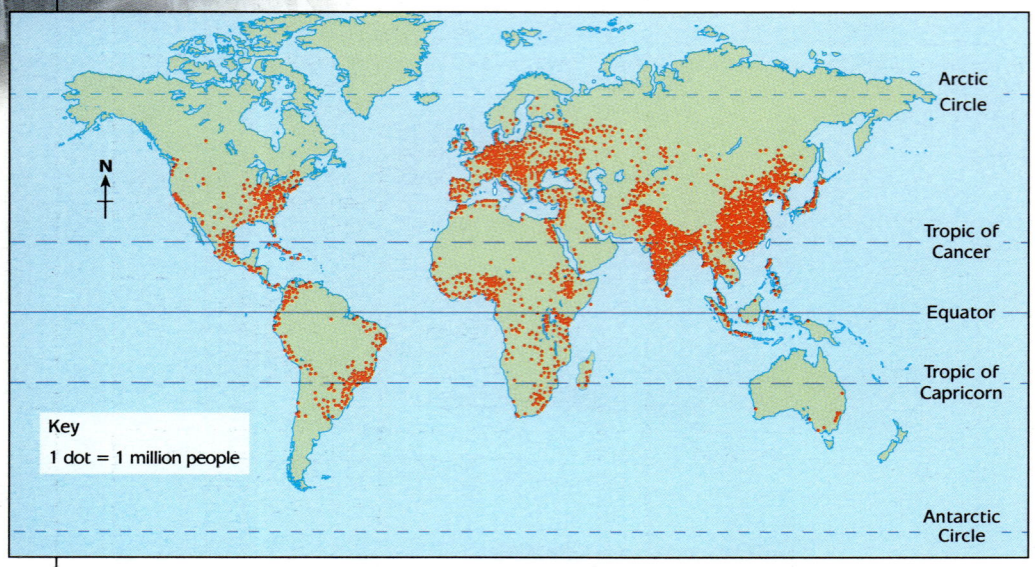

Figure 1 Dot map showing world population distribution.

Key: 1 dot = 1 million people

Population means people; there are over five billion people living in the world today. They are unevenly spread across the Earth's surface. Some parts of the world are very **densely** populated while others are almost totally deserted. The *distribution* of the population is the way people are spread out across the surface of the Earth. This is shown in **Figure 1** as a **dot map**.

The *density* of population is the number of people who live in an area, measured in people per square kilometre. **Figure 2** is a **choropleth** (shading) map showing the world's population density.

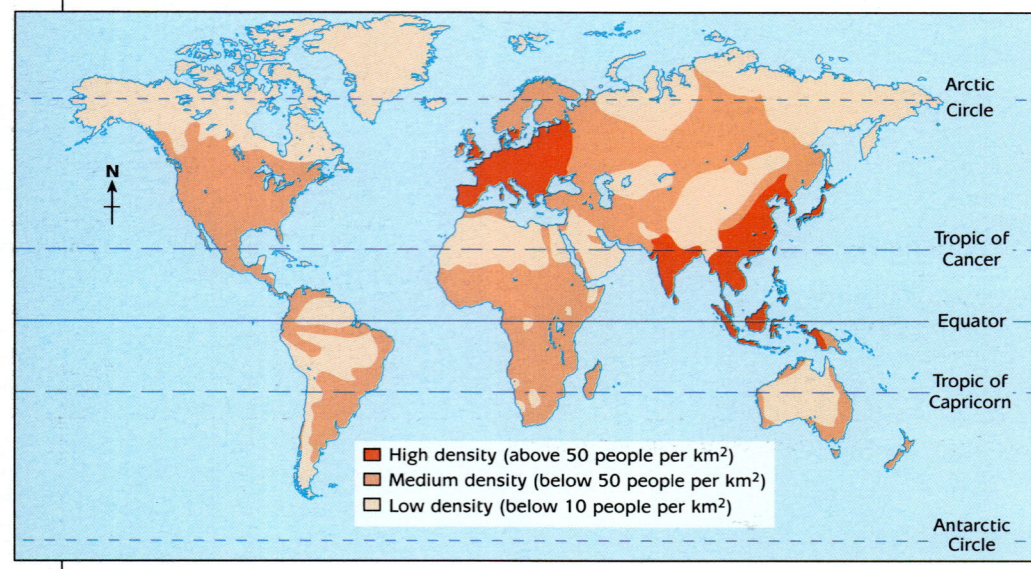

The world's population distribution can be divided into three main categories:

1. Areas with high densities of people (over 50 per km²): South and east Asia, Europe and the north-east of North America
2. Areas of medium population density (less than 50 per km²): California, the coast of Brazil, the Nile valley in Egypt and south-east Australia
3. Areas with low population densities (less than 10 per km²): Sahara desert in North Africa, northern Russia and Canada.

Europe and Asia have over 85 per cent of the world's population. This is partly because these areas have been settled for a very long time. In some textbooks they are referred to as the 'Old World'. However, they are only a small part of the Earth's land surface. Large parts of the world have very few people – the 'almost empty' areas cover 64 per cent of the land area.

The distribution of population also varies with latitude. In the southern hemisphere there are very few people because the land area is so small. In the northern hemisphere very few people live north of 60°N. The majority of the world's population (over 80 per cent) live between 20°N and 60°N, although this area also contains some of the highest mountain ranges and the world's largest deserts.

Figure 2 Choropleth map showing world density of population.

- High density (above 50 people per km²)
- Medium density (below 50 people per km²)
- Low density (below 10 people per km²)

PHYSICAL FACTORS	Reasons for areas of high density	Reasons for areas of low density
Relief	Lowland which is flat or gently sloping such as river flood plains, e.g. Ganges valley in India	Mountainous areas with high altitude and steep slopes, e.g. Alps, Andes
Climate	Moderate climates with no extremes. Enough rain and warm temperatures to allow crop growth, e.g. UK, Japan	Extreme climates: very cold, very hot and too dry, e.g. tundra, Sahara
Soil	Thick fertile soils such as loam and alluvium, e.g. south-east England	Thin, rocky and acid soils, e.g. hot deserts, mountains
Vegetation	Areas of open woodland and grassland, e.g. Pampas in Argentina	Very dense jungle which is difficult to penetrate, and swamps, e.g. Amazon Basin
Accessibility	Coastal areas with easy access, e.g. coasts in South America, UK	Interior areas with poor access, e.g. central South America
Resources	Plenty of water, timber, minerals such as coal, oil, copper; opportunity for fishing, e.g. coalfields in Western Europe	Few economic resources, e.g. southern Chile, Sahel

HUMAN FACTORS	Reasons for areas of high population density	Reasons for areas of low population density
Economic	Large, rich markets for trade Good infrastructure (roads, railways, services) and access to imports and exports, e.g. Japan, Europe, USA Skilled and varied labour force, e.g. in the large towns and cities, especially in the MEDCs	Poor trading links and markets Poor infrastructure (roads, railways, services) and limited access, e.g. The Sahara, Amazon Basin, interior Australia Limited job opportunities, including agriculture, e.g. Amazon Basin, Sahara, tundra, Alaska
Social	Some groups of people prefer to live together for security and companionship, e.g. Japanese, Americans	Some groups of people prefer to be more isolated, e.g. Scandinavians
Political	Stable government, e.g. Singapore, Taiwan	Unstable governments and civil war, e.g. Afghanistan

Figure 3 Reasons for different densities of population.

Explaining the population distribution

The world's population distribution is affected by both physical factors and human factors (**Figure 3**). Physical factors such as relief, soils and climate can encourage high densities of population. **Densely** populated areas are likely where there are areas of low, flat land with fertile soils and a temperate climate. However, where the climate is very hot or very cold, where there are high mountains or deserts, the environment is hostile to people and these areas are often only **sparsely** populated (**Figure 4**).

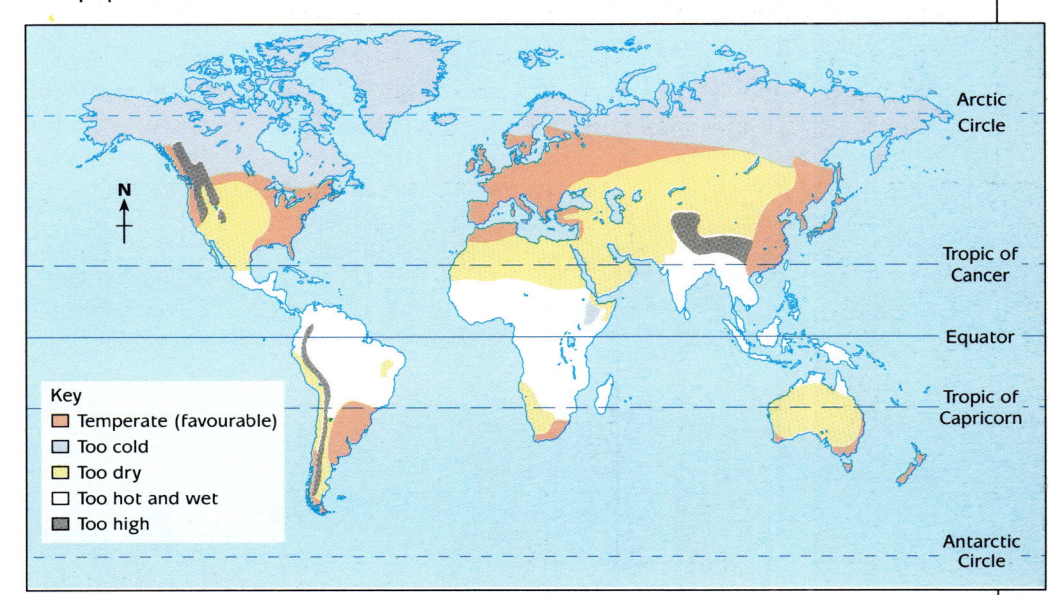

Figure 4 Limitations on population density.

Key
- Temperate (favourable)
- Too cold
- Too dry
- Too hot and wet
- Too high

Case Study – Population distribution in the UK

A country of varying densities

The UK is part of Western Europe, one of the areas of the world with a very high population density. However, as **Figure 1** shows, the population density is not high everywhere in the UK. The population distribution in the UK is very uneven. There are great differences from one area to another, from densities of under 10 per km² in the remote upland areas to densities of over 1000 per km² in the cities.

The sparsely populated areas in the UK are mainly upland areas (**Figure 2**) such as the Pennines, Dartmoor and the Scottish Highlands. The upland areas have a harsher climate than the lowlands. The terrain is rugged and the steep slopes make the building of communications and settlements difficult. The steep slopes, thin soils and short growing season prevent crop growth. The areas are often remote, with poor access and few services. In the uplands there are limited employment opportunities. The main occupations are extensive sheep farming, forestry, quarrying, the water industry (reservoirs and HEP) and tourism. Larger concentrations of people are only found where a resource has been developed, such as at Aviemore for winter sports or around the slate quarries in Snowdonia.

The high-density areas in the UK are the conurbations, the large cities and the industrial areas, e.g. Tyneside, Merseyside and Greater London (**Figure 2**). About 80 per cent of the UK population lives in towns and cities and over 50 per cent in the seven largest city areas, the conurbations. Most of the conurbations in the UK, except Greater London, are former coalmining areas which were developed during the Industrial Revolution. London has very high densities of population because of its importance as the capital city, and as an important port. The areas of high density are located in the lowlands where the relief is gentle and the climate more pleasant. There are dense networks of communications including roads, railways, airports and ports.

Large areas in the UK have medium densities of population (20–200 people per km²). These are mainly fertile farming areas with market towns and villages, such as East Anglia or places with small industrial towns and villages, such as County Durham with its landscape of former mining villages and small towns.

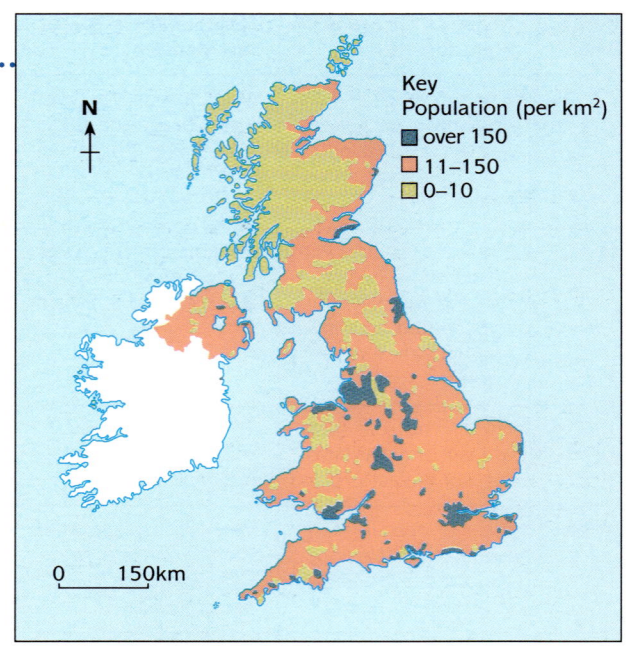

Figure 1 Britain's population density in 1994.

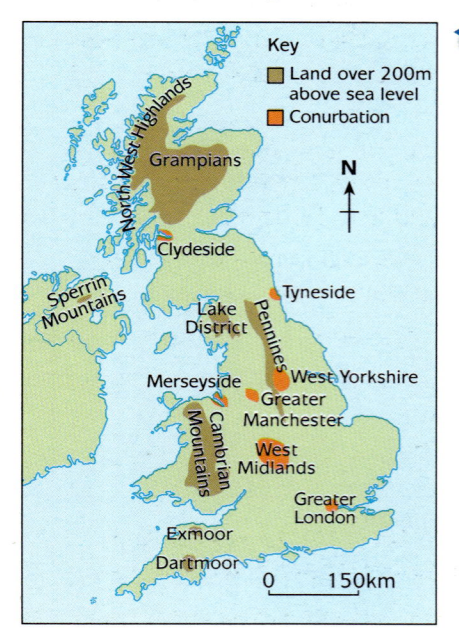

Figure 2 Upland areas and conurbations in Britain.

ℹ Conurbations

A conurbation is a huge urban area created by the growth of one or more cities which merge with each other and engulf smaller towns and villages.

Population distribution in Brazil

In the interior of Brazil, population densities are low because of extremes of physical factors such as infertile soils and a humid climate. The coast of Brazil has a moderate climate and the soils are suitable for intensive agriculture. At the coast human factors, such as better accessibility and the long history of settlement, help explain the high densities.

Figure 5 Very high densities of population are found in the coastal cities, such as Rio de Janeiro.

The Amazon Forest

The main factors causing the low population densities are **physical factors** and the remote interior location.

- Equatorial climate is hot (28°C) and wet (over 2000mm) all year with high humidity.
- Density of the jungle vegetation makes it difficult to penetrate and to clear, and communications are poor.
- Soils are infertile and easily leached and eroded once the trees are removed.
- Diseases spread quickly, e.g. yellow fever.
- Traditional type of farming is shifting agriculture, which can only support low population densities.

Manaus, a port and city, is a pocket of high density of population on the banks of the Amazon River. It has some impressive buildings, like the Opera House, built in the nineteenth century with profits from the rubber trade. In recent years, the opening up of the Amazon Basin has seen an increase in population density with people working in the mines, plantations and cattle ranches. Some reservations have been set up for the native Indians. Despite all this, population densities remain at less than 1 person per km² even today.

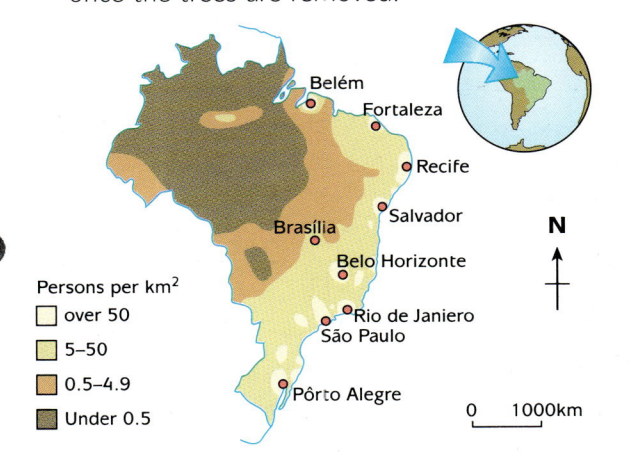

Figure 3 Brazil.

Figure 4 Few people live in the Amazon Basin.

The south-east coast

High population densities are due to:

- fertile agricultural land used for vegetables, fruit and cattle as well as large coffee plantations
- large towns and cities such as Rio de Janeiro, São Paulo, with its commercial and industrial dominance, and Belo Horizonte
- excellent communication links and a wide variety of employment and services
- a focus for in-migration from all parts of Brazil
- high concentrations of people in the cities, and high birth rates.

Activity

For *either* the UK *or* Brazil, describe and explain the pattern of population density.

Population change

A population may increase or decrease over time. How a population changes depends on the birth rate, the death rate and migration (see information box). A population grows if the birth rate is higher than the death rate, i.e. there is a **natural increase**, but some countries have a natural decrease where the death rate is greater than the birth rate. In some countries migration can have a large impact on population size.

World population growth
Figure 1 shows that the population of the world grew very slowly up until the middle of the 20th century. Then there was a population explosion, when population increased very rapidly. Today the growth rate is still high, although the rate of growth seems to be starting to slow down. The world's population is continuing to grow because in many countries the birth rate is higher than the death rate, causing the population to increase.

Growth in the developed world
Figure 2 shows how the MEDCs began with high birth and death rates. Over time both birth rates and death rates in the MEDCs fell to a low level, although the birth rate remained slightly higher, leading to steady population growth. In many MEDCs natural increase today is low and in some, such as Germany and Sweden, the birth rate is actually lower than the death rate.

Growth in the developing world
The biggest contribution to world population growth, especially since the 1950s, has been in the developing countries in Africa, Asia and Latin America. Initially both birth rates and death rates were high (**Figure 2**) giving a low natural increase. However, in the LEDCs as death rates began to fall the birth rates remained high. This caused a massive population explosion and very high natural increase. Even today, although birth rates are still falling, population growth remains high in many LEDCs.

Understanding population terms

Crude birth rate – the number of live births per 1000 population per year.

Crude death rate – the number of deaths per 1000 population per year.

Natural increase – the birth rate minus the death rate.

Annual population growth – the birth rate minus the death rate plus or minus migration.

Migration – the movement of people either into or out of an area.

▲ **Figure 2** Population growth in the developing and developed worlds.

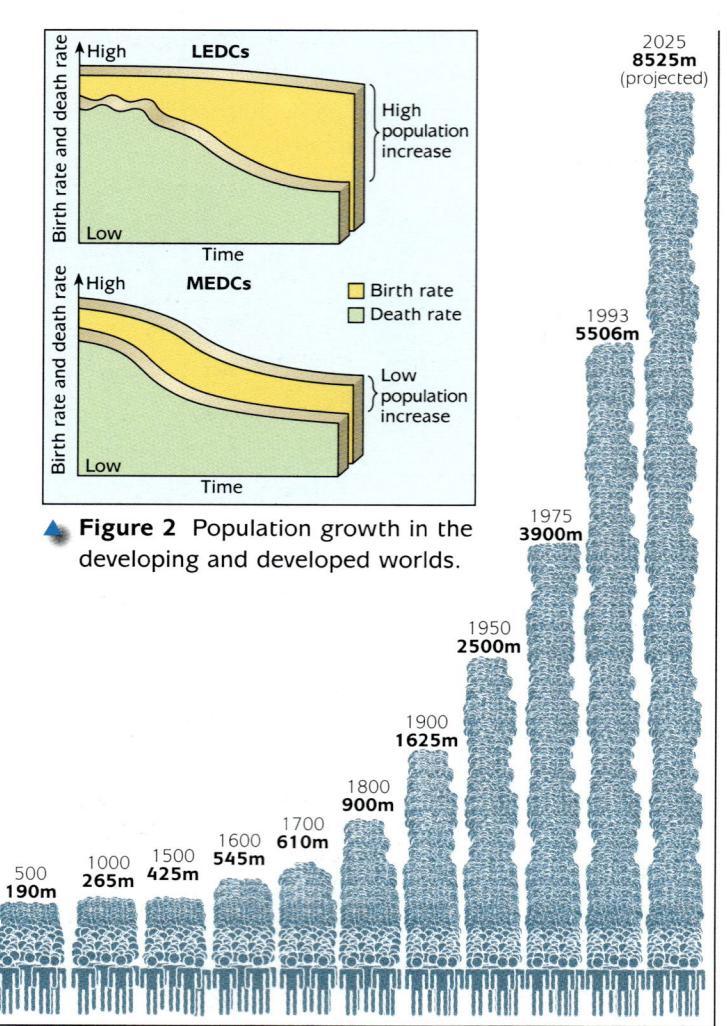

▲ **Figure 1** Growth of world population between 10 000BC and AD2025. Each person on the graph represents four million people.

10 000 BC	4m
5000 BC	5m
4000 BC	9m
3000 BC	14m
2000 BC	27m
1000 BC	50m
500 BC	100m
0	170m
500	190m
1000	265m
1500	425m
1600	545m
1700	610m
1800	900m
1900	1625m
1950	2500m
1975	3900m
1993	5506m
2025	8525m (projected)

Chapter 8 Population

The Demographic Transition Model (or Population Cycle)

Many countries in the developed world have passed through four stages in their population growth, shown in **Figure** 3.

Stage 1 High birth rate and high death rate

When birth rate and death rate are both high (about 35 per 1000) then the natural increase is very low, giving only a small population growth or no change at all. Examples of populations at Stage 1 are rare today because of the spread of modern medicines and new farming techniques. Perhaps only a few remote tribes in the Amazon Forest which have little contact with the outside world are still in Stage 1. The UK was at Stage 1 before the Industrial Revolution, up to about 1750.

Reasons for a high death rate include:
- diseases such as cholera, bubonic plague
- famine and malnutrition
- lack of clean water and sewerage facilities
- lack of medical care and drugs.

Stage 2 The birth rate remains high and the death rate begins to fall

At the start of Stage 2 both birth and death rates remain high. Reasons for a high birth rate are:
- Economic
  - many children mean more workers in the fields.
- Social
  - no birth control or family planning
  - couples have large families in the hope that a few will survive childhood
  - more children to support the parents in old age
  - children are regarded as a sign of virility in some cultures.
- Political
  - governments in Muslim and Catholic countries encourage large families and do not provide much education about family planning.

During Stage 2 the birth rate remains high but the death rate starts to fall to about 20 per 1000 people. By the end of Stage 2 there is a large difference between the birth rate and the death rate. This gives a high natural increase and a rapid growth in population. The death rate falls especially in the urban areas where an increasing proportion of the population live. This results from:
- improved medical care including vaccination, hospitals and medicines
- cleaner water supplies and improved sewage facilities
- an improvement in the quality and the quantity of food supplies.

The UK passed through Stage 2 during the Industrial Revolution between 1750 and 1900. At this time new medicines were being discovered and people learned about the importance of hygiene and cleanliness. In the UK, water mains and sewerage systems began to be built in many of the growing towns and cities. The same developments are taking place in many developing countries today, although some of the poorest, such as Bangladesh and Nigeria, are still in the early stages of Stage 2 of the population cycle.

Stage 3 The birth rate starts to fall

The death rate continues to fall but more slowly, to about 15 per 1000, but the most important change is in the birth rate. The birth rate also starts to fall, to about 20 per 1000 population. This means there is still high natural increase but the population growth begins to slow down. The birth rate begins to fall due to:
- introduction of family planning and birth control

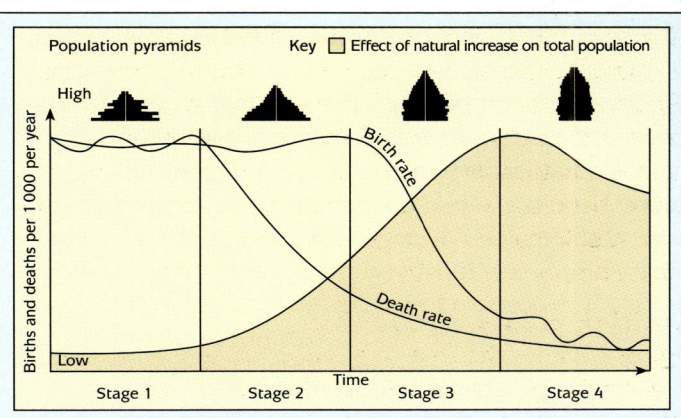

Figure 3 The Demographic Transition Model.

- improvement of medical care so that fewer children die (lower infant mortality) and there is less need to have such large families
- more people in cities where it costs more to support children, while fewer people live and work on farms, requiring less labour
- the materialistic society in which people are more interested in buying TVs, fridges and motor bikes than in having large families
- the provision in developed countries of state old age pensions, so that old people are not dependent on their children for support in old age
- more women staying in higher education, marrying later and pursuing careers.

The UK passed through Stage 3 between about 1900 and 1950. Today many LEDCs are in Stage 3, e.g. Argentina and Brazil. China has also moved to Stage 3 as a result of the government's one-child policy, which has reduced the birth rate from over 30 per 1000 in 1960 to 18 per 1000 in 1994.

Stage 4 Birth and death rates both low

In Stage 4 the death rate and the birth rate are both low, although both may fluctuate slightly from year to year. This gives a very low natural increase or a steady population. Many MEDCs, such as the countries of Europe, the USA and Japan, are at Stage 4 today.

If all the countries in the world were at Stage 4 then **zero population growth** would be much closer. Many people hope that world zero population growth is achieved before too long. They are worried about the speed at which the Earth's resources are being used up, about levels of pollution and about how the ever-growing population will be fed, clothed and housed.

The Demographic Transition Model was originally proposed with only four stages. However, some people now suggest that a fifth stage is needed. In Sweden the birth rate in 1996 was 11 per thousand and the death rate in 1996 was 12, giving a natural increase of –0.1 The minus sign indicates that more people are dying than are being born, causing a negative natural increase or a decline in the population.

Figure 4 Stages in the Demographic Transition Model.

Population structure

Most countries conduct a **census** every ten years to find out the characteristics of the population, including age, sex and ethnic composition. The information on age and sex can be used to draw a **population pyramid**, sometimes called an age–sex pyramid. The pyramids in **Figure 1** use horizontal bars to show the percentages of males and females in a population in each five-year age group (0–4, 5–9, 10–14 years, etc.). From a population pyramid it is possible to suggest in which stage of the Demographic Transition Model a country is placed. In **Figure 1**, Ethiopia is at Stage 2 while France is at Stage 4 (**Figure 4**).

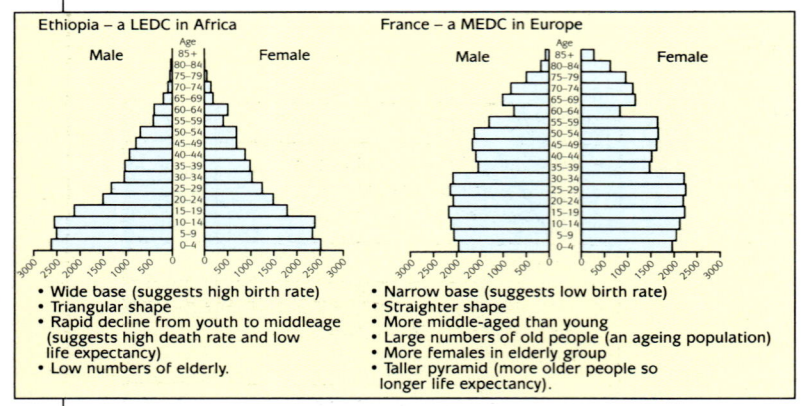

Ethiopia – a LEDC in Africa
- Wide base (suggests high birth rate)
- Triangular shape
- Rapid decline from youth to middleage (suggests high death rate and low life expectancy)
- Low numbers of elderly.

France – a MEDC in Europe
- Narrow base (suggests low birth rate)
- Straighter shape
- More middle-aged than young
- Large numbers of old people (an ageing population)
- More females in elderly group
- Taller pyramid (more older people so longer life expectancy).

▲ **Figure 1** Population pyramids for Ethiopia and France in the 1990s.

It is also possible to use a population pyramid to work out the **dependency ratio**. Children under 16 years old and people over 65 years are the dependent members of a society. They are dependent on the adult (16–64 years) population, which is usually the economically active (people working) or wealth-producing sector.

In Ethiopia in 1991, 46 per cent of the population were aged 15 or under, and 4 per cent were over 65. Thus 50 per cent were dependants and 50 per cent were adults, giving a dependency ratio of 1:1. Every dependant relies on one adult for support. The ratio is high because of the very large numbers of young people.

In the same year in France, 18 per cent were aged 15 or under, and 15 per cent were over 65 – 33 per cent were dependants and the remaining 67 per cent adults. This gave a dependency ratio of 1:2, which means that every dependant relies on two adults for support.

Although the dependency ratio is much lower in France than in Ethiopia, there are many more aged people in France who are dependants. France's population is an ageing population. People's **life expectancy** (the average number of years they are expected to live) has increased with improved medicines and medical care.

Some pyramids have irregular shapes with bulges or gaps at certain age groups especially where migration is greater (**Figure 2**). Bulges are often the result of in-migration to a town, region or country. Many cities in the developing world have a bulge in the male population between 20 and 40 years old as a result of the in-migration of young males to the city to look for work. In the same way a mining settlement often has a greater proportion of young males. Many rural areas in LEDCs have a gap in the population of young males, indicating the out-migration to the cities.

In the UK, some towns, like Eastbourne, have become popular for retirement, with couples who lived and worked in the cities. These retirement towns often have a top-heavy pyramid (**Figure 2**); there are more elderly people in the town in comparison with the rest of the population. The pyramids also show that there are more women in the elderly sector and more of them live longer. On average women have a longer life expectancy than men.

▼ **Figure 2** Age–sex pyramids for Eastbourne (UK) and Zambia (Africa).

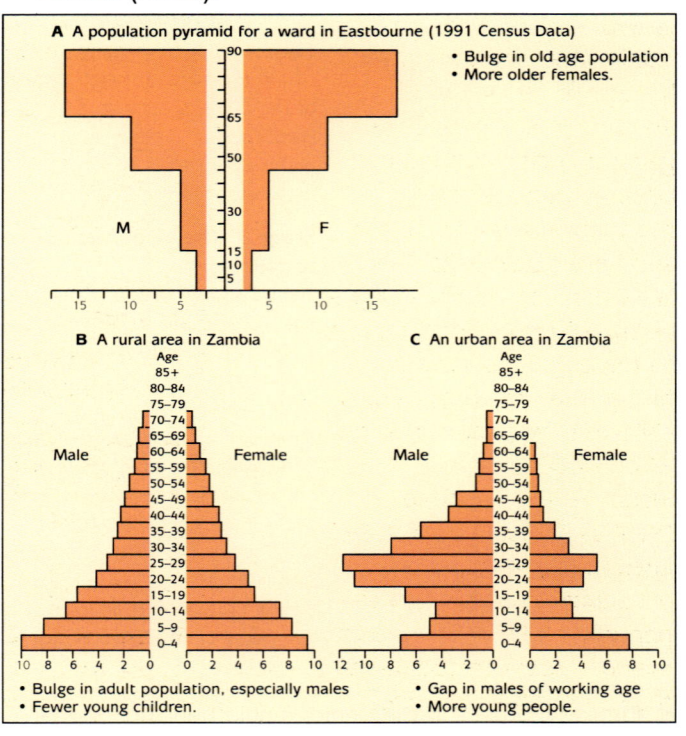

A A population pyramid for a ward in Eastbourne (1991 Census Data)
- Bulge in old age population
- More older females.

B A rural area in Zambia
- Bulge in adult population, especially males
- Fewer young children.

C An urban area in Zambia
- Gap in males of working age
- More young people.

Population problems

The world population continues to grow, but this simple statement hides great differences around the world. In the developing countries rapid population growth continues to cause problems, while in some developed countries governments are concerned about ageing populations and a declining workforce.

MEDCs: the ageing population

In many MEDCs, the life expectancy of the people has increased considerably (**Figure 3**). Better health care, vaccines, surgery and medicines mean that people are living much longer. At the same time the economically active population is declining, so the increase in the elderly population will put a great strain on resources. The elderly require special services and often an increased level of care as they get older. The growth will also mean more need for services, e.g. care homes, meals on wheels, warden-assisted homes and geriatric medical care. In addition there are the economic costs of pensions and housing benefits. It is likely that some resources will be transferred from the young to the old. Schools with falling rolls, youth clubs and children's hospital wards may all be closed and the resources used to fund facilities and services for the aged. More people will be encouraged to have a private pension, and state pensions may be means-tested rather than a right for everyone.

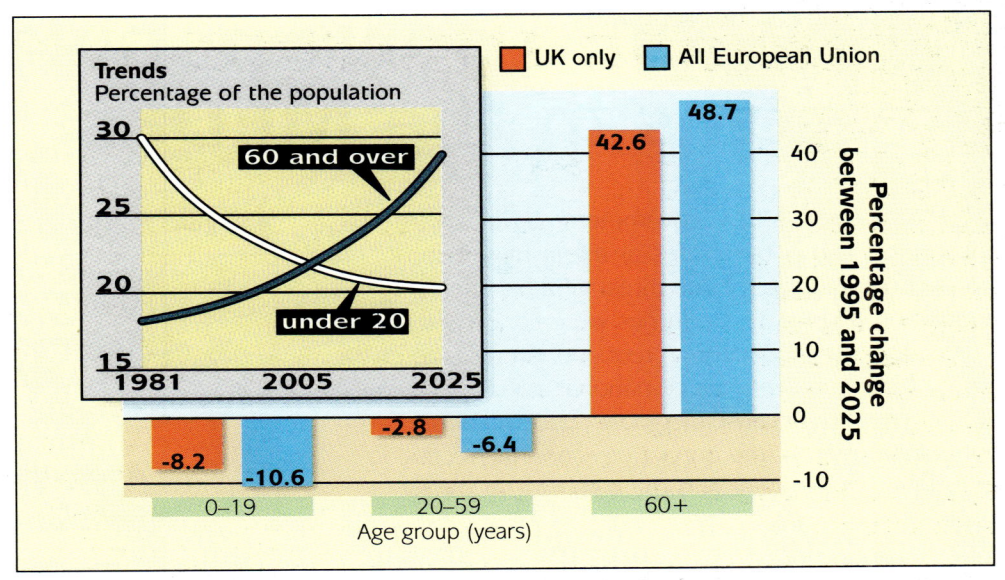

▲ **Figure 3** The generation gap.

LEDCs: More and more people

The greatest population problem facing many LEDCs is still rapid growth. Countries such as Bangladesh and Nigeria still have very high birth rates. It will take a long time for the growth to slow down. With such large numbers of young people in the population, even limiting each couple to one child would still mean a large population growth for many years to come. For many of the LEDCs the rate of population growth is crippling and presents many problems (**Figure 4**), resulting in low living standards and poverty.

In rural areas:
• overgrazing and overcultivation • water, land and air pollution • deforestation and soil erosion.

In urban areas:
• overcrowding and the growth of shanty towns • water, land and air pollution • traffic congestion.

In the country as a whole:
• shortages of resources, food and raw materials • unemployment and under-employment • lack of money for basic health care and schooling • rising crime, political coups, huge debts • low living standards.

▲ **Figure 4** Problems of population growth in LEDCs.

Activities

1 Calculate the dependency ratios for the following continents:

Continent	Young people <16 years (%)	Old people >64 years (%)
Africa	88	6
Asia	57	8
Europe	31	19
North America	33	17

b Explain the differences in your results.

2 a What is the main population problem in
(i) MEDCs
(ii) LEDCs?
b Explain how the MEDCs may cope with their population problem.
c Describe the problems caused by the high population growth in many LEDCs.

Attempts to solve population problems in the MEDCs

In the past, some MEDC governments have actively encouraged higher birth rates or the in-migration of guestworkers to reduce the threat of a decline in population (**Figure 1**). Countries were concerned about a decline in the labour force, reduction in the size of the armed forces and the loss of national status. Today such policies are rare because of global concern about population growth, the impact of economic recession causing unemployment and the high cost of family allowances.

Advertising for people!

Islanders in the Shetlands have been so worried about their dwindling population that they have advertised in national magazines for people to set up home on the island (**Figure 2**). Study the table to find out what the island has to offer and why the advertisements may not work.

The Shetland Islands want a population explosion

Residents of Fetlar are seeking 'youngish people or families with some capital and an entrepreneurial spirit' to travel to the island. Fetlar is a small island, just fourteen square miles in area. It lies nine miles east of Shetland's main island. Its population was once over 200 but is now down to just 80. The small primary school has only six children. The local shop is about to shut as the owners have decided to concentrate on crofting. Local people are worried that other services will close if the population continues to fall.

▲ **Figure 2** Fetlar in the Shetland Islands advertises for inhabitants: report in *The Daily Telegraph*, 16 April 1991.

Attractive for migrants?	Unattractive for migrants?
• Fresh air, open space and a mild climate • Very few cars – no congestion or pollution • Crime-free • Licensed community centre • Electricity • Taxes £45 per year • Relatively cheap housing • Birdwatching.	• Strong winds – it feels cold because of wind chill • No pub or hotel • High living costs – 15 per cent higher than on the mainland • Need to travel to the mainland for most shopping • Lack of employment – the only people with full-time jobs are the schoolteacher and the nurse • Remote.

▼ **Figure 1** Attempts to increase a country's population.

- ADVERTISING
- Accepting immigrants
- High family allowances
- Tax incentives
- Banning contraceptives ✗
- Crèches for working mothers
- Medals for Supermums
- 3-year job protection for mothers

France

Throughout the 20th century France's population has grown only slowly. Various measures have been tried to encourage higher birth rates:

- government discouragement of the use of contraceptives
- tax incentives for larger families
- increased family allowances for families with three or more children.

However, most couples in recent years have limited their family to two children. The extra costs of a larger family were considered too high, and many women wanted to return to their careers. In recent years the Government has been unable to afford the high taxes and compensation payments to encourage women to have larger families. As a result, the average has fallen to 1.8 children per family.

Creating more space: reclamation and drainage

In many MEDCs industrialization and urbanization have concentrated more and more people into towns and cities. In some MEDCs the extra living space has been achieved by land reclamation and drainage.

Chapter 8 Population

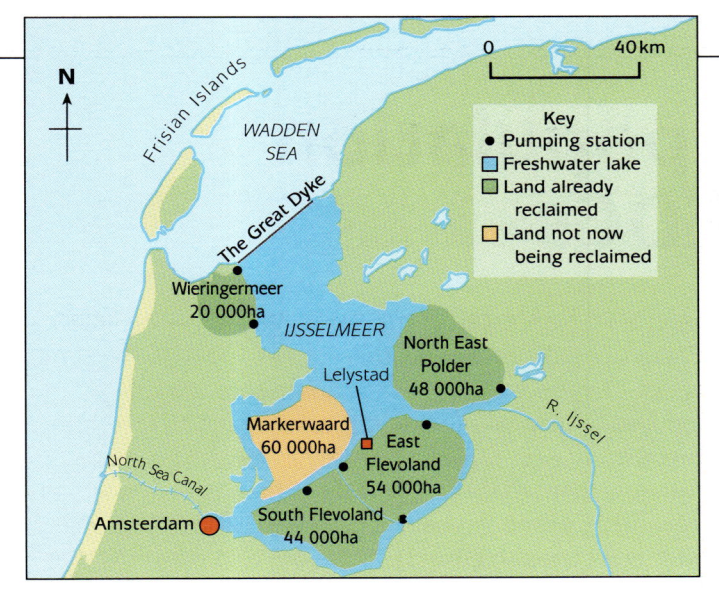

▲ Figure 3 The Zuider Zee Scheme.

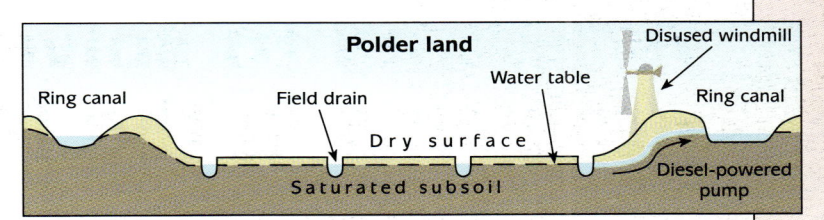

▲ Figure 4 Cross-section through a polder.

The Netherlands is one of the most densely populated countries in the world. It is also very low-lying – 40 per cent of the country lies below sea level. More space was needed for homes, industry and farmland in order to house and feed a growing population. The country was also short of fresh water and had a coastline vulnerable to flooding. Anything that reduced those problems was doubly welcome.

The Zuider Zee Scheme

The solution was the Zuider Zee Scheme in the north-west of the country. The plan was to reclaim and drain five large **polders** (Figure 3). A polder is an area of land reclaimed from the sea. In 1932 the enclosing dam across the entrance to the Waddenzee was completed. The barrier allowed a large freshwater lake, the Ijssel Meer, to be created, improving the supply of fresh water. A road was built on the top of the dam which improved communications to the north of the country. The barrier also shortened the Netherlands coastline by over 700km, reducing the threat of flooding.

Once the barrier was complete, work began on constructing the polders. A ring dyke was built around the area to be reclaimed, with a ring canal on the top (Figure 4). At first windmills were used to drain the sea water from inside the dyke. Later diesel and electric pumps did this work. The water was pumped into the ring canal which emptied into the sea. Drainage was put in to remove excess water, and salt-loving plants were grown to reduce the salt content of the soils. Large applications of fertilizer and constant pumping to remove water allowed the polders to be used for agriculture after about ten years. The landscape has a unique appearance. It is flat and largely treeless and criss-crossed with a network of drainage channels. The landscape appears planned, with farms, villages and towns often in a linear pattern on the higher land created by the dykes.

The land uses have changed on the polders. At first they were mostly used for farming, but more of the space on later polders is used for homes and recreation. The East Flevoland polder in particular has a new town called Lelystad, and this polder acts as an overspill for Amsterdam.

Activities

1. Using **Figure 1** as a guide, describe how countries can attempt to increase birth rates and solve labour shortages. Support your answer with examples.

2. Describe and explain how the Netherlands responded to problems caused by population growth.

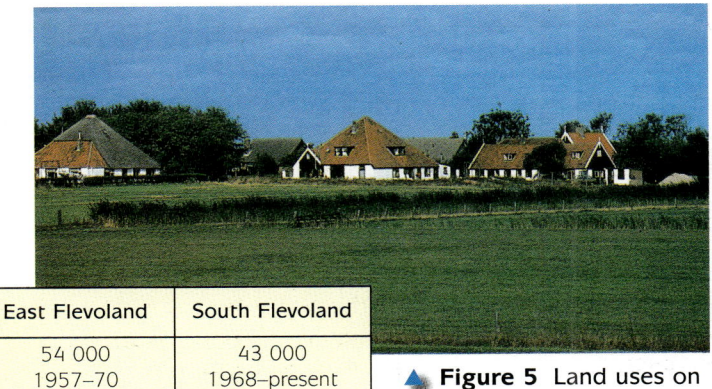

▲ Figure 5 Land uses on the polders.

	Wieringermeer	North East Polder	East Flevoland	South Flevoland
Total area (ha)	20 000	48 000	54 000	43 000
Period of development	1930–40	1942–58	1957–70	1968–present
Percentage of:				
Farmland	87	87	70	50
Residential land	1	1	8	18
Woodland, nature reserves and recreation	3	5	16	25
Canals, dykes and roads	9	7	6	7

Attempts to solve population problems in the LEDCs

The LEDCs have two difficult tasks:
1. to control the size and growth of their populations
2. to cope with the consequences of past, present and future high population growth.

Controlling population growth

Many governments in LEDCs have recognized that their greatest problem is the high birth rate. Some countries, such as India and Ethiopia, have implemented family planning policies to try to reduce birth rates and family size (**Figure 1**). The policies have varied from persuasion and incentives, as in Sri Lanka, to passing strict laws reinforced by severe punishment, as in China. Some countries, such as Iraq and Saudi Arabia, have shown little interest in controlling their population. In most cases this is due to religious beliefs. In Muslim and Catholic countries religious teaching opposes any form of contraception.

China's 'one child' policy

In the 1980s China's population was already over 1000 million. The Government decided that the existing 'two child' policy was not sufficient to reduce population growth. China's population would continue to grow at least until 2025, by which time there would be 1.8 billion Chinese. The Government introduced the 'one child' policy in the hope that the population would stabilize at about 1.2 billion early in the 21st century. **Figure 2** shows an example of the advertising information used by the Chinese Government.

The policy of 'one couple, one child' is very strict. It is virtually illegal to have more than one child and families are criticized and fined; forced abortions and sterilizations have also been reported. The policy has been quite successful in the cities, but 80 per cent of China's population are peasant farmers living in the rural areas. Chinese couples in the countryside want large families to help with work in the fields and to look after them in old age. Chinese culture has always held boys in higher esteem than girls, and there have been reports of infanticide where girl babies have been killed by couples who want sons (**Figure 3**). There are also concerns that the nation is breeding a society of spoilt children, mostly boys, who will have difficulty later finding partners because of the shortage of women.

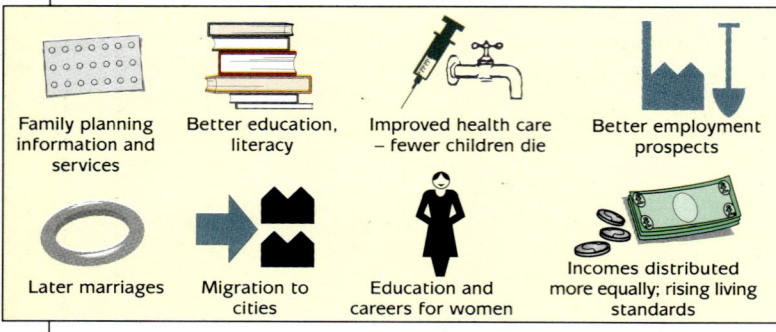

▲ **Figure 1** What changes birth rates?

- Family planning information and services
- Better education, literacy
- Improved health care – fewer children die
- Better employment prospects
- Later marriages
- Migration to cities
- Education and careers for women
- Incomes distributed more equally; rising living standards

WHY HAVE ONLY ONE CHILD?

For you with one child:
Free education for your one child.
Family allowances, priority housing and pension benefits.

For those with two children:
No free education, no allowances and no pension benefits.
Payment of a fine to the state from earnings.

To help you
Women must be 20 years old before they marry.
Men must be 22 years old before they marry.
Couples must have permission to marry and have a child.
Family planning help is available at work.

REMEMBER: One child means happiness.

▲ **Figure 2** Part of the Chinese Government's advertising campaign.

Chinese resist 'one child only' policy

By GRAHAM EARNSHAW in Peking

A Chinese peasant grasped a double-headed axe and confronted three birth officials, shouting: "If you force me to have a vasectomy, I'll kill all of you." It was a small incident which ended in the peasant paying a large fine, and probably having a vasectomy.

The effects of the current policy, from forced abortion and sterilization to female infanticide, are extremely worrying. The one-child-only policy has been generally successful in the cities, but the peasants, who make up 80 per cent of China's population, are proving to be very stubborn.

The peasants want a lot of children to help work the fields and to look after them in old age. And they prefer boys to girls to the extent that they are willing to kill their daughters to make sure their one child is male.

▲ **Figure 3** China's 'one child' policy – report in *The Daily Telegraph*, 30 May 1983.

Coping with the consequences of high population growth

Rapid population growth causes great problems for LEDCs. The countries need to stop further city growth and to attempt to solve the problems that already exist. Most LEDCs cannot afford to provide the housing, food, jobs and services that most people take for granted in the MEDCs. The cities also continue to grow very fast, partly due to high birth rates but also because of the high rates of rural-to-urban migration. LEDCs have tried various ways to provide food and shelter for the growing population and to stop the sprawling shanty towns, the congestion and the overcrowding in the cities.

The problems of high population growth can be classified into:

- environmental problems such as pollution and soil erosion
- socio-economic problems such as unemployment and poverty
- political problems such as how to plan and pay for housing, education and food.

The environmental consequences of population growth

In urban areas, the growth in population leads to overcrowding, traffic congestion, pollution and the sprawl of shanty towns into the countryside (**Figure 4**). In rural areas a growing population leads to greater demands for shelter, food and water. Pressure on the land increases as people grow more crops and keep more animals. In marginal farming areas, such as the Sahel (**Figure 5**) in North Africa, this has caused **overgrazing** and **overcultivation**. Soils have become **salinized** (salty) and useless for farming. The pressure of people and animals is particularly high around villages and wells. The wells become depleted, the vegetation trampled and the bare soil subject to erosion by wind and rain. In some areas the land is actually turning into desert, a process called **desertification**. In some rural areas population growth has led to out-migration to the towns and cities. The migration is **age-** and **sex-selective**, with mostly young adult males leaving the rural areas. This leaves behind the elderly, the very young and mostly women, and this can lead to farmland being abandoned or less carefully tended due to the shortage of skilled and fit labour.

- Overgrazing and overcultivation
- Desertification
- Depleted water supplies
- Pollution of land and water
- Deforestation
- Soil erosion and gullying
- Global warming and climatic change
- Traffic congestion
- Air pollution
- Open drains with sewage along streets
- Loss of farmland as shanties grow
- Land pollution – rubbish tips, litter
- Visual pollution – skyscrapers and shanties
- Demand for water leads to reservoirs
- Destabilization of hillsides – landslides.

▲ **Figure 4** The environmental consequences of population growth.

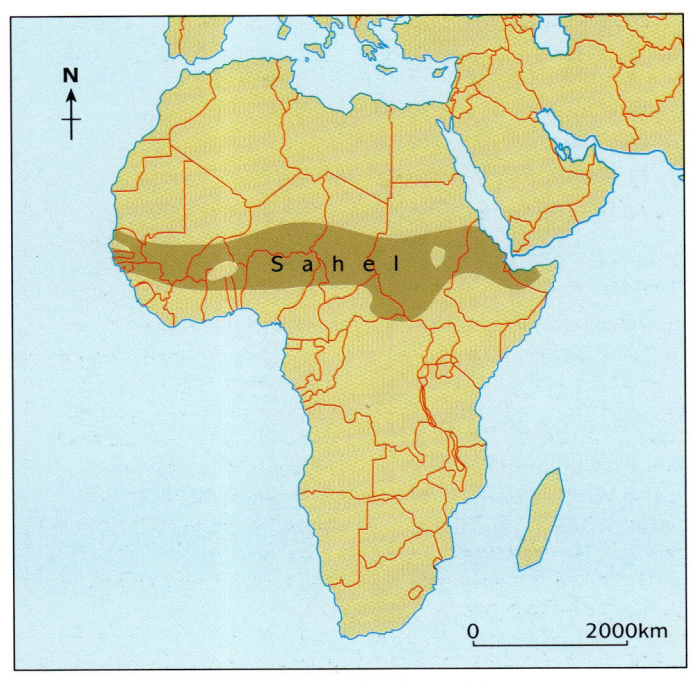

▲ **Figure 5** The Sahel region in North Africa.

Test questions

1. What are the main population problems in the LEDCs? (3 marks)

2. a Name two countries with birth control policies and two with weak or no policies. (4 marks)
   b Suggest reasons for the different approaches taken by governments. (3 marks)

3. For China:
   a describe the birth control policy implemented (6 marks)
   b evaluate the success of the policy. (4 marks)

Case Study – Solving population problems

Transmigration in Indonesia

Figure 1 Indonesia, population density and core and periphery.

Indonesia is a collection of islands to the north of Australia (**Figure 1**). Most of the islands have an equatorial climate and are covered in rain forest. The population in 1995 was about 200 million and population growth is high, with a birth rate of 25 per 1000 and a death rate of 9 per 1000.

Indonesia can be divided into a **core** area that includes the big cities and islands of Java, Madura and Bali, and a poorer **periphery**. Sixty per cent of the population live on Java itself. As well as high population growth, many migrants move in search of work to the main island of Java, and especially to Jakarta, the capital city.

The Government first tried to stop Jakarta's growth by moving government departments to other cities. But the impact was very small-scale compared with the level of migration into the city. The Government realized that the only solution was to provide places where the opportunity to get a job was as high as in Jakarta. They established the **transmigration policy** which aims to resettle people from the core to the periphery in new farming areas set up by the Government (**Figure 2**).

The migrants are given free transport, free land and housing and other assistance such as food and fertilizer for the first twelve months. Even though more people apply to migrate than the scheme can accommodate, it still makes little impression on the overcrowding problem in Java. The scheme has experienced a variety of political, environmental and socio-economic problems.

Political problems
- The migration has only had a small impact because it moves far fewer people than the population increase on Java.
- The administration is inefficient.
- The costs to the Government are high.
- The programme relies on aid from abroad, e.g. from the World Bank.

Environmental problems
- Many islands have infertile acid soils.
- About 10 per cent of new settlements have already failed because of the poor soils.
- Some sites have been badly affected by volcanic activity or flooding.
- The rain forests, which are the world's second largest after those in the Amazon Basin and contain over 100 mammals found nowhere else in the world, have been damaged.
- Forty-nine million hectares of forest have been cleared in the past 30 years for logging and agriculture.
- When the vegetation is cleared the soils are soon leached, making them useless for farming.

Socio-economic problems
- Conflict between the traditional farmers and the newcomers who were given money and land.
- Productivity is low, leaving some farmers still needing support after a year.
- Some native tribes have lost land and been forced to move to other areas.

Figure 2 Resettlement in Indonesia's rain forest.

Irrigation in Egypt

The Sahara desert stretches across much of North Africa. Libya and Egypt include large areas of desert. Libya has a population of 5 million but Egypt has 60 million people. How can Egypt support such a huge population? The answer lies with the River Nile. Over 99 per cent of Egypt's population live on only 4 per cent of the land area (**Figure 3**).

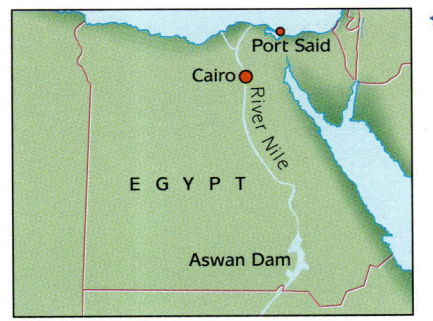

Figure 3 Egypt's population distribution.

Since the 1960s Egypt's response to population growth has been to increase the water supply and expand the area of irrigated farmland. In the 1960s the Aswan Dam was built to control the flow of the Nile and stop the annual floods which brought fertile silt and water to the rice fields. There have been about 20 land reclamation schemes along the Nile, which have increased the irrigated and cultivated land by almost two million hectares. The area of cultivated land has doubled from 4 per cent to 8 per cent of the total. Water is released from the Aswan Dam at times of low flow to maintain the river level. Farmers use a variety of techniques to lift the water out of the river. Traditional methods include the shaduf (**Figure 4**), although increasingly diesel and electric pumps are being used by the wealthier farmers. The water is then fed along open channels to the fields where it floods the small patches of land separated by banks of clay soil called *bunds*. The farmers can now produce two or three crops from the same land area in one year. The schemes have increased the water supply, created more land for people to farm, and increased food supplies.

However, the building of the dam and the expansion of farmland have also caused problems for the environment. Some of the irrigation schemes have made the soils salty and unusable. Over two million hectares of land have been affected and large stretches are now abandoned. The building of the Aswan Dam flooded some important archaeological sites. Lake Nasser behind the dam and the irrigation channels have increased the threat of disease, e.g. bilharzia which is transmitted by water snails, and malaria by mosquitoes. The huge quantities of silt once deposited on the Nile flood plain are now trapped behind the Aswan Dam. Lake Nasser is gradually silting up and eventually it will need to be dredged or abandoned. The farmers now need to buy expensive chemical fertilizers to keep the soil healthy, and the Nile delta at the river mouth is becoming smaller because it is starved of its supply of sediment.

Figure 4 A shaduf lifting water into irrigation channels.

Activities

1. You are working for an advertising agency in Jakarta, Indonesia, which has won the contract to design the advertising material for the transmigration programme. Design a poster suitable to be displayed around the city.

2. Imagine you are a migrant in one of the new resettlement areas. Write a letter to friends still in Jakarta who are thinking about moving too. Tell them about the advantages and disadvantages of your move.

3. a. Why was the Aswan Dam needed in Egypt?
   b. Make a copy of the table below and complete it to show the advantages and disadvantages of building the Aswan Dam.

Advantages of the Aswan Dam	Disadvantages of the Aswan Dam

Case Study – Solving population problems

Migration

Sometimes the annual growth rate of a country's population does not match up with the statistics for the birth and death rates. Jamaica has a birth rate of 27 per 1000 and a death rate of 6 per 1000. The natural increase is therefore 21 per 1000 but the annual growth rate is only 12 per 1000. This difference is explained by **migration** (the movement of people). More people have **emigrated** (moved away) from Jamaica to other countries than have moved into Jamaica. The difference between the numbers of immigrants and emigrants gives the **migration balance**. Jamaica has a net migration loss because it has lost more people through emigration than it gained through immigration. Hong Kong has a birth rate of 18 per 1000 and a death rate of 5 per 1000. The natural increase is 13 per 1000 but the annual growth rate is 33 per 1000, reflecting a net migration gain. Hong Kong has many more immigrants than emigrants.

Types of migration

There are many different types of migration (**Figure 1**).

Compulsory or **forced migration** occurs when people have no choice about moving. Forced migrants who move to another country are called **refugees**. The reasons why they move include:

- *Physical reasons* such as earthquakes or floods. In 1997 victims of the volcanic eruptions in Montserrat, a Caribbean island, fled the island – some came to the UK.

- *Human reasons* such as war or persecution. Forced migration occurred on a huge scale in the past, with the slave trade, and the Jewish persecution in World War II. In the 1970s Idi Amin in Uganda forced the Ugandan Asians out of the country. In Africa there are many millions of refugees (**Figure 2**) as a result of famine and civil war.

▼ **Figure 2** African refugees.

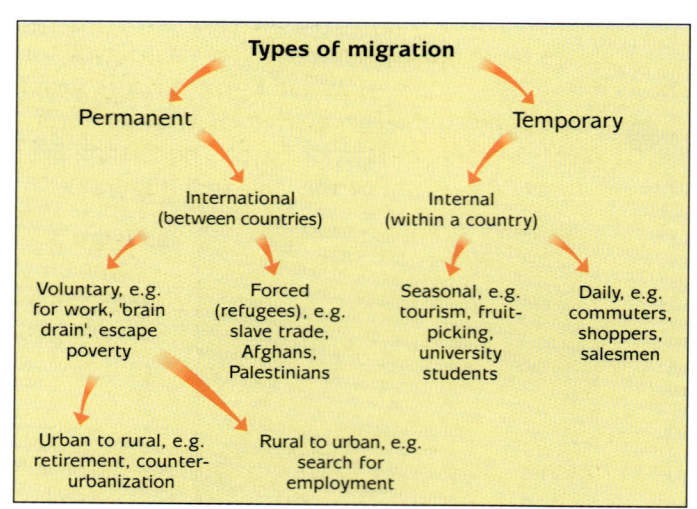

Figure 1 Types of migration.

Types of migration

- Permanent
  - International (between countries)
    - Voluntary, e.g. for work, 'brain drain', escape poverty
    - Forced (refugees), e.g. slave trade, Afghans, Palestinians
  - Urban to rural, e.g. retirement, counter-urbanization
  - Rural to urban, e.g. search for employment
- Temporary
  - Internal (within a country)
    - Seasonal, e.g. tourism, fruit-picking, university students
    - Daily, e.g. commuters, shoppers, salesmen

Voluntary migration is when the migrant makes the decision to move. Today most migration is voluntary. The decision is usually the result of balancing the advantages and disadvantages of the movement (**Figure 3**). There will be both **push** and **pull** factors involved. Push factors are the things people dislike or the disadvantages of where they live. There may be no work, few services and a low standard of living. Pull factors are the attractions or advantages of the place they are moving to. The location may be nearer to relatives, offer a better education or have a warmer climate.

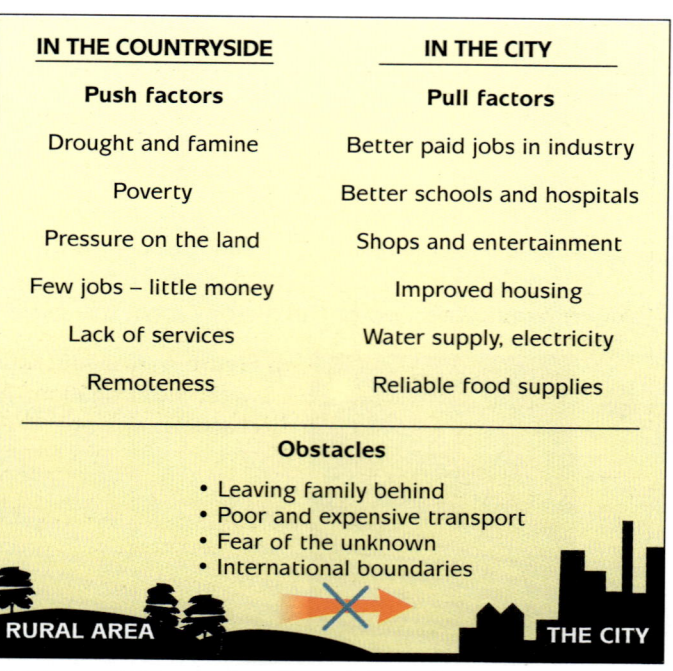

IN THE COUNTRYSIDE	IN THE CITY
Push factors	**Pull factors**
Drought and famine	Better paid jobs in industry
Poverty	Better schools and hospitals
Pressure on the land	Shops and entertainment
Few jobs – little money	Improved housing
Lack of services	Water supply, electricity
Remoteness	Reliable food supplies

Obstacles
- Leaving family behind
- Poor and expensive transport
- Fear of the unknown
- International boundaries

RURAL AREA → THE CITY

▲ **Figure 3** The push–pull model of migration.

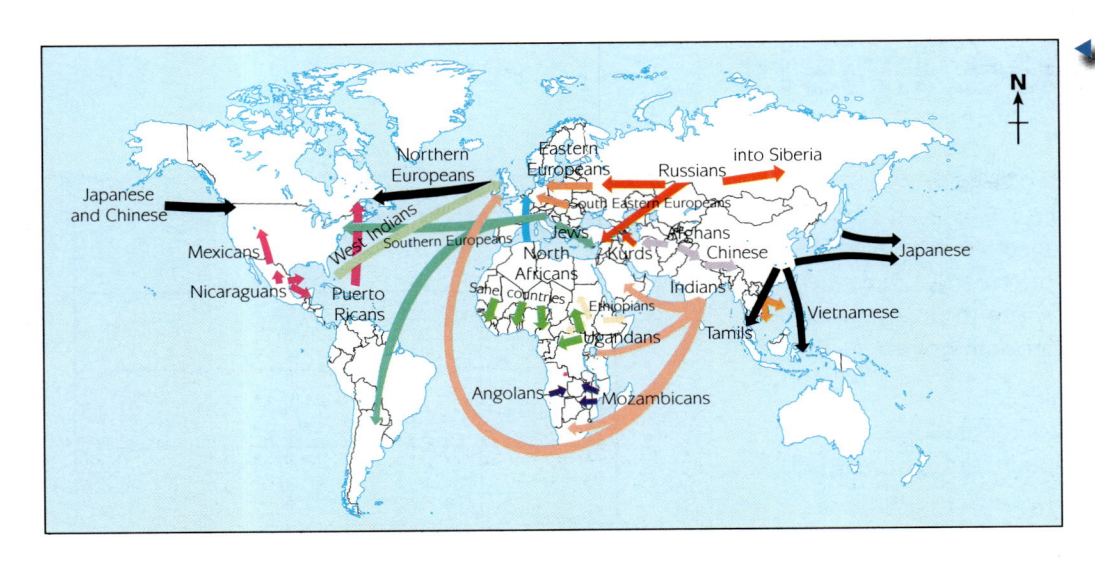

Figure 4 Some important international migrations in the 20th century.

International migration

In the 20th century international migrations – those that cross country borders – have decreased in importance. In the 19th century, large numbers of people moved voluntarily to different countries in the hope of colonizing new areas. Examples include the Pilgrim Fathers who sailed to New England on the east coast of America, and the white Europeans moving to South Africa to set up and manage gold mines and sugar plantations.

Some of the migrations were forced, such as the slave trade, and the movement from Ireland during the potato famine. **Figure 4** shows examples of international migrations. In recent decades, the major international migrations have been of three types.

- *From poor to rich countries*: these include the huge movements from Mexico into the southern parts of the USA. The migrants who move in search of work and a higher standard of living are often called economic refugees.
- *From drought-hit countries* in the Sahel region in Africa to neighbouring African countries.
- *Movements of political refugees* such as Jews returning to Israel and the emigration of Palestinians to live in huge refugee camps in neighbouring Jordan and the Lebanon.

Such international migrations have both advantages and disadvantages for the countries and people involved. These are shown in **Figure 5**.

	Advantages	Disadvantages
For the host country Economic	An extra source of labour. May bring skills and money to the country, e.g. brain drain of doctors from UK to USA, voluntary workers to LEDCs. Help to develop areas and extract resources.	A strain on the country's resources, especially in the LEDCs. Increased unemployment. Need to provide housing, food, medical care, education.
Social	Cultural exchange brings new skills and ideas.	May increase racial tension, violence and discrimination.
For the losing country Economic	May reduce burden on the country, with fewer mouths to feed and provide for. Money sent back by migrants is important foreign exchange. Families improve local economy by spending in local shops and on services.	A loss of labour – often the young males who have the entrepreneurial skills move.
For the migrant and family Economic	May earn more money and have a higher standard of living – stable employment with a salary/wage.	Higher living costs in the host country for housing, food, clothing.
Social	Meet new people and broaden cultural understanding.	May result in family separation if only the main worker migrates, e.g. Turkish males going to West Germany to work.

Figure 5 Advantages and disadvantages of international migration.

The refugee crisis

Strictly speaking, **refugees** are people who have been *forced* to move out of their country. However, some definitions also use the term refugee for people who have been **internally displaced**, or forced to move *within* their country. Most refugees are made to flee their homes by *human* or *political* rather than *natural* causes.

Political
- religious, political or racial persecution
- civil war.

Natural
- environmental disasters such as floods, drought, earthquakes and volcanic eruptions.

The numbers of refugees have grown enormously in recent years (**Figure 1**). In 1995 the United Nations suggested that there were over 14 million refugees in the world, although giving an accurate figure is difficult because most refugees are illegal immigrants and governments are sometimes unsure of just how many there are. Most refugees are children and the majority of adults are women. Most refugee movements are between neighbouring countries and over 80 per cent of all refugees are in LEDCs (**Figure 2 and 3**), the very countries that find it difficult to provide for their own population.

Refugees living in other LEDCs often live in extreme poverty, lacking food, shelter, clothing, education and medical care. They have no citizenship, few, if any, rights and virtually no prospect of improvement. Very few refugees are ever able to return to their home country.

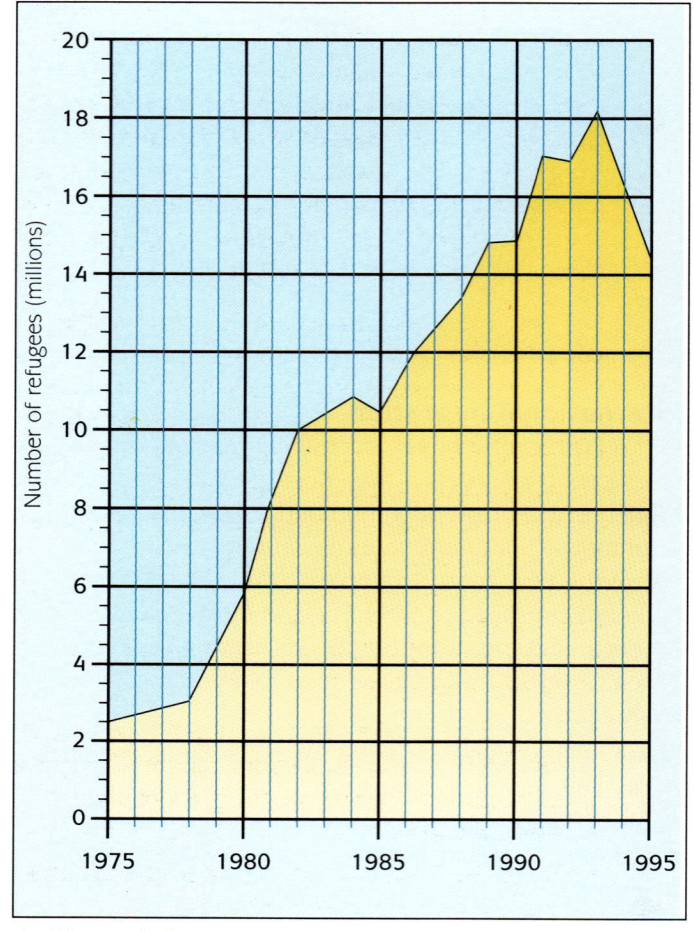

Figure 1 Growth of the world refugee population.

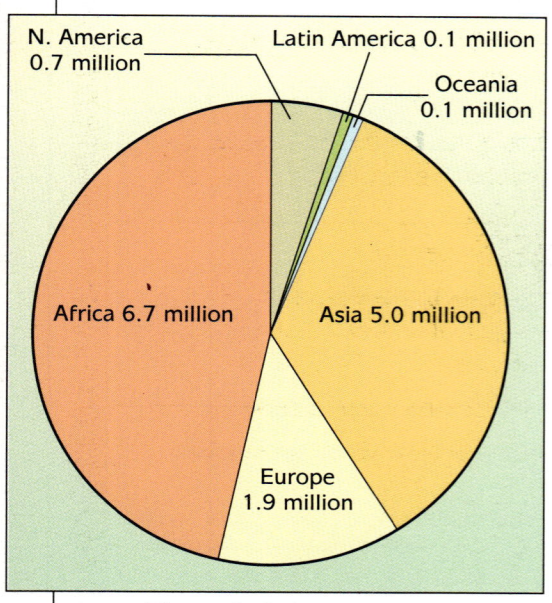

Figure 2 Refugees by region.

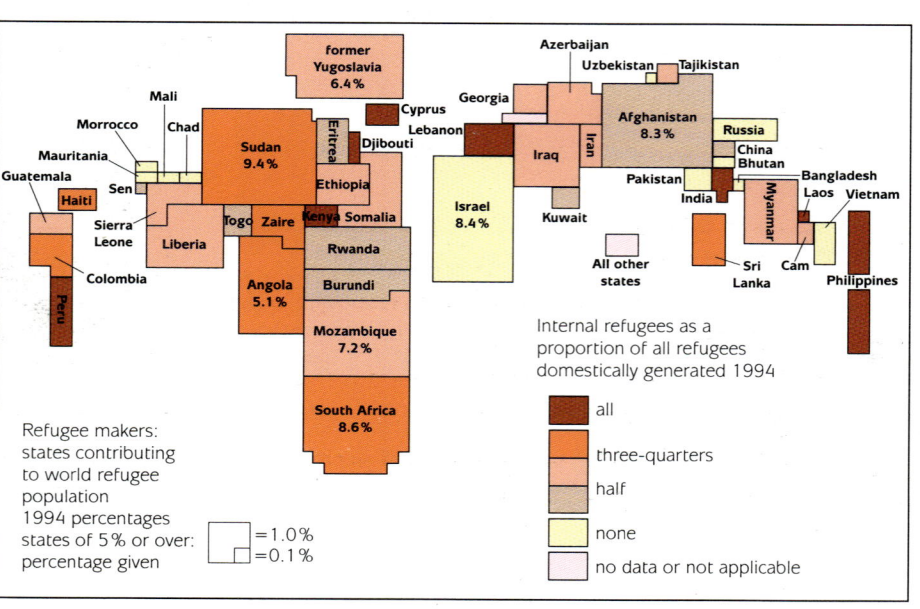

- N. America 0.7 million
- Latin America 0.1 million
- Oceania 0.1 million
- Africa 6.7 million
- Asia 5.0 million
- Europe 1.9 million

Figure 3 Refugee makers – where the refugees come from.

Refugee makers: states contributing to world refugee population 1994 percentages states of 5% or over: percentage given

- former Yugoslavia 6.4%
- Sudan 9.4%
- Afghanistan 8.3%
- Israel 8.4%
- Angola 5.1%
- Mozambique 7.2%
- South Africa 8.6%

Internal refugees as a proportion of all refugees domestically generated 1994
- all
- three-quarters
- half
- none
- no data or not applicable

Palestinian refugees

For hundreds of years the great majority of people living in Palestine were Arabs. But in the first half of the 20th century many Jews were concerned about anti-semitism and the persecution of the Jews in Hitler's Germany. By the end of World War II many Jews were desperate for the creation of a Jewish state. The Jews claimed Palestine was their homeland because of references in the Bible to it being the birthplace of the Jewish religion and the 'land flowing with milk and honey'.

In 1948, the Jews declared the creation of the state of Israel which replaced the country of Palestine. War broke out between Israel and her Arab neighbours and many Palestinians fled Israel. **Figure 4** shows the destinations of the Palestinian refugees. Most of the refugees settled in neighbouring Arab countries such as the Lebanon, Syria and Jordan.

Destination	Number of refugees
Jordan	1 072 561
Gaza	603 380*
West Bank	479 023*
Lebanon	328 039
Syria	314 039

*Now under Palestinian self-rule so not really refugees, although their status and the daily reality of their lives makes them still displaced and disadvantaged.

▲ **Figure 4** Destinations of Palestinian refugees.

Impact on the Lebanon
- There are seventeen overcrowded refugee camps (**Figure 5**).
- The Lebanon, already struggling to cater for the needs of its own population, cannot supply the refugees with shelter, clothing, food and medical supplies.
- There has been civil war between the Christians and the Muslims in the Lebanon.
- Several wars have been fought between Israel and the Palestine Liberation Organization (PLO) in the Lebanon.

Impact on Israel
- Wars with the Lebanon have been costly in lives and money.
- There is hostility and lack of trust between Israel and her Arab neighbours.
- Frequent bombings and attacks occur in border regions.
- Fewer Palestinian Arabs mean there is more land for the Jews to settle.
- Jobs have become available for the Jews in Israel.

◀ **Figure 5** Refugee camp in the Lebanon.

- Greater social cohesion is possible in an almost totally Jewish state.
- It is easy to establish schools and synagogues with only a single religion.

Impact on the refugees in the Lebanon
- They are free from the hostility they experienced in Israel.
- They have lost their homeland.
- They suffer appalling living conditions in makeshift shelters with little food, clothing, money or other services.
- Unhygienic living conditions cause disease.
- They have lost their rights and have no say in their own destiny.

Internal migration

Migrations which take place *within* a country are called internal migrations. Today, this is the commonest type of migration. Many thousands of people move house every year, but often within the same region or even the same urban area. As the distance increases the numbers of migrants tend to decrease. **Figure 1** shows some different types of internal migration.

In the MEDCs **rural to urban migration** – the movement from the countryside to the towns – began earlier and the rate was slower than in LEDCs. In the UK rural to urban migration began during the Industrial Revolution when towns were developing and industries mushrooming (**Figure 2**). Many people left the countryside where new farming practices required less labour. They flocked to the towns to work in the coalmines, steelworks, shipyards and textile mills. The same happens today in the developing countries, where people leave the countryside to seek employment in factories and services in the cities.

Rural depopulation has continued in many developed countries, especially from the most remote upland regions. **Figure 3** shows the **push** and **pull** factors for the MEDCs.

In recent years in the MEDCs there has also been **urban depopulation**, the flight from the cities. Many of the very large urban areas, the conurbations, have seen a fall in their population (**Figure 4**). People are escaping from the air and noise pollution, crime, poor housing and overcrowding to go in search of better housing in more peaceful rural surroundings, in suburbanized villages or New Towns. Greater London, for example, declined from 8.2 million people in 1951 to 6.9 million people in 1991. This process is called **counter-urbanization** – the movement of people from the urban areas, particularly the inner city to the rural–urban fringe and beyond.

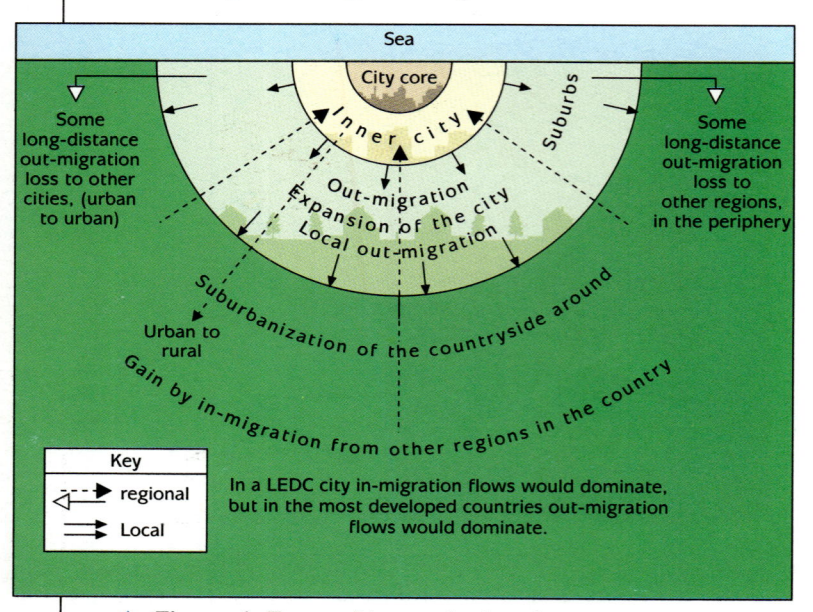

▲ **Figure 1** Types of internal migration.

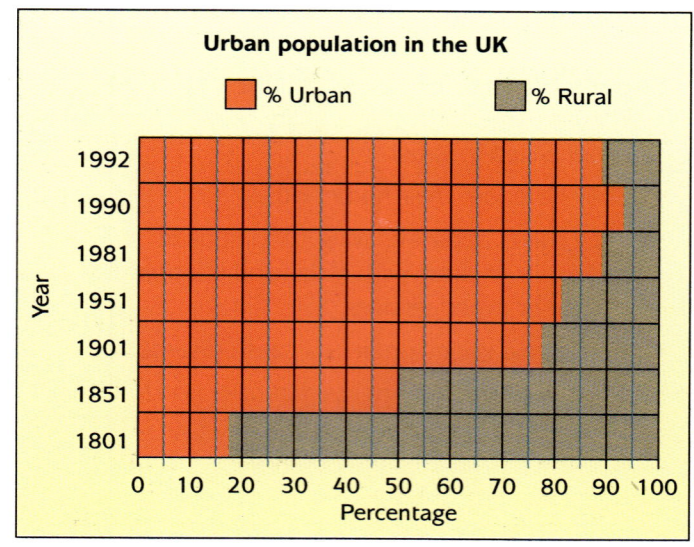

▲ **Figure 2** The urban population in the UK.

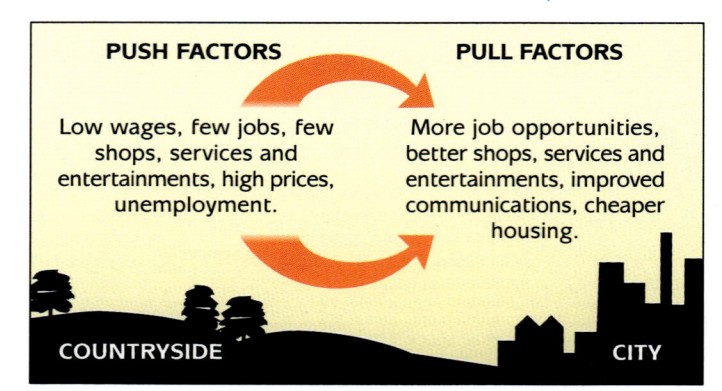

▲ **Figure 3** Push and pull factors for rural-to-urban migration in the developed countries.

PUSH FACTORS: Low wages, few jobs, few shops, services and entertainments, high prices, unemployment.

PULL FACTORS: More job opportunities, better shops, services and entertainments, improved communications, cheaper housing.

Year	Liverpool	Manchester	Birmingham
1801	82 000	75 000	71 000
1851	376 000	303 000	233 000
1951	789 000	703 000	1 100 000
1991	510 000	449 000	1 007 000

Source: *Philip's Geographical Digest*, 1996–7

▲ **Figure 4** The changing population of Liverpool, Manchester and Birmingham.

Internal migration in the UK

Figure 5 shows how the population changed in the regions of the UK between 1981 and 1991.

The main population movements are summarized below.

Out-migration from rural and upland areas
Example: the Scottish highlands, the Pennines.

Physical push factors:
- Climate is harsher.
- The relief of the land is steep and hilly.
- Soils are waterlogged, thin and acid.
- The areas are remote and accessibility is poor.

Human push factors:
- Limited services and employment opportunities.

Out-migration from declining heavy industrial areas
Examples: north-east England, South Wales.

In the Industrial Revolution these were wealthy, growing regions which attracted large numbers of people searching for work in the coalmines, shipyards, steelworks and textile mills. However, since the end of World War II these regions have been in decline. Coalmines, shipyards, steelworks and textile mills have all contracted or closed down. In the 1980s unemployment was over 50 per cent in some areas. New industries had not been attracted in sufficient numbers to soak up the thousands of jobs lost by the closures. The only solution for many people was to move away to find jobs elsewhere in the country.

Out-migration from inner city problem areas
Examples: Greater London, Birmingham, Glasgow and Newcastle.

Many people have left the inner city areas in the UK because of a variety of social, economic and environmental push factors (**Figure 6**).

In-migration
Many people choose to live in the countryside and commute to work in the large towns and cities. Improved transport links and faster cars and trains make long-distance commuting possible. They prefer the more peaceful country life in attractive market towns and villages. The environment is more pleasant with less congestion, air and noise pollution. In some areas house prices may also be cheaper. Devon, Cornwall and traditional tourist resorts along the south coast, such as Bournemouth, have also seen population growth. Pensioners from towns and cities have migrated to these areas, attracted by the pleasant climate and attractive scenery.

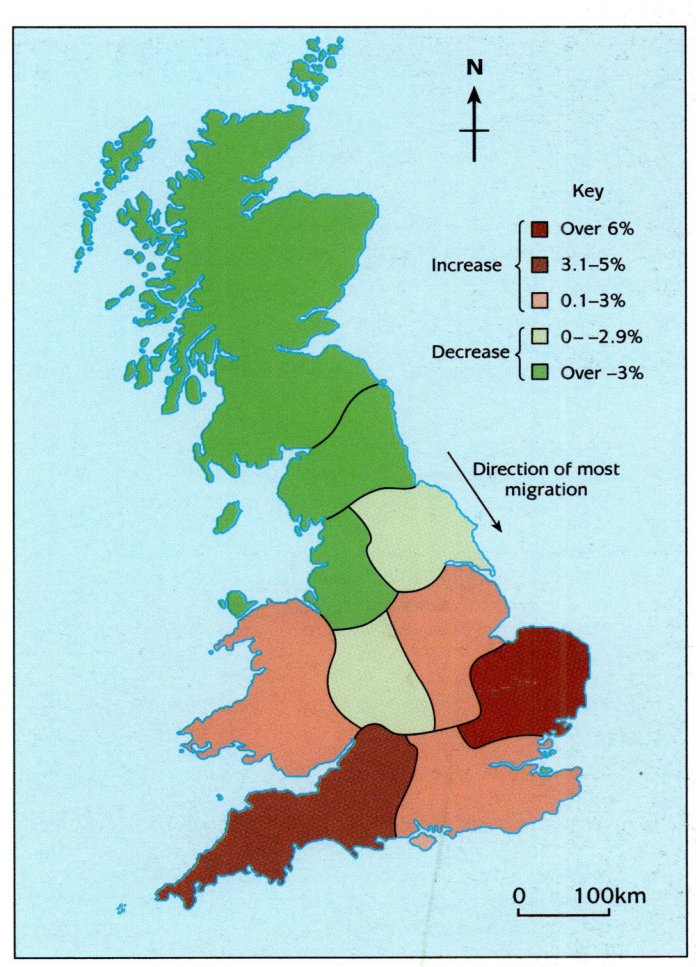

Figure 5 Population change in England and Wales, 1981–91.

Environmental	Socio-economic
Old terraced housing	Declining industries
Air and noise pollution	Unemployment
Derelict land and buildings	Low incomes
Lack of open space	Poor access to motorways
Vandalism and graffiti	High crime rates

Figure 6 Push factors of the inner cities.

Test questions
1. a Show on a single graph the data in **Figure 4**. (6 marks)
   b Describe and explain the trends shown on the graph. (6 marks)
2. Choose one area of decline and one area of growth from **Figure 5**. Describe and explain the reasons for the growth and decline in your chosen areas. (8 marks)

Rural to urban migration in the LEDCs

Push factors (the reasons why people leave the countryside):
- pressure on the land, leaving too little for people to live on
- overpopulation resulting from high birth rates
- starvation as a result of too many people for the available food supply
- overgrazing and overcultivation causing soil erosion and limiting food production
- hard work, long hours and little pay for farmers
- natural disasters such as drought, hurricanes, floods and volcanic eruptions
- dilapidated and poor-quality housing
- shortage of education, health and welfare facilities
- lack of electricity, water and sewage services
- lack of investment from governments, who spend most money in urban areas.

Pull factors (the reasons why people move to the cities):
- improved employment opportunities, a greater variety of jobs with higher wages
- expectations of improved housing with services such as water and electricity
- improved quality of life and standard of living
- the availability of schools, doctors, hospitals and entertainment
- more reliable sources of food
- the experience of life in modern, dynamic cities.

Figure 1 Rural push and urban pull factors.

In the LEDCs people began to move from the countryside to the towns in the early 20th century. This **rural to urban migration** has dominated in the past 50 years, with the rate of movement accelerating. In Nigeria, just 5 per cent of the population was urban in 1921 but by 1991 this had risen to 30 per cent. Lagos, with a population of 8 million, is expanding at the rate of 10 per cent per year. Early in the 21st century its population is expected to have doubled to 16 million.

The movement has been age- and sex-selective. It is mostly the younger males who have migrated to the cities, especially the capital cities and ports. The rural people are attracted by the job opportunities, the chance of a better education and the modern dynamism of the city presented in the media. These, and other pull factors, can be seen in **Figure 1**, along with the push factors that force people away from the rural areas.

The rural migrant leaves the home village with a **perception** of city life based upon radio programmes, magazines and letters from relatives already in the city.

The reality may be very different. They often have little money and need either to build their own shanty or to stay with friends or relatives until they are established. Some end up sleeping rough in the streets (**Figure 2**). Life in the shanty towns is covered in more detail in Chapter 9.

Figure 2 Sleeping rough in Goa, India.

Test questions

1 a What is meant by the terms:
   (i) birth rate
   (ii) death rate
   (iii) natural increase? (3 marks)
  b Draw a diagram to show the Demographic Transition Model. Label the four stages. (7 marks)
  c Describe the main features of a population pyramid at Stage 2 and Stage 4 of the Demographic Transition Model. Include sketches of the two pyramids. (4 marks)
  d Choose one of the following population problems and describe how a country may attempt to solve it:
   • high birth rate
   • an ageing population
   • the need for more space
   • the need for more food
   • a declining population. (6 marks)

2 a Describe and explain the pattern of internal migration in the UK in the past 40 years. (10 marks)
  b Describe and explain the rapid growth of cities in the LEDCs. (10 marks)

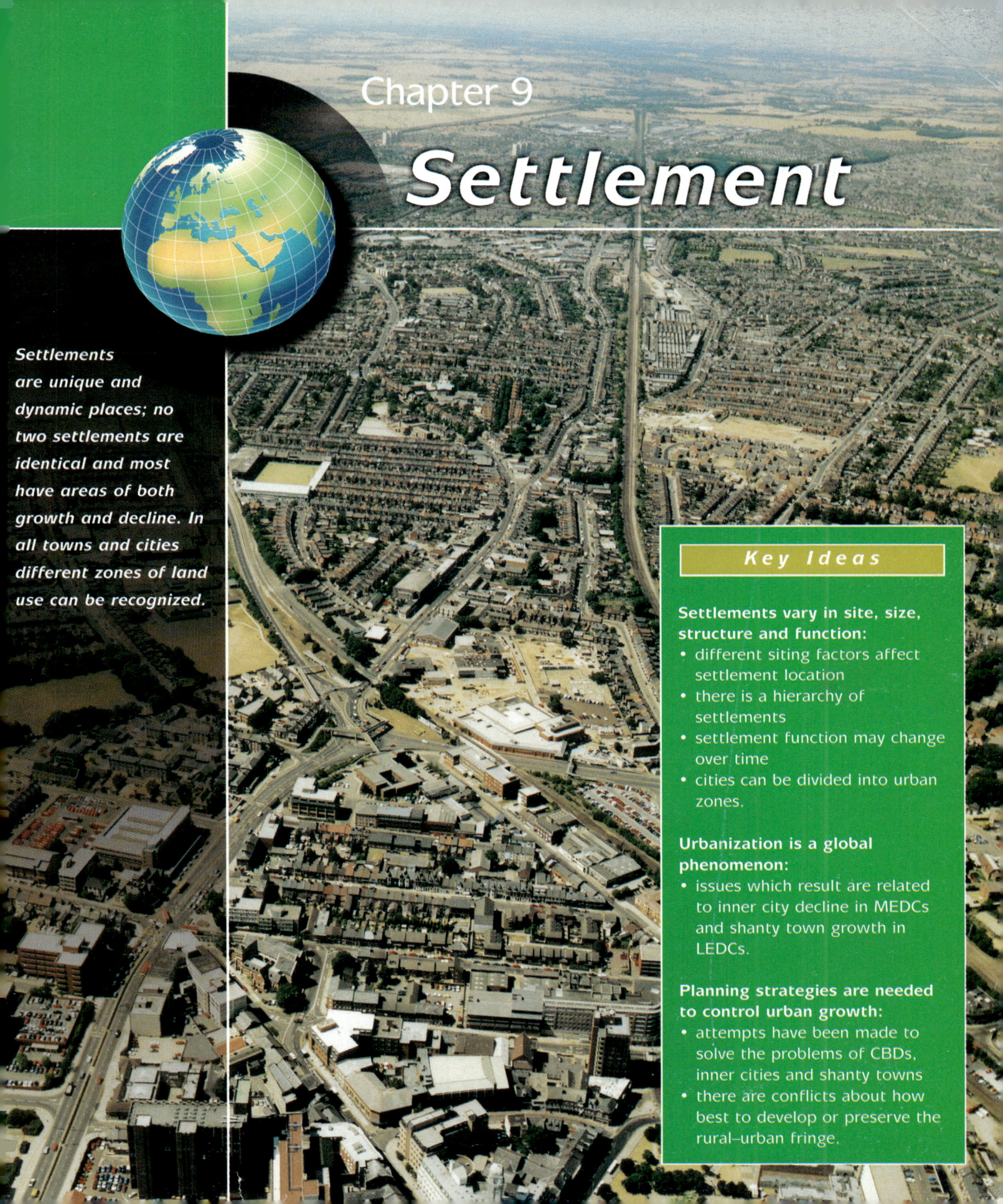

Chapter 9
Settlement

Settlements are unique and dynamic places; no two settlements are identical and most have areas of both growth and decline. In all towns and cities different zones of land use can be recognized.

Key Ideas

Settlements vary in site, size, structure and function:
- different siting factors affect settlement location
- there is a hierarchy of settlements
- settlement function may change over time
- cities can be divided into urban zones.

Urbanization is a global phenomenon:
- issues which result are related to inner city decline in MEDCs and shanty town growth in LEDCs.

Planning strategies are needed to control urban growth:
- attempts have been made to solve the problems of CBDs, inner cities and shanty towns
- there are conflicts about how best to develop or preserve the rural–urban fringe.

Settlement: site, situation and growth

Settlements are places where people live and work. In most countries there is a whole range of different-sized settlements, from individual farms and hamlets through to huge sprawling cities.

The physical land on which a settlement is built is called the **site**. Early settlements were located with great care. People had to grow their own food, find their own water supply, use the resources of the local area and even defend themselves against hostile neighbours. Think about how different life is today, especially in developed countries. Most families buy their food in huge supermarkets, there is electricity, piped gas and water supplies. Defence is no longer a factor.

Over time some settlements grew, others remained small, while some disappeared from the landscape. **Figure 1** shows the remains of an abandoned settlement on the Isle of Arran in Scotland. Settlements which grew were those with a good **situation**. The situation of a settlement is its location in relation to the surrounding area. A good situation is an area with the potential for settlement growth. Some settlements were at a route focus or bridging point. These encouraged trade which led to growth. Others were in rich farming areas and became market towns into which local farmers brought their produce for sale.

Site factors
Water supply

Water is essential for life. In arid or dry areas settlements locate near rivers, streams, wells or springs. These are called **wet-point sites**. In the chalk and

▲ **Figure 1** An abandoned settlement on the Isle of Arran, Scotland.

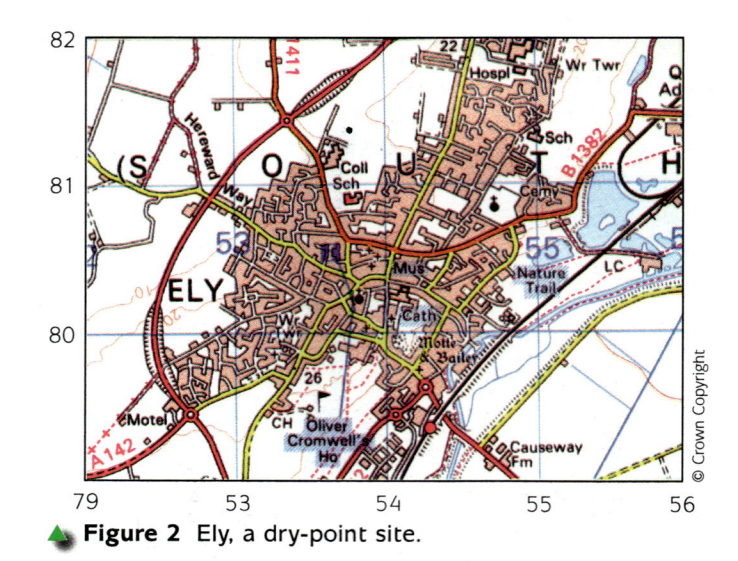

▲ **Figure 2** Ely, a dry-point site.

limestone areas of Britain there is often a line of spring-line settlements at the base of escarpments (page 27).

In some locations the land is marshy and prone to flooding. Settlement in these locations tends to locate on valley sides, gravel terraces or small hills above the flood plain. The Fenland area of Britain was once a marshy lowland and many of the settlements, such as Ely in Cambridgeshire (**Figure 2**), are sited on small mounds. These are **dry-point sites**.

Aspect and shelter

In the northern hemisphere the south-facing (*adrêt*) slopes are warmer than the cooler north-facing (*ubac*) slopes (**Figure 3**). The south-facing slopes are also sheltered from cold north or north-easterly winds. More settlements are sited on the south-facing slopes in the northern hemisphere and also on the lower hillslopes where there is even more shelter.

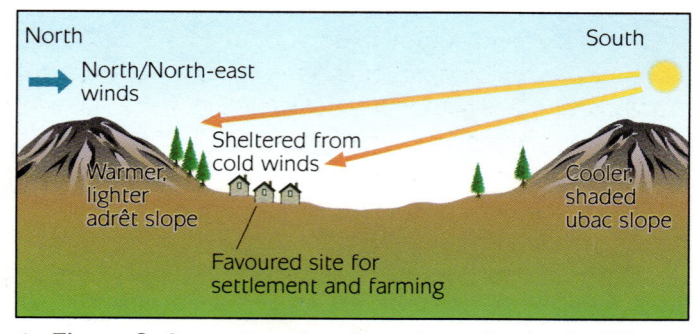

▲ **Figure 3** A cross-section through a valley in the UK running from west to east.

Defence

There are large numbers of settlements today which have the remains of castles, forts or town walls. This indicates just how important selecting a defensive site was in earlier times. In southern Italy there are many hilltop towns and villages. The people were driven onto the hilltops by invaders. Here they felt safer and could see any attackers approaching. Other defensive sites include Durham City (**Figure 4**), located on the inside of a huge incised meander, and Corfe Castle (**Figure 5**), sited at a gap within a ridge of chalk. The original site of Paris in France was on an island in the middle of the River Seine because it was a good defensive site, surrounded by water.

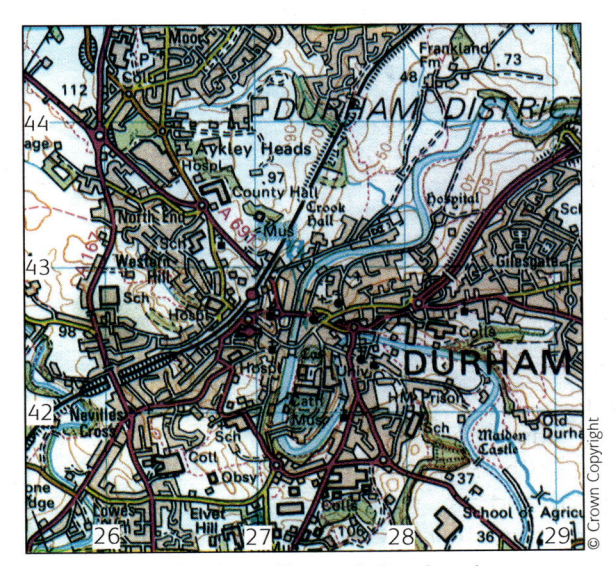

▲ **Figure 4** Durham City: a defensive site.

Resources

It was essential that early settlers had access to the resources they needed. A food supply was vital, so the areas with the most fertile soils often supported more settlements as more people could be fed. There is a higher density of rural settlement on the fertile loams and boulder clay soils in East Anglia than in the Pennines or the Chilterns where soils are thinner and less fertile.

Early settlements often relied upon timber for fuel as well as for building materials, so nearby woodland was an advantage. In other areas settlements were sited near a quarry or mine for building materials and mineral resources. County Durham has many examples of villages which only developed because of the local coal seams which could be mined. In Alaska and the oil-rich countries in the Middle East some settlements owe their existence to the oil reserves found nearby.

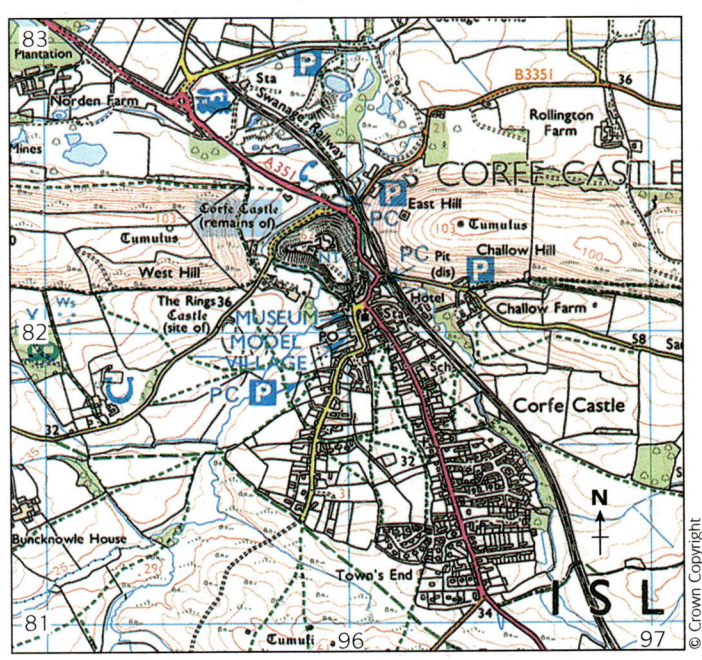

▲ **Figure 5** Corfe Castle: potential for growth?

Communications

Settlements often grew at **bridging points** or fords, around a crossroads, in gaps through hills or at a junction of valleys. Good communications often gave the settlement an advantage over others so that it grew as a **route focus** and attracted trade from other local settlements. Further encouragement to growth was given if the settlement had a castle, cathedral or monastery. The settlement grew as more people were needed to provide services for the soldiers or monks. The sketch map in **Figure 6** shows the site of Berwick-upon-Tweed in Northumberland and the reasons why it has grown into a town.

▲ **Figure 6** Sketch map of Berwick-upon-Tweed.

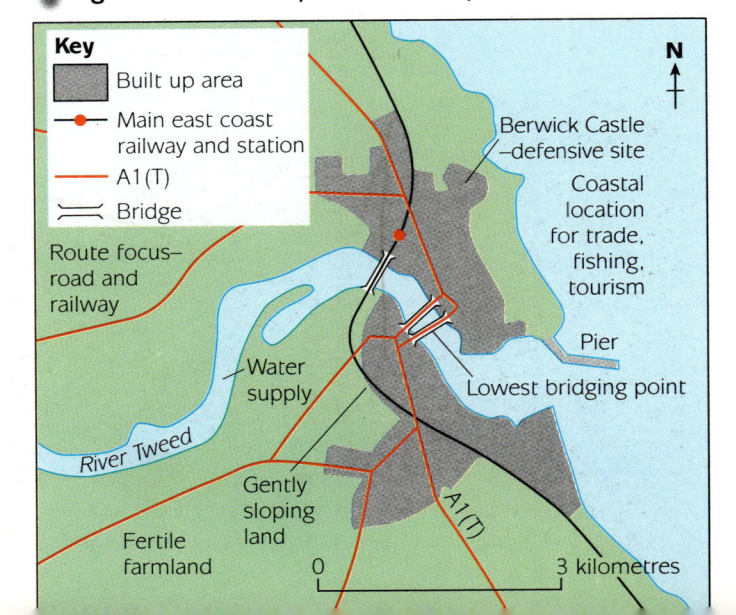

Hierarchy of settlement

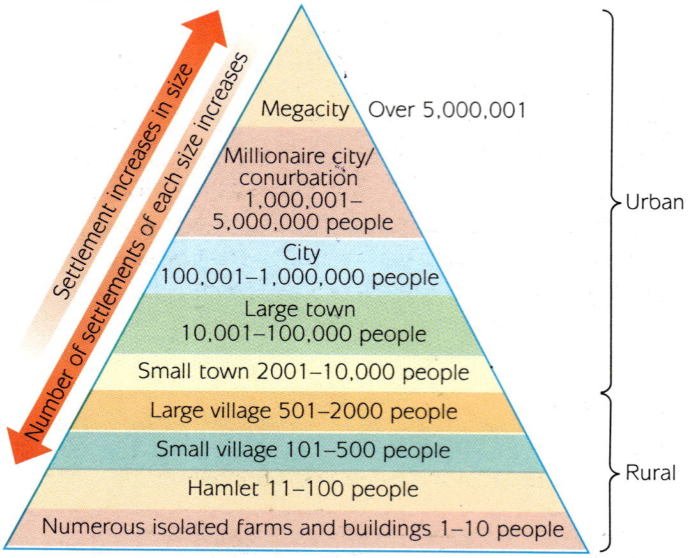
Settlement increases in size
Number of settlements of each size increases
Megacity Over 5,000,001
Millionaire city/ conurbation 1,000,001–5,000,000 people
City 100,001–1,000,000 people
Large town 10,001–100,000 people
Small town 2001–10,000 people
Large village 501–2000 people
Small village 101–500 people
Hamlet 11–100 people
Numerous isolated farms and buildings 1–10 people
Urban
Rural

Figure 1 **A hierarchy of settlements according to population size.**

A settlement hierarchy arranges settlements in order of importance, with individual farms and hamlets at the bottom and the single largest city, which is usually the capital city, at the top. Three different measures are often used:

- the size of the settlement in terms of its population
- the range and number of services
- the sphere of influence or the size of the area served by the settlement.

Settlement size

Figure 1 shows a hierarchy of settlements according to population size. There is no agreement about the size of a hamlet, a village or a small town. In Britain today, many villages have grown enormously with the addition of modern housing estates. Their populations have grown to over 2000 people, yet they would still be called villages because they do not fulfil all the requirements of a town, such as the wider range of services and employment opportunities.

Major shopping centre.
Several central covered centres.
Several suburban and edge-of-city centres.
One covered area in city centre.
Many shopping streets.
Several edge-of-city centres.
Several shopping streets.
One or two edge-of-city centres.
One main shopping street and market.
One village shop.
None

Figure 2 **A hierarchy of settlements based upon services.**

Services

The shops and services in a settlement provide the local population with its needs. The larger a settlement, the more services are needed to provide for the population. **Figure 2** suggests a hierarchy based upon the services in settlements of different sizes.

Sphere of influence

The sphere of influence is the area served by a settlement, sometimes called its **catchment area** or **hinterland**. The larger the settlement, the greater the number and variety of shops and services and the wider the area from which people will travel to use the centre. London's sphere of influence is the whole country. Outside London towns such as Plymouth, Newcastle, Leeds and Norwich serve local regions. Market towns serve smaller villages and farms in the area. A village only serves itself and some surrounding farms.

Smaller settlements tend to have fewer shops and services than larger settlements. The shops, such as a general store, newsagent, small supermarket and chemist tend to provide low-order or **convenience goods** such as newspapers, bread and milk. In larger settlements there are more shops and services. They include shops selling convenience goods but there are also department stores and specialist shops selling jewellery, sports equipment and furniture. These are called high-order or **comparison goods**. The types of goods and services in a settlement are linked to the following.

1. **The threshold population** – the minimum number of people required to support a service so that it remains profitable. In the UK this is about 300 for a village shop, 500 for a primary school, 25 000 for a shoe shop, 50 000 for a medium-sized store and 100 000 for a large one.
2. **The range of a good** – the maximum distance people are prepared to travel to use a shop or service. Most people do not travel great distances to buy a newspaper or do their shopping but they are prepared to travel further to purchase clothes, jewellery or furniture, which are more costly and bought less often.

Functions of a settlement

The function of a settlement is its purpose – why it is there and the 'work' that it does. It can be assessed by looking at the occupational structure of the settlement. Towns can be classified according to their function, as shown in **Figure 3**. Many of the larger towns and cities are multi-functional, probably with a mixture of residential, industrial, commercial and educational functions.

Description	Definition
Towns with a balanced occupational structure	No single employment group dominates
Fishing towns	Fishing employs over 5 per cent of workers in the town
Mining towns	Mining employs over 20 per cent of workers in the town
Quarrying towns	Quarrying employs over 20 per cent of workers in the town
Engineering towns	Engineering employs over 15 per cent of workers in the town
Chemical towns	As for engineering
Shipbuilding towns	As for engineering
Transport towns	As for engineering
Resort towns	Personal service and entertainment employ over 20 per cent of workers in the town
Commercial towns	Commerce and finance form the largest single group, employing over 10 per cent of workers

▲ **Figure 3** A classification of towns by function.

Many settlements in Britain have changed their function over time. In some cases the original function no longer applies, such as the defensive function. Most settlements began with farming as their main function. Over time mechanization has reduced the need for farmworkers and therefore many villages, especially those close to large urban areas, now house workers in all types of employment who travel elsewhere to work. These settlements are called **commuter** or **dormitory villages**. They have often expanded with the addition of a new housing estate, and the residents commute to work in the cities nearby. In County Durham and South Wales many villages began as farming settlements. During the Industrial Revolution many new villages were created and some existing villages found themselves close to coal seams that could be mined. These villages expanded, with pit head workings, rows of colliery terraces, railway lines and new services, e.g. churches, public houses and schools. By the mid-1990s many village mines had closed. The earlier closures led to a decline in population and shops and services closed as people moved to find jobs in mines elsewhere. Today many of these villages have become dormitory settlements with the addition of a modern housing estate. **Figure 4** charts the history of Shincliffe, a former farming and mining village in County Durham.

Activities

1 Using a map of your local area and **Figures 1** and **2**, complete a copy of the table below.

Settlement hierarchy	Population size	Example from my local area	Functions
Conurbation			
City			
Town			
Village			
Hamlet			
Isolated farms			

2 a Define the term **sphere of influence**.
  b Giving reasons, state where you and your family would go to buy:
     (i)   a magazine and some sweets
     (ii) the weekly food shopping
     (iii) a new three-piece suite and clothes.

3 Study **Figure 4**.
  a How has the function of the village changed over time?
  b Describe and explain how the population of Shincliffe has changed.

Farming settlement — Middle Ages — Population growth — Mine opened — Population decline — Mine closed — Population growth — Commuter settlement — 2000

▲ **Figure 4** A changing village: Shincliffe in County Durham.

Urban growth

Urbanization is a process of urban growth which leads to a greater proportion of people being concentrated into towns and cities. In Britain, where urbanization has been going on for a long time, about 80 per cent of the population live in urban areas (**Figure 1**).

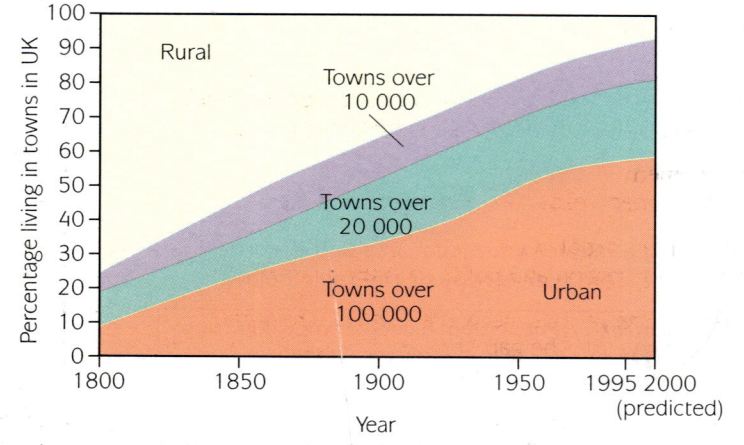

▲ **Figure 1** Urban population growth in the UK, 1800–2000.

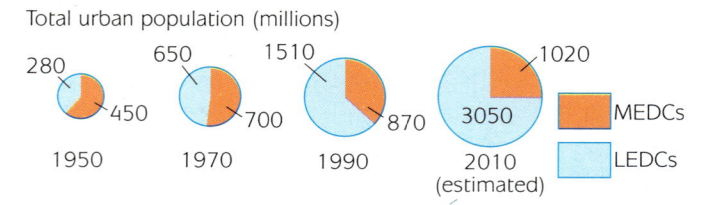

▲ **Figure 2** The world's urban population, 1950–2010 (in millions).

Cities in developed countries (MEDCs)

Towns and cities in MEDCs grew rapidly during the Industrial Revolution. In Britain this was mainly in the 19th century. At the time there was an Agricultural Revolution. New farm machinery meant less labour was needed on farms, so people moved to towns where there were plenty of new jobs available in new factories, mines and shipyards. Urbanization was happening. Although growth was quite rapid, about 10 per cent per annum, there were enough jobs for people, and mine and factory owners built houses for their workers.

Towns and cities continued to grow into the 20th century. This was a result of both push and pull factors (page 121) causing rural depopulation, particularly from the remote rural areas. However, in the late 20th century, some cities are seeing a loss of population from the run-down inner city areas. At the same time redevelopment schemes in the inner cities are attracting people back. Cities themselves have also continued to expand into the countryside but with no growth of population. People marrying later, the elderly living longer and the higher divorce rates have created smaller families. People also prefer to live in larger houses with bigger gardens.

Cities in developing countries (LEDCs)

The rapid growth of cities in LEDCs in the second half of the 20th century is much later than in MEDCs. The growth has been phenomenal, with rates reaching over 20 per cent per annum. The main causes of urbanization in the LEDCs are:

- rural to urban migration, a result of both push and pull factors (page 121)
- high rates of natural increase among the youthful population of these cities
- the concentration of industry and all other modern economic activities, making the cities a natural magnet for young people looking for work.

World urbanization

In the 20th century the rate of urbanization has been very rapid (**Figure 2**). While the world's population doubled between 1950 and 1990, the urban population trebled, and most of this growth has been in the cities of the LEDCs. There are two striking features of urbanization in the late 20th century:

1 Before 1950 most of the world's largest cities were in the MEDCs of the northern hemisphere (**Figure 4**). Since 1950 the growth of cities in the LEDCs has been rapid. Now, the developing countries, mostly located in the tropics, have most of the world's largest cities and the largest number of urban dwellers. The total population living in cities in the LEDCs is much greater than in the MEDCs, although the percentage of the population which is urbanized is lower.

2 A second feature of the urbanization process has been the growth of really large cities (**Figure 3**). In 1900, a city of over 1 million inhabitants was considered large. At the time there were only two, London and Paris, and they were described as **millionaire cities**. Now, there are over 300 millionaire cities and the ten largest cities in the world all have a population of over 10 million – these are sometimes called **megacities**. Deciding which is the largest city in the world is a problem. In many countries, collecting accurate census information is difficult and with rapid in-migration to a city it is impossible to have an accurate record. Mexico City is often said to be the world's largest city, with a population of about 20 million, while some say the largest is Tokyo.

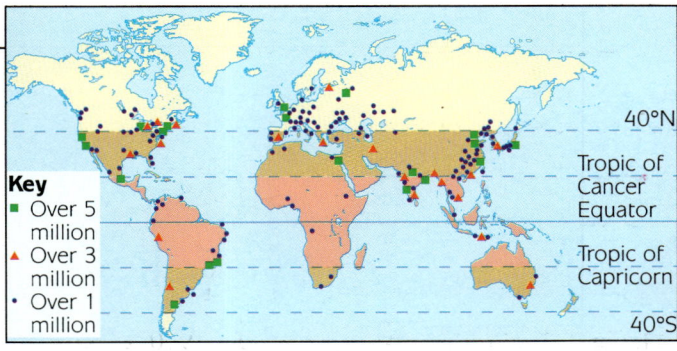

Figure 3 Growth and distribution of 'millionaire' cities.

Figure 5 Market traders arrive from the countryside to sell their produce.

Urbanization in the LEDCs has advantages and disadvantages:

Advantages

1 Economy
It stimulates the economy and farming around the city. Farms increase production and may switch from subsistence (growing food to feed the farmer and his family) to commercial (food grown for profit) to provide a surplus of food for sale in the cities.

2 Services
People have access to better services such as water supply, electricity, medical care and education.

3 Improved income
Casual, poorly paid work in the **informal sector** in the city still pays more than farmwork in rural areas. Many migrants arrive in the city and find that no work is available in the factories. They find work in the informal sector as street traders, selling fruit or shoe-cleaning or in workshop industries based in people's homes.

4 Opportunities for improvement
- Living in shanty towns is seen as a step on the ladder to improvement for the future generations – the slums of hope.
- Jobs in the informal sector may provide some skills and training which enable the migrant to gain a better job in the future.
- It eases some of the population pressure in rural areas and some funds flow back to the migrants' villages.

Disadvantages

1 Housing
Social and economic problems of housing provision lead to vast illegal shanty towns. Living conditions are appalling.

2 Employment
Unemployment leads to a large informal sector.

3 Other urban problems
There is congestion and pollution in the cities.

4 Widening the gap between the rich and the poor
Growth highlights the gap between rich and poor, which can lead to strikes and protests.

5 Problems in the rural areas
The rural areas may have insufficient able-bodied workers to farm the land. Agricultural production can fall.

Activity

1 Study **Figure 1**.
   a Copy and complete the table below.

Year	% of the population in urban areas in UK
1800	
1900	
1950	
2000 (projected)	

   b Describe how the rate of urban growth in the UK has changed since 1800.
   c Suggest reasons for the changes you notice in **b**.
   d In 1995 what percentage of the population lived in:
      (i) towns over 100 000
      (ii) towns between 20 000 and 100 000
      (iii) towns between 10 000 and 20 000
      (iv) rural areas?
   e From **d**, what is the relationship between the size of the urban area and the percentage of the urban population?

2 Describe and explain the changes in the growth and location of the world's urban population.

Rank order 1970		1995		2010 (estimated)	
1	New York (16.5)	Tokyo (26.8)		Tokyo (28.7)	
2	Tokyo (13.4)	São Paulo (16.4)		Bombay (24.3)	
3	London (10.5)	New York (16.3)		Shanghai (21.5)	
4	Shanghai (10.0)	Mexico City (15.6)		Lagos (20.8)	
5	Mexico City (8.6)	Bombay (15.1)		São Paulo (20.1)	
6	Los Angeles (8.4)	Shanghai (15.1)		Jakarta (19.2)	
7	Buenos Aires (8.4)	Los Angeles (12.4)		Mexico City (18.2)	
8	Paris (8.4)	Beijing (12.4)		Beijing (17.8)	
9	São Paulo (7.1)	Calcutta (11.7)		Karachi (17.6)	
10	Moscow (7.1)	Seoul (11.6)		New York (17.3)	

Source: United Nations Population Division, 1995

Figure 4 The world's largest cities (figures in millions of people).

Urban morphology

Urban land uses are the shops, industries, offices, housing, parks and open space found in larger settlements (towns and cities). Urban areas tend not to have a jumble of different land uses. Each type of land use usually clusters together to give distinctive **zones** such as the **Central Business District** (CBD), where shops and offices are concentrated. Other zones are formed by industrial areas and the vast suburban housing areas. **Morphology** is the term used to describe the internal structure of a city. Various urban models have been developed to show the arrangement of land-use zones within cities.

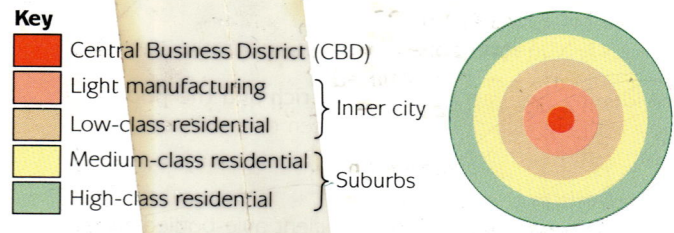

Key
- Central Business District (CBD)
- Light manufacturing ⎫ Inner city
- Low-class residential ⎭
- Medium-class residential ⎫ Suburbs
- High-class residential ⎭

▲ **Figure 1** The Burgess model.

Urban models for cities in MEDCs

The Burgess model (**Figure 1**), developed in the 1920s, has five concentric rings representing five land-use zones. The zones are arranged in a circular pattern around a Central Business District (CBD).

The Burgess model is based upon two main ideas:

1. Cities grow outwards from the original site and hence property becomes younger as the outskirts of the town are reached. The original site is generally where the CBD is located today.

2. Land costs are highest in the CBD where land is in short supply and, traditionally, accessibility is greatest. Only high-profit-making businesses can afford to locate in the CBD. Away from the city centre, costs decrease and more land is available, allowing industries and housing to locate here.

Hoyt's model in **Figure 2**, developed in the 1930s, combines concentric rings with sectors of land use. The model contains the same five land-use zones as in the Burgess model but was designed later. Transport routes had become more important as a locational factor for industry and a sector of industry was added to the model with a zone of low-class housing alongside. The low-paid workers lived adjacent to the factories because they were unable to afford high travel costs to work.

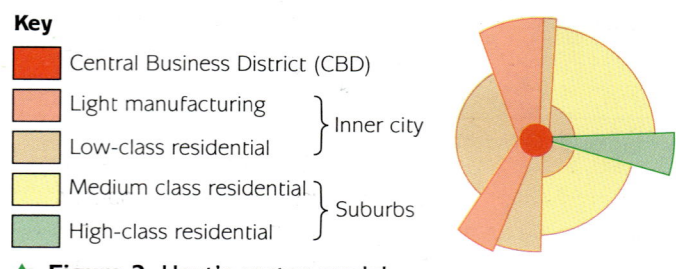

Key
- Central Business District (CBD)
- Light manufacturing ⎫ Inner city
- Low-class residential ⎭
- Medium class residential ⎫ Suburbs
- High-class residential ⎭

▲ **Figure 2** Hoyt's sector model.

An urban model for a city in LEDCs

The model in **Figure 3** is based upon cities in Brazil. As in all of the models, the CBD is located centrally. All CBDs also tend to look very similar, with skyscrapers and Western-style shops. The model also has an industrial zone located along a road or railway, which matches the Hoyt model. However, there are some striking differences between the models. The city in the developing world is much less regular, with more zones. The land uses are less well segregated. There is only a very small high-class sector, mostly located near the CBD or on prime sites, such as near a beach, as in Rio de Janeiro, or on high ground with a good view. There is no evidence of any middle-class housing zone similar to the suburbs of the cities in the developed world. The largest zone is that of the shanty towns which may begin close to the CBD and stretch vast distances to the outskirts of the city. The shanties may occupy wasteland or swamps within the city, or some of the steeper slopes. The developing world city also has no traditional industrial areas. Industries are mostly modern factories in zones along lines of communication. Most of the industries have 'followed the people' to the city, unlike in the MEDCs where the people moved to the cities because work was available.

Key
- Central Business District (CBD)
- Elite group
- Zone of upgraded self-built houses
- Modern factories along main road
- Zone of active improvement of housing
- Shanty towns/ squatter settlements

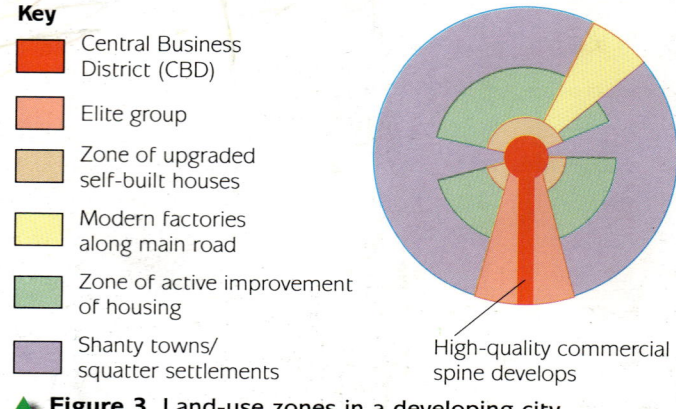

High-quality commercial spine develops

▲ **Figure 3** Land-use zones in a developing city.

Urban zones in British cities

1. The **Central Business District** is at the heart of the city, where the settlement was originally sited. On an OS map it can be recognized by historic buildings, where several main roads meet, a high density of buildings and bus and railway stations, often at the edge of the CBD.

2. The **Inner City** zone grew during the Industrial Revolution. It is a mixed zone of terraced housing and industry. The terraces were built along narrow streets, giving them a grid-like appearance. Some of the industries cluster together in an industrial zone alongside railway sidings, canals or rivers. Some inner city areas have been redeveloped with high-rise blocks of flats with open spaces between.

3. The **suburbs** began to expand after World War I. These housing estates have an irregular road pattern with avenues and cul-de-sacs. Houses are more varied, with semi-detached and detached properties.

4. In the **rural–urban fringe**, different land uses may be found, some rural, such as farmland and forestry, and some connected to the city, such as golf courses, airports, and out-of-town shopping centres.

5. Throughout the urban area **recreational facilities** may be found, such as parks, and sports fields.

6. **Industrial estates** have been built on the fringes of many towns and cities, where there is more space for single-storey factories and car parks.

▼ **Figure 4** OS map of Luton, Beds., 1:50 000 (2cm = 1km).

Activity

Study **Figure 4**, the OS map of Luton.
a Which urban zone is represented by each of the six grid squares outlined in black?
b Describe the land uses in each of the six squares.
c Describe and explain the pattern of land uses in Luton.
d To what extent does the pattern of urban zones fit the Burgess or the Hoyt model?

The Central Business District

The typical Central Business District (**Figure 1**) dominates the commercial and cultural activity in a city. In many large cities it is immediately recognizable by the tall skyscrapers, the neon lights at night and the very high density of buildings, traffic and people. The CBD is usually highly accessible. It is the focus of roads, with bus and railway stations nearby. The largest urban areas often have a mass rapid transport system such as the London Underground and Newcastle Metro. The CBD usually has the highest density of bus services and taxis in the whole of the urban area. Although the residential population is only very small, during the day and evening the CBD is crowded with people working, shopping or seeking entertainment.

Main functions of the CBD

Shops
The CBD is usually at the top of the shopping hierarchy in a city. It has the widest range of shops and the largest department stores. Shops mainly sell comparison or high-order goods and they draw their customers from a wide sphere of influence. The highest land costs are in the centre of the CBD. Here, in the **core** of the CBD (**Figure 2**), are found large department stores and branches of many national chains of shops. Smaller, often privately owned, shops are located on the edges of the CBD in the fringe area called the **frame**. Some shops, such as clothing, shoe and jewellery shops, tend to cluster together to take advantage of competition, while others are more dispersed, such as newsagents and chemists.

Offices
Banks, building societies, solicitors, company headquarters, insurance companies and government offices occupy high-rise office blocks or the upper floors above shops in the CBD.

Culture and entertainment
Parts of the CBD 'come alive' at night as the theatres, cinemas, clubs, bars and restaurants attract customers. Certain parts of cities have become famous for their nightlife, such as London's West End and Newcastle Quayside.

The CBD of a city is not static; it is a dynamic area going through phases of growth and decline. Pass through any CBD of a large city to see areas in decay, with closed shops and a rundown appearance, and others that appear lively, smart and successful. The CBD also

▲ **Figure 1** Leeds CBD.

experiences problems of traffic congestion, parking and pollution as well as those caused by lack of space and shortage of land. Local planners have implemented a variety of different schemes to attempt to solve the problems of the CBD.

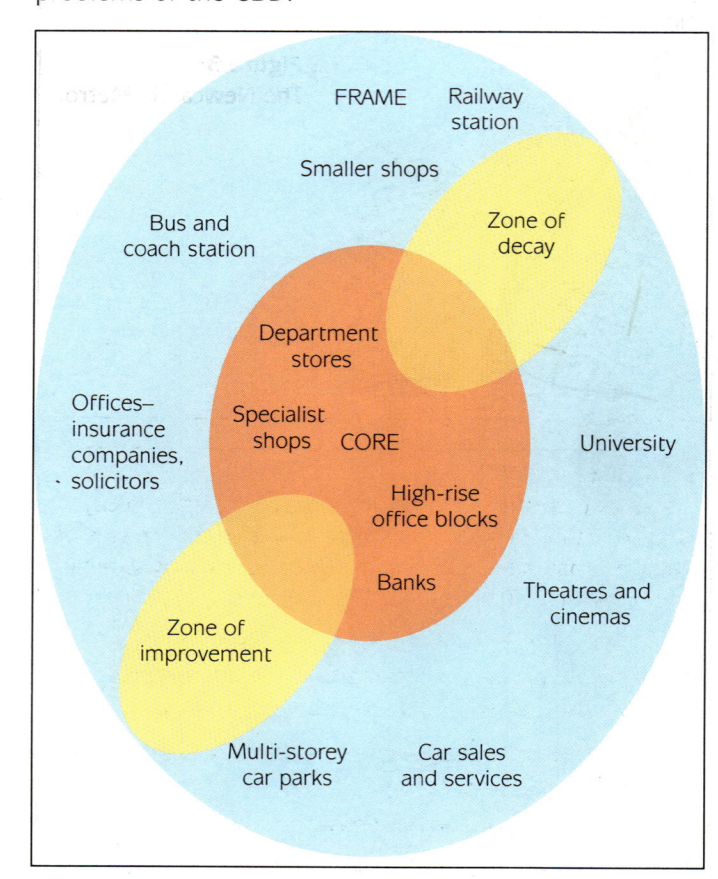

▲ **Figure 2** The core and frame in the CBD.

Problems and attempted solutions in the CBD

Traffic congestion

Towns grew and the street patterns were established before the motor car was invented. Now high car ownership and the concentration of shops, services and employment in the CBD create massive problems of congestion and parking in city centres. Roads are often narrow, with little pavement space, and in some cities the rush-hour traffic is in danger of causing 'grid-lock'. Attempted solutions include:

- ring roads and by-passes to divert traffic not going into the city centre
- urban motorways and flyovers
- public transport schemes such as 'park and ride', the Newcastle Metro (**Figure 3**), trams in Manchester
- multi-storey car parks
- pedestrianization of high streets.

In the late 20th century the emphasis is shifting from accommodating the motor car to schemes to ban or charge cars for going into the city centre. Environmentally friendly forms of transport are being encouraged, such as buses which run on methane, and electric cars. Integrated public transport schemes such as metro systems are a high priority for many local authorities to reduce the number of cars in city centres, especially cars containing just one person. In Leeds lone motorists are now charged a toll along certain roads.

Figure 3 The Newcastle Metro.

Pollution

Water, land, air and noise pollution are all common in city centres. Pollution is thought to contribute to the stresses of living in urban areas and to some diseases, such as asthma and bronchitis. Attempted solutions include:

- laws against litter and dumping sewage in rivers
- improved provision of litter bins and road sweeping
- Clean Air Acts that allow only the use of smokeless fuels
- clean fuel technology and vehicles which run on methane gas or electricity
- banning heavy lorries from passing through city centres
- increased planting of trees and shrubs.

Lack of space and the high cost of land

Competition for land has led to high prices, and growing firms find it difficult to find space. In some CBDs the smaller retailers have been forced away from the city centre because of the high costs. Attempted solutions include:

- high-rise buildings to increase the floor area available
- new retailing areas in out-of-town shopping centres (**Figure 4**) in the suburbs or rural–urban fringe in a process called **decentralization**.

Figure 4 The Gateshead MetroCentre.

Urban decline

Parts of some CBDs have declined. Shops and offices have closed down and the empty buildings are vandalized (**Figure 5**). City centres compete with out-of-town shopping centres to cater for the growing demands of shoppers. Attempted solutions include:

- redevelopment of zones of decline in the CBD such as King's Cross and Covent Garden in London and Eldon Square in Newcastle
- expansion of the CBD into areas of the inner city – old factories and substandard terraced housing have been cleared, rehousing the occupants in the suburbs or New Towns and filling the space with new shopping and office developments.

Figure 5 Decline in the West End of Newcastle upon Tyne.

Test questions

a List six characteristics of the CBD. (6 marks)
b Using **Figure 2**, describe four differences between the core and the frame of the CBD. (4 marks)
c Suggest reasons why so few people live in the CBD. (3 marks)
d (i) Name the four main problems in the CBD. (4 marks)
  (ii) Describe how planners can attempt to solve *one* of these problems. (3 marks)

The inner city

Figure 1 Back-to-back terraced housing for workers in the inner city.

Figure 2 Once Victorian terraces for the middle classes, now multiple-occupancy flats and bedsits for students and ethnic minorities.

The inner city is the zone between the Central Business District and the suburban housing areas. In British cities the inner city grew during the Industrial Revolution. Factories were built on the edges of the historic towns, now the CBD. The industries mostly located alongside rivers, canals or railways. High-density terraced housing (**Figure 1**) was built nearby to accommodate the workers moving from the countryside to take up jobs in the factories. The housing was cheap and often poor quality but it was close to the workplace so people could walk to work. Factory owners and wealthy business people also lived in the more desirable areas of the inner city. Their housing was also terraced, but larger, often three- or four-storey including basements and attic rooms where the servants would live (**Figure 2**). Local services catered for the needs of the people, including corner shops, schools, public houses, churches, libraries and parks. This resulted in a mixture of land uses in the inner cities.

In the 1960s and 1970s many local authorities tried to improve parts of the inner cities that were suffering from decay. The main problems were poor housing and a decaying environment. The old terraces with no proper kitchens, bathrooms or central heating were thought to be old-fashioned and below modern-day standards of housing. The answer at the time was the high-rise flat (**Figure 3**). In Glasgow 262 multi-storey blocks of flats were built from 8 to 31 storeys high. In most cities, including Glasgow, the flats have been a disaster. Many have been demolished after only about 30 years, while the terraces had stood for over 100 years.

In addition, many inner cities were affected by efforts to solve problems of traffic congestion in the CBD. The congestion was tackled by building huge multi-storey car parks, ringroads, flyovers and urban motorways for which part of the inner city was used.

In the 1980s and 1990s the inner cities continued to decline and the problems worsened. In some areas, such as Brixton, Liverpool and Manchester, there was much unrest and riots broke out. Most inner city areas suffered from serious environmental, social and economic problems (**Figure 4**). The riots led to an enquiry and a report by Lord Scarman, after which a new phase of inner city regeneration began.

Figure 3 High-rise flats – the 1960s answer to the problems of inner cities?

Environmental problems

Housing:
- Decaying terraced housing
- Poorly built tower blocks

Pollution and decay:
- Air, land and water pollution
- Derelict warehouses and churches
- High levels of graffiti and vandalism
- Traffic congestion.

Poor services:
- Lack of open space and poor facilities.

Social problems
- Above-average concentration of pensioners, lone parents, ethnic minorities and students
- High levels of disease, illness and overcrowding
- Rising crime rates
- Poor police and community relations

Economic problems
- Poverty and low income
- High unemployment, often over 50 per cent male unemployment
- Declining industries
- Poor access to motorways and airports
- High land values.

Figure 4 The environmental, social and economic problems of British inner cities.

Improving the inner cities

Urban renewal and urban redevelopment have taken place in many inner cities since the 1970s. Now it is much more common for local communities to be involved in the planning of the changes. Consultation with the local people is less likely to lead to disaster, and the people value the changes and feel greater ownership of their environment. New schemes have also tried to attract people back into the inner city. Some schemes include the creation of executive-style apartments to encourage wealthier people to return to the inner cities. Attractive, modern riverside apartments are a feature of many riverside development schemes, including the London Docklands, St Peter's Wharf in Newcastle upon Tyne and Salford Docks in Greater Manchester.

> **Information box**
>
> **Urban renewal** – the renovation and improvement of existing buildings.
>
> **Urban regeneration** – 'knock it all down and start again'.

Improving Glasgow's inner city areas

Glasgow's inner city

Comprehensive Development Areas (CDAs) were first proposed in the 1950s. The CDAs were areas targeted for improvement. Grants and tax exemptions were given to companies locating in the CDAs. The Gorbals area of Glasgow was a CDA and the early schemes had a policy of 'Knock it all down and start again'. Large numbers of the tenement buildings (**Figure 5**) in the Gorbals were demolished to be replaced by high-rise flats. The policy was abandoned in 1974 after high-rise flats were seen to be a mistake – the inner city had gradually become empty of people, creating a 'dead heart'.

▲ **Figure 5** A Glasgow tenement.

Glasgow Garden Festival (1988)

The Garden Festival was planned on 39 hectares of derelict land in the dockland area of Glasgow's inner city. The area has 1100 new houses and flats, a new road, a business park and 4.5 hectares of open space based upon one of the parkland theme areas of the festival.

The Govan initiative (1986–94)

This was a partnership between the public and private sector that aimed to regenerate the local economy by encouraging new business into the area. The Govan area is a patchwork of different land uses with blocks of industry, housing, services and derelict land and buildings. Improvements have included:

- 'start-up' units for businesses
- landscaping schemes to improve vacant land
- education, training and advice on home and industrial security
- the reopening of the one remaining shipyard
- skills training programmes.

Turning tower blocks into pagodas

A renovation scheme is going to great lengths to disguise two grim towers of 1960s council flats in Paisley near Glasgow. The architects have decided to replace the flat roofs with Japanese pagoda-style roofs in blue aluminium. The two towers have also received blue and grey panelling bolted on top of the original concrete.

The original high-rise flats were cold, poorly insulated and prone to condensation. They had become sordid places to live. It cost £1 477 000, a fraction of the cost of building 112 new homes from scratch. The scheme has been so successful that there are plans to refurbish five similar tower blocks.

▲ **Figure 6** Adapted from *The Daily Telegraph*, 14 October 1994.

Residential environments

In most British cities the sprawling suburbs cover the greatest land area. The suburbs are mostly residential, housing the population of the city. Moving towards the outskirts of a city the housing becomes younger and the density decreases.

Local Authority housing

In the 1930s, new council estates were built in the suburbs, often still within walking distance of factories or close to main roads with access to public transport. In the 1960s, as inner city terraces were cleared, new council estates were built further out in the fringes of the suburbs. A greater effort was made to vary the size and type of the accommodation provided, with single-storey terraces, maisonettes with two or three storeys, and high-rise tower blocks. The estates often had free-standing garages and more open space.

The Victorian terraces of the inner city

High-density housing was built in back-to-back terraces. Built in long straight rows, they give a grid-iron street layout. They were originally built as two-up two-down houses with no separate bathroom and kitchen. They each had a backyard with an outdoor toilet and coal store. No gardens or garages were provided. Today many have been improved with the addition of a two-storey extension to provide kitchen and bathroom, double-glazing, and central heating. Car parking can still be a problem as there is no space for garages.

Rural–urban fringe | Suburbs | Inner-city | Central

Chapter 9 · Settlement

Inner city redevelopment

Two phases of redevelopment can often be recognized:

1 The high-rise flats built in the 1960s by local authorities to rehouse people from the demolished terraces.

2 More recent modern housing built by private builders in varied styles, sizes and prices. Some are aimed at first-time buyers, while executive apartments have been built in prestigious locations, for example on riversides, in an attempt to diversify the social structure of the inner city.

Inter-war housing

Typically these are semi-detached houses with bay windows and metal window frames. Most have front and back gardens but at first, few had garages as car ownership was still unusual. Some of the housing was in estates, and some was built along main roads as ribbon development.

Post-war private housing

More recent housing has a greater variety of styles and designs. Some large private housing estates have been built, while smaller patches of land within the suburbs have been used for in-fill housing development. In the 1990s there has been an increase in the building of very expensive executive-type housing, costing over £250 000 per unit. These estates are well planned and spacious and less uniform in their layout.

| district | Inner-city | Suburbs | Rural–urban fringe |

The rural–urban fringe

The rural–urban fringe is another area of mixed land uses. It lies beyond the suburbs at the edge of the built-up area.

Urban sprawl

The growth of cities has caused urban sprawl outwards into the countryside, engulfing small villages, farms and woodland. Land is in demand for housing, industrial estates, business parks, out-of-town shopping centres, bypasses, airports, recreational amenities and public utilities such as waterworks and sewage farms. Much of the growth in the past was haphazard and cities have gradually increased in size. Now planning authorities are actively involved in trying to control the growth of urban areas. There are many conflicts and issues surrounding the rural–urban fringe.

Motorways and bypasses

In the 1980s car ownership and road building were encouraged. The result has been enormous pressure on the existing road network, congested city centres and villages damaged by the weight and noise of traffic. The solution in the 1980s and early 1990s was to build more roads, but many of the schemes attracted considerable opposition from local people and conservation groups (**Figure 1**). By the late 1990s public opinion and Government policy were changing. Increasingly schemes plan to reduce the amount of

11 January 1996
Protesters Halt By-Pass Work Again

6 May 1994
Road Protesters Ready For Battle on Solsbury Hill

14 June 1995
Carrageway duel to save the Blackdown Hills

18 February 1996
Newbury protesters told how to destroy

▲ **Figure 1** No more roads, please!

traffic improving public transport, charging tolls on motorways, putting up the cost of fuel and car parking in town centres and encouraging more environmentally friendly forms of transport. Many new road schemes planned for the late 1990s and the early 2000s have been scrapped.

Commercial and industrial developments

Out-of-town locations have many advantages (**Figure 2**) to the developers of business parks, shopping centres and industrial estates:

- plenty of space for large superstores, single-storey factories and car parks
- cheaper land than in urban locations
- access to motorways and airports
- a large labour pool and market from the nearby suburban population
- open space, pleasant countryside
- cleaner, less congested environment.

In the 1980s and 1990s cities rushed to build on the rural–urban fringe. New industrial estates, business

▲ **Figure 2** Doxford International Technology park on the outskirts of Sunderland.

parks and out-of-town shopping centres mushroomed. Such developments provide the suburban population with improved shopping and employment opportunities. However, it is now clear that these developments bring disadvantages too:

- increasing urban sprawl
- loss of agricultural land and public open space
- loss of trade in traditional city centres
- increasing pollution and traffic congestion.

Increasingly, local authorities are applying stricter planning controls in the rural–urban fringe to protect the environment and to counter the damage caused to existing city centres and industrial areas.

Conservation and green belts

Green belts were the first attempt to halt the sprawl of cities. They are areas of green and open land on the margins of towns and cities, perhaps 10km wide, in which urban development is restricted. Britain's first green belt was created around London. Following the 1946 New Towns Act a ring of New Towns was built beyond the green belt, to house the overspill population and people made homeless by redevelopment in the inner city. Many other towns and cities also created green belts (**Figure 3**) – as recently as 1998, the Department for the Environment announced a new green belt around Durham City. Green belts have had some success but in the 1990s there have been pressures to release green belt land for development, and many exceptions have been allowed to the 'no building' policy. The orbital motorway or M25 around London was partly built on London's green belt. Several hundreds of hectares of green belt land have been released north-east of Newcastle upon Tyne for new housing. Many local people and members of conservation groups oppose the loss of green belt land and want the policy to be more strictly enforced.

THE GREEN BELTS
Since the 1947 Town and Country Planning Act, green belts have been established around major towns to check urban sprawl.

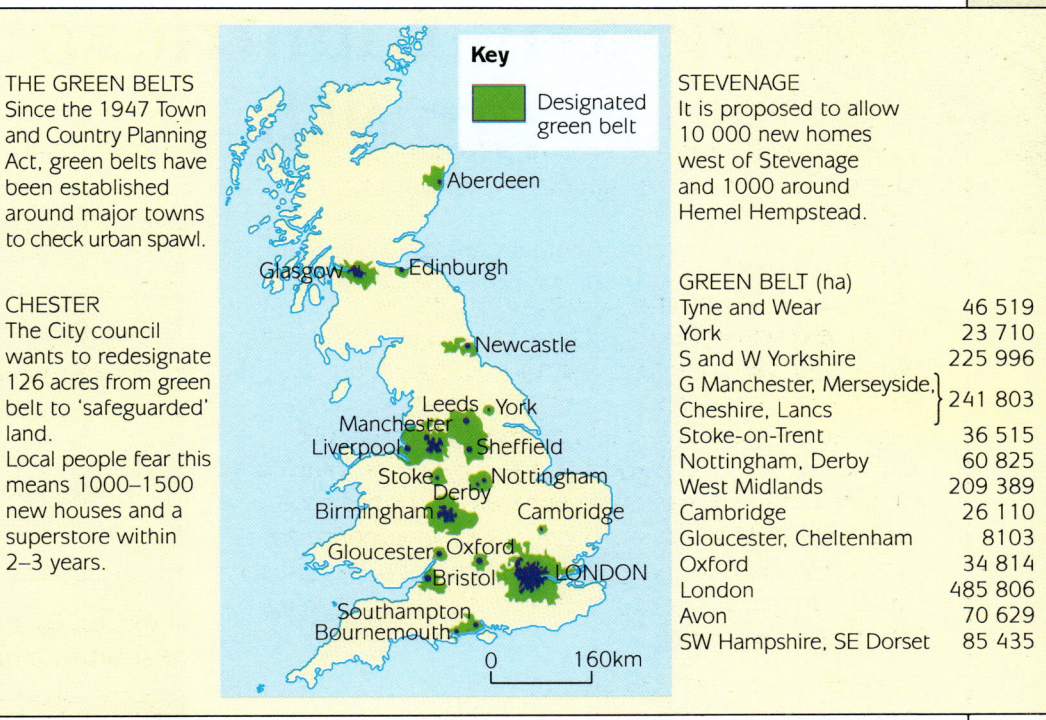

CHESTER
The City council wants to redesignate 126 acres from green belt to 'safeguarded' land.
Local people fear this means 1000–1500 new houses and a superstore within 2–3 years.

STEVENAGE
It is proposed to allow 10 000 new homes west of Stevenage and 1000 around Hemel Hempstead.

GREEN BELT (ha)
Tyne and Wear	46 519
York	23 710
S and W Yorkshire	225 996
G Manchester, Merseyside, Cheshire, Lancs	241 803
Stoke-on-Trent	36 515
Nottingham, Derby	60 825
West Midlands	209 389
Cambridge	26 110
Gloucester, Cheltenham	8103
Oxford	34 814
London	485 806
Avon	70 629
SW Hampshire, SE Dorset	85 435

▲ **Figure 3** Green belts in the UK, 1995.

Hobby farming

Green belts around towns and cities have protected some farmers by preserving the farmland. However, in unprotected areas of the rural–urban fringe, farmers have to compete for land with businesses which can make higher profits from the land than farming. Some farmers have also had increased problems with vandalism, sheep worrying, theft and crop trampling as the urban areas have gradually expanded.

For most of the 20th century people have argued against the loss of valuable agricultural land to the bulldozer. However, in recent years this argument has lost some of its importance. The intensification of agriculture and the overproduction of farm produce has led to European policies of 'set aside' where farmers are paid *not* to farm the land. Other pressures such as the beef crisis, the reduction in subsidies and the children of farmers preferring to seek employment in cities have meant the sale of many farms in the rural–urban fringes. The farms are rarely sold in one unit as working farms.

▲ **Figure 4** Hobby farming.

The farmer makes a greater profit on the sale if there is planning permission for housing, industry or commercial functions or if the land is sold in separate plots. The demand by urban dwellers for a piece of the countryside has led to a growth in small plots used for **hobby farming**. The land may be used to grow fruit and vegetables or to keep a few chickens, goats and sheep. '**Horsiculture**' is also very common as the urban dweller demands space for horse riding close to their suburban home. The owners of the plots often erect stables, sheds, greenhouses and even a new house, leading to the gradual urbanization of the countryside (**Figure 4**).

Developing countries: the problems of urban growth

There is a great gulf between the rich and poor in cities of the developing world. There are relatively few rich people but vast numbers of the poor. The rich live in very comfortable homes, either detached with gardens or in apartment complexes with security systems, air-conditioning and maid service. The children are healthy and well educated and many go to university and into well-paid jobs. Many of the rich live in areas close to the CBD with easy access to the shops and services. In contrast, the numbers of poor people are swelling all the time as more and more migrants arrive from the rural areas. Urban growth has been so rapid and on such a large scale in developing countries that the cities are facing serious problems.

Traffic congestion and pollution
As in cities in MEDCs, traffic congestion and pollution are major problems. Traffic congestion can be even more acute than in MEDC cities – in south-east Asia, cars, buses and lorries compete for road space with scooters, donkeys, cows, rickshaws and pedestrians. The accident rate and air and noise pollution levels are all very high. On 17 March 1992 all children in Mexico City were told to stay at home as air pollution had reached dangerously high levels.

Unemployment and poverty
New factories have been built in many LEDC cities but job creation cannot keep pace with the demand for employment. There are large numbers of unemployed. Many more are underemployed in the informal sector as street pedlars, shoe-shiners or domestic servants. The shortage of well-paid employment leads a large sector of the population to live in poverty in the cities.

Housing shortages
The rapid rate of growth of the cities has created a shortage of housing, particularly low-cost affordable housing. As a consequence vast, sprawling shanty towns have developed.

Problems caused by the growth of shanty towns
Housing
Most large cities in developing countries are surrounded by spontaneous and makeshift shanty towns (**Figure 1**). In Mexico City, Calcutta, Mumbai (Bombay) and São Paulo, over 50 per cent of the population live in shanty towns. Shanty towns have different names in different parts of the world – *favelas* in Brazil, *barriadas* in Peru and *bustees* in Calcutta.

Figure 1 Shanty towns on a hillside in Rio de Janeiro, Brazil.

The shanties are sited on any spare land the migrants can find. This includes steep slopes (as in Rio de Janeiro and Lima), swamps and rubbish tips. The areas used are often avoided by others because they are prone to landslides, flooding or industrial pollution. The shanty towns are illegal settlements and the people are squatters. The shacks and shelters are homemade, built from anything the people can find, including bits of wood, sheets of corrugated iron, cardboard, polythene and five-gallon oil drums. They are a real fire hazard. Typically, there are usually only one or two rooms where the family eats, sleeps and lives. Most shacks lack basic amenities such as electricity, gas, drainage, running water and toilets. In the *bustees* of Calcutta one water tap and one toilet may be shared among 30 people. The sewage often runs down the streets (**Figure 3**) and pollutes the water supply, leading to diseases such as cholera and typhoid. Washing and drinking-water supplies are very unhygienic. There is often no refuse collection, and any spare space becomes filled with rubbish, another breeding ground for disease.

Transport

Many of the shanty towns lack any basic transport infrastructure. Roads may only be dirt tracks, and few people own a bicycle, let alone a car. Most rely on walking or public transport. Many people who have to travel long distances to work in industrial areas or the CBD find the costs of the overcrowded and infrequent public transport too high.

Food and health

Families live in poverty, with little money for food or clothes. Many families, and especially the children, suffer from malnutrition. Local shops, often dirty and fly-ridden, sell a limited range of poor-quality foods. People live on one or two staple foods that lack the proteins, vitamins and calories of a healthy balanced diet. Infant mortality rates are high because babies are the most vulnerable to disease.

The lack of clean water and sanitation encourages water-borne diseases such as dysentery, typhoid and diarrhoea. Diseases spread very quickly because of the high density of people and housing (**Figure 2**). Health care is often too expensive and too far away. Life expectancy is low.

Figure 2 Sewage running down an open drain in Goa, India.

Education

Many children do not go to school or only manage to attend primary school. They remain illiterate and lack the skills to gain jobs, and frequently leave school early to earn money to help the family survive. Children as young as six years old may do some shoe-shining or roadside selling.

Employment

There are usually no jobs in the shanty towns. Migrants from rural areas are often poorly educated with few skills. Many join the informal sector of employment as street traders, roadside mechanics and domestic servants. Others use their home as their place of work and sell food, clothes, wood and metal. Few people are unemployed but most are underemployed, their work taking up few hours in the week and earning very little. A few may get jobs in local factories but travelling to work is very expensive, the wages are poor, the conditions of work dreadful and the hours long. Those who manage to earn a reasonable wage often build a better home or even move.

Social problems

The stress of living in the shanty towns leads to frequent breakdown of marriages and an increase in crimes, especially vandalism and theft. In some cities there are large numbers of children who live on the streets, a product of the social problems in the shanty towns.

Case Study – Brazil

Solving the problems of cities in the developing world

Nearly all large cities in the developing world suffer similar problems: vast sprawling shanty towns, a lack of basic amenities and services, inadequate transport and widespread pollution. However, the countries themselves have little money to spend on improvements. Cairo in Egypt and São Paulo in Brazil have both attempted to solve some of the problems, but have not had much lasting success. The two cities illustrate just how difficult it is for a country to solve the problems of urban growth with limited funds.

In Brazil the attempted solutions can be classified into those targeted *within the city* and those that try to *open up the interior* and to divert some of the growth into the countryside.

Schemes in the city

Self-help schemes

Although the shanty towns are illegal, the Government has realized that they cannot remove them. The people are so poor that it is difficult to build them homes and charge the rents necessary. One solution in São Paulo in Brazil has been to establish **self-help schemes** (**Figure 1**). The Government puts in basic services such as water, sewerage and electricity and provides cheap building materials, such as breeze-blocks. The families then build single-storey homes with a water tank and indoor bathroom. The building helps to develop a community spirit and the houses are relatively cheap, hygienic and fire-resistant. However, the residents must be able to co-operate with each other and to plan the improvements. In Brazil these 'improved' shanty towns are known as the **periferia**.

▲ **Figure 2** The underground train system in São Paulo, Brazil.

Transport and pollution

In São Paulo an underground train system (**Figure 2**) has been constructed to reduce the numbers of cars on the road, to cut down on accidents and to help control pollution. The system is also a reliable, cheap alternative for people travelling from the shanty towns to the CBD where most employment is available. The authorities are also trying to zone land uses more strictly, with separate areas for housing and industry, stricter pollution controls and the dirtiest industries encouraged to move to the outskirts of the city.

Opening up the interior

New towns

In Brazil a new capital city, Brasilia, was planned and opened in 1960 (**Figure 3**). One aim was to divert some of the rural migrants away from the already overcrowded cities at the coast, such as Rio de Janeiro and São Paulo. The population of Brasilia has grown to over 1 million, but the shanty towns of the coastal cities are still growing and *favelas* have begun to appear in Brasilia where the housing is too expensive for many rural migrants.

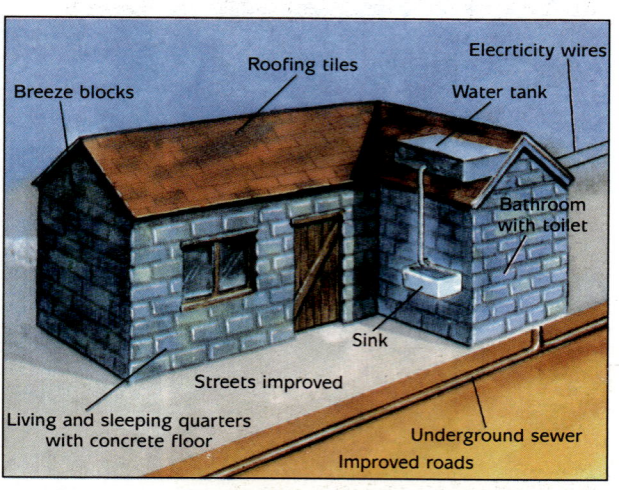

▲ **Figure 1** Self-help scheme in São Paulo, Brazil.

Expanding towns

Many migrants move in stages from their local village to a small town, then to a medium-sized town and finally to one of the large cities. The Government has attempted to slow the movement to the largest cities by developing some of the smaller towns, building low-cost homes and attracting new industries to provide employment.

Developing the Amazonian rain forest

The Brazilian Government has tried to reduce the numbers of rural migrants, especially from the drought-stricken north-east, moving to the large cities at the coast. Roads such as the Trans Amazonian Highway have been built through the forest and plots of land made available for settlers. Many of the landless peasants from the north-east migrate to Amazonia rather than to São Paulo. However, the Government also tries to solve rural problems where they exist and reduce migration flows by breaking up large farm estates and redistributing the land to the peasants.

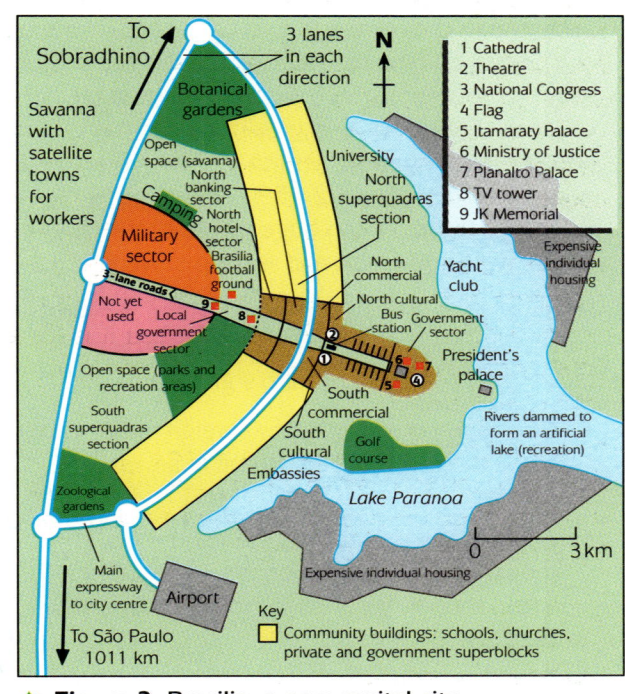

Figure 3 Brasilia, a new capital city.

Cairo

By 1995 Greater Cairo's population was over 12 million, making it one of the world's megacities. Growth has been rapid and continuous since the 1950s, so rapid that the authorities cannot keep pace with the influx of people. Problems in Cairo include the need for:

- low-cost affordable housing
- utilities such as piped water, electricity, paved roads and sewers
- services such as schools, health centres and hospitals
- solutions to the problems of traffic congestion and pollution
- employment for large numbers of rural migrants.

Cairo has different housing problems from most cities in the developing world. There are no shanty towns, but brick-built houses are built illegally on state-owned land or **green land** – the land next to the River Nile irrigated for agriculture on the fringes of the city, and protected by law to ensure a food supply for the people. These 'informal' houses now cover over 80 per cent of the land area of Greater Cairo. Elsewhere, in the 'Cities of

Figure 4 'Cities of the Dead', Cairo.

Figure 5 Overcrowded and unstable rooftops in Cairo.

the Dead' (**Figure 4**), 2–3 million people have set up home in the tombs of Old Cairo, and in the old city centre homemade huts have been erected on rooftops. Some of the buildings are in danger of collapse (**Figure 5**). Every Cairo citizen has an average living space of less than 2 m². The overall population density is 32 759 persons per km². Cairo also suffers from huge traffic problems, smog, water pollution and leaking sewers.

Despite the country's money shortage, Egyptian authorities have begun a number of projects to tackle the problems of Cairo's growth:

- One scheme is funded by foreign aid to repair and extend the city's crumbling sewerage system.
- A huge new ring road encircles the city to reduce traffic congestion, and a modern metro line is able to carry over 1 million commuters each day.
- The Zabbaleen people and their donkey carts (**Figure 6**) are licensed as the official refuse collectors and recyclers for the city slums.
- New satellite and dormitory towns such as Tenth of Ramadan City have been built to house overspill population. However, the rents are often too high and employment is lacking. Few people can afford the cost of travel to Cairo for work.

Figure 6 The Zabbaleen – official refuse collectors in Cairo's slums.

Test questions

1. **a** What is the difference between the site and the situation of a settlement? (2 marks)
   b List four site factors important for early settlements. (4 marks)
   c With the aid of a sketch map, describe the site of one settlement that you have studied. (6 marks)
   d Explain why the original site factors are less important today. (3 marks)
   e Explain why some settlements grew more than others. (2 marks)
   f Explain the meaning of:
      - sphere of influence
      - hierarchy of settlement. (2 marks)
   g What is the relationship between the population size of a settlement and the number of services? (1 mark)

2. **a** Draw a labelled diagram to show the location of the following urban zones of a city:
      - suburbs
      - industrial area
      - Central Business District
      - inner city (4 marks)
   b Describe the characteristics of two of the urban zones named in **a**. (6 marks)
   c List four problems of inner cities in developed countries. (4 marks)
   d What are the advantages and disadvantages of redevelopment schemes to improve life in the inner cities? (6 marks)

3. **a** What is a shanty town? (2 marks)
   b Give two reasons why shanty towns have grown in many LEDC cities. (2 marks)
   c Describe and explain the problems of the shanty towns for the inhabitants and local authorities. (8 marks)
   d Using one or more case studies, describe some solutions being applied to the problems of the shanty towns. (8 marks)

Chapter 10
Agriculture

Wheat growing in the British countryside. Why did the farmer choose to grow crops on the land?

Key Ideas

The farm as a system:
- farming is a system with inputs, processes and outputs.

Agricultural activity varies from place to place:
- physical factors (relief, soils, climate) and human factors (market, capital, labour, politics) result in different farm systems
- farming systems may be commercial or subsistence, intensive or extensive
- there is a wide range of farm types in the UK.

Agricultural change can have advantages and disadvantages:
- in LEDCs farming has been affected by the Green Revolution, irrigation, soil conservation and the use of appropriate technology
- in countries in the European Union, farming has been affected by hedge removal, soil erosion, quotas and subsidies.

Types of farming

The farm as a system
Farming is a business and it may be studied as a system with a series of inputs, processes and outputs:

INPUTS → PROCESSES → OUTPUTS

Inputs are what goes into the system. They may be physical inputs, such as the climate, relief and soils, or human inputs, such as labour, capital, machinery and seeds. **Processes** are the activities on the farm which turn the inputs into outputs. **Outputs** are the products of the system, such as crops, wool, meat and money. The outputs should be greater in value than the inputs so that a profit is made. Figure 1 shows a range of possible inputs, processes and outputs in farm systems.

Types of farming
There are many different ways of classifying or grouping farm types (Figure 2).

Around the world there are many different types of farming (Figure 3), but the pattern is not haphazard. Certain regions of the world have a particular farming type that is dominant. For example, in much of Western Europe farming is mixed, in North Africa there are large areas of nomadic herding and in south-east Asia there is intensive rice growing. The world distribution of farm types can be partly explained by the physical environment, which has a strong influence on agriculture.

Inputs	Processes	Outputs
Physical environment:	Planting	Milk
Relief	Ploughing	Cereals, e.g. wheat, corn
Soils	Spraying	Vegetables, e.g. potatoes, cabbage
Climate	Harvesting	
Drainage	Feeding stock	Oilseed rape, sugar beet
		Fruit, e.g. apples, strawberries
Human environment:	Shearing	Eggs
Labour	Dipping	Cattle, pigs, sheep
Machinery and fuel	Milking	Wool
Fertilizers, chemicals	Crop storage	Poultry
Animal feeds		Hay and straw
New animals and seeds		Animal feedstuffs
		Wastes, including manure

▲ **Figure 1** The farm as a system.

- **Arable, pastoral or mixed:** Some farms are **arable** farms and only grow crops, other farms are **pastoral** and concentrate on rearing animals. In some areas farmers both grow crops and rear animals on **mixed** farms.
- **Subsistence or commercial:** Many farmers, particularly in the LEDCs, are **subsistence** farmers producing food only to feed themselves and their family. In MEDCs most farming is **commercial**. The farmers grow crops and rear animals to sell in order to make a profit.
- **Intensive or extensive:** Intensive farms have high inputs of labour or capital (money) in order to achieve high outputs per hectare or **yields**. The farms are usually quite small. Some examples include intensive rice growing in south-east Asia or market gardening. Extensive farms are usually much larger with low inputs and outputs per hectare, such as the shifting cultivators in the Amazon Basin.
- **Sedentary or nomadic:** Most farming is **sedentary** – that is, settlement is permanent and the landscape is farmed every year. **Nomadic** farmers move around to find fresh pasture for animals or new plots of land to cultivate.

▲ **Figure 2** Classification of farm types.

▼ **Figure 3** Types of farming.

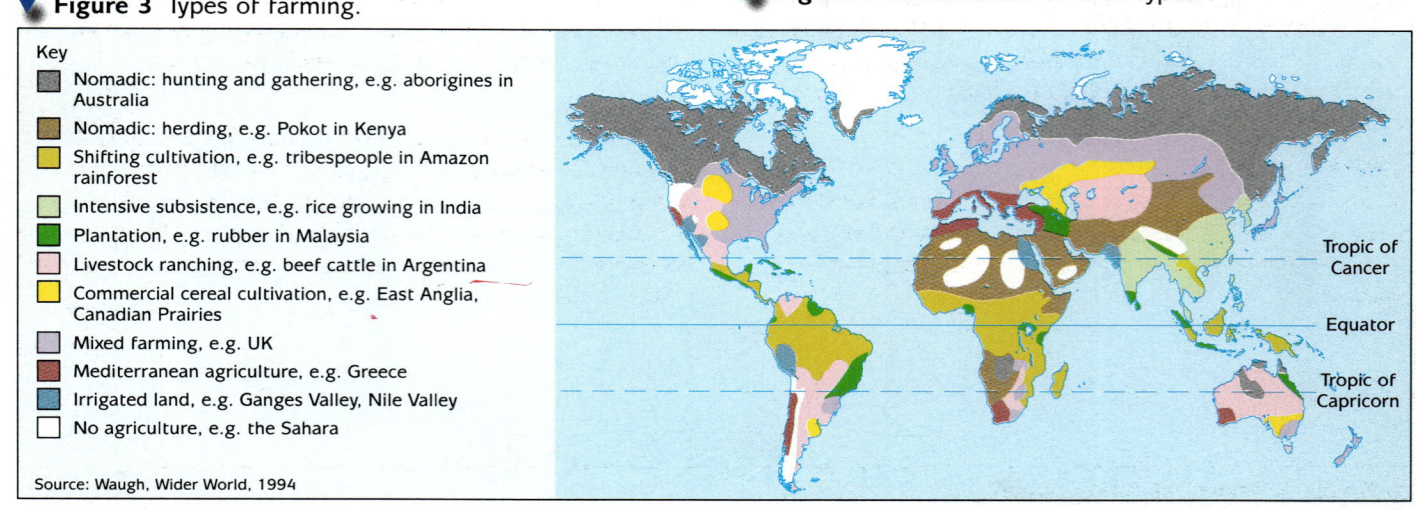

Key
- Nomadic: hunting and gathering, e.g. aborigines in Australia
- Nomadic: herding, e.g. Pokot in Kenya
- Shifting cultivation, e.g. tribespeople in Amazon rainforest
- Intensive subsistence, e.g. rice growing in India
- Plantation, e.g. rubber in Malaysia
- Livestock ranching, e.g. beef cattle in Argentina
- Commercial cereal cultivation, e.g. East Anglia, Canadian Prairies
- Mixed farming, e.g. UK
- Mediterranean agriculture, e.g. Greece
- Irrigated land, e.g. Ganges Valley, Nile Valley
- No agriculture, e.g. the Sahara

Source: Waugh, Wider World, 1994

Factors affecting farming

Deciding whether to grow crops or rear animals is affected by the physical conditions and human factors in an area (**Figure 4**). The physical conditions are often the most important. Sometimes the farmer may have several choices, especially in an area with fertile soils and a temperate climate. In other areas, the choice may be limited by infertile soils, lack of water or a short growing season.

PHYSICAL FACTORS

Rainfall
All crops and animals need a reliable source of water. Different crops require different amounts of water. Wheat, for example, does not need more than 600mm a year and grows well in south-east England. The mountainous areas of England (**Figure A**) have over 1000mm of rainfall, which is too damp for wheat.

Temperature
Most plants stop growing when temperatures fall below 6°C. The number of months the temperature is above 6°C determines the length of the growing season. In some countries the growing season is too short for any crops to be grown. Different crops also have different temperature ranges within which they grow well. Wheat grows well in areas with a temperate climate while rice prefers hot temperatures in tropical and sub-tropical locations.

Sunshine hours
The number of sunshine hours is important, especially for the ripening of crops. Grapes need long hours of sunshine to ripen and grow well in the Mediterranean countries.

Soil type
Crops grow best on deep, fertile, free-draining soils, while less fertile soils prone to waterlogging are best used for pastoral farming. In the upland areas of the UK soils are thin, acidic and often rocky, and are unable to support crops, whereas in the lowlands the richer, fertile brown earths are more suited to agriculture.

Relief
Mountainous areas are colder than the lowlands and slopes are often too steep for farm machinery so most farming is pastoral. The lowlands with gentle relief are more easily farmed.

▲ **Figure A** Hill sheep farming dominates in uplands such as the Lake District where the poor physical conditions make crop growing difficult.

HUMAN FACTORS

Labour
Labour is in abundance in some countries, such as India and Bangladesh. Here, rice growing absorbs huge numbers of people in planting and harvesting. In other areas such as the Pennines in the UK the population density is low and hill sheep farming is adapted to low inputs of labour.

Finance
The profit a farmer makes affects the amount that can be invested in machinery, fertilizer, seeds and animals, and how much the farmer can afford to pay in wages for the family and any farmworkers.

Market
If a farmer is to make a profit there must be a market for the produce. In the past, farms close to towns and cities in the UK often concentrated on dairying and market gardening in order to supply fresh foods quickly to the large urban population. Today, many farmers have contracts with supermarkets, e.g. Sainsbury's, and other food companies such as Bird's Eye which guarantee a market for their produce.

Politics, loans, grants and subsidies
In some LEDC countries loans have been available to farmers to buy machinery, seeds and fertilizers. In the European Union there is a complicated system of subsidies which has encouraged farmers to specialize in different crops.

Tradition
Many farms have practised the same type of farming for generations. Tradition is important in rural communities. Also, it is very costly to change farming practices. Imagine the cost of converting from a cereal farm with its seed drills and combine harvesters to a dairy farm with milking parlours and cattle.

▲ **Figure 4** Factors affecting farming.

Farming in the UK

In the UK many farmers combine a number of different activities on their farms. However, as **Figure 1** shows, in certain areas particular crops or types of livestock are dominant. The pattern of land use in the UK is a result of a variety of physical and economic factors.

Cereals

Arable land covers 27 per cent of the land area in the UK. The most important arable crops grown in the UK are the cereals wheat and barley. Wheat growing is concentrated in the south and east of the UK (see pages 150–53). The physical conditions in this area encourage arable farming to dominate. The **relief** (**Figure 2**) of the land is mostly less than 200m above sea level and flat or gently undulating. Large machinery such as combine harvesters can easily be used. **Soils** are mostly fertile boulder clay or loams, which are free-draining and easy to plough. The **climate** is a major influence on where cereals are grown. In the south and east of England summer temperatures are high, averaging over 16°C (**Figure 3**) and there is ample summer sunshine to ripen the crops. Winters are cold with frequent frosts which help to break up the soil ready for ploughing in the spring and to kill soil pests.

Sheep

Sheep are raised for their meat and wool. There are over 30 million sheep in the UK and, as **Figure 1** shows, the main areas of rearing sheep are in the uplands, land over 400m above sea level (see pages 154–55). The steep terrain of the upland areas makes the land unsuitable for the large machinery needed to grow crops. Sheep, however, are sturdy and sure-footed, able to cope with the slopes and uneven terrain. Soils in the uplands are often thin, acidic and infertile, unsuitable for crop growing. In many areas the land is covered with moorland vegetation, including heather, bracken and rough grassland. The sheep graze on the open moors and hills where other livestock such as beef and dairy cattle could not survive because of the poor quality of the grassland. In the uplands, winters are cold, often with snow, and summers are also cooler than in the lowlands. Rainfall is high, often over 1000mm a year, and there is much more cloud cover. Hill sheep-farming areas are too cold, have too much rainfall and too little sunshine to be successful crop-growing areas.

Market gardening

Market gardening is the growing of vegetables, fruit and flowers (**Figure 4**). This type of farming is very intensive. Most market gardens are small in area but have very high inputs of labour and capital. There is a large labour input in planting, irrigating, fertilizing, spraying and harvesting the crops. Expenditure is also high on fertilizers, seeds, sprays, and heating and lighting for greenhouses.

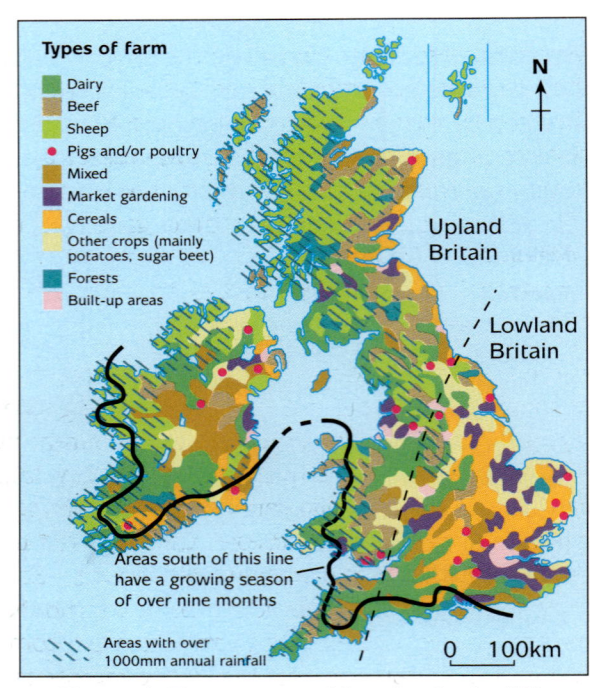

▲ **Figure 1** The pattern of farming in the UK.

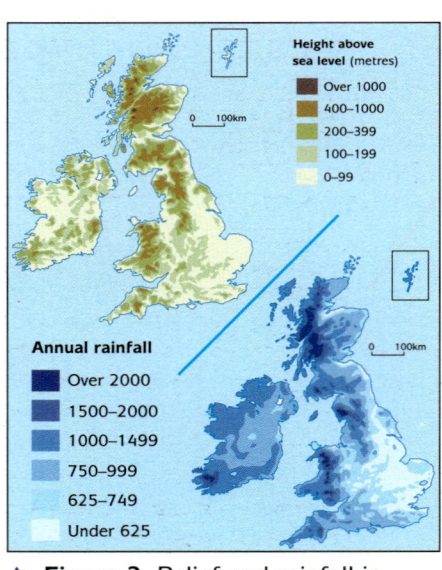

▲ **Figure 2** Relief and rainfall in the UK.

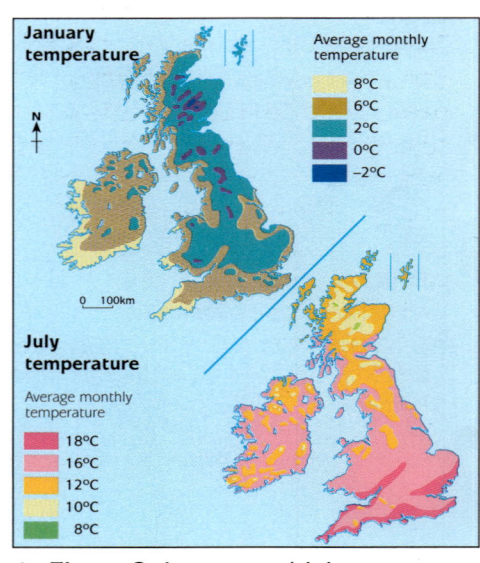

▲ **Figure 3** January and July temperatures in the UK.

Market garden crops need to be transported quickly to the market where they are sold. The crops are perishable and in most cases they need to reach the shops within 24 hours of being picked. When communication links were poor and methods of transport slow, market gardens developed on the fringes of cities, with easy access to the market for the produce. This can still be seen in the pattern of market gardening in **Figure 1**. Today, transport developments and new varieties of plants which are less perishable allow tomatoes from Guernsey, flowers from Kenya and strawberries from Israel to be in our shops in perfect condition.

In the UK most market gardens are in the south and east to take advantage of the physical conditions. The flat, low-lying relief, adequate rainfall and warm, sunny summers (**Figure 2**) all encourage market gardening. In East Anglia and the Fens the many market gardens take advantage of the fertile, light and stone-free soils which warm up quickly, encouraging seeds to germinate. In the south and east the crops can be grown outdoors without the need for artificial heating in greenhouses. Economic factors are also important. The vast population in London and the south-east provides a large market for the produce and there are ample communication links by road and railway to take the produce to the market quickly.

Figure 4 Market gardening.

Dairying

The pattern of dairying in the UK is influenced by both physical and human factors. Dairying is important in the lowlands of south-west Britain where the rainfall is high and winter temperatures are mild. Dairy cattle (**Figure 5**) are grazed on flat or gently sloping land in areas where high rainfall allows a rich growth of grassland. **Figure 3** shows that average temperatures even in winter are above 5°C so the pasture continues to grow all year round. Farmers only need to provide small amounts of additional winter fodder, and the cows can graze outdoors for longer in the year. This reduces costs for farmers.

Dairying, like market gardening, is influenced by distance to market. The perishability of the milk makes daily collection and transport to dairies essential. For this reason some areas of dairying in the UK are adjacent to large cities so that the milk can reach the supermarket shelves and people's doorsteps within 24 hours.

Figure 5 Dairy cattle.

Activities

1 Copy and complete the table to show the factors that affect the pattern of farming in the UK:

	Cereal growing	Hill sheep farming	Market gardening	Dairying
Distribution in the UK				
Named example(s)				
Physical factors:				
Relief				
Climate:				
Summer temperatures				
Winter temperatures				
Rainfall				
Sunshine				
Soils				
Human factors				

2 Write an essay to **a** describe and **b** explain the pattern of farm types in the UK as shown on **Figure 1**.

Case Study – East Anglia

Arable farming

East Anglia (**Figure 1**) includes the counties of Norfolk, Cambridgeshire, Suffolk and the northern part of Essex. It is the most important arable farming region in the UK mainly because of its physical advantages of climate, relief and soils (**Figure 2**). The farming is both intensive and commercial. Most farms are large, over 200 hectares, and highly mechanized using huge combine harvesters and specialist machinery for sowing and harvesting oilseed rape and sugar beet. The crops are **cash crops**, sold for profit to the many local mills and factories. Wheat is bought by flour mills and used for cakes, flour and animal feed. Barley is used to make malt for the brewing and distilling industries as well as being sold as animal fodder. Carrots, peas and potatoes are sold to local freezing and canning factories. Sugar refineries buy up large quantities of sugar beet.

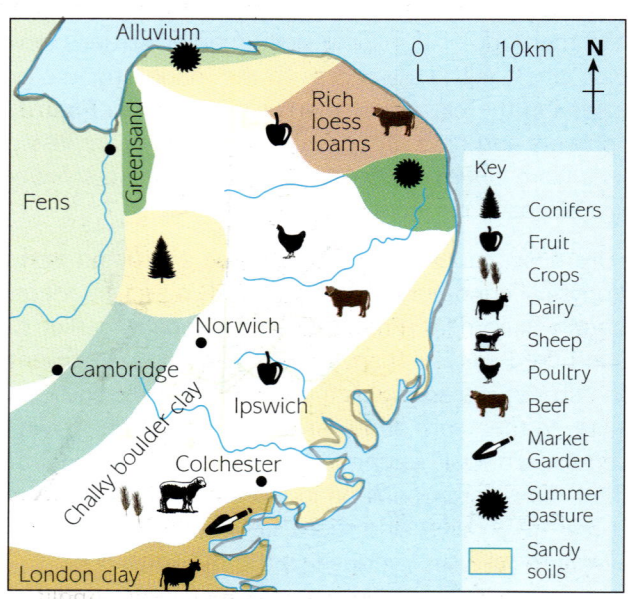

Figure 1 Soils and land use in East Anglia.

Physical conditions	Impact on land use
Climate	
Warm summers, 17°C	Crops grow well and ripen.
Rainfall under 700mm per year	Sufficient for crop growth, no waterlogging
Slight summer rainfall maximum	Rainfall in season when crops most need it
Long hours of sunshine in summer	Ripens the crops
Winter frost	Breaks up the soil and kills pests, does not affect crop growth
Relief	
Flat or gently sloping	Easy to use machinery
Lowland, most less than 100m above sea level	Roads and railways have been easy to construct
Soils	
Mostly fertile boulder clay soils left behind by the ice sheets at the end of the Ice Age	Fertile soils suitable for growing cereals, sugar beet and potatoes
Infertile sandy soils, e.g. Breckland	Breckland is planted with pine trees, other areas have been fertilized and used for market gardening, cereals and sugar beet. The light sandy soils heat up quickly and seeds germinate fast.
Loam soils	Very fertile, good for vegetables, fruit and cereals; retain plant foods and moisture, easily penetrated by roots
Waterlogged soils and marshland of the Norfolk Broads.	A little dairying.

Figure 2 Physical conditions for farming in East Anglia.

East Anglia also benefits from some favourable human factors. It is situated in the east of England to the north of London. That densely populated region provides a large and wealthy market for the produce. In the south of the region more farmers specialize in market gardening and dairying. The flat relief has enabled a dense network of communication links to develop, such as the main East Coast railway, the M11 link to London and the A1, which allow the rapid transport of the produce. Since joining the European Union many of the farmers in East Anglia have benefited from the Common Agricultural Policy (CAP). They have received subsidies for growing certain crops, e.g. wheat, oilseed rape and linseed.

An intensive, commercial arable farm

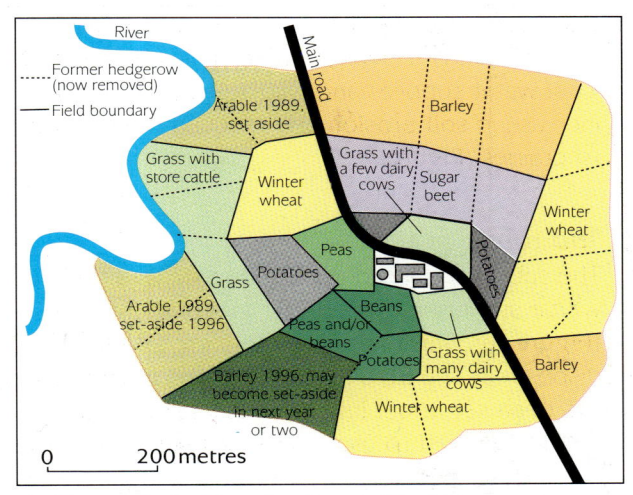

▲ **Figure 3** An East Anglian arable farm.

Figure 3 shows an arable farm located north of Norwich, which is typical of many in East Anglia.

Changes on the farm in East Anglia
In the 1940s and 1950s farming in East Anglia was very different from today. The farms were smaller and the landscape was made up of small hedge-lined fields. The farmers practised the famous Norfolk four-course crop rotation. Some crops, such as wheat and barley, remove large quantities of nitrogen from the soil while others, such as clover, replace nitrogen. Animals were also kept as part of the rotation. They provided a valuable source of manure. Most of the farms were mixed farms, employing large numbers of people. Since the 1950s there have been many changes and the farms have become increasingly intensive.

Chemicals
The crop rotation has largely disappeared as chemical fertilizers allow the more profitable wheat and barley to be grown year after year in the same fields. Increased use of herbicides and pesticides has also increased farm productivity.

Land reclamation
Across East Anglia the desire to produce more crops led to more land being cultivated, a process called **extensification**. Areas of sandy soils were fertilized and cultivated, marshes were drained and areas of woodland cleared.

	O	N	D	J	F	M	A	M	J	J	A	S
Temperature °C	11	7	4	4	4	6	8	12	15	17	17	14
Rainfall mm TOTAL: 650	64	69	61	61	46	38	48	43	43	66	53	58

Mechanization
Fields were made larger by removing hedgerows, and smaller farms were joined together to become larger. This increased profit margins by allowing a greater scale of mechanization.

Improved buildings
Drying sheds for grain and temperature-controlled storage buildings for apples and potatoes have improved the storage of crops.

Agribusiness
In East Anglia **agribusiness** is a significant feature of the farming. It is associated with large-scale, capital-intensive farms. The farms are owned by large companies and run by a farm manager. The owners include processing factories, supermarkets and even companies whose main operation is nothing to do with farming, such as insurance companies. The large companies use high-technology and **agrochemicals** to obtain maximum yields from the land. The farms are intensive with high inputs of machinery and fertilizers, so more crops are produced from the land using less labour.

Activities
1. Describe the relief, climate and soils of the farm in East Anglia.
2. Describe the layout and land use on the farm.
3. Explain the changes in farming in East Anglia since the 1950s.

Case Study – East Anglia

Politics and farming in East Anglia

In the UK, agriculture employs only 2.5 per cent of the working population and creates just 1.25 per cent of the national wealth. Yet it is considered to be so important that it has its own Government department, MAFF (the Ministry for Agriculture, Fisheries and Food). The industry also enjoys a very high level of government financial support through membership of the European Union. The Common Agricultural Policy (CAP) (**Figure 1**) has brought many changes to farming in East Anglia.

> The initial aims of the CAP were:
> - to increase productivity and to achieve self-sufficiency
> - to give all farmworkers a fair standard of living
> - to keep prices of agricultural products stable
> - to maintain food supplies
> - to ensure 'reasonable' prices for customers.

▲ **Figure 1** The Common Agricultural Policy.

The CAP measures are funded from VAT on goods in the EU member countries and from levies charged on imports from outside the European Union. East Anglia has benefited from the CAP in the following ways.

1 Price support policies

A target price is set for farm produce each year, which it is hoped will be the farmers' selling price. A threshold price is also set, which is the minimum price set for imports and is always higher than the target price so that EU producers cannot be undercut. A third price, the intervention price, is set that is lower than the target price; if selling prices fall to the intervention price the EU buys up the product, hoping to push selling prices up by reducing the amount available. This policy guarantees farmers a good price for their crops.

2 Subsidies

One of the first aims of the CAP was to increase food production so that the EU became more **self-sufficient** in foodstuffs (**Figure 2**). This was achieved by pricing policies and by giving subsidies to farmers. In East Anglia the drive to produce more wheat in order to receive subsidies led to an increased use of chemical fertilizers and pesticides, the removal of hedgerows (**Figure 3**) and woodlands and the draining of wetlands, all to increase yields. However, the changes threatened local water supplies and wildlife, caused an increase in **soil erosion** and reduced the landscape to prairies (**Figure 4**).

Too much grain

The subsidies caused overproduction and then wheat surpluses created vast grain mountains (**Figure 5**), which are costly to store and to dispose of. The EU's response to the grain surplus has been set-aside, introduced in 1992. Farmers are not allowed to use at least 20 per cent of their

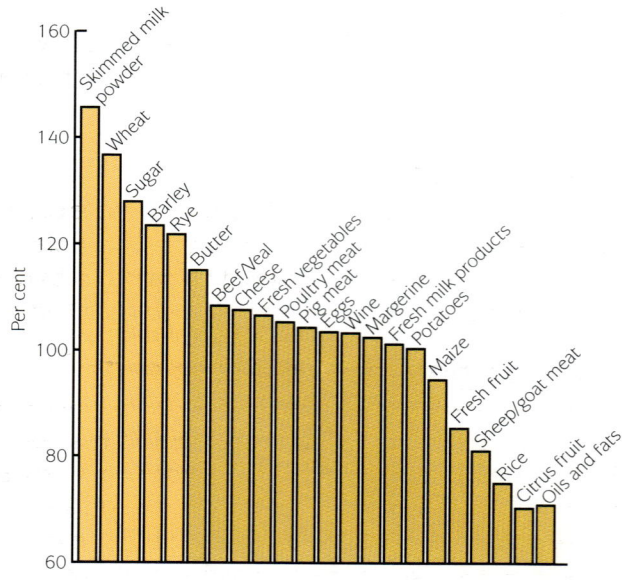

▲ **Figure 2** EU self-sufficiency in foodstuffs, 1991.

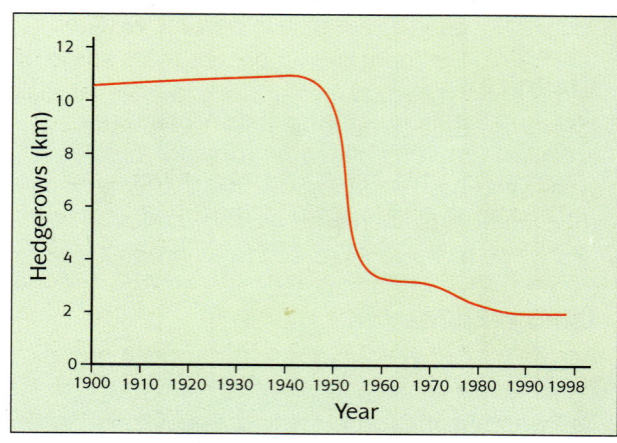

▲ **Figure 3** The decline in hedgerows in Cambridgeshire, East Anglia, 1900–1998.

Chapter 10 Agriculture

Figure 4 'Prairieization' – the monotonous East Anglian landscape.

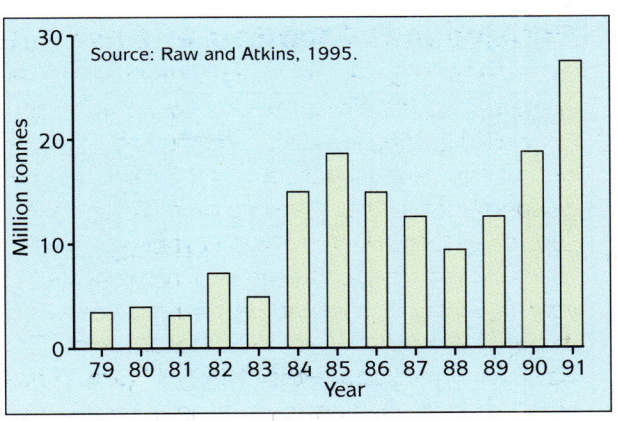

Figure 5 Stocks of EU cereals 1979–1991.

arable land for five years. The land can be left fallow, planted with trees or used for non-agricultural purposes. In addition, since 1995 support for cereals has been cut. Instead, farmers are paid for their set-aside land. In 1995, UK farmers were paid £253 per hectare for fallow, £140 per hectare for cereals and £445 per hectare for oilseed rape.

Too little oil

One food shortage in the EU was vegetable oil, a problem that could be solved by growing more oilseed rape. This was achieved by paying subsidies to the seed-crushing companies, who then had to pay the farmers a good price. The growing of oilseed rape began in Hampshire in 1973 but soon spread throughout East Anglia and to many other arable areas. The crop gave a good return to the farmer and also had other advantages. The seed has a 40 per cent oil content and the residue after oil removal is high in protein, making it valuable for livestock feed. The crop improves the structure and fertility of the soil, making it a useful 'break' crop before wheat is grown. However, the growth of oilseed may begin to decline; the subsidy was removed in 1996 because the EU was approaching self-sufficiency.

Damaging the environment

The drive to increase output and profits has not always been beneficial to the environment. Between 1945 and 1975 over 45 per cent of Norfolk's hedgerows disappeared to increase the size of fields. Hedgerows take up valuable agricultural land (**Figure 6**) and limit the size of machinery that can be used, but they are also important wildlife habitats. The hedgeless landscape loses some of its charm and is turned into a monotonous flat plain similar to that of the Prairies in North America.

The increased use of chemical fertilizers and pesticides is also blamed for polluting the land and water supplies. Many of the chemicals, in large enough quantities, can seep into streams causing **eutrophication**, a loss of oxygen. This may kill the stream life, damaging the whole ecosystem. Strict guidelines are now in force about the types and amounts of chemicals that are allowed to be used. Farmers can also be heavily fined for pollution of watercourses.

Figure 6 The advantages and disadvantages of hedgerow removal.

Case Study – East Anglia

Case Study – The Lake District

Hill sheep farming

Physical

Relief	– high mountains, steep slopes and little flat land
Soils	– thin, rocky, acid and leached (podzols)
Climate	– temperatures fall by 1°C for every 160m above sea level. Temperatures are much lower than in the lowlands (14°–15°C in summer). The growing season is short and there is high rainfall, over 2000mm on the Fells. There is more cloud cover, snowfall and hill fog.
Accessibility	– twisting steep gradients make access difficult; many roads are very narrow. The main access routes are along valley floors in the Lake District. Today, the M6 passes along the eastern edge of the area.

Human

Market	– a small local market and limited transport
Labour	– the uplands are sparsely populated so little labour is available. The farms cannot afford many workers and are well adapted to a small labour force.
Capital	– there is often little profit to reinvest so farming methods stay the same.
Tradition	– the farming has changed very little over the years, retaining the 'One man and his dog' image.
Politics	– subsidies and grants have been paid to the farmers to guarantee a minimum standard of living.

▲ **Figure 1** Factors affecting farming in the Lake District.

In the upland areas of Britain, a variety of *physical and human factors* (**Figure 1**) combine to make the grazing of sheep the main farming activity. Breeds of hill sheep such as the Swaledale (**Figure 2**) can survive the extremes of weather and the poor-quality pasture. The hill farmers make a living by selling the wool and the fattened sheep and lambs for meat. The hill farms cover a large area of land and use little machinery and labour. This makes hill farming one of the most extensive forms of pastoral farming.

▲ **Figure 2** The hardy breeds of sheep are sure-footed on the rugged terrain in the Lake District.

A farm in the Lake District

Hill farms in the Lake District have three zones of land use. **Figure 3** is a land use map of a Lake District farm. During the summer the sheep graze on the **open fell** which begins about 300m above sea level. The farmer rarely owns this land but shares the grazing rights with other farmers in the parish. The land is open moorland with no fences or dry-stone walls. The coarse grasses mixed with heather, bracken and marsh give poor-quality grazing land.

The lower slope of the fell, called the **intake**, is often owned by the farmer. The land is enclosed by dry-stone walls and some of the pasture may have been improved by adding drainage and fertilizers. The slopes are still exposed and moderately steep, with acid soils leached by the heavy rain. The best land, the **inbye**, is on the valley floor but it is only a small part of the total land area. Here the soils are more fertile and the land more sheltered. The intake and the inbye are used to graze the sheep during bad winter weather when they are also fed supplementary feeds of hay, silage and turnips. The sheep are also here during lambing and shearing when the animals need to be closer to the farm. Parts of the inbye may be used to grow crops of hay and turnips which provide the winter fodder. Some hill farmers

Case Study – The Lake District

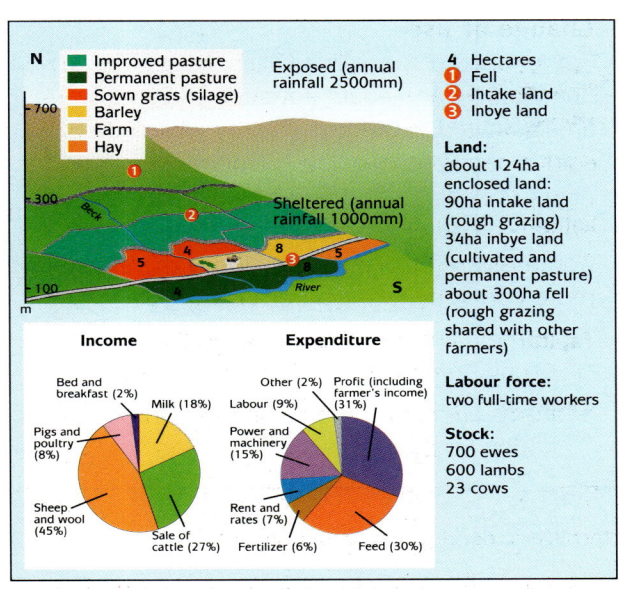

Chapter 10 Agriculture

▲ **Figure 3** Profile of Fell Farm in the Lake District.

	1977	1986	1995
Farmers (full-time)	980	893	828
Farmers (part-time)	270	302	331
Total	1250	1195	1159

▲ **Figure 4** The numbers employed as hill farms decline.

also keep small herds of dairy or beef cattle which graze on the valley floor or lower slopes. A milk herd is a useful addition to the farm, providing a weekly income to the farmer. On many hill farms the organization of the farm revolves around maintaining the sheep and cattle which together provide over 90 per cent of the farm income.

Recent problems and changes
Problems
Hill farming is a vulnerable business – the farming is not always profitable. The land is marginal, a severe winter can deplete the stock, and the removal of EU subsidies may cause many farmers to go bankrupt. In recent years the farms have become less profitable. Fuel, fodder and machinery costs have risen but lamb prices have collapsed. As older farmers retire, fewer young people are willing to carry on the hill farming tradition (**Figure 4**). More attractive work and higher wages can be found in the towns and cities or in tourism in the Lake District National Park. The tourists also cause conflict with the farmers. The vast majority of visitors to the Lake District are sensible and follow the Country Code, but a small minority leave gates open, cause sheep worrying by allowing their dogs off the lead, break down the dry-stone walls, camp indiscriminately and leave litter. In addition, many farmers are at odds with the National Park Authority because they feel that they are not allowed to make progress and to invest in their farms because of the strict planning regulations.

Changes – improvements in farming
Many farmers have increased the quality and the quantity of their output of meat and wool. The stock has been improved by buying in better animals to breed from and pasture has been improved by greater additions of fertilizer. Grants for new farm buildings have been available. At Fell Farm grants were used to build a shed for the cows to winter in and a slurry tower to store the organic waste. The slurry is spread on nearby fields as manure. Many hill farmers also claim subsidies from the CAP policy for Less Favoured Areas (LFAs). LFAs are 'areas in danger of depopulation and where the conservation of the countryside is necessary'. However, current reforms of the CAP may see a reduction in hill farm subsidies. More grants are now being paid for farmers to conserve the countryside by planting and conserving hedgerows, restoring dry-stone walls and allowing natural meadowland to flower and seed before cutting for hay. This is to encourage a greater **biodiversity**, or variety of animals and plants.

▲ **Figure 5** Diversification in the Lake District.

Case Study – The Lake District

Changes – diversification

Many farmers have seen their profits fall and feel threatened by sheep quotas and reduced grants. As a result of this, they have been forced to diversify. In a National Park like the Lake District, farms have started to provide facilities for visitors, such as campsites, holiday homes in converted barns, bed and breakfast, farm visits, pony-trekking and farm shops (**Figure 5**). Other types of diversification also exist, such as fish farms, small workshops and farm woodlands.

Change of use

Some farms, especially smaller ones, have proved uneconomic and could not survive. Some were amalgamated with farms nearby while others were sold in separate lots. The buildings were sold for high prices as second homes while the land was bought by other farms or by the Forestry Commission for plantations. Today there are also more part-time farmers because:

- farmers are supplementing their income by taking on other employment
- farms are sold off in small lots and bought as hobby farms.

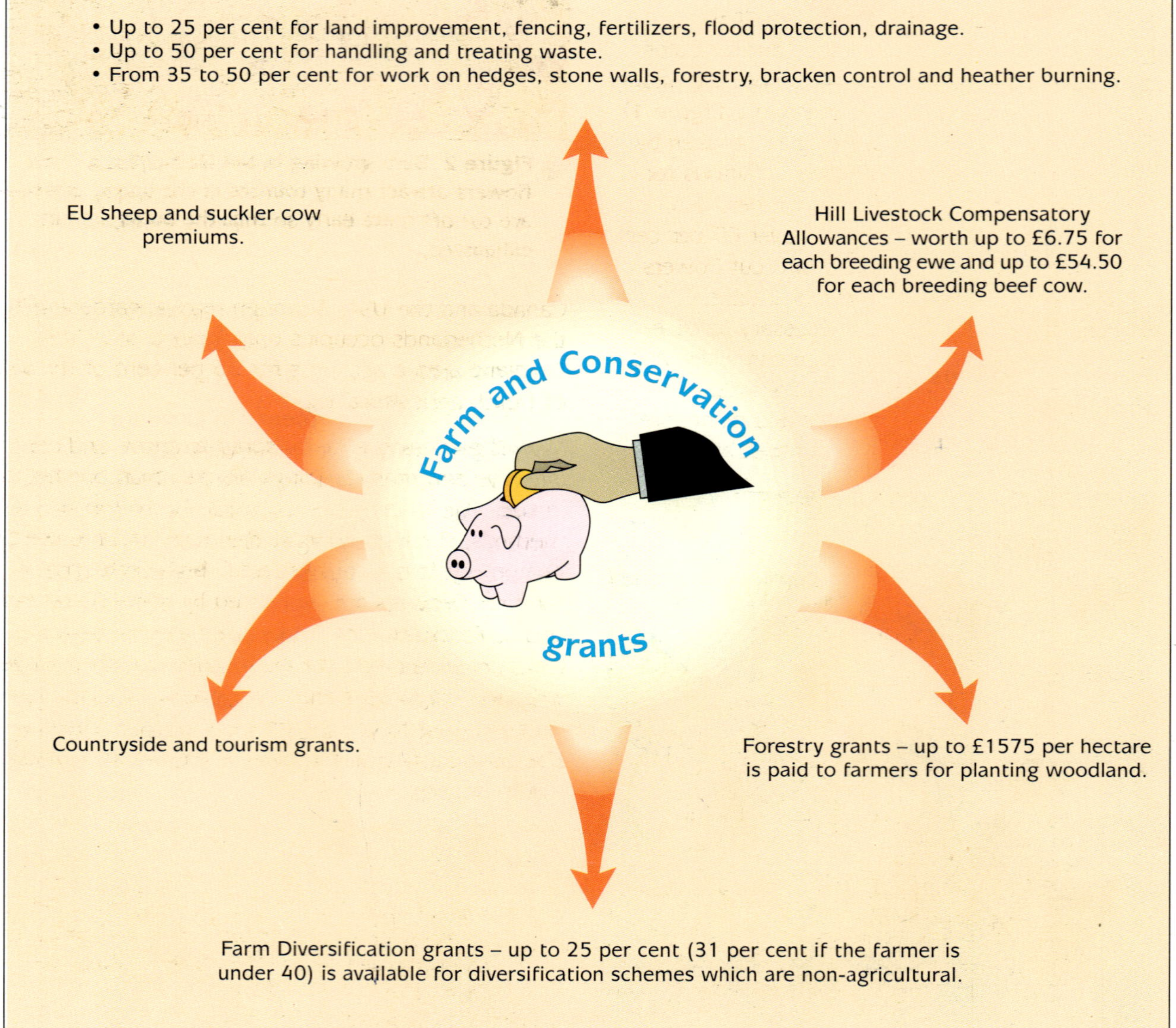

Farm and Conservation grants

- Up to 25 per cent for land improvement, fencing, fertilizers, flood protection, drainage.
- Up to 50 per cent for handling and treating waste.
- From 35 to 50 per cent for work on hedges, stone walls, forestry, bracken control and heather burning.

EU sheep and suckler cow premiums.

Hill Livestock Compensatory Allowances – worth up to £6.75 for each breeding ewe and up to £54.50 for each breeding beef cow.

Countryside and tourism grants.

Forestry grants – up to £1575 per hectare is paid to farmers for planting woodland.

Farm Diversification grants – up to 25 per cent (31 per cent if the farmer is under 40) is available for diversification schemes which are non-agricultural.

Source: LDNP, Choices for Farmers, GCSE Resource Guide 3, 1989

▲ **Figure 6** Grants available to farmers.

Chapter 10 Agriculture

Market gardening and bulb growing in the Netherlands

The Netherlands is one of the most *intensively* farmed countries in the world. In part this is due to the skill of the Dutch farmers but it also reflects the high land values. The Netherlands is a densely populated country where land is scarce. Farming must be profitable to compete with other land uses.

Market gardening and bulb growing are concentrated in a strip of land behind the coastal sand dunes in the west of the Netherlands (**Figure 1**). The relief is low-lying and flat, and soils are very light and sandy. The soils warm up and dry out quickly, which helps seeds to germinate; free drainage is important for bulbs such as tulips and hyacinths. The most important area for market gardening is Westland (**Figure 1**). Seen from the air it is a 'sea of glass' broken by slender chimney stacks. The area is famous for the production of tomatoes, cucumbers and lettuce, although in recent years over 60 per cent of the farmers have diversified into cut flowers and pot plants which are more profitable (**Figure 2**). The change was necessary to cover the rising costs of heating the greenhouses, and severe competition in the EU. A considerable proportion of the flowers, bulbs and plants are *exported* to other European countries and to Canada and the USA. Although market gardening in the Netherlands occupies only 5 per cent of the farmland area it accounts for 25 per cent of the value of Dutch agricultural exports.

▲ **Figure 2** Bulb growing in the Netherlands – the flowers attract many tourists in the spring but they are cut off quite early so that the bulbs are not exhausted.

Market gardening is both *labour-intensive* and *capital-intensive* and many holdings are less than one hectare in size. The farming is successful due to the intensive methods, the high value of the crops and the use of technology. It is a sophisticated, **high-tech** type of farming. Growers are supported by scientific research and advisory services. There are many cooperatives which provide credit for the growers to buy fertilizers, irrigation equipment and other products. Cooperative auctions exist to sell the growers' output. The co-operative auction at Aalsmeer is the world's largest flower auction.

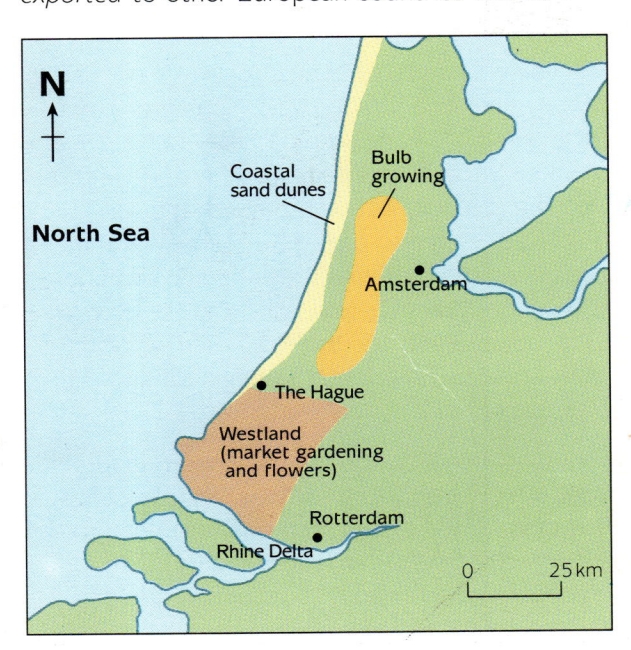

▲ **Figure 1** Factors affecting farming in the Netherlands.

Activity

a Using **Figure 1** and the text, complete a table showing factors affecting market gardening in the Netherlands. Use the headings **Physical factors** and **Human factors**.
b What is intensive farming?
c Why is farming so intensive in the Netherlands?

Case Study – Market Gardening

Farming in the developing world

Three-quarters of the world's population live in the developing world, and over 70 per cent of these people are engaged in farming. Much of the produce from farming in the LEDCs is for *subsistence*, to feed the farmer and his family.

Shifting cultivation

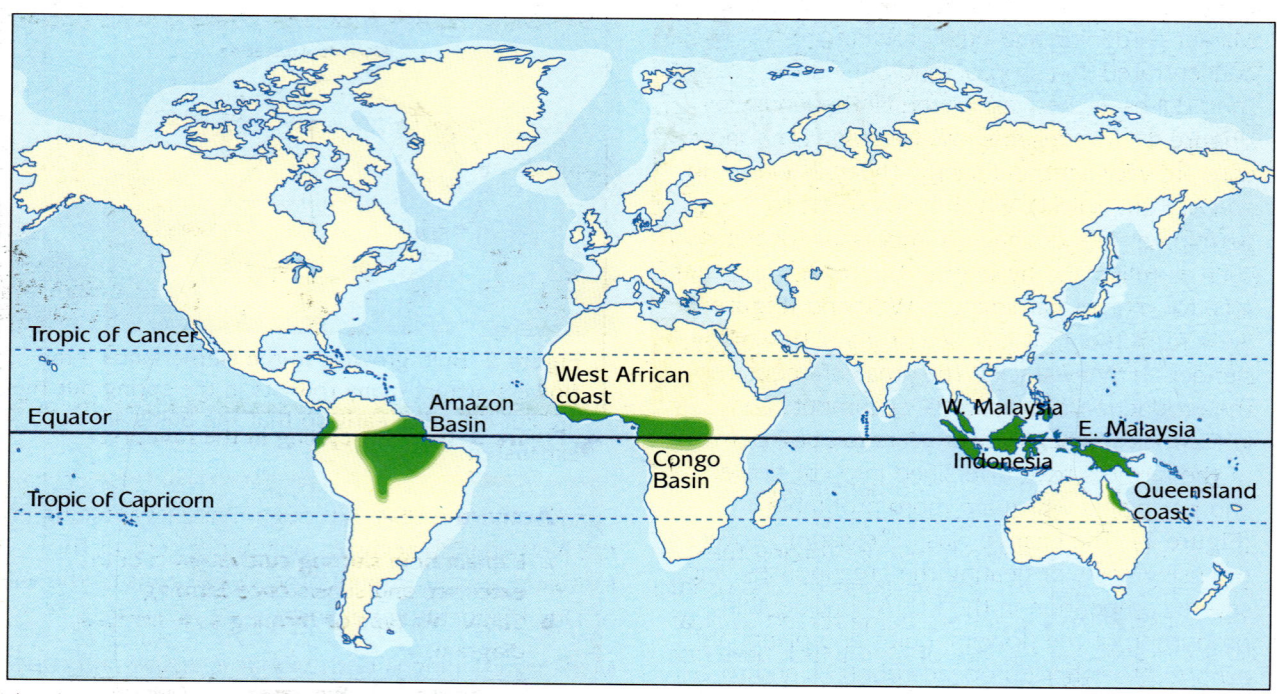

▲ **Figure 1** The world distribution of areas of shifting cultivation.

Shifting cultivation is a traditional form of subsistence agriculture once found in many areas of tropical rainforest, such as the Amazon basin and Indonesia (**Figure 1**). Today this extensive form of agriculture is only found in the inaccessible and least 'exploited' areas of rain forest.

In the Amazon basin, the Amerindians use **machetes** to clear about one hectare of forest. After time enough to allow the vegetation to dry, the trees and undergrowth are burned, the ash being used to fertilize the soil. This is also known as 'slash and burn'. In the clearings, called **chagras**, the women plant and grow crops such as manioc, yams, beans and pumpkins (**Figure 2**). The farming is all done by hand with only simple tools. The men supplement the diet by hunting for tapirs and monkeys, fishing and collecting fruits from the forest.

The soil very quickly loses its fertility. Once the tree canopy has been removed, the source of humus for the soil has gone and the heavy rains can strike the bare ground. This causes soil erosion and the leaching of minerals down through the soil (**Figure 3**) (see also page 95). Harvesting the crops removes more nutrients from the soil and after four to five years yields decline and the plots have to be abandoned. The tribe will then 'shift' to another part of the forest to begin the cycle all over again.

Shifting cultivation needs a high labour input and large areas of land to provide enough food for a few people. The abandoned clearings need to be left for over 50 years to allow the forest to regenerate and the soils to recover. Traditionally, shifting agriculture was in harmony with the environment. It is a wasteful method of farming

Chapter 10 Agriculture

Case Study – Shifting cultivators

▲ Figure 2 A chagras in the Amazon basin.

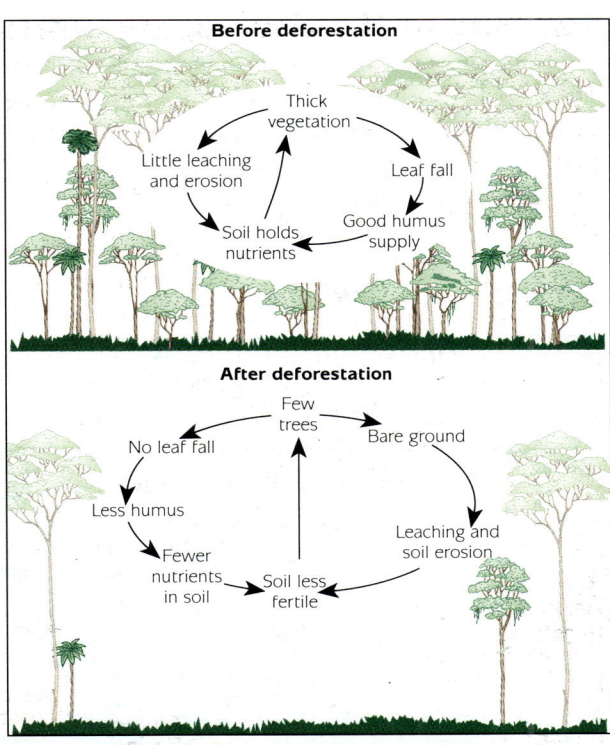

▲ Figure 3 Nutrient cycling in the rainforest.

but less harmful to the environment than permanent agriculture. Recently, new developments in the rain forest are forcing the tribes into smaller and smaller areas of land or into reservations. The Indians are being forced to clear for a second time patches of land which have not yet fully recovered. The soils are being damaged beyond repair, making it impossible for the rain forest to re-establish. Large numbers of Indians have also died from 'Western' diseases or been killed by developers. Many have decided to leave the rain forest and join other migrants in the shanty towns of the large urban areas.

Activity

a Explain how shifting cultivation is both extensive and subsistence farming.
b Show this type of farming as a systems diagram:

Inputs	Processes	Outputs

c Describe the problems and changes in this type of farming.
d Suggest ways in which farmers and their families could break out of the poverty trap.

Plantation agriculture

A plantation is a vast agricultural estate in the tropics, often occupying 2000–3000 hectares. It is a highly efficient, intensive and well organized farming unit that resembles a factory rather than a traditional farm. Plantations are commercial enterprises, often growing a single **cash crop** for export to developed countries. This is called **monoculture**. A tremendous variety of crops are grown on plantations, including coffee, tea, cocoa, rubber, bananas (**Figure 1**), oil palm and cotton. Many plantations were begun by the colonial powers. Companies from the developed world set up the plantations to provide their own countries with tropical foods, beverages and raw materials that they were unable to grow themselves. Today, many are still owned and operated by the huge **multinational** or **transnational** corporations (TNCs) which have their headquarters in the developed world, for example Unilever (**Figure 2**), Dunlop and Nestlé. The plantations are both capital-intensive and labour-intensive. In the past, local labour was augmented by the use of slaves or the in-migration of workers from other areas. **Figure 3** shows the advantages and disadvantages of plantations to the developing countries.

Unilever is a giant Anglo-Dutch TNC, one of the largest industrial companies in the world. It includes some 500 companies in 80 different countries, employs over 250 000 people and sells over 1000 different products. Unilever's headquarters, manufacturing and research and development sites are mostly located in the MEDCs. Unilever is the world's largest producer of margarine, ice-cream and packaged tea. Many of the products, such as Flora, Oxo and Persil, and companies such as Bird's Eye, Wall's and Lever Brothers, are household names.

In 1992 Unilever employed 120 000 people in LEDCs where it owns and operates plantations and factories.

Advantages of plantations	Disadvantages of plantations
Exports earn large amounts of foreign exchange which can be used to improve the economy and services in a country.	Plantations often occupy the most fertile soils which would be better used to grow food crops for the local people.
TNCs bring expertise, skills and knowledge which can be taught to the local people.	Some countries export plantation cash crops only to import food crops which they could be growing themselves.
Many jobs are provided for the local people, raising their living standards and having a spin-off in the local economy.	TNCs take most of the profits back to the developed countries, particularly as much of the value-adding (processing and packaging) takes place out of the producing country.
Plantations provide houses, schools, health clinics and services, such as electricity and water, which improve standards of living.	Local people may be exploited as cheap labour.
Roads and railways are often built, improving the infrastructure.	The growth of a single crop makes plantations very susceptible to disease, poor weather and the fluctuations in world market prices.
Some plantation products provide a local food supply. Unilever's palm oil production in Malaysia is sold locally.	

▲ **Figure 3** The advantages and disadvantages of plantations.

▲ **Figure 1** A banana plantation.

Planted land area of Unilever's plantations

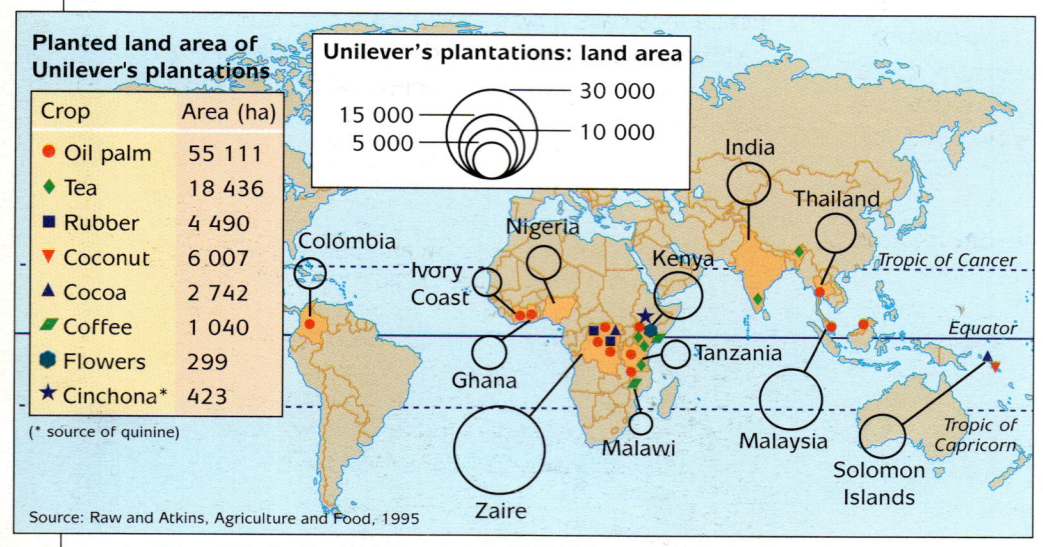

Crop	Area (ha)
● Oil palm	55 111
◆ Tea	18 436
■ Rubber	4 490
▼ Coconut	6 007
▲ Cocoa	2 742
／ Coffee	1 040
● Flowers	299
★ Cinchona*	423

(* source of quinine)

Source: Raw and Atkins, Agriculture and Food, 1995

▲ **Figure 2** Unilever's plantations (1993).

A rubber plantation

Malaysia has a hot, wet equatorial climate (pages 76–77) and gentle relief that are perfect for rubber trees. No part of the country is very far from the coast, allowing easy export and import of goods. Rubber is one of Malaysia's main cash crops.

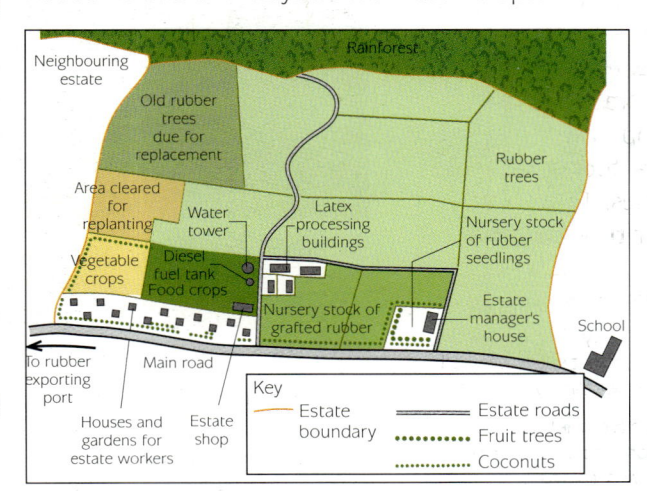

▲ Figure 4 A rubber plantation in peninsular Malaysia.

One of the largest plantation schemes is the **Jengka Triangle Project**, located in the centre of the state of Pahang. It has 40 500ha of oil palm and rubber, and houses over 9000 families. There are 23 schemes in the region. Within each scheme the plantations are arranged in separate sections (Figure 4) with trees at different stages of growth. The trees are first tapped when they are about six years old and they produce latex for about 20 years. At any one time about 60 per cent of the land has mature trees, 20 per cent young trees and 20 per cent is being cleared for replanting. The tapping and collecting are done early in the morning and the latex is taken to the processing factories. The latex and dry rubber are used for making tyres and other products.

Problems and effects on the environment

Plantations are an example of large-scale interference with the ecosystem. The natural rain forest is destroyed and the initial clearance exposes bare ground to the damaging effects of weather. Heavy machinery compacts the soil. Erosion may be severe and cause silting of rivers, and landslides. Soils are generally poor. It is often necessary to use **soil conservation** techniques.

▲ Figure 5 Techniques for soil conservation

Soil conservation techniques

1 The growing of cover crops
This is widely practised in new development schemes such as the Jengka Triangle Project in Malaysia. Leguminous crops are planted between the rows of young oil palm and rubber trees to protect the topsoil. The leguminous plants also help to restore fertility by adding nitrogen to the soil.

2 Bunds and pits
Bunds are raised banks of soil which enclose a depression or pit. They are constructed near young trees to slow down soil erosion and trap the soil as it is washed away.

3 Terracing
Terracing is used on steep slopes to prevent soil erosion. The steep slopes are levelled by building steps or terraces which follow the contours of the slope.

4 Fertilizers
Plantations have a high capital expenditure on fertilizers such as potash and nitrates. In recent years fertilizers have been applied by spraying from aeroplanes or helicopters.

Activity

1. Both shifting cultivation and plantation agriculture take place in the hot, wet tropical rain forests. Describe the similarities and differences between the two farming systems. Consider the following: physical conditions, intensive or extensive, scale of operation, subsistence or commercial, environmental impact.

Intensive subsistence rice growing in south-east Asia

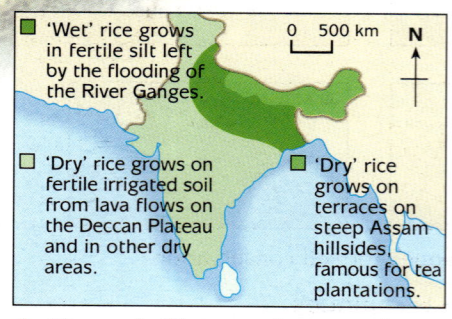

Figure 1 Rice growing areas in India and Bangladesh.
- 'Wet' rice grows in fertile silt left by the flooding of the River Ganges.
- 'Dry' rice grows on fertile irrigated soil from lava flows on the Deccan Plateau and in other dry areas.
- 'Dry' rice grows on terraces on steep Assam hillsides, famous for tea plantations.

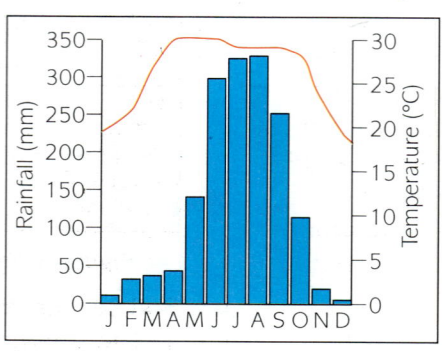

Figure 2 The monsoon climate.

Figure 3 Planting rice.

South-east Asia is one of the most densely populated areas in the world and rice is the **staple** or main food crop. Rice growing is uniquely linked to the monsoon climate and the high densities of population. Most farmers are *subsistence* farmers who grow the rice to feed themselves and their families. Rice grows best in areas with heavy **monsoon** rains or where ample **irrigation** water can be provided. The flood plain and delta of the River Ganges in India and Bangladesh (**Figure 1**) have many advantages for rice growing.

The growing of rice is hard work and usually involves the whole family (**Figure 3**). The typical farmer's year is shown in **Figure 4** – in some years the farmer grows a second crop on the same land, either beans, lentils or peas. The farmers may also keep a few chickens for eggs and meat.

Problems of rice growing

1 Flooding
The River Ganges frequently floods and under normal conditions the floodwaters are useful, providing the water and fertile silt for the paddy fields. Sometimes the floods are catastrophic, and they destroy the rice crop.

2 Drought
In some years the monsoon 'fails'; rainfall is lower than expected and the rice crop is ruined.

Month	Things to do
January	Plant crops: peas, beans and lentils.
February	Weed fields. Look after crops.
March	Harvest crops.
April	Finish off odd jobs before monsoon starts.
May	Get seed bed ready for rice, weed, spread ash and manure on fields. When the rains come, sow rice seed.
June	Weed fields.
July	Plough in manure.
August	Move rice plants to another field. Plant them out 25cm apart.
September	More weeding. Add manure.
October	Rice plants begin to flower. Weeding.
November	Monsoon is over. Rice ripens.
December	Harvest and thresh rice.

Source: Adapted from: Longman *Geography for GCSE*, 1997: 162

Figure 4 The lowland rice farmer's year.

3 Shortage of land
Large areas are owned by big landowners and there are many landless peasants. In addition, traditionally when a man dies his land is divided among his sons. The units become too small to support a family.

4 Population growth
India has a high rate of population growth and new methods of farming are needed to feed the population.

Physical factors
- A monsoon climate (**Figure 2**) with heavy rains and high temperatures provides ideal conditions for rapid growth of rice.
- Heavy alluvial soils provide an impervious muddy layer.
- Flat flood plains make the flooding of fields easier; terraced hill slopes can be used for 'dry rice' in areas such as Assam.
- There is a water supply from the River Ganges and from wells.

Human factors
- Rice gives high yields per hectare, which helps to feed the large population.
- Water buffaloes are used for work and as a source of manure for the fields.
- Rice seeds are stored from one year to provide the next year's crop.
- Rice growing is labour-intensive.
- Many people can work in the paddy fields ploughing, planting, harvesting and threshing.

Chapter 10 Agriculture

The Green Revolution

In the 1960s India needed more and better food and an improved standard of living for its people. The Government implemented the Green Revolution, which involved technological changes to increase food output.

- Indian farmers were given seed of **high-yielding varieties** (HYVs) of drought-resistant Mexican wheat such as IR8, with an average yield of 5.0 tonnes rather than 1.5 tonnes per hectare. Because the plants were fast growing, ripening in four months instead of five, a second crop could be grown. This is called **double** or **multiple cropping**. HYVs had shorter and stiffer stems that were more resistant to wind and rain and more plants could be planted per unit area.
- More fertilizers were used as the HYVs were more demanding on soil nutrients.
- Tractors and mechanized ploughs were used instead of water buffalo.
- Grants and loans were made available to farmers to purchase new seeds and equipment.
- Irrigation schemes were built to ensure adequate water supplies.

Successes	Failures
• Farmers who could afford the HYVs and fertilizer increased yields by three times.	• Many poor peasants could not afford to buy HYVs and fertilizer so their yields did not change.
• Faster-growing plants allowed multiple cropping each year.	• Poorer farmers who borrowed money could not pay it back and their debts increased, forcing some of them to move to the city.
• Farmers could grow wheat, maize and vegetables as well as rice, giving more variety in the diet.	• The HYVs need more fertilizers and pesticides, which are expensive.
• Increased output created a surplus to sell in the cities, raising the farmers' income and standard of living and reducing the costs of imports.	• Irrigation schemes were needed and many farmers lost their homes and land.
• Higher incomes allowed more fertilizer and machinery to be bought.	

▲ **Figure 5** Successes and failures of the Green Revolution.

Figure 5 shows that the Green Revolution had its successes and failures.

Overall, the introduction of the Green Revolution widened the gap between the rich and poor farmers – the rich became richer and the poor became poorer.

Irrigation

The monsoon rains in India are irregular and sometimes inadequate for rice to grow. The new HYVs and multiple cropping also require far more water. This has increased the importance of irrigation to water the land artificially. In the Ganges valley several different techniques, both traditional and modern, are used to irrigate the land.

1. **Wells** are a traditional method of irrigation in the Ganges valley. They are used where surface water is in short supply and there are water supplies underground. Holes are dug to reach the water table and each well can irrigate one or two hectares of land. It is a very cheap method of irrigation for many of the poor farmers. Traditional methods of lifting water from the well are the *shaduf* and the *sakia* (a waterwheel) operated by donkeys or oxen (**Figure 6**). The Green Revolution is replacing these with modern electric or diesel pumps. Deep, modern **tube wells** are being dug. Electric pumps are used to bring water to the surface, and up to 400ha of land can be irrigated from one tube well.

◀ **Figure 6** A *sakia* or waterwheel. Oxen turn the wheel and cowhide buckets are lifted and emptied into field ditches.

2. **Inundation canals** are used in the Ganges valley. These are canals dug on the sides of a river to lead water into the fields when the river level rises and floods. The canals are cheap to build and maintain, and they are able to bring valuable nutrients from the flood water to the fields, reducing the need for expensive fertilizers. However, irrigation canals also cause problems of waterlogging and salinization through the upward movement of salts in the soil. The canals attract disease-carrying insects, and evaporation rates are high.

Appropriate technology

The Green Revolution brought with it the need for cheap sources of power and more water for irrigation. Some LEDCs followed the example of the developed world and built large dams to provide a water supply and electricity. However, many of these schemes have major disadvantages for the subsistence farmers (**Figure 1**) who cannot afford new electric or diesel pumps, fertilizers, HYV seeds and pesticides. Many have borrowed money and now find themselves in **debt**. The increased yields have not been sufficient to repay the debt, and high interest rates make repayment impossible.

Many subsistence farmers would have been better off using **appropriate technology**. It involves:

- using small dams and individual wells (**Figure 2**)
- using renewable energy sources such as wind, solar power and biogas (**Figure 3**) rather than expensive electricity or imported oil
- setting up labour-intensive projects to use the cheap labour force rather than machines
- providing tools and techniques designed to use local resources and skills
- avoiding hi-tech machines which need expensive fuel and spare parts imported from abroad
- setting up low-cost schemes using technologies the local people can afford, understand and control
- establishing projects that are sustainable and in harmony with the environment.

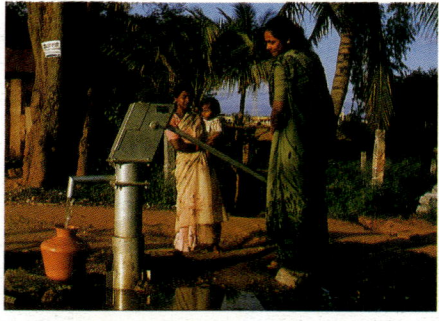

Figure 2 Appropriate technology – a well in Northern India.

Figure 3 A biogas plant.

Locals lose homes and land.

Stagnant water increases water-borne disease.

Little or no compensation for the locals.

Influx of foreign workers bring disease and introduce different cultures and moral standards.

Loss of floodwater and silt. Locals may need pumps to obtain water for irrigation and money for fertilisers.

▲ **Figure 1** The disadvantages of the large-scale project.

Test questions

1. a What is subsistence farming? (2 marks)
   b Using Figure 3 page 146, describe the world distribution of subsistence farming. (3 marks)
   c Choose *one* of the following types of subsistence farming:
      - Shifting cultivation
      - Rice growing.
      (i) Name a country and location where the chosen farming is practised. (2 marks)
      (ii) Describe the physical factors which favour this type of farming. (6 marks)
   d (i) What is the Green Revolution? (1 mark)
      (ii) Explain the advantages and disadvantages of the Green Revolution to developing countries. (6 marks)

2. a Describe the differences between intensive and extensive farming. (3 marks)
   b Choose one type of intensive farming:
      - arable farms in East Anglia
      - plantations
      - market gardening in the Netherlands.
      (i) Describe how the farm type is intensive. (4 marks)
      (ii) Draw a systems diagram for the farm:

Inputs	Processes	Outputs

      (6 marks)
   c (i) Define diversification. (1 mark)
      (ii) Choose one farm you have studied. Describe the ways it has diversified. (4 marks)
      (iii) Give two reasons why the farmer has diversified. (2 marks)

Chapter 11
Industry

Cambridge Science Park, an example of a modern development on a greenfield site

Key Ideas

Industrial activity can be classified:
- primary, secondary, tertiary and quaternary are the four types of industry.

Industry is a system:
- as with all systems there are inputs, processes and outputs.

Industrial location is influenced by many factors:
- locational factors include raw materials, energy, capital, labour, transport and government
- the relative importance of these varies according to the type of industry.

Industry changes over time:
- on a global scale the changing nature of industry has led to the growth of newly industrializing countries (NICs) and multi-national corporations.

Types of industry

Four types are usually recognized – primary, secondary, tertiary and quaternary. These mean simply first, second, third and fourth, and refer to the order in which they developed.

1 Primary industry

Primary industries extract **raw materials**, which are natural products untreated by people, from the land or sea. Although many are truly natural products, some are farm products from plants and animals. Mining, quarrying, forestry, farming and fishing are all examples of **primary industries**. People who work in these industries have occupations in the primary sector.

Examples of raw materials

Minerals, e.g. crude oil
Metals, e.g. iron ore and bauxite
Vegetation, e.g. wood
Plants, e.g. cotton
Plant products, e.g. cocoa and rubber
Animal products, e.g. wool and hides

Figure 1 Herding in Egypt – starting young in primary industry.

2 Secondary industry

When raw materials are manufactured, they are *changed* by one or more manufacturing processes – by manual (hand) labour, by machines, by being heated, by having water or chemicals added – until they are made into something different. These manufactured products are **secondary** products. People making goods in factories work in the secondary sector, because manufacturing is classified as a **secondary** industry. Secondary industries also include building and construction.

Figure 2 A factory making dyes in Leicester – an example of secondary industry.

3 Tertiary industry

Many industries neither produce a raw material nor make a product. Instead they provide services to people and to other industries. The long list of services in the Information Box on page 167 still misses some important services out, such as education (schools and teachers) and broadcasting (TV and radio). The list includes essential services used every day, such as water and electricity, and others equally essential but used less frequently, such as doctors. Others are optional services, such as tourism, leisure, sport and entertainment, that make life more enjoyable and interesting. These services are examples of **tertiary** industries. These tertiary industries increase and multiply as countries and people become more wealthy.

Examples of manufacturing industries

Raw material	Manufacturing process(es)	Manufactured goods
Crude oil	Refining using heat	Petrol, plastics, polythene
Wood	Hand carving	Wooden ornaments
Cotton	Spinning and weaving by machines	Clothes, sheets, towels
Oranges	Squeezing with machines and adding water	Fruit juice

Types of services

Health, e.g. doctors and dentists

Local Council, e.g. refuse collection and care services

Local services, e.g. water, gas and electricity

Communications, e.g. phone and cable companies

Transport, e.g. buses and trains

Retail, e.g. supermarkets and stores

Financial, e.g. banks and building societies

Sport and leisure, e.g. sports centres and tennis clubs

Tourism, e.g. hotel staff and tourist guides

Figure 3 The downtown business district at the southern tip of Manhattan in New York.
Its skyline is dominated by the twin towers of the World Trade Centre, each more than 100 storeys high. The area houses the Wall Street Stock Exchange and offices for all the world's major banks, insurance and trading companies. Tertiary industries are concentrated in city centres everywhere, but this is one of the world's greatest concentrations. There are service sector jobs for over 50 000 people in the twin towers alone.

4 Quaternary industry

In recent years high-technology has become a great part of everyday life in MEDCs. How many people in your class have access to a computer at home? Until a few years ago only businesses had computers. Now they are on sale among the washing machines and fridges in electrical shops. Research and development (R&D) has made this possible. Most big companies have an R&D department that researches and develops new products at the frontiers of technology. Such high-technology research-based industries are called **quaternary** industries. Their highly skilled, and often well paid, staff work in the quaternary sector of employment. Silicon Valley, not far from San Francisco in California, is famous for its concentration of high-tech companies which rely upon the fruits of research. In the UK the growth of the quaternary sector has brought 'Silicon Glen' in the central lowlands of Scotland, the 'Technology Corridor' west of London, and over 40 Science Parks attached to Universities.

Activities

1. State the primary sector occupations associated with the raw materials listed in the first Information Box on page 166.

2. Name three different manufactured products which can be made from each of the following raw materials:
   - grapes
   - iron ore
   - pine trees.

3. Name the main raw material used for manufacturing each of the following:
   a bread b cheese c beer
   d soft drinks cans e electrical wire.

Figure 4 Changes in employment in different types of industry in the UK since 1841.

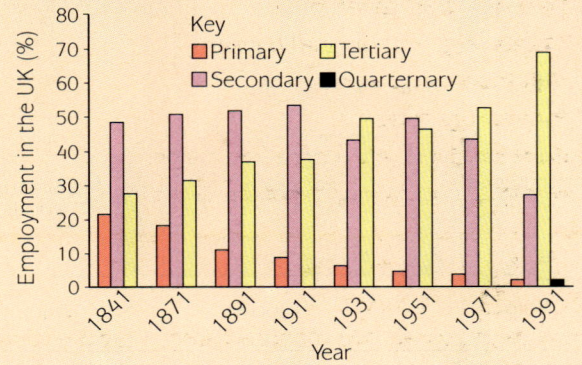

4 a From **Figure 4** give the year:
   (i) when primary employment fell below 10 per cent for the first time
   (ii) when secondary employment was at its peak
   (iii) after which tertiary employment has remained the greatest.

b State the evidence from **Figure 4** for the following features of employment, which happen as a country becomes more economically developed.
   (i) The primary sector decreases in importance.
   (ii) The tertiary sector increases in importance and becomes the most important.
   (iii) A small quaternary sector develops.

c (i) For 1991, state the percentages given in **Figure 4** for the four sectors of employment.
   (ii) Plot these on a pie chart and give a key to the sectors.

Industry as a system

All systems have inputs, processes and outputs. A simple version of the factory system is given in **Figure 1**. Raw materials (an input) go into the factory at one end. They are worked upon and changed (processes) in the factory. Manufactured goods (output) come out of the other end of the factory and are transported away to market. A factory is also a business. For it to survive, the factory needs to make a profit. The combined costs of obtaining the inputs and undertaking the processes must be lower than the value of the outputs that are sold (**Figure 2**).

Of course, the system is more complicated than this. Many factories use more than one kind of raw material. Some factories, such as in the car industry, use many component parts made in other factories. There are several inputs; a fuller list is given in **Figure 3**. The company owning the factory pays for the inputs, although in some cases the cost may be reduced by government grants. Although the real interest is in goods for sale, most factories produce waste as a by-product of processing raw materials. Some wastes are produced as gases and burnt off into the atmosphere, but there are also solid and liquid wastes which need to be treated and disposed of, and that costs money. When factories make profits, they go to the owners or shareholders. However, most companies re-invest some of the profits back into the factory for greater profits in the future.

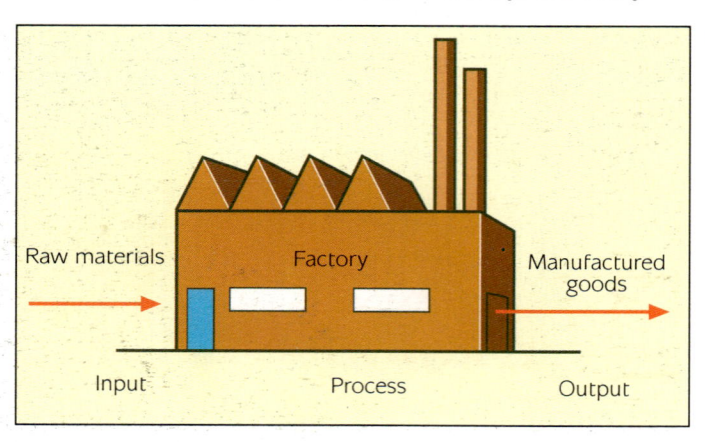

Figure 1 A simple factory system.

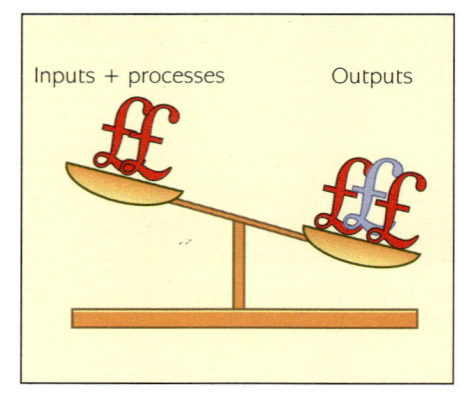

Figure 2 A profitable factory.

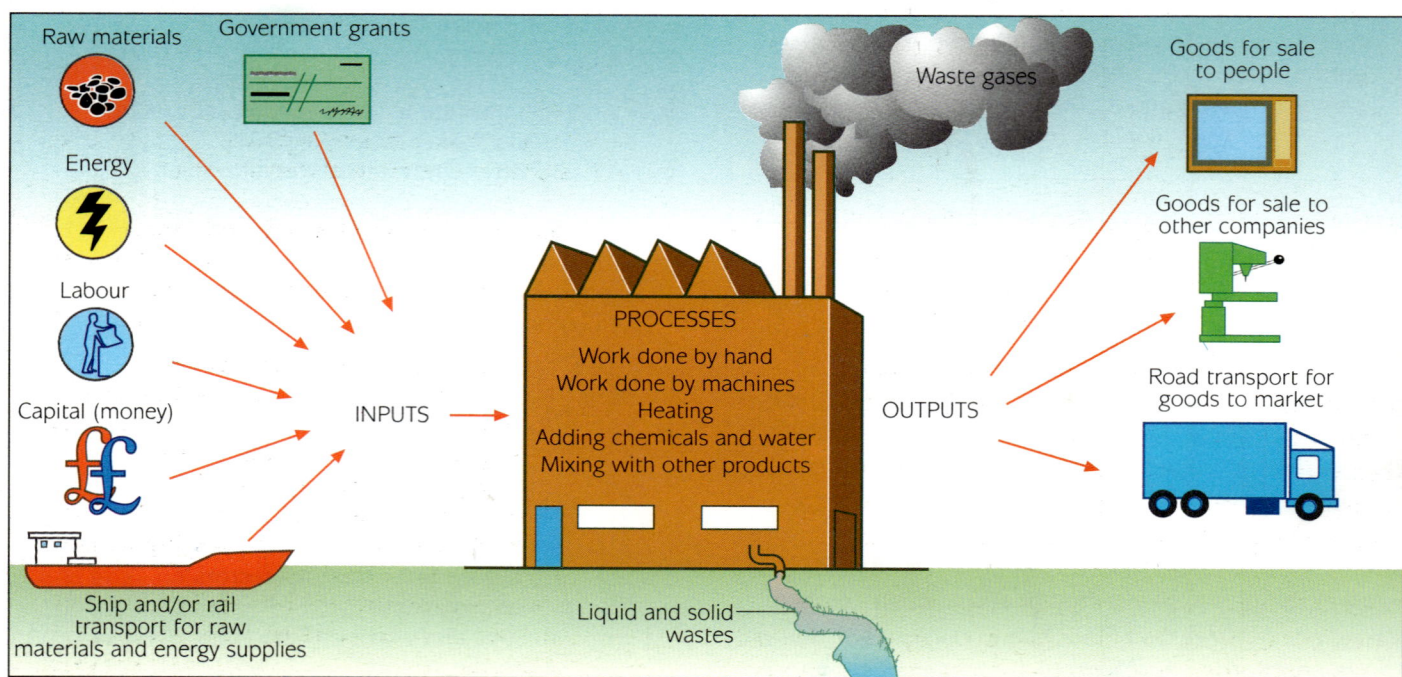

Figure 3 Factory system for a manufacturing industry.

Figure 4 Types of manufacturing industry.

```
         Primary      Secondary    Tertiary    Quarternary
         industry     industry     industry    industry
```

Heavy industries
Characteristics
- Large-scale industries.
- Big plants covering large areas of land
- Capital intensive–big investment needed to set them up.
- Make large products often bought by other manufacturing companies.

Examples: Steel, oil-refining, chemicals, engineering, and ship building.

Light (consumer) industries
Characteristics
- Make small products, mainly to be bought by individuals.
- Most are small-scale, suitable for factory units on industrial estates.
- Only a limited amount of investment capital is needed.

Examples: Electrical goods, clothing, food-processing and toys.

Hi-tech industries
Characteristics
- Make high-value products using modern technology.
- Heavy capital investment in research and development.
- Many are sufficiently small to be housed in units on business parks.

Examples: Computers, business systems, microprocessors and communications equipment.

Figure 5 View over Teesside, one of the largest concentrations of heavy industry in the UK.

Types of manufacturing industry

Manufacturing industries make goods from raw materials and/or assemble parts made by other companies. A three-fold division of manufacturing industry is often used – heavy, light and high-tech (**Figure 4**).

Some heavy industries refine minerals, such as crude oil, into many different products, which can then be used by other industries to make a multitude of smaller products. Others smelt metals, such as iron ore, into steel, and these are produced in many different shapes and forms depending upon what they are going to be used for. The works may cover large areas of land; pollution from their chimneys may be obvious many kilometres away. They do not add to the scenic beauty of the landscape, but they are necessary industries because they provide the materials many light industries use for making consumer goods (**Figure 5**).

Light and high-tech industries can be combined under one heading – **footloose** industries. The term **footloose** refers to their greater freedom to choose a location compared with heavy industries. This freedom comes from having low raw material demands and the need only for small factories, which means that suitable sites are widely available. The final products, being high in value and low in weight, can be easily distributed anywhere by road. New factories typically have pleasant locations on the edges of towns surrounded by green areas.

Test questions

1 Definitions.
  a Define 'manufacturing industry'. (1 mark)
  b Define the term 'footloose industry'. (2 marks)
  c What is meant by 'high-tech' industries? (3 marks)
  d State the main features of heavy industries. (4 marks)

2 Photograph interpretation: use **Figure 5**.
  a State the physical features of the area shown in **Figure 5**. (2 marks)
  b Draw a labelled sketch based on the photograph to show the locations and features of the heavy industries. (5 marks)
  c Some of the people from the housing areas on the photograph are happy to live there, but others are not. Suggest why people have different views about living near heavy industries. (3 marks)

Factors affecting industrial location

If a manufacturing company is going to be profitable, the directors need to consider the location for their factory carefully. Most consider the costs of inputs for locations in several different areas. After deciding upon the area with the greatest number of favourable factors, they look for a suitable site. Sometimes there are two or three equally attractive locations where costs are similar. In these cases the availability of government financial aid for one of the locations may be the deciding factor. Sometimes when advantages are similar the choice of final location can be based on quite irrational human decisions such as nearness to a good golf course or a successful football team.

The type of manufacturing industry strongly influences decisions about location. Another simple example can be used (**Figure 2**). If the three locational factors – nearness to raw materials, markets and labour force – are considered to be of equal importance, point A is the logical position for the factory. However, for Factory 1 nearness to raw materials is the most significant factor with the greatest pulling power. The position of Factory 2 suggests that market is the most important factor in choosing a location. Factory 2 may make goods that are perishable, or of low value and heavy to transport. What goods regularly bought in the shops could be made in Factory 2?

Transport
Movement of raw materials by water (sea and inland waterways) or over land (road and rail). Movement of manufactured goods to market (roads are used for part or all of the journey). Many manufactured goods transported in countries which are interchangeable between road, rail and ship. Air cargo sometimes used for light, high-value goods.

Greater weight/amount of raw materials needed by heavy industries – transport costs are very important. Speedy delivery and easy transport to markets are significant for light/consumer goods.

Other communications
Dramatic growth in fax, phone, cable, on-line computer systems and e-mail. Global communication is now faster and easier than ever imagined.

Greater freedom for location worldwide. Less need for office staff in the factory as people can work from home. Newspapers are printed near markets both at home and overseas, but this has all happened too recently for the wider effects on location to become clear.

Capital
Money used to set up industry. Invested in the factory building and on the machines inside it. The money comes from bank loans or shareholders, sometimes with contributions from governments (or EU).

Heavy industries in hi-tech industries need capital most. It is more likely to influence choice of country or region rather than exact location within it.

Market
The buyers of goods whether other companies or individual consumers. Market size reflects both the number of buyers and their wealth. Location of market – whether concentrated in one place or widely dispersed.

Heavy industries making large and bulky products must either have a market close by or access to cheap transport (e.g. next to the sea). Light industries making perishable goods need either markets close by or a location next to a fast transport link (motorway, high-speed train, airport).
Least affected are industries making light, high-value and non-perishable products.

Government
Role can be positive, cutting out restrictions and providing industrial sites. Industry can be attracted to a country or region by grants and cheap loans. Role can be negative by refusing planning permission or increasing business taxes.

The higher the capital investment, e.g. for a heavy industry or a large factory such as a car plant, the more attractive government money is. Government incentives are usually reserved for areas of high unemployment to which industries are unwilling to move.

Labour
Numbers, quality and cost of workers is important. Sufficient numbers of workers, with the skills required, are needed. Average wage rates can vary significantly between regions and countries.

Access to highly educated, skilled labour is often most important factor for hi-tech industries. Cheap labour matters most for labour-intensive industries, e.g. textiles. Labour is of little importance in modern highly mechanized industries, e.g. oil-refining and petrochemicals.

▲ **Figure 1** Factors affecting the location of manufacturing industries.

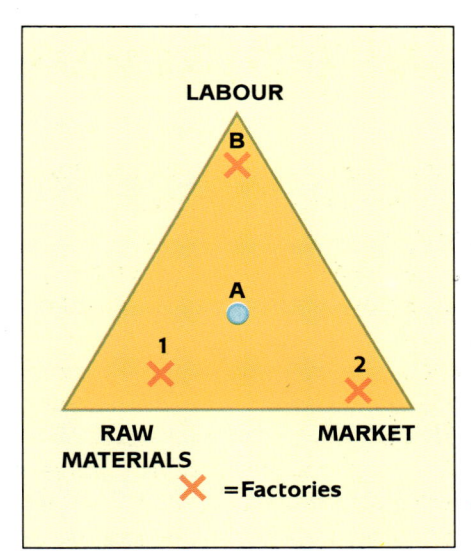

Figure 2 Factory locations.

Raw materials

Materials from which the goods in the factory are made. Examples include metals, minerals, wood, plant and animal products. Heavier and bulkier than the finished goods

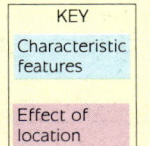

KEY
Characteristic features

Effect of location

Often low in value and expensive to transport – they attract industries toward them. Heavy industries most likely to be attracted – they consume a lot of raw materials.

Site needs

Most important are cost and availability of land. Flat or gently sloping land is preferred – cheaper to develop.

Heavy industry needs a large area of flat and cheap land. Light industry needs less land and may consider other factors such as appearance

Energy

Energy is needed for changing raw materials into manufactured goods. Burning fuels such as coal, oil and gas provides heat. Energy sources such as electricity drive machinery.

Heavy industries most attracted – they use the most. Electricity is available everywhere – allows lighter industries to be footloose.

Activities

1. a Why is Factory 1 on **Figure 2** located in a position associated with heavy industries?
   b Name two examples of *consumer goods* which are:
      (i) perishable
      (ii) low in value but heavy.
   c (i) What type of industry would you expect to be located at point B on **Figure 2**?
      (ii) Justify your choice.

2. **Figure 3** shows the relative costs of transporting iron ore by sea.

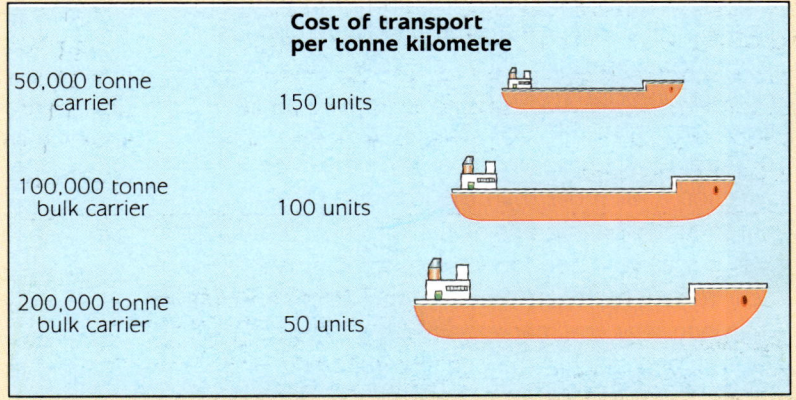

	Cost of transport per tonne kilometre
50,000 tonne carrier	150 units
100,000 tonne bulk carrier	100 units
200,000 tonne bulk carrier	50 units

   Figure 3 The relative cost of transporting iron ore by sea.

   a Describe what **Figure 3** shows.
   b Why are many modern steelworks next to deepwater harbours?

3. Decision-making. The directors of an oil company have already decided to locate a petrochemical works in the area shown in **Figure 4**. The letters A, B, C and D indicate the positions of four sites that are being considered. The supply of crude oil will come by super-tanker.

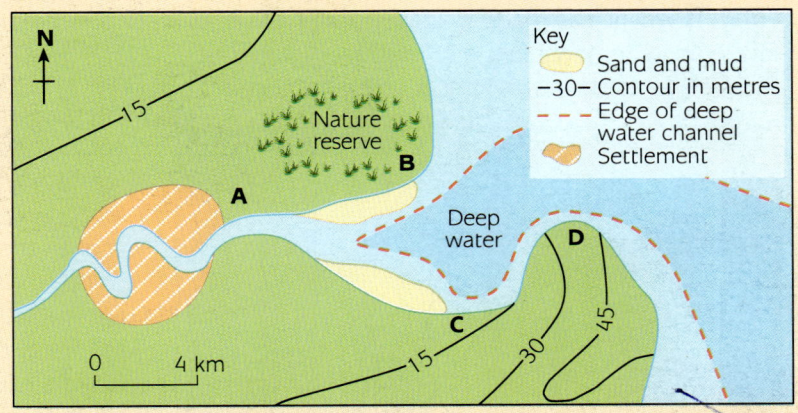

   Figure 4 Sites for a petrochemical works.

   a From the evidence available on the map, which site would be most suitable for the location of a petrochemical works? Give reasons to support your choice.
   b Explain why you considered the other three sites less suitable.
   c What other information about this area, not given on the map, could have influenced the decision about choosing a site?

Case Study – Teesside

Heavy industry

Heavy industries have been located around the estuary of the River Tees for more than a century and they remain a dominant feature of the landscape, as Figure 5 on page 169 shows.

Steel-making – historical background

Iron and steel industries began to develop along the south bank of the Tees between Middlesbrough and Redcar in the 19th century because all the **raw material** and **fuel supplies** were locally available – iron ore from the Cleveland Hills, coking coal from the Durham coalfield and limestone from the East Durham plateau (**Figure 1**). The iron ore, coal and limestone weighed a lot more than the iron and steel products that came out of the furnaces. Transport was not as well developed as it is today. A location near to raw materials made more economic sense than one near the market, although large markets for iron and steel in the engineering works and shipyards which lined the banks of the rivers Tyne and Wear were not far away.

Steel-making on Teesside in the 1990s

Of these early advantages for steel-making, only the supply of limestone still exists today; the coal mines and shipyards have all closed. However, British Steel recognizes that Teesside still has many locational advantages for a modern steelworks, which is why it has made massive capital investments in new plant and machinery. Most of the steel is made in the Redcar works (square 5625 on **Figure 2**) which is a modern plant built in the 1980s. Investment in the steelworks continues, and it continues to be upgraded with the latest technology.

Transport is perhaps the key factor. The Tees estuary is wide, sheltered and deep. It is navigable for large bulk ore carriers. British Steel can buy iron ore from any country in the world where the price is right – from Brazil or Australia or Liberia – knowing that a cheap means of transport exists which can deliver ore to the steelworks' own terminal (squares 5425/5525).

The River Tees is equally useful as the starting point for the export of steel by sea to EU and other overseas **markets**; these were developed by British Steel to make up for market decline in the UK when big steel-using industries such as engineering and shipbuilding contracted. A railway line runs next to the works for distribution to other parts of the UK. The long history of steel-making means that a **labour** supply with the necessary skills and experience exists.

Finally, the **site** factors are ideal. Plenty of little-used flat land was still available upon which to build the Redcar steelworks, despite the long history of industry here. This type of land on the sides of a river estuary has few other uses, and it is therefore cheap, which is important when a large site is needed.

Other heavy industries on Teesside

Similar locational advantages attracted the chemical industry to the banks of the Tees. The early works set up by ICI at Billingham (just off the western edge of the OS map) were based upon local raw materials such as rock salt, gypsum, and coal as the fuel. Since 1950 the major expansion has been oil-based. An oil pipeline from the Ekofisk field in the North Sea brings crude oil ashore at the terminal near Seal Sands. Super-tankers can use the Tees. As you can see from the OS map, the north bank is covered by oil-storage tanks, refineries and chemical works; however, the largest industrial complex is the Wilton Works on the south bank. This is an ICI petrochemical factory producing many petroleum-based products, such as plastics and synthetic fibres, which are used by light industrial firms to make consumer goods.

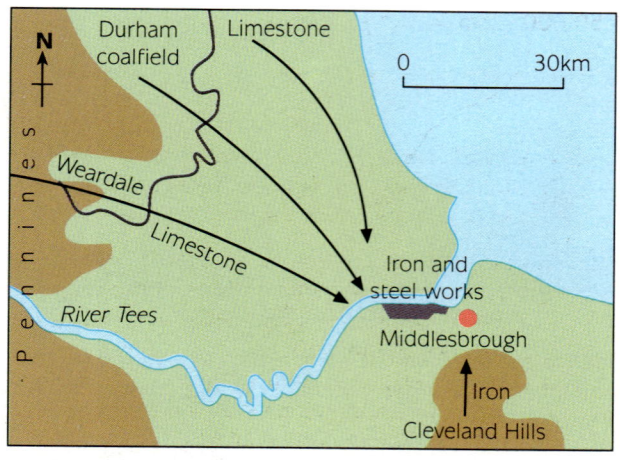

Figure 1 Sources of supply for the early iron and steel works.

Chapter 11 Industry 173

Case Study – Teesside

▲ **Figure 2** OS map of the Tees estuary at a scale of 1:50 000 (2cm = 1km).

Activities

Use **Figure 2** for answering questions 1–3.

1 On a sketch map:
  a show where the steelworks are located
  b label their site features.

2 a Describe the physical features of the River Tees which allow it to be used by large ships.
  b (i) Name three human aids to help ships navigate the river.
   (ii) Describe how each one is useful.

3 a Describe the pattern of roads and railways.
  b Give one physical and one human reason for the high density of roads in the area.

4 'Teesside – a case study of a region of heavy industry'. Using information from these pages and page 169, make notes using the headings:
  a Examples of industries
  b Where they are located
  c Factors which influence their location
  d Likely environmental problems.

Case Study – Motorway corridors out of London

Footloose industries

New industrial regions, in which the industrial structure is dominated by **footloose** industries, are most likely to be located next to motorways. The growth industries they contain are often referred to as **sunrise** industries. There are many of them along motorway corridors, such as the M11, M23, M3 and M4 (**Figure 1**). The greatest concentration of all is along the M4 corridor in the section between London and Reading. **Light** industries abound, including electrical goods, car parts and many food companies. Many of the **high-tech** companies are engaged in research and processing involving micro-electronics for computers and telecommunications equipment. High-tech companies here include Digital, Oracle and NEC.

increasingly important EU market. They also benefit from nearness to London's three main airports for international business links.

Specific advantages for high-tech industries

Labour is a key locational factor. The availability of highly skilled research scientists and engineers is very important. The presence of several universities has helped to provide a pool of graduates, and universities offer research facilities as well. The long-established presence of aerospace research in the Bristol area, undertaken by companies such as Rolls-Royce and British Aerospace, has been a further attraction for some companies. Another important consideration is where these specialist

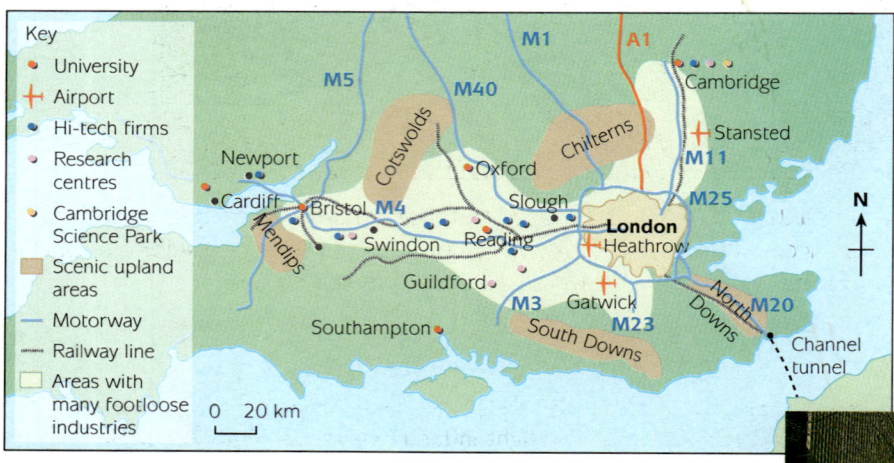

▼ **Figure 1** Industrial corridors along motorways out of London.

General advantages for the growth of light industries

Locations next to motorways would suggest that **transport** is the most important factor in deciding their location. Since they use or assemble parts of no great weight or bulk made by other industries, transport to market is more significant than raw material assembly. The wealthiest and most concentrated market in the country is in Greater London and the surrounding counties. Being close to this market is an enormous locational advantage. At the same time, there are motorway connections to the rest of Britain, and a high-speed rail link follows the M4 corridor between London and South Wales. Some parts of these corridors benefit from closeness to the routes to the Channel Tunnel and ports for access to the

▲ **Figure 2** Both food and high-tech companies are located in the industrial estate in square 7169 on the OS map. Scale 1:50 000 (2cm = 1km).

Figure 3 Part of Reading at a scale of 1:50 000; 2cm = 1km.

Case Study – Motorway corridors out of London

workers prefer to live. Areas of pleasant countryside are close enough to be accessible at weekends, they are near airports for holidays abroad, and everywhere is within easy reach of London for big sporting events, exhibitions and West End shopping and shows.

Activities

1. **a** 'The M4 corridor – case study of an area important for footloose industries': make notes using the headings:
   (i) Examples of industries
   (ii) Factors which favoured their growth.
   Use information from the text and add specific information to it (such as numbers for motorways, names for Universities and airports, etc.) from **Figure 3**.
   b Draw a labelled sketch map to show the transport advantages of the area.

2. Find square 7169 on the OS map, in which the industrial estate at Worton Grange is located. Two companies located there are shown in **Figure 2**. The large building next to the M4 is part of a brewery.
   a Describe (i) its site and (ii) its situation in relation to the rest of Reading.
   b Explain the advantages of its location for light industries such as food and drink.

3. Reading is attracting people as well as industries. Look at **Figure 4** which was taken in square 7570 in 1995.

Figure 4

   a Describe the photograph and map evidence that Lower Earley is an area of recent growth.
   b Using **Figure 3**, suggest why planners do not want Reading to grow any further to the east and south.

The Rhine–Ruhr region

Figure 1 North Rhine–Westphalia.

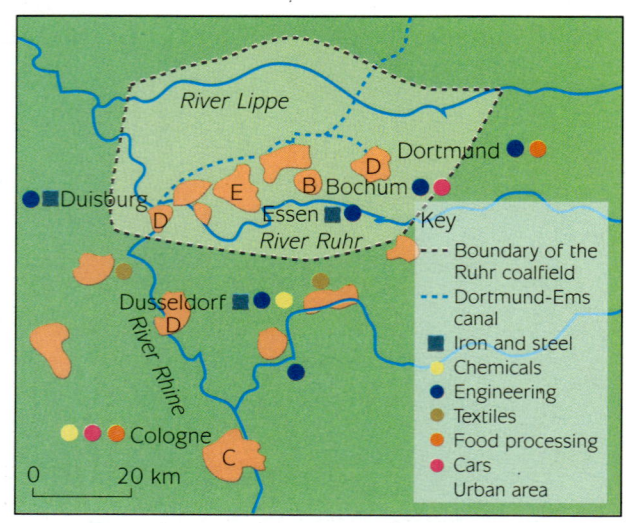

Figure 2 Industries in the Rhine–Ruhr region.

North Rhine–Westphalia is the richest and, with 18 million people, the most populous of the German states. The River Rhine flows through it towards its western edge. The largest town is Cologne (Köln) with a population of about one million (**Figure 1**). Within this state is the single greatest concentration of industry anywhere in the EU. The Rhine–Ruhr region covers the Ruhr coalfield and nearby areas in the Rhine valley.

Types of industries

For over a hundred years the region's economy was dominated by coalmining (a primary industry) and by the secondary industries which depended upon coal – textiles, steel-making and smelting metals, heavy engineering and chemicals. Today heavy industries remain important and oil-refining has been added to the list; of the consumer industries, food-processing is the most important.

Factors for the growth of industry

The Ruhr coalfield is Europe's largest **energy** supply, with massive reserves. It has a variety of types of coal, including high-quality coking coal. The amount and the quality of the coal attracted heavy industries. Heavy industries are large consumers of energy; by locating in the Ruhr they made considerable savings on transport costs. For the chemical industry coal was also a **raw material** because various products can be manufactured from it.

Such was the concentration of steel and metal-smelting industries in the area between Duisburg and Dortmund that they created their own **market**. Industries using the metals, such as heavy engineering, and industries needing machines for their factories, such as textiles, set up in the Rhine–Ruhr region as well. The smaller companies and lighter industries benefit from a location in the state with the richest and largest market in Germany. The region also occupies a central position within the EU, and benefits from a wider market of over 300 million people.

The River Rhine is used for water **transport**. It is a busy highway for barge traffic and gives a link to the North Sea and the world shipping lanes. Convoys of push-barges can move up to 9000 tonnes at a time. Moving bulky and heavy raw materials by barge is cheaper than using rail or road. The Rhine waterway therefore reduces the disadvantages of the region's inland location for heavy industries. Canals, such as the Dortmund–Ems canal, lead from the Rhine to serve steel towns such as Dortmund.

Industrial change since 1950

Industrial decline in the Rhine–Ruhr region has not been as rapid as in many other coalmining and heavy industrial regions in Europe because of:

- the amount and quality of Ruhr coal
- the productivity and prosperity of German industry

- the central position of the region within the EU
- the water links along the River Rhine.

However, there have been changes.

1. There has been a decline in the number of workers in the heavy industries and coal-mining. For example, the number of miners dropped from over half a million in the 1950s to under 100 000 by 1995. Numbers have only been kept by government subsidies and guaranteed markets for coal in electricity and steel.

2. Some non-traditional manufacturing industries, are now well established. Motor vehicle production climbed from sixteenth in order of importance in 1950 to fifth in 1995.

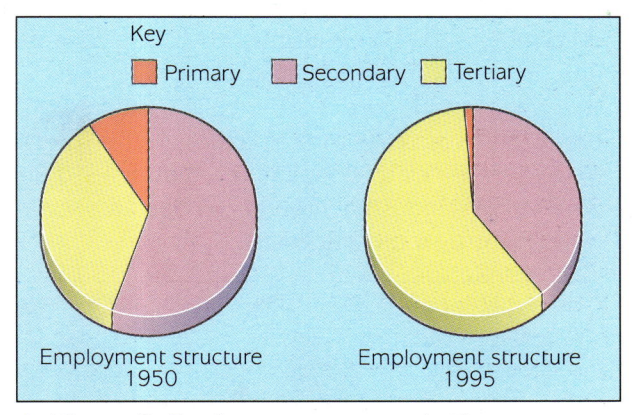

▲ **Figure 3** Employment structure in the Rhine–Ruhr region, 1950 and 1995.

3. There has been a rise in the importance of the tertiary (service) sector. Cologne, for example, has become a telecommunications and media centre. It is an attractive city on the banks of the Rhine with good transport links. In the region there are 130 000 media sector jobs.

The main problems

1. Unemployment – it has not been possible to replace all the jobs lost.
2. Overdependence upon mining and heavy industry, which still need to lose more workers.
3. An environment showing the effects of over 100 years of mining and heavy industry. The massive task of landscaping waste tips and pit heaps, cleaning up water courses, planting trees and preserving green wedges between built-up areas has been operating for over 20 years but the work is not complete.

Activities

1. **a** On a sketch map, show the location of five different manufacturing industries in the Rhine–Ruhr region.
   b Explain why the largest concentration of heavy industries in Europe developed here.
   c Describe some of the environmental problems which are caused by mining and heavy industry.

A. 1950 Top eight industries	B. 1995 Top ten industries	C. 1995 Ten largest companies
1 Textiles	1 Chemicals	1 Veda AG – chemicals
2 Coal-mining	2 Machinery	2 RWE – energy
3 Food	3 Food	3 Telekom – telecommunications
4 Steel and heavy metals	4 Electronics	4 Bayer – chemicals
5 Chemicals	5 Motor vehicles	5 Thyssen AG – steel and machinery production
6 Construction	6 Construction	6 Metro-gruppe – trading
7 Machinery	7 Steel and heavy metals	7 Rewe gruppe – retailing
8 Electronics	8 Petroleum-refining	8 Aldi-Gruppe – trading
	9 Coalmining	9 Ruhrkohle AG – mining
	10 Textiles	10 Mannesmann AG – machines and electronics

▲ **Figure 4** Changes in importance of different industries in the Rhine–Ruhr region, 1950–1995. Ranking is by turnover (a measure of volume of trade).

2. Use **Figure 4** to answer the following:
   a (i) State the two industries with the greatest change in position between 1950 and 1995.
      (ii) For one of these industries, suggest reasons for the change.
   b From column C:
      (i) name two companies operating in the tertiary (service) sector
      ii) name the company that is a primary industry.
   c Give evidence for the following:
      (i) Heavy industry remains important in 1995. ii) The tertiary sector has increased in importance.

Case Study – The Rhine–Ruhr region of Germany

Industries in less economically developed countries

The economies of many LEDCs are still dominated by primary activities, mainly farming. This is reflected in their employment structures; typically more than 50 per cent of the workforce are employed in agriculture (**Figure 1**).

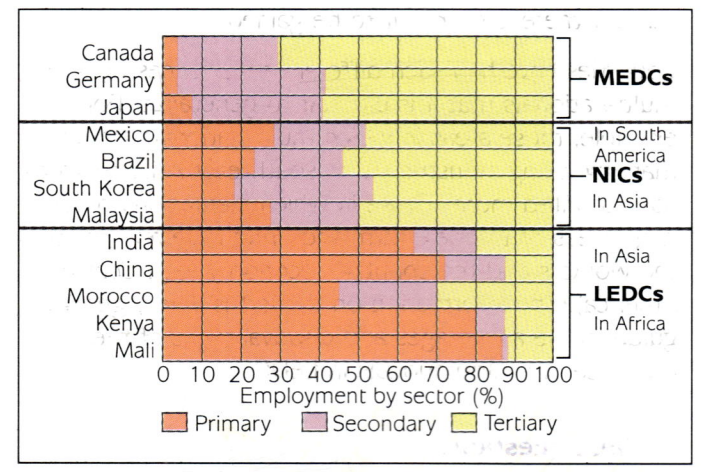

Figure 1 Employment structures for selected countries with different levels of economic development.

In countries in sub-Saharan Africa, farming is the way of life for almost everyone. In Mali, for example, trading and a tiny amount of craft industry and food-processing are confined to the capital city, Bamako, or to desert trading outposts such as Timbuktu. The employment pattern is the reverse of that in MEDCs.

On the scatter graph (**Figure 2**) the percentage employed in agriculture has been plotted against the country's wealth. This has been done for the ten main South American countries. Whilst the relationship is not perfect, you would have no problem drawing in a 'line of best fit'. A negative relationship is clearly shown – as the wealth of a country increases, the percentage employed in agriculture decreases.

In some LEDCs the secondary and tertiary sectors are now important. Look at Mexico, Brazil, South Korea and Malaysia in **Figure 1**. These countries are some examples of **newly industrializing countries** (NICs), so-called because there has been sufficient industrial growth for it to make a substantial contribution to the economy. Also the LEDCs' share of world manufacturing has increased, even though the concentration in MEDCs, where only one-quarter of the world's people live, remains overwhelming (**Figure 3**). The LEDCs' share was predicted to increase further, although this forecast was made before Asia's economic troubles in 1997–1998. Some of this industrial growth has been associated with investment by **multi-nationals**.

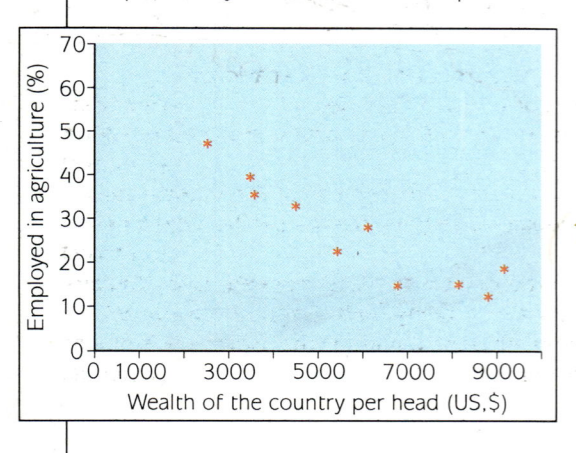

Figure 2 Relationship between wealth and percentage employment in agriculture in South America.

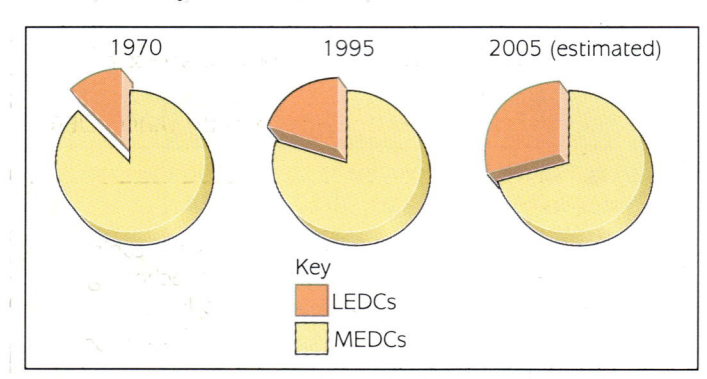

Figure 3 Percentage share of world manufacturing output.

Multi-national corporations

These are large companies which have business interests in many different countries. Their business interests can be many and varied and include mining, plantation farming and manufacturing. The headquarters of most of these companies are in MEDCs (**Figure 4**), but they are truly **global companies**. They will set up operations in MEDCs and LEDCs alike, wherever there is an opportunity for profit. Many companies with well-known brand names are multi-nationals; some are named in **Figure 4**.

Advantages and disadvantages of multi-nationals

Countries in which these companies operate have benefited from economic growth. Those countries with

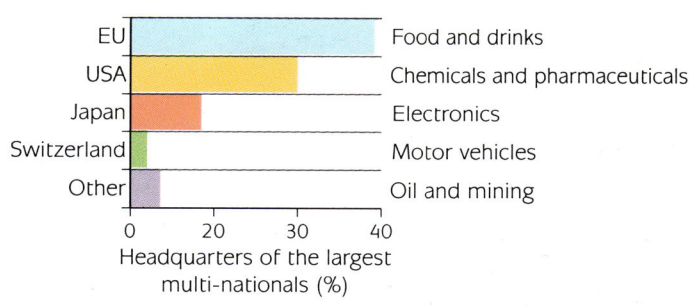

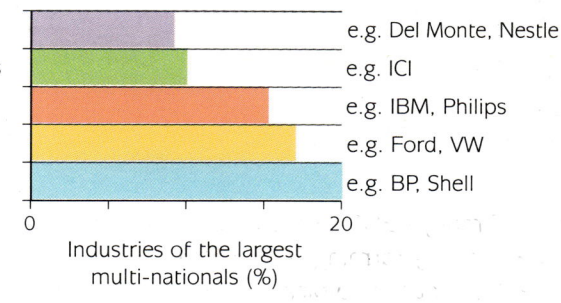

▲ Figure 4 Some characteristics of multi-nationals.

Advantages

- They bring CAPITAL, TECHNOLOGY, KNOWLEDGE, EXPERTISE and SKILLS which the country does not possess.
- They set up INDUSTRIES such as MOTOR VEHICLE MANUFACTURE, ENGINEERING and CHEMICALS, for which an LEDC does not have the necessary technology and capital.
- They bring or encourage improvement of the TRANSPORT INFRASTRUCTURE which can be used by local people and other companies.
- They create JOBS especially with assembly industries (e.g. electrical goods and electronics) and labour-intensive light manufacturing, such as clothing, sports goods and toys.
- They increase EXPORTS because of their access to markets worldwide.
- There may be OTHER BENEFITS from the MULTIPLIER EFFECT and SPIN-OFFS.

Disadvantages

- There are FEW JOBS when the industries are capital-intensive, such as oil and chemicals, and technology rather than people is used to do the work.
- LOW WAGES give the feeling that the company has moved there to exploit the workers.
- Companies AVOID TAXES and EXPORT THE PROFITS, so that the host country gains little financial benefit.
- INDUSTRIES are EXPORT-DEPENDENT, which puts them at the mercy of changes in world demand and prices over which they have no control.
- ONLY A LIMITED RANGE OF INDUSTRIES are chosen, not for the best needs of the country but for their earning potential to the company.
- POOR SAFETY RECORDS and INADEQUATE POLLUTION CONTROLS take advantage of the absence or weak enforcement of regulations, working to standards below those that would be allowed in the country where the HQ is located.

no attractions for multi-nationals, mainly in Africa and Asia, are among the world's poorest countries. However, the multi-nationals are motivated by profit rather than by a desire to achieve economic development for their host country; they are the world's most competitive companies and will leave a country as quickly as they came if there is no profit to be gained.

Countries have had such different experiences with multi-nationals that it is difficult to generalize. For example, those areas in which multi-nationals set up manufacturing industries (e.g. south-east Asia) seem to have profited more. Those in which plantations cover large areas of the best farmland bring little reward to the workers and the country's economy (e.g. Central America). The information on the left is a very general guide to the advantages and disadvantages of the presence of multi-nationals in LEDCs.

Test questions

1. **a** (i) What is meant by a newly industrializing country? (2 marks)
   (ii) Describe how its employment structure is different from that of other LEDCs. (3 marks)

2. Read the following report.

   Bhopal, Central India, December 1984

   A leak of gas from a pesticide plant, owned by Union Carbide, an American multi-national corporation, killed over 2500 people. It affected the health of up to a quarter of a million people, most of whom were slum dwellers. They had been attracted to the city by its rapid industrial growth and were unaware of the risk of living next to a factory producing toxic chemicals.

   The cause of the accident was put down to design faults in the plant's safety systems, made worse by a decline in maintenance standards. Significantly, in the USA plants producing these chemicals are required to be located 50km away from settlements.

   a State three characteristics of multi-national corporations like Union Carbide. (3 marks)
   b (i) How could Union Carbide have reduced the risk of a gas leak? (2 marks)
   (ii) Why was there a greater loss of life in India than there would have been from a similar works in the USA? (3 marks)
   c At the time the plant was being planned, many Indians were in favour of it being built. Suggest reasons why (i) the people of Bhopal and (ii) the Indian government were in favour. (7 marks)

Newly industrializing countries (NICs)

Manufacturing industry is not shared out equally among LEDCs. In the 1970s, growth was most impressive in South America. Multi-nationals from North America such as Ford, from Europe such as Philips and Volkswagen, and from Japan such as Sony, were investing heavily in Brazil. This was the continent's largest market and restrictions on imports encouraged production within Brazil. Since then the most impressive growth has been in East Asia, where the main attraction for investors from overseas is low-cost labour with some skills. Although wage rates have risen with economic growth, in the mid-1990s wage rates in the Far East remained well below those in the USA and EU (**Figure 2**).

The advantages of East Asia for industrial location

1. **Cheap labour supply:** Wages are low by world standards. Asian workers are reliable and work hard for long hours, often in factories that would not meet all the health and safety standards of those in the West. Labour is the most important factor.
2. **Transport:** All countries in the region have access to the main shipping lanes. The use of containers has reduced the cost of transporting manufactured goods by sea, which was always the cheapest way to transport goods over long distances.
3. **Market:** Although many factories were set up to export all their products, home markets within the Asian countries are increasing as people become more prosperous.
4. **Government:** Although many governments discourage the import of manufactured goods, they encourage the import of capital and technology to establish factories and provide employment.

The four countries which maintained significant growth rates – Hong Kong, Singapore, Taiwan and South Korea – are known as 'Tiger Economies'. Other NICs in the region trying to match them are Thailand, Malaysia, Indonesia and the Philippines. They are known for a wide range of industries from heavy industries (steel, ships and petrochemicals) to light consumer industries (electrical goods and clothes), as well as high-tech industries (micro-chips, semiconductors, computers and word-processors). Hong Kong and Singapore are also great trading and commercial centres.

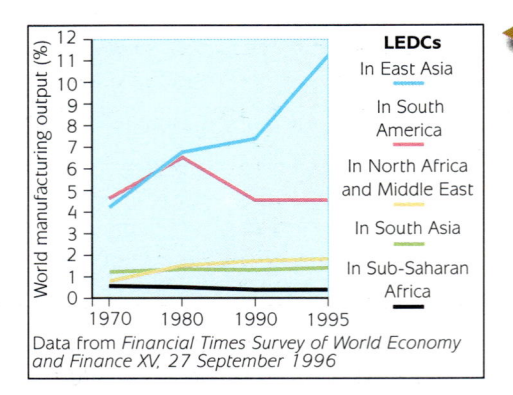

Figure 1 Shares of world manufacturing production of LEDCs in different parts of the world, 1970–1995.

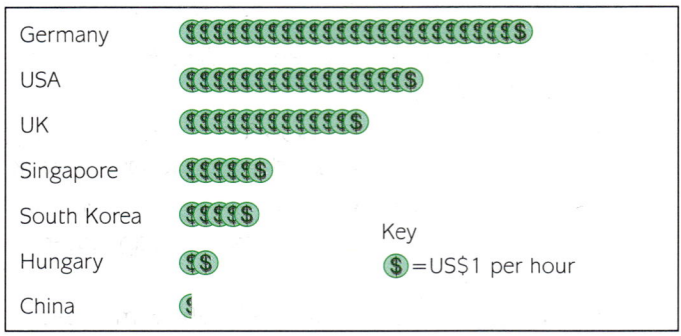

Figure 2 World manufacturing labour costs in the mid-1990s (US$ per hour).

Figure 3 Hong Kong's CBD – prosperity comes from manufacturing and trading.

Problems caused by rapid growth

In the dash for growth, people's health and the environment have been neglected. Working conditions and practices in the factories are often hazardous. Waste leaves the factories untreated so that some rivers have become dead with industrial waste. Air pollution is a serious problem in those cities with heavy industries; smog causes severe breathing problems.

Most of the industrial growth is based upon ever-increasing exports which makes the countries vulnerable to a world recession.

Chapter 11 Industry

Case Study – South Korea

Industry in an LEDC

Total population: 44 million
Capital city: Seoul (12 million)
Top four industrial conglomerates:
1 Samsung – semiconductors, electronics, shipbuilding, petrochemicals
2 Hyundai – vehicles, construction, electronics, shipbuilding
3 LG (Lucky Goldstar) – electronics, petrochemicals, consumer products
4 Daewoo – cars, electronics, shipbuilding, construction.

Industry	World ranking
Shipbuilding	1
Petrochemicals	5
Textiles	5
Cars	6
Electronics	6
Steel	6

In 40 years South Korea has changed from a poor country with few resources to one of the world's top ten industrial countries (**Figure 4**). Why?

All the general reasons given for East Asia on the opposite page apply:

- a cheap but efficient workforce that was willing to work twelve hours a day for six days a week
- almost everywhere on the peninsula is within 100km of the sea for access to cheap water transport
- its main markets are in the Pacific Rim (USA, Japan, Australia and Hong Kong) and its protected home market has increased
- a government that puts up many barriers to the import of manufactured goods that would compete with its own industries.

The special factor in South Korea is the way in which its industries are organized. Thirty *chaebol* (the Korean term for conglomerates or large corporations) are responsible for three-quarters of industrial output. The largest of these family-based *chaebols* are active in several areas of industry. Their size has supported their aggressive export drives and underpinned their ruthless desire to become leading world players in certain industries. Samsung, Hyundai and LG are now multi-national corporations with big investments in MEDC countries such as the UK.

▲ **Figure 4** South Korea; the main concentration of industries is in and around Seoul.

ℹ Problems

- Air pollution from traffic and industrial fumes in Seoul.
- Strikes because of low wages and poor working conditions.
- Faulty goods – the drive for growth has been at the expense of quality.
- Currency crisis in 1997/98 – has growth been too fast?

Activities

1 On an outline map of East Asia, shade and name the newly industrializing countries.

2 **a** Describe what **Figure 1** shows about East Asia's share of world manufacturing output.
  b State how it is different from that of LEDCs in other regions.

3 Explain fully why many clothes, sports goods and electrical appliances on sale in shops in the EU are manufactured in East Asia.

4 In what ways is South Korea **a** similar to, and **b** different from the other NICs of East Asia?

Changes in industrial location in the UK

The two trends examined below in a UK context occur in many MEDCs. The growth of out-of-town locations started in the USA before spreading to Europe. It is now happening around big cities in LEDCs in Asia and South America. The EU has a regional development policy for assisting poorer areas. All EU countries have areas that need help if they are going to develop.

The growth of out-of-town locations

The traditional location for manufacturing industry is near to the centre of towns and cities. The canal-side location of the dye works shown in Figure 2 on page 166 is an example. If clearance creates space for new building, these areas are called **brownfield** sites – ones that have already had urban land uses on them. These sites are not particularly attractive to modern footloose industries. Their preferred location is on **greenfield** sites – rural open land which has never been built on, out of town, usually in the rural–urban fringe.

Advantages of greenfield over brownfield sites include:
- cheaper land
- more space
- closer to motorways
- less traffic congestion
- easier to landscape to create a pleasant environment.

Many urban land uses – factories, offices, shopping centres, houses and roads – compete for greenfield sites. Not everyone is happy with these trends, which raises further issues. What about preservation of the Green Belt?

A variety of names are used for the new industrial areas created in and around urban areas. **Industrial estate** is a term used where many of the tenants are manufacturing companies. Where there is a mixture of two or more of the following – light manufacturing industries, service industries, retail outlets, leisure complexes, distribution warehouses, administrative offices and research establishments – they are called **business parks**, particularly if offices and research industries dominate. Figure 1 shows that Worton Grange is carefully designed with a low building density and set among landscaped surroundings (see also page 174). This is not easily achieved on brownfield sites, which is why pressures on the rural–urban fringe are so strong.

▲ **Figure 1** Worton Grange on the edge of Reading.

The idea of **science parks** came from the USA. Unlike business parks, these always have a direct link with a University. Universities are places where research is undertaken. By providing a pleasant working environment, the intention is that research and development can be linked to successful business possibilities. There are about 40 science parks in the UK, of which one of the first, largest and most successful is the Cambridge Science Park. An aerial view of the park can be seen on page 165 and its location is shown on page 174 (Figure 1).

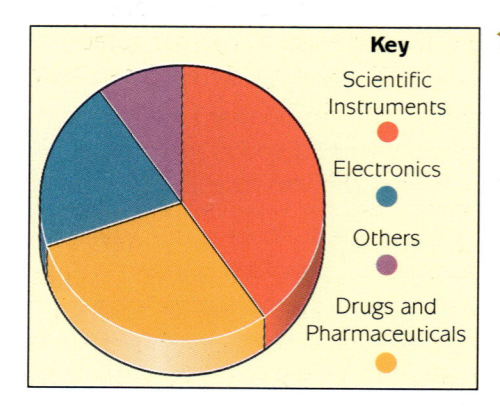

◀ **Figure 2** Types of companies in Cambridge Science Park.

Key: Scientific Instruments, Electronics, Others, Drugs and Pharmaceuticals

ℹ️ Cambridge Science Park

Opened in 1972
Established by Trinity College, Cambridge
Over 50 hectares landscaped with lakes and trees
Nearly 100 tenants employing about 2500 people

Areas in need of government assistance

Figure 3 shows the traditional industrial regions of Britain. With the exception of London, all these industrial regions were close to coalfields. This showed coal's

Figure 3 Traditional industrial regions in Britain.

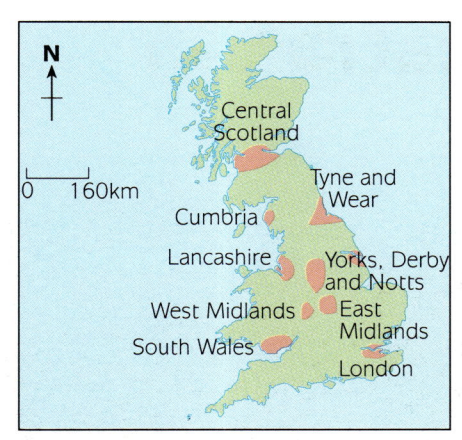

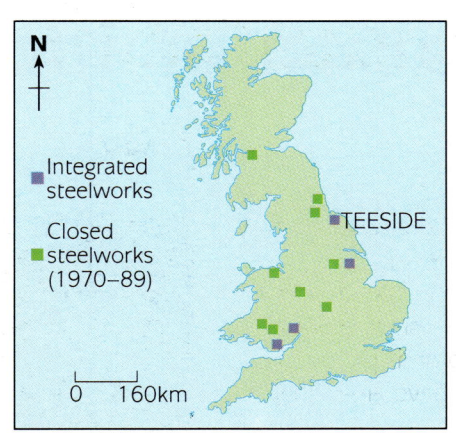

Figure 4 The British steel industry, 1970–1995.

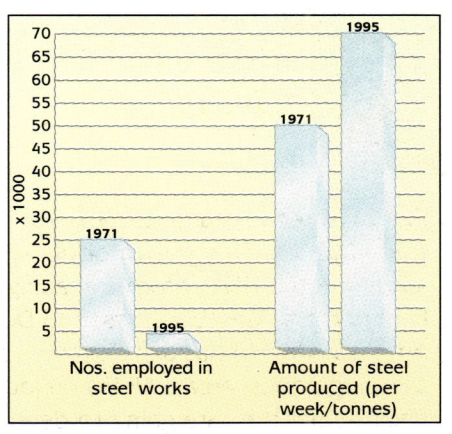

Figure 5 Steel output on Teesside, 1971 and 1995.

dominance as a fuel for 200 years from the beginning of the Industrial Revolution to the 1950s. Being difficult and expensive to transport, industries went to the coal. Although there is little direct use of coal by manufacturing industries today, the areas shaded in **Figure 3** still include many of the country's main manufacturing regions. For modern light and high-tech industries the pulling power of motorways has replaced that of coalfields. The reasons are given in the case study on pages 174–75.

There has been a great decline in heavy industries. Failure to modernize made the shipbuilding industry unable to compete with East Asian shipyards, notably those in Japan and South Korea (page 181). Those heavy industries that have survived, such as steel, have undergone such great changes that they are barely recognizable as the same industries. British Steel has closed most of its plants. Steel-making is concentrated in only four places where the locational advantages are the greatest (**Figure 4**). One of these is Teesside (pages 172–73). **Figure 5** gives some interesting information about steel output on Teesside which highlights the increasing use of modern technology. Even profitable heavy industries have shed workers.

The decline of coalmining and heavy industries mainly affected the northern and western parts of Britain. The preferred location for the growing number and range of footloose industries was in the south and east, where unemployment rates were lower anyway. The UK government and the EU have regional policies through which financial and other forms of assistance can be given to areas of job losses (**Figure 6**). This is an example of a political factor influencing industrial location. Without it, Central Scotland, north-east England and South Wales would become industrial deserts.

Activities

1 'Case study of a Science Park – Cambridge': put information together using the following headings as guidance:
   - definition of Science Park
   - location
   - appearance
   - types of companies
   - reasons for growth.

2 a From **Figure 6**, describe the distribution of assisted areas in the UK.
  b Explain the main features.

3 Choose one assisted area in the UK and research information for:
  a why assistance was needed
  b how the assistance has been used.

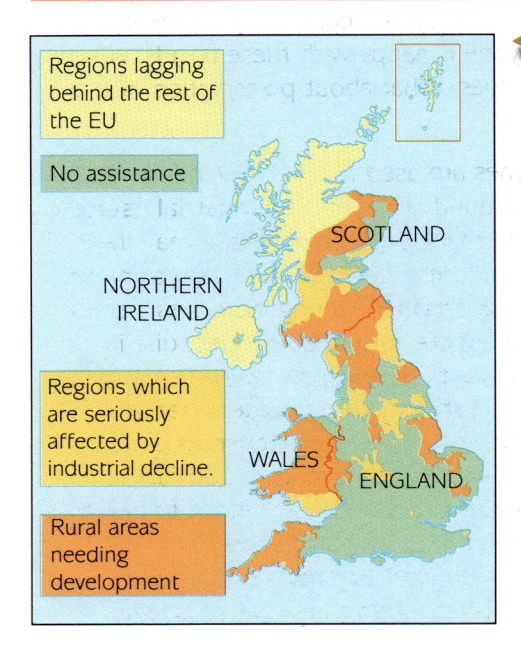

Figure 6 Assisted areas of the UK in 1996.

The globalization of industry

Industry is international.
- Industrial countries trade in global as well as home markets.
- Large companies set up factories locally and in other countries where the locational attractions are greater.

The UK is not an industrial island cut off from the rest of the world. It is part of the EU. Multi-national corporations like Ford operate within the EU as if it were all one country (**Figure 1**).

During the 1990s South Korean companies have made substantial investments and promised more, showing how large industrial corporations from LEDCs also realize the importance of becoming global if they are to sustain growth. Samsung already produces microwave ovens on Teesside; LG, with an existing plant in north-east England at Washington, chose South Wales in 1996 for their proposed investment to make TV monitors and semiconductors. Look at the enthusiastic newspaper headlines about investments into the UK by South Korean multi-nationals (**Figure 2**).

However, being part of the global industrial community means that the UK and EU are also at the mercy of events in other parts of the world, such as the East Asian financial crisis of 1997/78 (**Figure 3**).

In April 1998 LG announced that although it wished to proceed with its investment plans in Wales, it could not raise the funds due to economic changes in East Asia. Another problem is a world oversupply of semiconductors. Further, there is a worry in the UK and EU that investments from multi-nationals will be channelled instead into eastern Europe.

Eastern Europe is close to the wealthy EU markets, but has substantially lower costs of production. Look at wage rates in Hungary in Figure 2 page 180. Multi-nationals go where they can make most profit.

This is all part of the globalization of industry which, has its advantages and disadvantages.

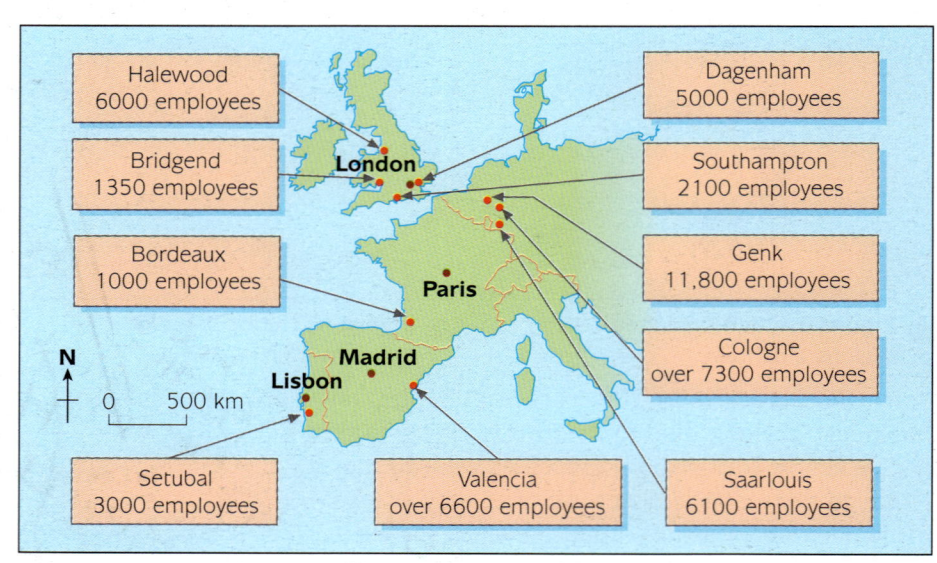

▲ **Figure 1** Ford's main production sites in Europe, 1997.

Locations shown on map:
- Halewood 6000 employees
- Bridgend 1350 employees
- Bordeaux 1000 employees
- Setubal 3000 employees
- Dagenham 5000 employees
- Southampton 2100 employees
- Genk 11,800 employees
- Cologne over 7300 employees
- Valencia over 6600 employees
- Saarlouis 6100 employees

Hyundai to build £2.4bn plant in Scotland
Fife semiconductor facilities will create 2000 jobs in an area troubled by unemployment
WELSH JOY AS LG CHOOSES NEWPORT
Decision will be a new boost to Silicon Glen

▲ **Figure 2**

Hyundai delays £3bn Scots plan
Korean crisis forces factory investment to be put on hold
Asian crisis will slow world growth

▲ **Figure 3**

Fear of the central Europe boat coming in
The north-east of England has a good inward investment record but former communist states offer serious competition.

▲ **Figure 4**

Chapter 12
Managing resources and tourism

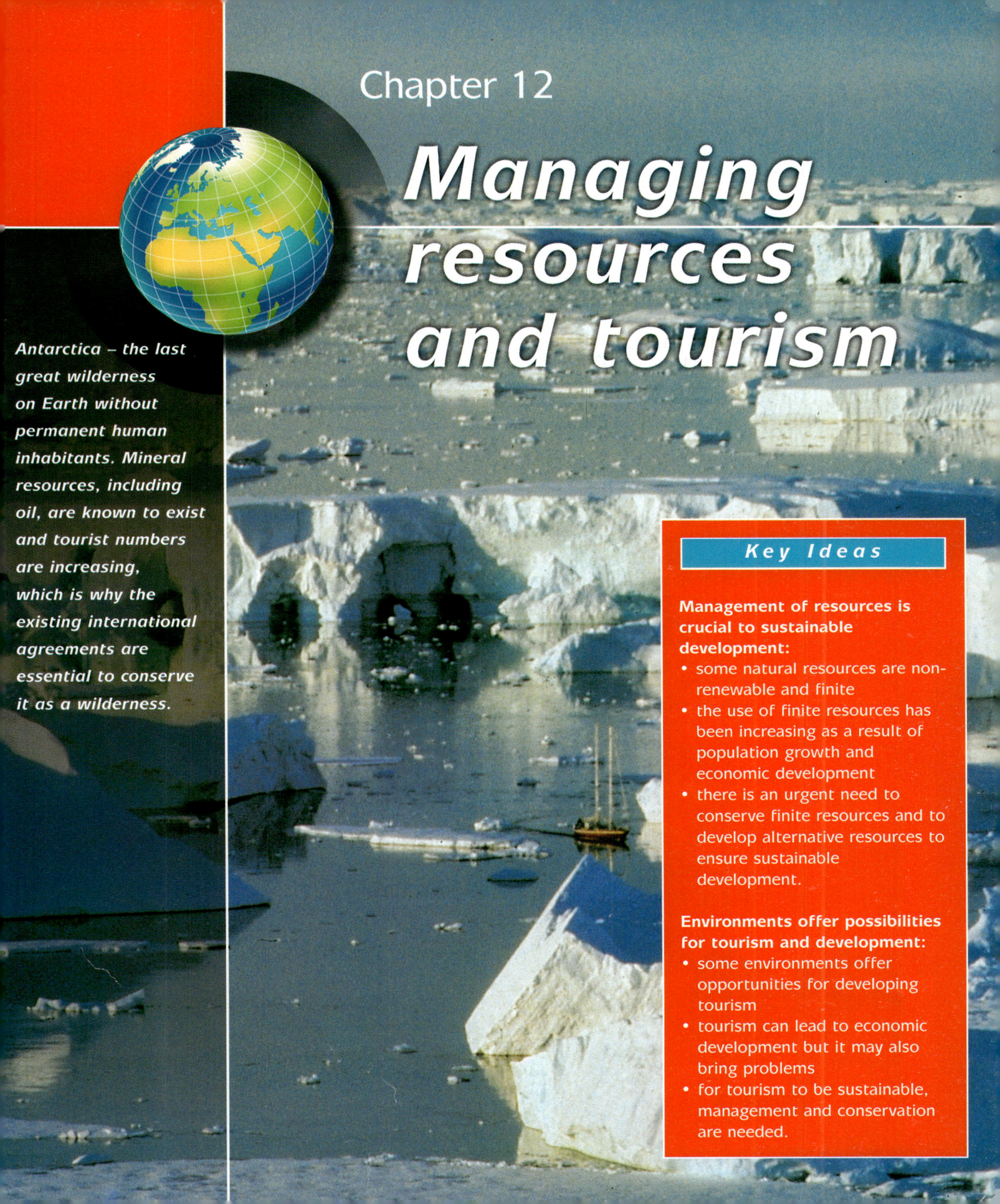

Antarctica – the last great wilderness on Earth without permanent human inhabitants. Mineral resources, including oil, are known to exist and tourist numbers are increasing, which is why the existing international agreements are essential to conserve it as a wilderness.

Key Ideas

Management of resources is crucial to sustainable development:
- some natural resources are non-renewable and finite
- the use of finite resources has been increasing as a result of population growth and economic development
- there is an urgent need to conserve finite resources and to develop alternative resources to ensure sustainable development.

Environments offer possibilities for tourism and development:
- some environments offer opportunities for developing tourism
- tourism can lead to economic development but it may also bring problems
- for tourism to be sustainable, management and conservation are needed.

Resources

The Earth provides many natural resources without which human life would have been impossible. These resources are summarized in **Figure 1**.

For the earliest human inhabitants, natural ecosystems provided all their basic needs for survival. *Water* came from the atmosphere. *Food* was obtained either directly by eating plants and their fruit, or indirectly by eating the animals which fed on the plants. *Shelter* came from making use of wood and branches. *Clothes* for *warmth* were made either from plants or animal skins. For a long time humans survived by gathering and hunting. The natural resources upon which life depended, such as the forests and their products, were naturally replaced after use; in other words the resources were **renewable**. If population growth outstripped an area's resources, some people starved to death until the natural balance between numbers of people and availability of resources was restored.

Today, this total dependence upon natural resources exists only for small groups of people living in remote locations, such as some Indian tribes who live in the most landlocked parts of the Amazon rain forest. Although primitive, their way of life is **sustainable** because they cause little disturbance to the natural environment and, left to nature, forests and soils are examples of renewable resources.

Humans developed skills and were inventive. They 'invented' agriculture by learning how to cultivate formerly wild plants in fields and by domesticating animals from the wild. They 'invented' irrigation and were able to make use of fertile soils in areas otherwise too dry for cultivation. The net result was greater control over food supply, allowing more people to be fed.

However, as the world population grew there was more pressure on natural resources. Timber was usually the first of the natural resources to be destroyed as people cleared more land for farming. Pressure of population has led to deforestation in many places, and soil erosion in some, resulting in the loss of otherwise renewable resources.

As more food could be grown by fewer people, towns and cities began to grow as places in which people specialized in craft industries or trading. These greatly increased in size and importance from about 1750 as a result of the **Industrial Revolution**. This great change, or revolution, was again made possible by human inventiveness; this time it was the invention of the steam engine, which was capable of driving machines and led to the growth of factories. Towns dominated by factories, smoking chimneys and terraced houses for the workers developed in areas near to coalfields (**Figure 2**).

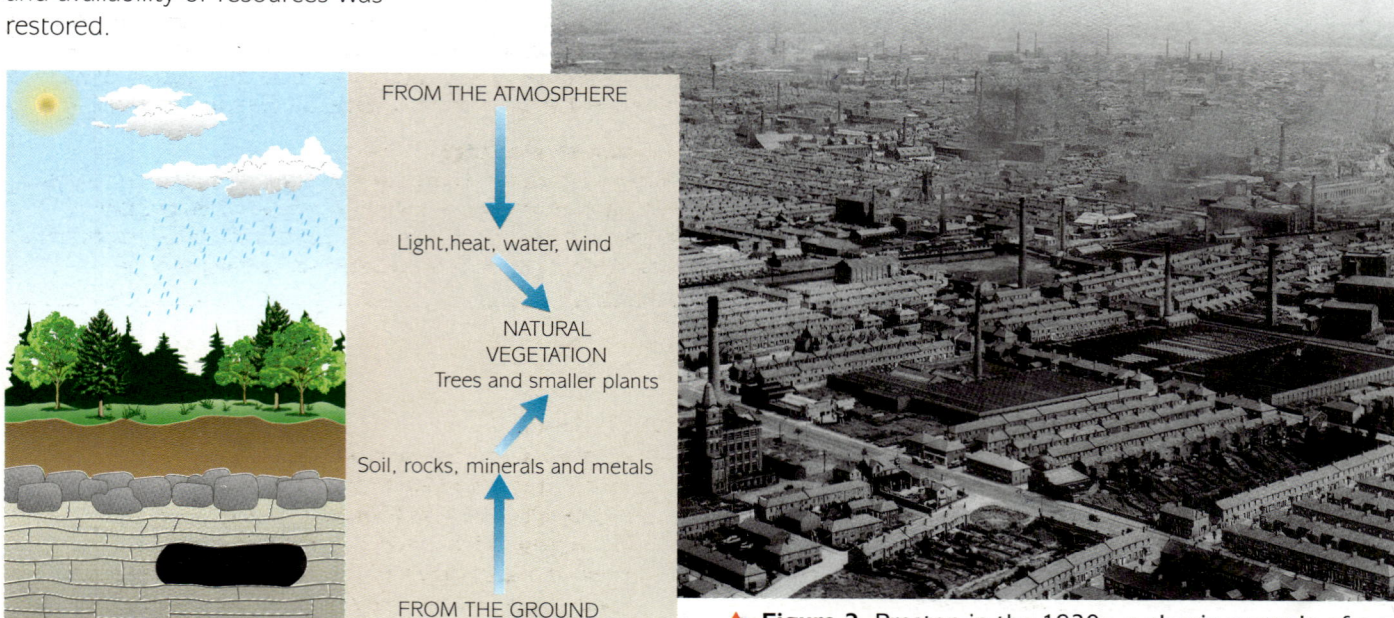

▲ **Figure 1** Some of the Earth's natural resources.

▲ **Figure 2** Preston in the 1930s, a classic example of a northern industrial town.

The natural resource upon which the Industrial Revolution was based was **coal**. Coal was used to heat the water which produced steam that drove the machines in the textile mills of Yorkshire and Lancashire. Heat from burning coal smelted the metals which fed engineering and shipbuilding industries. Burning coal led to the Transport Revolution, based upon the use of steam trains and ships. Other inventions followed. One of these was electricity; to generate it in large quantities, steam was needed to drive the turbine.

Although the Industrial Revolution began in Britain, it soon spread to other countries which had their own coal, such as Germany and the USA, which industrialized from 1870 onwards. During the past 100 years the number, range and diversity of manufactured goods have increased, leading to today's **consumer society** in the MEDCs. The changes since 1750 have been accompanied by a massive increase in consumption of the world's natural resources.

Essential terminology to a study of resources

A Fossil fuels

Which are the main ones?
Coal, oil (petroleum) and natural gas.

What makes them *fossil* fuels?
1. They have been formed from the decomposition or remains of plants and animals.
2. Their formation began many millions of years ago – about 300 million years ago for the UK's coal deposits from the Carboniferous period.
3. Massive numbers of plants and animals were needed to form just small amounts of fuel.

Why are they *fuels*?
When they are burnt, they give off heat which can be used directly as a source of power. For example, heat from coal furnaces smelts metals, petrol from oil drives car engines and natural gas heats the water in central heating systems.

Why are they described as *non-renewable*?
It takes a very long time to form even small deposits of fuel. It will take millions of years to replace the fuels that have already been used. One estimate is that the world consumption of fossil fuels in one year is the equivalent of one million years of formation.

Why are they also described as *finite*?
Fossil fuels being used today will not be replaced for millions of years. We have the deposits already discovered, which are called **reserves**. Although other deposits of coal, oil and gas are still to be discovered, there is only a limited (or finite) amount of each fuel on or close to the Earth's surface. There is not an unlimited amount – every time a tonne of fuel is used, that is a tonne less for future people on Earth to use.

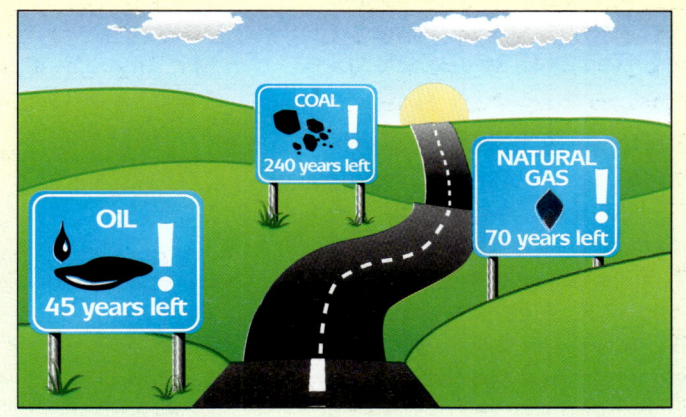

▲ **Figure 3** Length of life for known reserves of fossil fuels at present rates of consumption.

For how long will the fossil fuels last?
One estimate is shown in **Figure 3**. Estimates keep being revised based upon amount consumed and amount discovered, so they should be treated only as a guide.

B Other fuels

Are there fuels which are not fossil fuels?
Wood and animal waste (dung) are two examples. They give off heat when burnt and are therefore fuels. They are growing or being produced now and can be used immediately. They are renewable for as long as there are trees and animals.

C Sources of energy

Energy is a broader term than fuel. It includes the fossil fuels, which give off energy when burnt. This is called **primary energy**. Also included is electricity, which must be generated from another source. This is called **secondary energy**.

Activities

1. a Outline the differences between:
   (i) renewable and non-renewable resources
   (ii) fuels and energy.
   b (i) What is meant by a resource?
   (ii) Make a list of the Earth's natural resources under three headings:
   1 Fossil fuels 2 Other fuels
   3 Renewable resources.

2. Use **Figure 2**.
   a Draw a frame and make a labelled sketch within it of the urban land uses shown.
   b Describe the disadvantages of burning coal suggested by a study of this photograph.
   c State the changes which are likely to have taken place in this area between then and now.

Resource use

Natural resource use is vital to human survival. It is also vital to modern living. Energy sources provide the power for cooking, lighting and heating. They provide the power to operate machinery in factories and to run all modern forms of transport. Timber and metals provide raw materials from which manufactured goods are made.

World population growth

World population has increased and the rate of increase has speeded up, particularly in the second half of the 20th century and in the LEDCs (see Chapter 8). **Figure 1** summarizes the increase in total numbers of people. It took almost 100 years for world population to double from 1 to 2 billion, but then took less than 50 years for it to double from 2 to 4 billion. The pressure on the world's natural resources is increasing in line with world population growth.

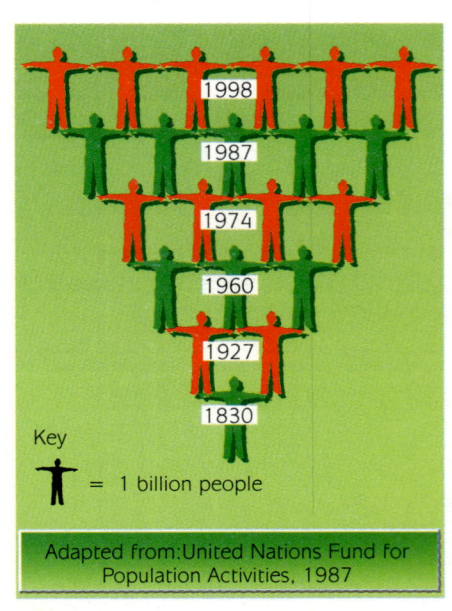

▲ **Figure 1** Total world population, 1830 to 1998.

World energy consumption

The other significant factor for resource use is that people everywhere are seeking an improved standard of living, which usually means an even greater demand for energy supplies. The homes of people living in MEDCs are packed with electrical goods. Electrical goods either do jobs that used to be done by hand, such as washing or washing up, or equipment for leisure and entertainment, such as televisions, stereo systems or computers. Private cars use more energy per person for the same distance travelled than do buses and trains. Once people have electricity in their homes, they want at least a television and a fridge. As the economies of LEDCs develop, and the standard of living of their population improves, factories, offices, means of transport and homes consume more energy. Therefore a combination of more people and higher levels of economic development explains the continued rise in world energy consumption (**Figure 2**), which is increasing on average by 2–3 per cent per year.

However, **Figure 2** does not include the consumption of energy sources such as wood or animal and crop wastes, because they are not traded. It is impossible to put a price on them or obtain statistics for the amounts used, although these fuels are often the main fuels used in rural areas, especially in many African and Asian countries.

Some people, societies and countries make low demands upon the world's resources. There is, for example, no direct relationship between total energy consumption and total population in a country. When a value of energy consumption per head is calculated, wide variations emerge (**Figure 3**). **Figures 3** and **4** highlight the high consumption of energy resources in MEDCs, and in North America in particular. Average consumption per head

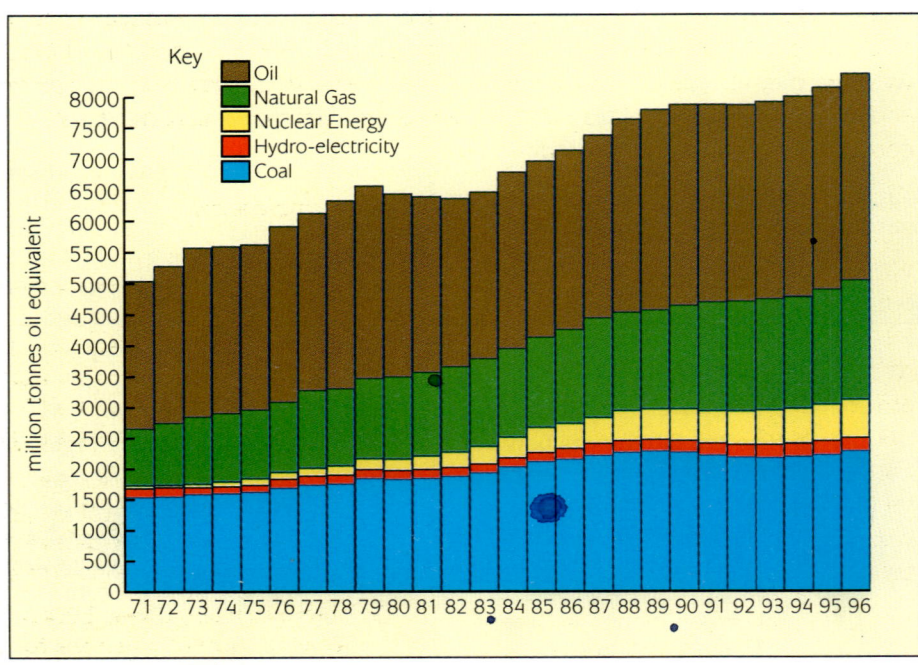

▲ **Figure 2** World commercial energy consumption, 1971–1996.

Rank	Country	Total consumption of commercial energy sources (million tonnes oil equivalent)	Total population (millions)	Energy consumption per head (million tonnes oil equivalent)
1	USA	2070	263	7.87
2	China	833	1218	0.68
3	Russian Federation	624	148	4.22
4	Japan	490	125	3.92
5	Germany	336	82	4.10
6	France	235	58	4.05
7	India	227	930	0.24
8	Canada	225	30	7.50
9	UK	218	59	3.69
10	Italy	152	58	2.62

▲ **Figure 3** The world's ten greatest consumers of energy, 1995.

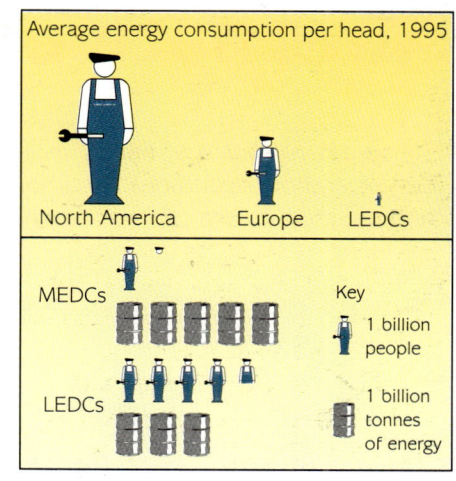

▲ **Figure 4** Differences in average energy consumption, 1995.

in North America is double that in Europe and more than ten times that of an LEDC.

Differences in levels of economic development explain some differences in energy consumption. Indeed, energy consumption per head is regarded as a reliable indicator of a country's level of economic development (Chapter 13). Much higher levels of economic activity are associated with well developed manufacturing and service sectors, which create the need for high levels of transport of goods and many movements of people. People have higher incomes (**Figure 5**) which allow them to travel by private car, take holidays and buy appliances. Each one has high energy demands. Compare the American lifestyle you have noticed in films and TV programmes with the tiny energy demand of an African farmer living in a village without electricity. Almost all tasks in the village are done by human energy; often fuelwood for cooking is the only fuel used.

Climate is another factor. Canada and many parts of the USA experience very cold winters. What would be called a 'big freeze' in Britain is normal winter weather in many places in North America. In contrast, summers in the centre and south are very hot; 'heatwaves' occur every summer which make air-conditioning a necessity in a way that it is not in Europe.

However, waste of energy is also a relevant factor. The American love of big cars is waning but has not been lost. There is not the same incentive to turn to smaller, more energy-efficient cars, when the price of petrol is less than one-third of the European average. North Americans tend to overheat their buildings in winter, while in summer the air-conditioning is quite severe.

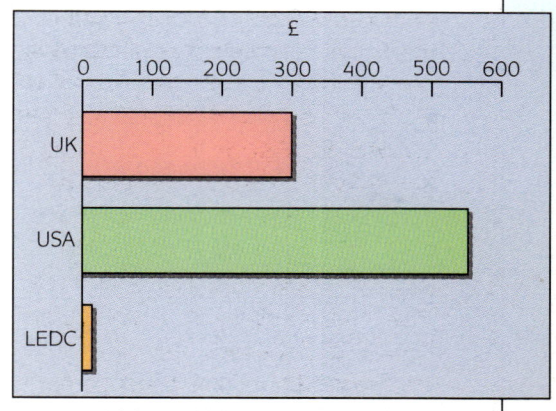

▲ **Figure 5** Average weekly family income, 1997.

Test questions

1 Use **Figure 2**.
  a Describe the changes in *total* world energy consumption between 1971 and 1996. (3 marks)
  b Name the fossil fuels shown. (1 mark)
  c Of the total world consumption of energy in 1996, how much was contributed by fossil fuels? (2 marks)
  d Name the only renewable energy source shown. (1 mark)

2 a Give the information which supports each of these statements:
    (i) More people live in LEDCs than in MEDCs. (2 marks)
    (ii) More energy is consumed in MEDCs than in LEDCs. (2 marks)
  b Explain why MEDCs use more energy. (5 marks)

3 Energy consumption in LEDCs is likely to increase during the next 50 years. Give two reasons for this. (4 marks)

Alternative sources of energy

An **alternative** source of energy usually means an energy source that can be used instead of fossil fuels. It is implied that it is also a renewable source of energy so that its use can be sustained long after fossil fuels have run out.

Why is there a need for alternative sources of energy?

A study of Figure 3 on page 189 shows just how great the contribution of fossil fuels to world energy consumption remains. Although there has been a slight increase over the years in the relative contributions from nuclear and hydro-electric power, the fossil fuels (oil, coal and natural gas) still account for over 90 per cent of the world's commercial energy supplies. Fossil fuels are convenient to use and remain relatively cheap. Trouble in the Middle East pushed up oil prices in the late 1970s and early 1980s, but oil prices have been low in the 1990s (**Figure 1**). A litre of petrol in the UK in 1998 would sell for less than 20 pence without the taxes added to it. For how much longer can this almost total dependence upon fossil fuels continue?

The *first* point to make is that, because they are fossil fuels, they do have a limited life expectancy (Figure 3 page 187). In 1960 the life expectancy of oil was estimated at between 40 and 50 years. The estimate is still the same at the millennium. What has happened is that new reserves of oil have been discovered and new technology has allowed the oil companies to recover a higher percentage of oil from existing wells. However, the recoverable deposits of oil are finite. At some time in the future the life expectancy of the oil reserves must start to fall if present levels of use continue.

The *second* important point is that burning fossil fuels has already contributed massively to atmospheric pollution and environmental damage (**Figure 2**). Vehicle exhausts emit a cocktail of gases, which includes oxides of nitrogen and sulphur dioxide, contributors to acid rain. These gases are emitted in much greater quantities from thermal power stations burning coal, which are seen as the largest single contributor to acid rain in Europe (**Figure 3**). The carbon stored in fossil fuels is released as carbon dioxide when they are burnt. The resulting greenhouse effect is believed to be responsible for global warming and consequent rises in mean sea level. People are becoming more environmentally conscious (even though most remain very interested in maintaining their own standard of living), and there is much more pressure upon the governments of MEDCs to tackle in a serious way the problems of pollution. Of all the world's major pollution problems, it is only the hole in the Earth's ozone layer for which fossil fuels are not blamed. This was probably caused by the release of chemicals into the atmosphere, particularly those containing CFCs.

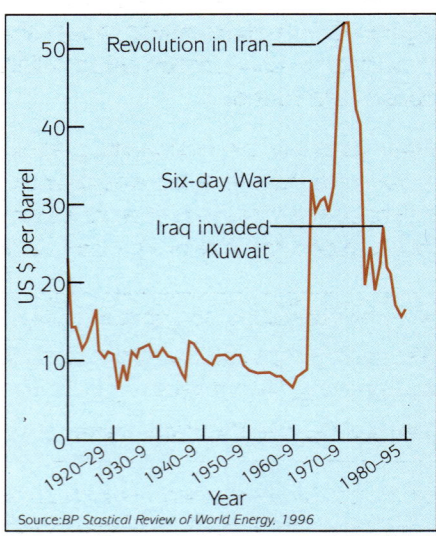

Figure 1 The price of crude oil since 1920 (in US$ per barrel adjusted for inflation).

Figure 2 Consequences of burning fossil fuels. From *Time International Magazine*, 29 January 1996.

"One day, my child all this could be yours"

Figure 3 Ferrybridge power station located next to the Yorkshire coalfield. It is power station number five in the league table for acid rain production in England and Wales.

A *third* point worthy of note is that coal, the fossil fuel with the longest life expectancy, is the one most disliked by environmentalists. Burning coal, especially low-grade deposits, produces more emissions of carbon dioxide and other gases than burning oil, while natural gas is relatively clean (**Figure 4**). However, unless cheap alternatives to fossil fuels are developed, an increase in coal consumption is forecast, particularly for Asia where large deposits are found.

What are the alternative energy sources to fossil fuels?
At one time the big hope was **nuclear power**. Huge amounts of power could be produced from a small amount of raw material (uranium). Nuclear Electric made the following claims in its advertisements:

> We *don't* contribute to global warming.
> We *don't* contribute to ozone depletion.
> We *don't* cause acid rain.
> **Are we the friends of the Earth?**

The advert focuses upon how much cleaner, and therefore how much more environmentally friendly, nuclear power is than fossil fuels. It does not say that radioactive waste is produced, which is dangerous to health and life for hundreds of years, and for which there is no secure long-term place of storage. Although scientists have repeatedly emphasized how safe nuclear power is, they have not been able to convince the public of this. Leaks of radioactive materials have not helped, but what really shattered public confidence in nuclear power was the explosion at Chernobyl in 1986. Information from a survey of the world nuclear industry is given in **Figure 5**. The title for the survey was 'A power needed but yet to be accepted'. Do you think this is an appropriate label for nuclear power?

Now that nuclear power is considered too risky, hopes lie with alternative sources, most of which make use of natural sources of energy such as the sun, water, wind, waves and tides. There are many *advantages* associated with using these as sources of energy:

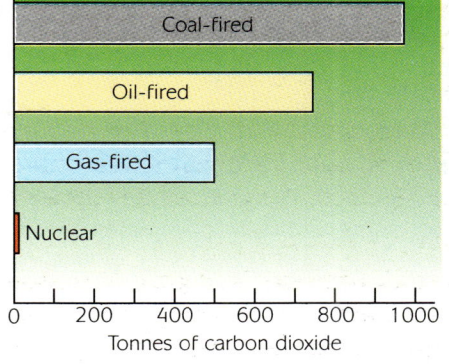

Figure 4 Carbon dioxide emissions from power stations.

Advantages of using natural sources of energy
1. They are natural sources, which are inexhaustible and will always be available. In other words, they are renewable sources of energy.
2. They are clean sources of energy which are not going to make further contributions to polluting the Earth.
3. There are several different types so that one or more of them must be present in every country, in contrast to fossil fuels. These have a very uneven distribution, with large deposits of oil and gas present in only a few countries.
4. Most can be small and serve local needs, avoiding costs of transmission.

Percentage of world electricity from nuclear reactors:	17 per cent
Total number of nuclear reactors in operation:	447
Total number of nuclear reactors under construction:	39

The top five nuclear countries:

	Country	Number of reactors in operation	Number under construction
1	USA	110	0
2	France	56	4
3	Japan	53	3
4	Russian Federation	36	3
5	UK	35	0

Nuclear power stations expected to be shut down between 2020 and 2030:

Western Europe	108
Eastern Europe	50
North America	75

Figure 5 Survey of world nuclear power reactors, 1995.

Activities
1. Explain why fossil fuels are:
   a cheap b in limited supply
   c dirty.
2. Put forward arguments in favour of:
   a using natural gas instead of coal
   b using nuclear power rather than oil
   c using alternative sources of energy rather than nuclear power.

Some alternative sources of energy

Alternative sources have their *disadvantages*. Some depend upon weather conditions that cannot be guaranteed: there are cloudy days when the sun does not shine and calm days when the wind does not blow. They also have some negative environmental effects. The photovoltaic panels (PVs) that turn sunlight into energy use toxic substances such as cadmium sulphide. Harnessing the energy of the tides involves building a barrage across an estuary, thereby interrupting water flow and possibly affecting marine life and changing rates of erosion and deposition.

However, the main factor that has held up their use is *greater cost*. Research is needed to develop the technology, which is expensive because success cannot be guaranteed. The incentive to undertake research is greatest when energy prices are high. However, low oil prices, and continued discovery of new reserves, have not encouraged as much investment in alternative sources of energy as environmentalists would like.

HEP (hydro-electric power)

HEP is the renewable alternative to fossil fuels that is used most. It is the only one included in world consumption graphs (Figure 2, page 188). Instead of heating water to produce steam using coal, oil or gas, running water is used to drive the turbines. The amount of electricity produced is controlled by the force and volume of water. Certain favourable physical conditions are essential, such as:

- fast-flowing water such as a waterfall
- high rainfall spread throughout the year
- a lake as a natural water store, or a narrow and deep valley to create a reservoir as an artificial store of water.

Once in operation the natural flow of water allows continuous production without any pollution. Costs per unit of electricity are lower than for thermal power stations. The water is not consumed and can be used for other purposes.

There are some drawbacks and problems. Sites with all the required physical conditions may not exist, especially close to centres of population where the electricity will be consumed. The plant is a high-cost investment, especially if a dam is needed, and it is expensive to put up the transmission lines to distant markets. Although environmentally friendly when producing power, building

▲ **Figure 1** Lake Nasser from the Aswan High Dam. *In large schemes, the high cost of building the dam and reservoir can often only be justified by including other uses in the scheme such as water supply, irrigation, recreation and flood control.*

large dams can have adverse environmental effects, such as flooding forests and destroying wildlife habitats. People may need to be forcibly relocated. The larger the dam, the greater is the size of any problems, but also greater is the amount of fossil fuels saved by the electricity generated.

Wind power

Two decades of research has produced a modern, electronically controlled wind turbine which stands over 30m high and has fibreglass blades 35m or more across. Placed close to one another, these form a wind farm (**Figure 2**). They are located in open, exposed places, usually on hilltops but sometimes along the coast. The technology is now well tested and costs are competitive with other sources of energy. Although the investment needed to set up a wind farm is high, the turbines are cheap to run. They are pollution-free and take up little land, and the ground between the turbines can still be used for farming. Local people are often less enthusiastic about them because they are noisy and can disrupt TV reception. Many turbines are needed to produce the same output as one thermal power station, and on calm days no power at all is produced.

▼ **Figure 2** Wind farm on Caton Moor in Lancashire.

Chapter 12 Managing resources and tourism

An HEP scheme: on the Yangtse river

In 1993 the Chinese Government began work in preparation for building the Three Gorges Dam, which will be a 200m wall of concrete. This will make it the largest dam in history, holding back a reservoir that is estimated to be over 600km long (**Figure 3**).

The power station is planned to supply 18 000 megawatts, which will supply a national power grid. The Chinese argue that this extra energy is vital to support the country's rapid economic growth and that it will reduce its contribution to global warming from burning coal. The giant turbines are expected to start generating power by 2003, although the dam will not be completed until 2009. Other aims are flood prevention and improving navigation. To build the dam and reservoir, 1.3 million people will have to be moved and more than 320 villages and 140 towns will be flooded by the muddy waters of the Yangtse. Flood waters will cover 40 000 hectares of China's best farmland. Also destroyed will be the habitat of rare river species (dolphins, sturgeon and alligators) and the bankside habitat of the few remaining tigers and giant pandas. It could produce a variety of disastrous side-effects, such as pollution of freshwater supplies and increased risk of landslides, and it could become clogged with sediment. Critics calculate that it will generate only a fraction of the power promised.

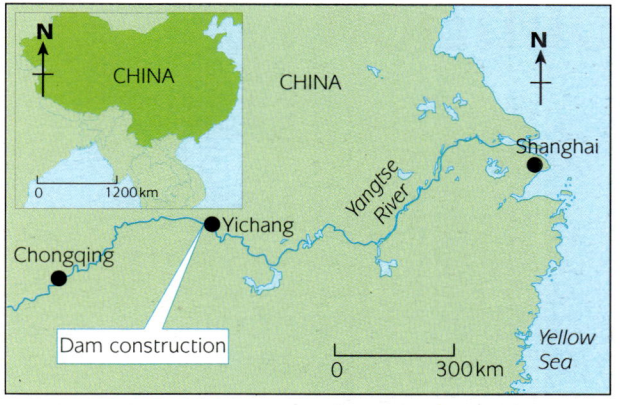

▲ **Figure 3** Location of the Three Gorges Dam.

Wind power resources

The UK has more potential for generating electricity by wind power than most of its European neighbours (**Figure 4**). Strong westerly winds are a feature of its maritime climate, and being an island country gives it a greater length of exposed coastline. Many of the upland areas are towards the north and west where westerly gales blow most frequently.

The 1989 Electricity Act paved the way for the Non-Fossil Fuel Obligation (NFFO) to encourage development of renewable energy technologies. In 1996 a campaign was launched for 10 per cent of the UK's energy needs to come from wind power by 2025. By 1996 there were already 550 wind turbines, producing electricity equivalent to the needs of 400 000 homes. By the time you read this there will be many more both on hilltop sites (see **Figure 2**) and next to the coast. Now that prices are below those of other electricity sources, wind farms are seen as a secure investment.

Generation method	Cost (pence per kilowatt hour)
Wind power in Scotland	2.7
Wind power in England and Wales	3.1
Power produced from fossil fuels	3.4

▲ **Figure 5** Average costs of electricity generation in the UK, 1997.

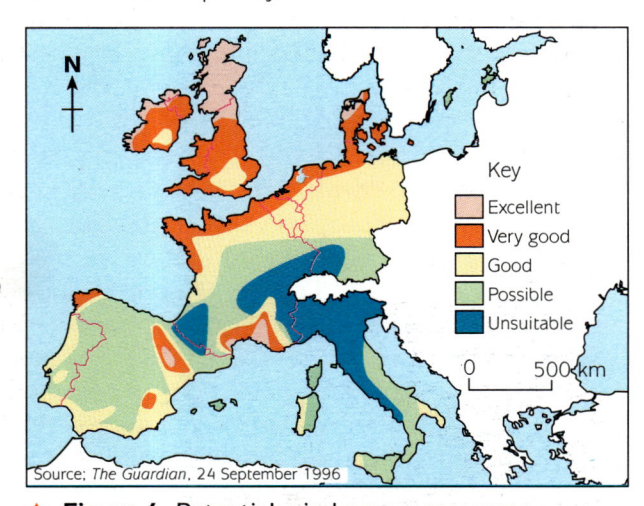

▲ **Figure 4** Potential wind power resources.

Case Studies – The Three Gorges Dam Project, China/Wind Power in the UK

Conserving resources and reducing pollution

Alternative forms of energy are beginning to reduce dependence upon fossil fuels, but fossil fuels will remain the main energy source for many years to come. In the meantime the gradual change towards renewable sources of energy must be supported by other measures and strategies, to ensure economic development that is sustainable well into the future without further damage to the environment. Two strategies are:

- to conserve resources by recycling and greater energy efficiency
- to establish pollution controls to reduce ozone layer damage, acid rain and global warming.

Conserving resources

Recycling is the recovery and conversion of waste products into new materials. One product commonly recycled is the glass bottle (**Figure 1**). Next to the bottle banks near supermarkets, there are often bins for waste paper (pulped down and made into new paper goods), clothes and textiles (converted into upholstery and blankets), and aluminium cans (melted down and manufactured into new containers). However, recycling is only worth while if it saves the natural resources without consuming a large amount of energy for reprocessing. Recycling aluminium cans is particularly worth while because reprocessing only consumes 5 per cent of the energy needed to produce aluminium from its raw material (bauxite). **Resource substitution** may be useful as well, for example making goods out of aluminium instead of from metals that are less easy to recycle.

We can all contribute to reducing energy consumption – by switching off lights when they are not needed, by using high-efficiency light bulbs, or by not using the car when it is possible to walk, cycle or use public transport. Small measures from many people can have a large overall effect.

For **energy efficiency**, however, the role of governments and companies is often more important. The UK Government has toughened up the energy efficiency standards for new buildings so that less heat is lost through walls, roofs and windows. You may have noticed energy-efficient labels on electrical goods in the shops, such as fridges, which is a government initiative. Combined heat and power schemes are encouraged. Next to some power stations are glasshouses heated by

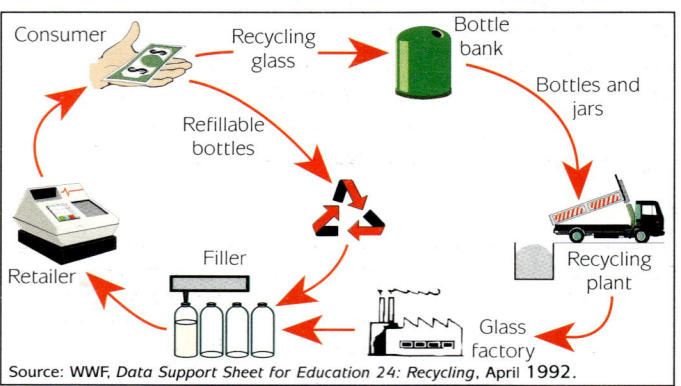

▲ **Figure 1** Recycling glass bottles.

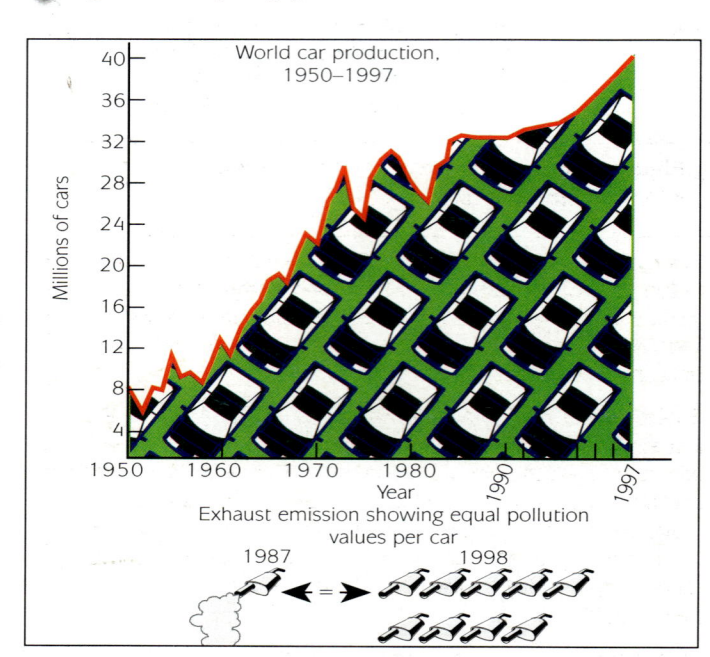

▲ **Figure 2** More but cleaner cars.

the water which has passed through the cooling towers. Supermarkets use the heat given off by their freezers to heat other parts of the store.

There is no evidence that people in MEDCs will stop using their cars, and people in LEDCs also have the same desire to own a car. At least cars can be made more energy-efficient and cleaner (**Figure 2**). Today's petrol car in Europe is 90 per cent cleaner than its ten-year-old counterpart. The car companies have been highly successful at reducing emissions of pollutants, such as oxides of nitrogen, carbon monoxide and hydrocarbons, mainly through the use of catalytic converters. Today the pressure is on them to achieve greater energy efficiency by reducing fuel consumption using improved engine technology.

Reducing pollution

Pollution moves across national boundaries. The hole in the ozone layer was first detected over Antarctica, but was not created there. The cause of much of the damage to trees in Scandinavia by acid rain can be traced back to the emissions from British power stations. Global warming is a world-wide problem and effective pollution controls need international agreement.

The hole in the ozone layer

Ozone-eroding gas	Uses	Controls under 1990 Protocol
CFCs	Refrigeration, air-conditioning, aerosols	Completely phased out by 2000
Halons	Fire extinguishers (especially in ships, aircraft and computer rooms)	All phased out by 2000 except for essential safety uses

▲ **Figure 3** International agreement – Montreal Protocol of 1987, strengthened in 1990.

Scientist: 'The agreement is still not stringent enough. Chlorine in the atmosphere will grow during the next ten years. I calculate that it will be 2030 before the chlorine level goes down to the level in 1986 when the hole was first announced.'

Environment Minister of an LEDC: 'India has just begun installing the technology to make CFCs, the chemicals which enabled the rich countries to have cheap refrigeration and air-conditioning. Now India is being asked to stop making them and to use expensive substitutes which have yet to be fully developed and which India does not have the technology to make. Why should India agree to the Protocol?'

Most countries are abiding by the Protocol. Countries such as India are being given financial and technological aid to help them meet the targets.

Acid rain

The UK emits far more sulphur dioxide every year than any other EU country. Of the total, 85 per cent comes from power stations burning coal and oil; some comes from car exhausts.

International Control – Directives of the EU, 1988

1 Large Plant Directive (power stations and factories)
Using 1980 as the baseline, the Directive calls for these reductions in emissions of sulphur dioxide in the UK:
- by 1993: minus 20 per cent
- by 1995: minus 40 per cent
- by 2003: minus 60 per cent.

Most of the reductions were to be achieved by 'scrubbing' the gases emitted to remove sulphur dioxide. The giant scrubbers are called 'flue gas desulphurization plants' (FGDs), but there have been delays in fitting these to the large power stations and the targets have not been met. The Government until 1997 tried to meet targets by switching from coal to gas as the preferred fuel for electricity generation. Increased use of renewables would help even more.

Emissions of nitrogen oxides had to be reduced by 30 per cent by 1998. This would be achievable by fitting nitrogen oxide burners to major power stations.

2 Vehicle Emissions Directive
This laid down 30 per cent cuts in emissions of oxides of nitrogen and hydrocarbons, later increased to 75 per cent. All new cars must be fitted with catalytic converters.

Global warming

Latest international treaty – from The Climate Change Summit in Japan, December 1997

Requirements of the Treaty
- MEDCs must cut emissions of carbon dioxide and five other gases by 2012 so that they are 5.2 per cent lower than in 1990.
- LEDCs need not make any cuts unless they choose to.
- Penalties for violating countries will be determined later.

Comment on the Treaty
It would take a 60 per cent reduction to make much of a dent in the greenhouse gases which built up in the atmosphere since the Industrial Revolution. Major coal-burning countries such as China and India are not required to reduce their emissions at all. Few countries met the targets agreed to at the previous summit in Rio. For what really needs to be done, see page 208.

Activities

1 Make a large version of the table below and fill it in.

	Definition and examples	Advantages	Problems
Alternative energy sources			
Recycling			
Energy efficiency			
Reducing pollution			

2 a Why is pollution an international problem?
  b Explain why international problems are difficult to solve.

Energy – a summary

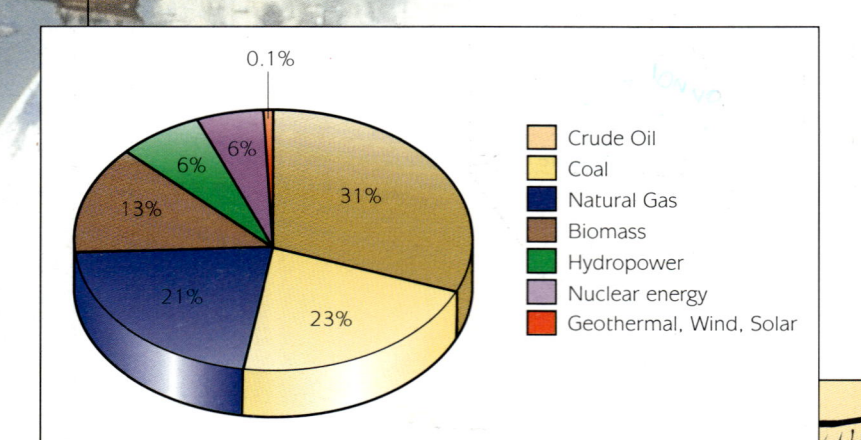

All sources of energy have their advantages and disadvantages. Past energy use has been dominated by fossil fuels (**Figure 1**). Future energy use is likely to be more of a mixture between fossil fuels and renewable alternatives. Much will depend upon price and availability.

◀ **Figure 1** World consumption of energy, 1996.
The chart shows the relative importance of all sources of energy, both commercial and non-commercial (such as biomass).

Pie chart values:
- Crude Oil: 31%
- Coal: 23%
- Natural Gas: 21%
- Biomass: 13%
- Hydropower: 6%
- Nuclear energy: 6%
- Geothermal, Wind, Solar: 0.1%

Fossil fuels
Coal, oil and natural gas are the fossil fuels formed from long-dead plant and animal matter.

Assessment
Renewable
No release of carbon dioxide
Does not pollute the air
Does not lead to local environmental problems
Safe
Cheap energy source ✓
Known technology ✓
Simple technology for use in remote areas (in LEDCs) ✓
Always available because it does not rely upon the weather ✓

Comment
The world economy and the way of life for most people is based upon them.

Biomass
Biomass includes vegetation and organic materials such as animal dung. Biofuels are the solid (e.g. wood) or liquid (e.g. alcohol) or gaseous (e.g. methane) fuels that are derived from them.

Assessment
Renewable ✓
No release of carbon dioxide
Does not pollute the air
Does not lead to local environmental problems
Safe ✓
Cheap energy source ✓
Known technology ✓
Simple technology for use in remote areas (in LEDCs) ✓
Always available because it does not rely upon the weather ✓

Comment
The pollution problems are much less severe than for fossil fuels. It is widely used in LEDCs where for many people in rural areas it forms their only source of fuel.
Reliance upon woodland has contributed to deforestation.
Land used for growing crops for biofuels, such as sugar cane for making alcohol, may take away land otherwise useful for growing food crops.

▲ **Figure 2** Assessment of different energy sources.

Chapter 12 Managing resources and tourism

Solar
The Sun's power can be used for generating electricity by using photovoltaic cells (PVs). Although it can also be used to heat water or to heat materials which retain the Sun's heat, the main commercial hope for the future is for electricity generation.

clear energy
s is produced by 'fission'.
an atom is split.
ng uranium.
heat produced drives steam
bines to generate electricity.

essment
newable
release of carbon dioxide
es not pollute the air
es not lead to local environmental problems
e
ap energy source
wn technology
ple technology for use in remote areas (in LEDCs)
ays available because it does not rely upon the weather

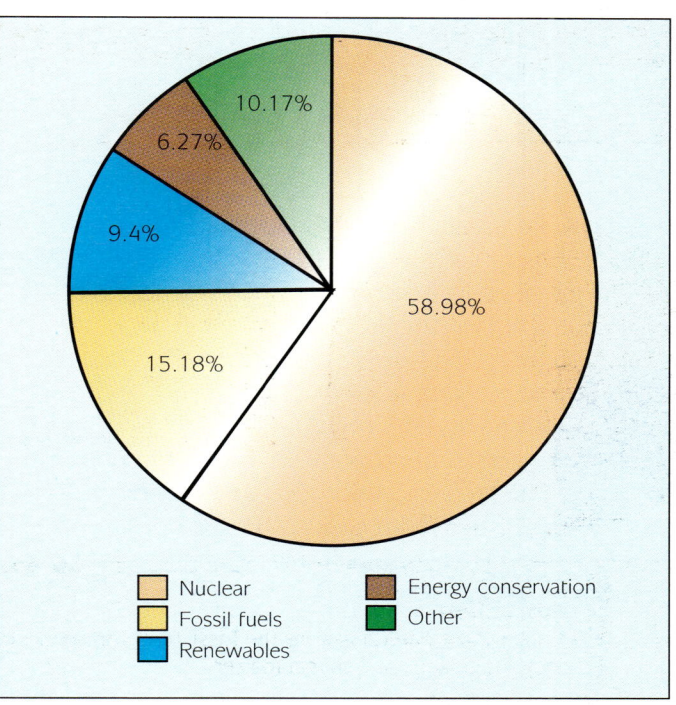

ment
ic confidence in it has been lost and there is the problem
hat to do with the radioactive waste which already exists.

Pie chart values: 58.98%, 15.18%, 9.4%, 6.27%, 10.17%

Legend:
- Nuclear
- Fossil fuels
- Renewables
- Energy conservation
- Other

▲ **Figure 3** How the MEDCs spent money on research and development for energy from 1979 to 1990.

Activities

1 Make an assessment and comment for HEP from large-scale schemes and for wind power as has been done for other energy sources in **Figure 2**.

2 Research information about one other alternative energy source (such as geothermal or tidal power).
  a With the help of a labelled sketch, describe how energy is produced from your chosen source.
  b Give an assessment and comment for it.

3 a On a divided bar graph, plot the values for world energy consumption in 1996 shown in **Figure 1**.
  b What percentage of energy consumption came from renewable energy sources in 1996?

4 a Approximately what percentage of research money went on renewables from 1979 to 1990?
  b Why is it likely that this percentage will have increased since 1990?
  c Explain why in the second half of the 21st century it is unlikely that the world will be totally dependent upon renewable sources of energy alone.

Where are the environments that favour tourism?

In the **UK** the coastline remains the most important location; 60 per cent of main holidays in the UK in 1996 were taken at coastal resorts. A beach is a necessity – if longshore drift is in the habit of washing it away, the Local Authority builds groynes. Spectacular coastal scenery close by, such as cliffs, caves, arches and stacks, helps, as also do scenic upland areas inland from the resort for day trips. Another factor of great importance is climate. The greatest concentration of large coastal resorts is along the south coast of England. Here the warmest summer weather and highest number of hours of sunshine are recorded.

Within the past 50 years scenic environments inland have increased in popularity. Pressure of visitors and conflicts between local people and visitors in areas of great scenic beauty led to the setting up of National Parks, made possible by The National Parks and Access to the Countryside Act of 1949. A **National Park** can be defined as 'an area of beautiful and relatively wild countryside'. Creating a National Park has two aims:

- to preserve and enhance an area's natural beauty
- to promote people's enjoyment of the countryside.

To achieve both aims is not an easy task – too many visitors destroy the peaceful and beautiful countryside they are all going to see. Rules and regulations are needed and they must be enforced, which is why each park is managed by its own National Park Authority.

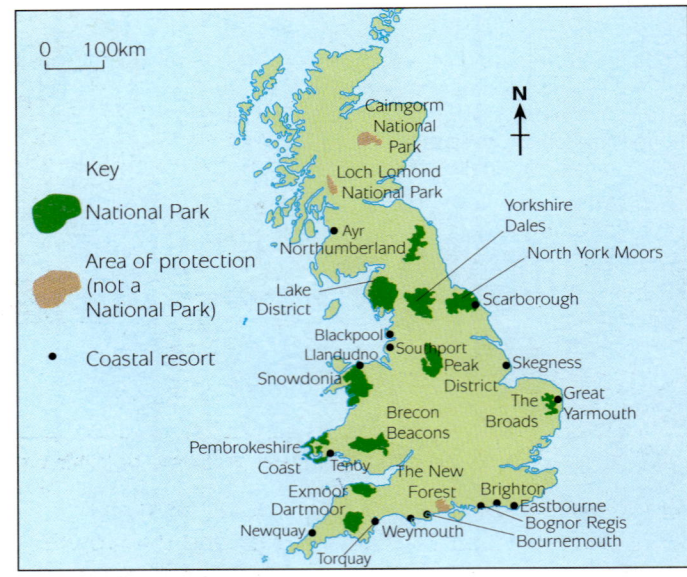

▲ **Figure 1** Coastal resorts and National Parks in the UK.

Management tasks are a mixture of the positive and the negative:

- managing the land, undertaking conservation work and planting woodland
- advising local landowners
- controlling developments
- providing access and setting up facilities for visitors, such as information centres, car-parks and picnic sites, while controlling where they are located.

▲ **Figure 2** Yorkshire Dales National Park. A: Improved footpath using local raw materials near Malham Cove; B: Roadside commercial enterprise, which would be discouraged.

Chapter 12 Managing resources and tourism

Figure 3 Some popular worldwide destinations.

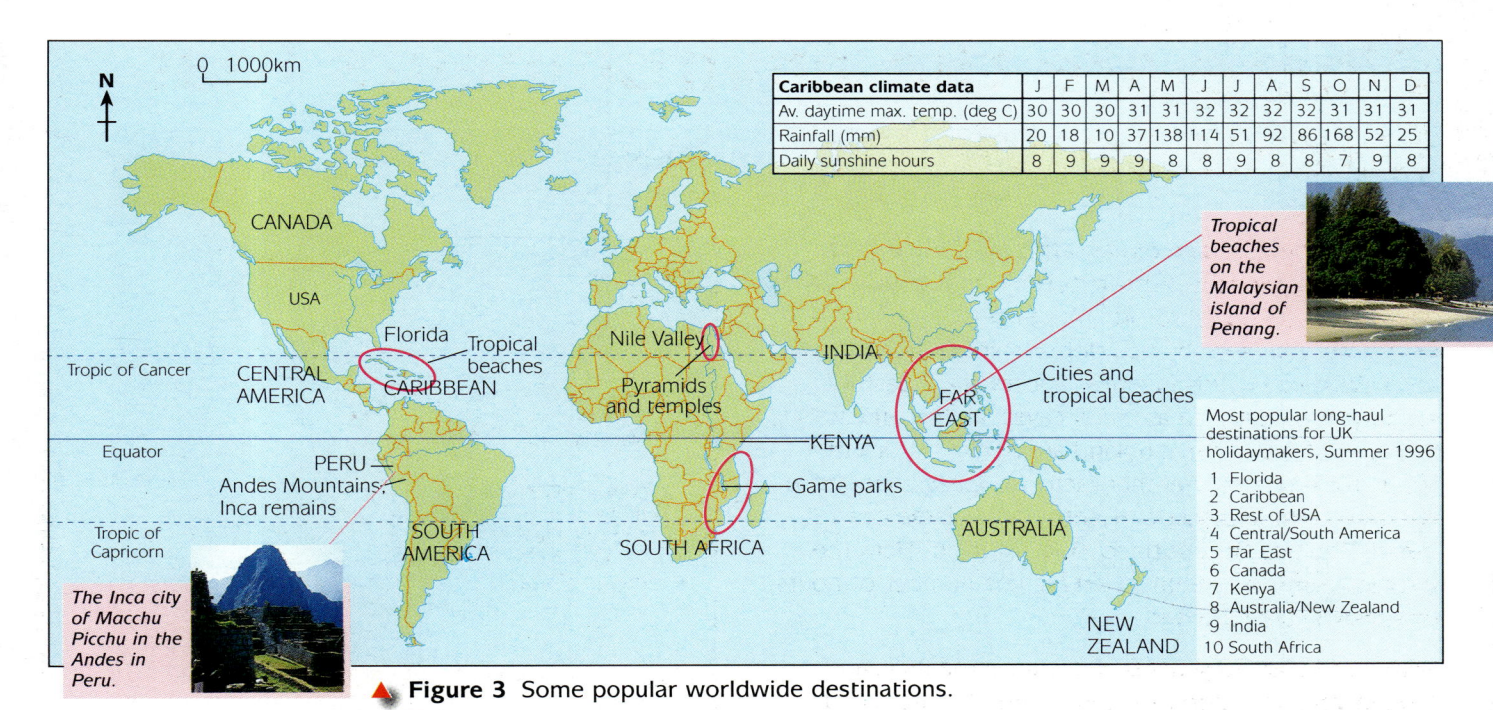

Caribbean climate data	J	F	M	A	M	J	J	A	S	O	N	D
Av. daytime max. temp. (deg C)	30	30	30	31	31	32	32	32	32	31	31	31
Rainfall (mm)	20	18	10	37	138	114	51	92	86	168	52	25
Daily sunshine hours	8	9	9	9	8	8	9	8	8	7	9	8

Most popular long-haul destinations for UK holidaymakers, Summer 1996
1. Florida
2. Caribbean
3. Rest of USA
4. Central/South America
5. Far East
6. Canada
7. Kenya
8. Australia/New Zealand
9. India
10. South Africa

World-wide tourism is a great growth industry. Increased leisure time, higher incomes and the growth of cheap and readily available air travel and package holidays have helped turn tourism into one of the world's fastest-growing industries. Tourism accounts for 8 per cent of world trade and is expected to become the world's largest industry by the year 2000. The popularity of long-haul holidays is growing. One purpose may be to visit relatives. Another is the desire to escape from winter weather for a warm tropical beach. This is why the peak season in the Caribbean stretches from December to April, which also coincides with the dry season there (**Figure 3**).

However, people's horizons are broadening and an increasing number wish to see environments and experience cultures different from their own. For many years Kenya dominated the African wildlife and safari market for tourists, but it is now facing stiff competition from South Africa. Central and South America have leapt up the chart of long-haul destinations as people have become aware of the region's natural attractions (mountains, waterfalls, glaciers, jungles and wildlife) as well as the monuments from earlier civilizations (Mayas, Aztecs and Incas).

The desire of people in MEDCs to travel, along with affordability, has opened up new economic opportunities for some LEDCs. Many LEDCs still depend too heavily upon the export of just one or two commodities, for their foreign exchange income. Until tourism arrived it was difficult to see how their income could be increased.

St Lucia is typical of many small island countries in the Caribbean. Bananas are the main export, but they are grown on smallholdings and the farmers cannot match the low prices of bananas grown by large companies on plantations in Central America. With only 150 000 people on the island, industrialization is not an option, so it is fortunate that visitors from North America and Europe find the climate and scenery there attractive.

Activities

1. a Describe the distribution of National Parks in England and Wales.
   b Plot the following data about visitor numbers to National Parks, on a bar graph:

   Visitors per year (millions)
Brecon Beacons	7	Northumberland	1
The Broads	3	North York Moors	11
Dartmoor	8	Peak District	22
Exmoor	3	Pembrokeshire Coast	13
Lake District	20	Snowdonia	11
Yorkshire Dales	9		

   c Why do you think there are such great differences in visitor numbers between the Parks?

2. Choose one of the National Parks.
   a Describe the physical (landscape) features which attract visitors to the Park.
   b Choose one of these features and explain its formation.

3. Find information about one of the tourist areas named in **Figure 3** (except Kenya). Design an Information Sheet to fit an A4 page which would be useful for a person intending to holiday there.

Case Study – The North York Moors

Focus on a National Park

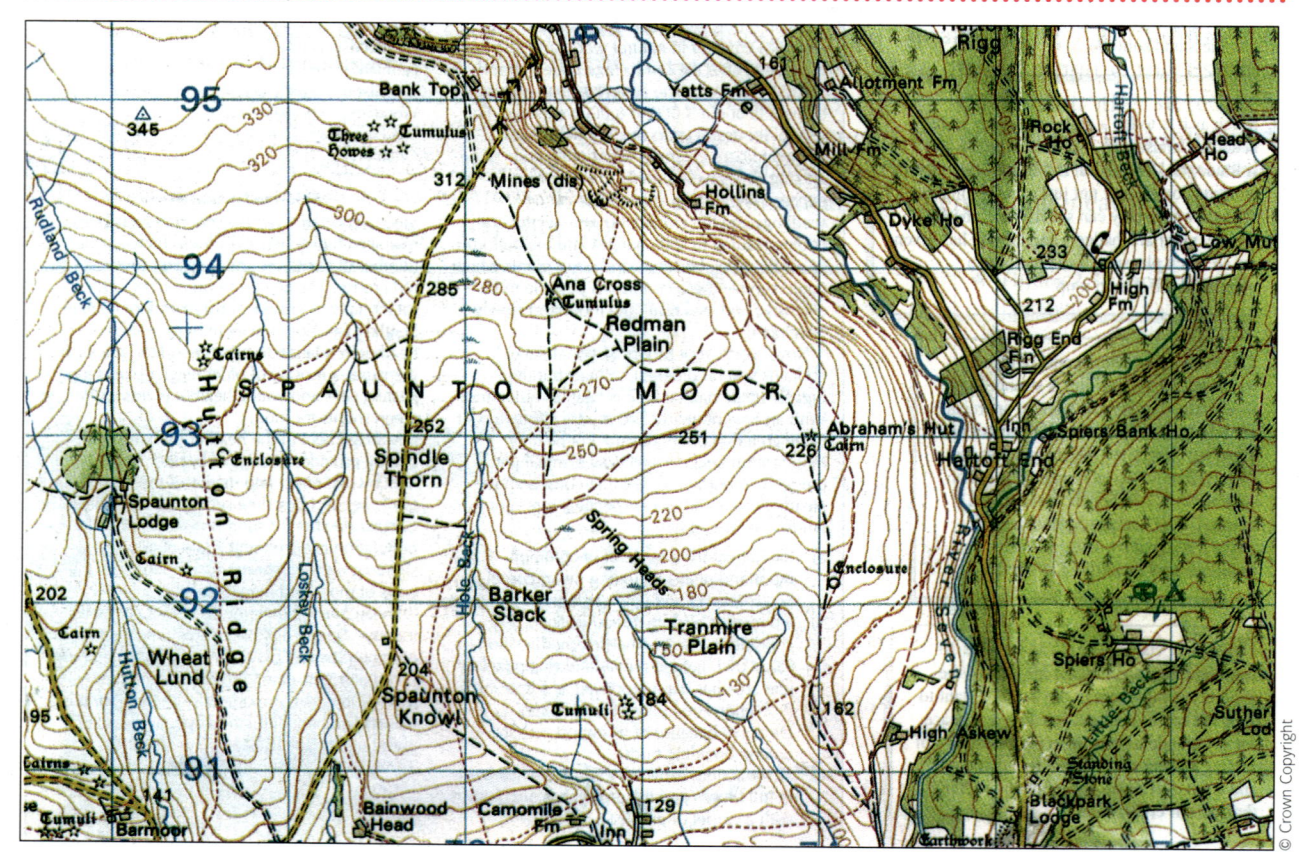

▲ Figure 1 The North York Moors National Park.

▲ Figure 2 Inland scene across the North York Moors.

▲ Figure 3 Rugged coastal scenery, North Yorkshire.

Chapter 12 Managing resources and tourism

Case Study – The North York Moors

ℹ The North York Moors National Park

Key facts about the Park
- created in 1952
- about 150 000 hectares in area
- population about 25 000
- about 11 million visitors per year.

Physical features and attractions
- plateau-like surface cut by river valleys (dales)
- heather-covered moorlands on the higher parts
- bracken, woods and farmland on the lower slopes
- spectacular coastal scenery with high cliffs
- wide bays with rocky wave-cut platforms.

Human attractions
- old fishing villages such as Staithes and Robin Hood's Bay
- churches and abbeys such as Rievaulx Abbey
- long-distance footpaths such as the Cleveland Way
- North York Moors Steam Railway from Grosmont to Pickering
- moorland villages in scenic settings, such as Goathland, the location for the TV series *Heartbeat*.

The Park's main problem – pressure from visitor numbers

The Park is close to densely populated urban areas, notably Teesside. On sunny summer weekends as many as 150 000 visitors may arrive in the Park, mostly by car, which leads to congestion on the roads and pressure on car-parking spaces. The visitors are not equally spread throughout the Park, and most make for the main tourist sites such as Robin Hood's Bay, Helmsley and Goathland, which become overcrowded. Places such as these which attract many visitors are known as **honeypots**. As with the other National Parks, this is only one of the problems that has resulted from the growth in tourist numbers.

The Threat To *Heartbeat* Country
How the popularity of the TV series is harming Goathland's environment

The popularity of the series, which depicts a policeman's lot on the North York Moors, has caused serious problems for the villagers of Goathland, the moorland community in which it is filmed.

Heartbeat's success brings more than a million fans to the village each year, trampling the grass, churning up the roadsides and causing horrendous traffic congestion with their inconsiderate parking. The tourist hoards are eager to see where their favourite show is set. The low estimate is for 1.25 million visitors a year, which means that on a busy day, with a staggering 700 cars parked in Goathland, it can take three-quarters of an hour to pass through the village.

The response to the problem has been to deter car-parking by significantly expanding the yellow lines in the village and installing curbs to protect particularly vulnerable roadsides, measures which are starting to prove successful.

David Brewster, the Head of North York Moors National Parks Services, which has a partial responsibility for tackling the problem, said, 'We are not trying to stop *Heartbeat* being filmed here. It does bring income into the area and into Whitby (estimated at £9m in 1996), but there are also significant problems and we have to do something to reduce the impact that flows from them.'

Parish council chairman Keith Thompson said, 'We have a concern for the environment and a duty of care for the village. The village evolved over a long period of time and we should not pass it on bespoiled when problems can be addressed. A lot of people in the middle of the village say they can sit in their gardens and ignore the people milling about outside but there has been some upset to quality of life. However, I don't think people resent the show because the visitors provide a livelihood for a lot of people.'

▲ **Figure 4** Adapted from *Yorkshire Life*, April 1997.

Activities

1. Draw a sketch map of the area covered by the North York Moors National Park. Locate on it some of the physical and human attractions for visitors.

2. Describe with the help of labelled sketches the physical attractions of this National Park.

3. a Make a chart showing costs and benefits of tourism for Goathland.
   b Why will some people in the village object more strongly than others to the great numbers of visitors?

Case Study – The North York Moors

Other problems and conflicts in National Parks

A Footpath erosion

Visitors who walk more than half a mile away from their parked car, number fewer than 50 per cent of those who visit the Parks. Dramatic landscape features at the end of a short and easy walk from the car-park, such as Malham Cove, have footpaths 'almost like motorways' leading up to them (**Figure 1**). There are still many keen walkers who love the hills. The long-distance footpaths such as the Pennine Way, the South Downs Way or the Cleveland Way, which is in the North York Moors, are very popular and well used. The regular pounding of boots soon removes the thin vegetation cover, exposing loose soil which, once eroded by people, is quickly washed away by the rain. As people look for more comfortable walking on the sides of the path, the zone of erosion is widened.

Management in National Parks includes footpath repairs. Steps made of local stone are one solution on steep hillsides (**Figure 2A** page 198). Slabs of stone are laid in flatter areas. Badly eroded sections may be fenced off and reseeded. Wooden rafts are laid across marshy ground.

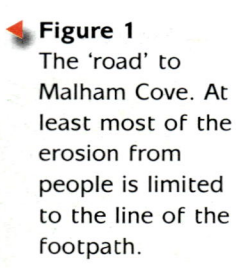

◀ **Figure 1** The 'road' to Malham Cove. At least most of the erosion from people is limited to the line of the footpath.

B Conflicts between local people and visitors

The basic cause of this problem is that making a living in upland areas, where most of the Parks are located, is never easy. Farming is the activity which covers most land. In the 1980s some farmers in the North York Moors reclaimed moorland into pasture to try to increase their farm income; according to some environmentalists this destroyed the beauty of the wild landscape and reduced wildlife habitats.

Extending the area covered by coniferous forests is even more contentious. Nearly 20 per cent of the open moorland on the North York Moors has been ploughed up and planted with conifers in the past 30 years, and there are some large stretches of forest (**Figure 2**) which dramatically affect the scenery and limit visitor access. The trees have economic value. However, some lessons have been learned over the years. It is now accepted that much can be done to improve the appearance by planting some deciduous trees as well, and to improve the attractions for visitors by developing forest walks, picnic sites and information points. Even so, visitors must be constantly reminded and warned against carelessly starting fires.

The other locally significant conflict, quarrying, was dealt with on pages 28–29. This is an old-established economic activity which can give permanent employment to significant numbers of local people. It does come as a shock to many first-time visitors to a Park to see works in the midst of splendid scenery (**Figure 3**). There are usually good reasons for the works being there, and their products may be essential to life in the city, from which most Park visitors come.

▲ **Figure 2** Coniferous plantation on the North York Moors.

▲ **Figure 3** Boulby potash mine within the North York Moors Park.

Tourism in an LEDC

KENYA SAFARI
7 nights

- **Day 1 London to Nairobi with British Airways**

- **Day 2 Nairobi to Aberdares**
  Transfer to the highlands of the Aberdare range and overnight at the Aberdare Country Club.

- **Day 3 Aberdare National Park**
  Transfer to The Ark, situated in the heart of the Aberdare National Park. In the evening enjoy floodlit game viewing.

- **Day 4 Aberdares to Sweetwaters**
  Transfer to the Ol Pejeta Rhino Reserve and Sweetwaters tented camp, overlooking one of the busiest waterholes in the reserve.

- **Day 5 Sweetwaters to Mount Kenya**
  After an early morning game drive, continue to the famous Mount Kenya Safari Club on the slopes of Africa's second highest mountain.

- **Day 6 Mount Kenya**
  A full day at leisure at the Mount Kenya Safari Club. Take an optional excursion to the Animal Orphanage or to Mount Kenya or treat yourself to an 'Aerial Safari', a 20-minute scenic flight over Mount Kenya.

KENYA COAST EXTENSION
7 nights

- **Day 7 Mount Kenya to Masai Mara**
  A short flight takes you to Masai Mara and the Mara Safari Club.

- **Day 8 Masai Mara**
  Another full day at the Mara Safari Club with morning and evening game drives. You can also take part in the walking safari or take an optional hot-air balloon ride over the Masai Mara Park.

- **Day 9 Masai Mara to Nairobi to Kenya Coast**
  After a short-flight transfer to Nairobi, travel by Kenya Airways to Mombasa. Ground transfer to the Turtle Bay Beach Club located 20km south of Malindi on a white sand beach within the Watamu Marine National Park.

- **Days 10–15 Kenya Coast**
  Spend a lively and relaxing week next to the sea. Use of the hotel's water sports and sports and fitness facilities is included at no extra cost.

- **Day 16 Kenya Coast to Nairobi to London**
  Fly back to Nairobi to connect with the overnight British Airways flight to London.

▲ **Figure 4** A typical holiday in Kenya.

Nairobi	J	F	M	A	M	J	J	A	S	O	N	D
Daytime temp. (°C)	25	26	26	24	23	22	21	22	24	25	23	28
Rainfall (mm)	88	70	96	155	189	29	17	20	34	64	189	115
Daily sunshine hours	9	9	9	7	6	6	4	4	6	7	7	8

Activities

1. Plot the climate statistics for Nairobi in **Figure 5** using the normal methods for temperature and rainfall and an appropriate method for sunshine hours.

2. Draw a sketch map of Kenya to show places that are visited by tourists.

3. Show the following tourist numbers in a pie graph.
   Tourists to Kenya in 1995:
   UK 24%;   Italy 8%;
   Germany 29%;   USA 6%;
   Switzerland 8%;   others 17%.
   France 8%;

Key facts (1995)

Total population	About 30 million	Main exports:	Coffee, Tea, flowers, fruit and vegetables worth US$ 1.2 billion
Birth rate	43 per 1000	Main imports	Oil, machinery, manufactured goods worth US$ 2 billion
Death rate	12 per 1000		
Annual rate of natural increase	3.1 per cent	Visible trade deficit	US$ 800 billion
GNP per head	US$ 270	Earnings from tourism	US$ 500 billion

▲ **Figure 5** Kenya.

Case Study – Tourism in Kenya

Kenya has two different environments attractive to foreign visitors:

- wildlife parks on the plateau
- the coastline of the Indian Ocean.

Many visitors spend one week on safari and one week on the beach, as in the holiday described on the previous page.

KENYA

One of the 'Big Five' that tourists can expect to see on safari.

Of all the countries in Africa, Kenya has some of the most prolific and most accessible game parks. Here you can observe some of the greatest examples of wildlife, including the 'Big Five' – elephant, lion, leopard, buffalo and rhino. Scenically stunning with vast expanses of savannah grassland and bush across the plateau of the highlands, it is blessed with beautiful mountains such as Mount Kenya, Africa's second highest peak. A tempting option for the more adventurous visitor is to take the three-day trek complete with porter, cooks and guides to the 5000 metre summit.

As to the beaches, the coastal strip from Malindi to beyond Mombasa has mile upon mile of white coral sand, lapped by the warm waters of the Indian Ocean, sheltered in parts by gently swaying palms. Why not take a trip in a glass-bottomed boat on to the reef where you can see over 240 species of fish and a wide variety of corals? And if you want something different, visit Mombasa – it is hot and dusty but there is a buzz of excitement in its colourful bazaars!

Safaris

Seeing animals in the wild, in their own natural habitat, free of any civilizing influences, is a life-enriching experience. Seeing them in Africa is truly awesome. While a bush safari is one of life's great adventures, we make sure that it is a comfortable one. You will travel in a specially adapted minibus with a guaranteed window seat, be guided by an English-speaking driver and accommodated in comfortable lodges.

▲ Figure 1

Interview with Kenya's Minister of Tourism and Wildlife in early 1997

Q What would you single out as the main achievements of the Kenyan tourist industry in the last 34 years?

A Tourism is a moving force behind world economic development. In Kenya the industry is our number two foreign exchange earner, accounting for 21 per cent of total foreign exchange earnings. In terms of jobs, over 11 per cent of total wage employment is accounted for by tourism. The industry also acts as a catalyst for development in related sectors such as agriculture, horticulture, transport and communications.

Q What are you doing to ensure that Kenya remains a favourite tourist destination?

A We are in the process of diversifying in terms of where tourists come from. With support from major tour operators, we hope to achieve a leading position as an ecotourism destination and avoid the negative environmental and socio-economic impact often associated with mass tourism. We have taken part in tourism promotional exhibitions in Poland, Japan, Hong Kong, Australia and New Zealand.

The first answer from the Minister of Tourism summarizes the **benefits** of tourism, both to the economy of Kenya and to the Kenyan people who depend for their living upon the continued arrival of foreign tourists. Kenya was ahead of most other East African countries in protecting its wildlife within National Parks, which cover 8 per cent of the country, and in providing luxurious accommodation in safari lodges and clubs. Kenya remained comparatively prosperous when neighbouring countries like Somalia, Ethiopia and Sudan were racked by civil war. The answer to the second question shows that tourist promotions are vital to keep the visitors coming and to reduce the heavy dependence upon visitors from Germany and the UK.

Chapter 12 Managing resources and tourism 205

Case Study – Tourism in Kenya

The problems

1 Falling numbers of tourists

Numbers of visitors have fallen since the peak of 900 000 in 1990 (**Figure 2**) and crashed in the second half of 1997 (**Figure 3**). The economic consequences are going to be severe.

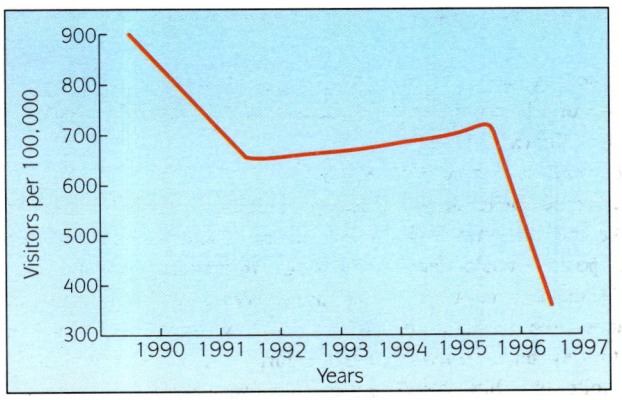

▲ **Figure 2** Number of visitors to Kenya, 1990–1997

2 Damage to the environment

There are also *environmental* problems. On the reefs, boats drop their anchors into the coral, which is a fragile, living community. People walk on the coral and some tourists take pieces of coral away as souvenirs. In the game parks, drivers are keen to get as close as possible to the animals; the army of minibuses surround and disturb animals (**Figure 4**). They churn up the ground in the wet season and the grassland is changed into a 'dust bowl' in the dry season. Particularly in the Masai Mara, there is too high a concentration of visitors in too small an area.

The Kenya Wildlife Service (KWS) is responsible for the game parks. It is under-resourced for the important work it needs to do, and although many

▲ **Figure 4** Lions and tourists in the Masai Mara.

Last week I was almost the only guest at Kilaeuni, a 56-room thatched safari lodge in Tsavo National Park. It is the high season for tourism in Kenya; in a normal year the park would be buzzing with zebra-striped minibuses with pop-up roofs.

But tourism in Kenya has collapsed. All over the country, parks and lodges are half empty. On the coast, hotels are closing for lack of business; the hawkers and beach boys are starved of their European prey; no one is buying their wooden masks, their polished elephants or their beaded Masai bracelets.

This year's tourist season has coincided, fatally, with the run-up to Kenya's election. Violence has already started. After the massacre of tourists at Luxor in Egypt, tourists are taking no chances. In August the violence in Kenya got too close to the tourists. A police station in the coastal resort of Likoni near Mombasa was attacked and seven police officers were killed. The members of a band that had been playing in a tourist hotel were murdered.

▲ **Figure 3** From *The Guardian*, 15 December 1997.

are well motivated, poorly-paid employees with limited experience of the work are more likely to be open to bribery. Some ignore poaching. Others take no action against minibus drivers who go off the roads to get close to the wild animals to earn higher tips from their tourist passengers.

3 Conflicts with local people

There are also *conflicts* between local tribespeople, the Masai, and the Kenyan authorities. When the game parks were set up, the Masai were driven off the land to make way for wild animals. Acute shortages of grazing land, coupled with rapid population growth, have forced farmers to move closer to the edges of the parks. Elephants trample their crops. Lions eat cattle. Villagers and tribespeople are injured, or sometimes killed, by wild animals, but they are not allowed to kill them. Few of these people gain anything from tourists visiting Kenya. The one hope is that soon, with new attitudes associated with **eco-tourism**, there might be an opportunity for groups such as the Masai to benefit from tourism for the first time.

Activity

Write up and illustrate 'Tourism in Kenya' as a case study using these four headings:

A Tourist attractions and their locations
B Benefits of tourism
C Problems
D Changes (you also need to look ahead to page 207).

The impacts of tourism

ADVANTAGES	DISADVANTAGES
A Environmental • Greater awareness of the need for, and interest in, conservation of landscape features, vegetation and wildlife, and preservation of ancient monuments. • Income from tourism/entrance fees may pay for management, conservation and repairs.	**A Environmental** • Destruction of the environment, and resulting loss of habitats, for the building of airports, roads, hotels, etc. • Loss of peace and quiet. • Pressure on landscapes frequently visited, such as footpath erosion and soil erosion. • Pollution problems such as litter or untreated waste going into rivers or the sea.
B Economic • Earns foreign exchange for a country from overseas visitors. • Increases the size of the domestic economy; people are employed in service occupations as tourism tends to be labour-intensive. There is also a greater market for souvenirs from craft industries and food from farms. • The infrastructure (airports, roads, water and electricity supplies), which is improved for tourists, can also benefit local people.	**B Economic** • Country does not gain the full benefits of income from overseas visitors – as little as 15 per cent of money spent on a holiday reaches the host country. A lot of materials and highly-paid staff may be imported. Money for development may be borrowed, increasing debts. • Numbers of visitors go up and down. • Many jobs created by tourism are unskilled, of low status, poorly paid and seasonal. • Some local people, such as farmers or fishermen, may lose their livelihoods in areas where tourist facilities are developed.
C Social/Cultural • Local cultures and traditions may be preserved. • Development of tourism may halt migration loss because of new employment opportunities.	**C Social/Cultural** • Local traditions may disappear even faster in favour of copying the visitors. • Tourists look down on local people and treat them badly.

▲ Figure 1 Advantages and disadvantages of tourism.

The last two case studies have shown that tourism, like other economic activities, has both positive and negative impacts upon people and the environment in those areas where it is important. These are summarized in **Figure 1**.

Most of these advantages and disadvantages apply to tourist locations anywhere in the world. However, the disadvantages may be more severe for LEDCs. For example, management and stewardship of the environment are more difficult because they lack the human expertise and money to be as effective as in MEDCs, as the example of Kenya showed.

Also, much of the technology and many of the materials essential for setting up the facilities and services needed for large-scale tourism in LEDCs have to be bought from MEDCs. Think what is needed before a new resort receives one tourist – airport, planes, paved road to the resort, buses, hotels with 'Western' facilities, services such as water, sewerage and electricity. How many of the materials and fittings needed would be manufactured in an LEDC such as Kenya? How much of the money for a holiday to Kenya costing £1500 per person goes to Kenya (**Figure 2**)?

Minimum benefit to an LEDC	Maximum benefit to an LEDC
• Book and pay for holiday in home country. • Travel on an airline from an MEDC. • Stay in luxury hotels owned by American or European companies. • Eat meals in the hotel.	• Pay for as little as possible in home country. • Travel on an airline from an LEDC. • Stay in small hotels or guest houses and pay locally. • Eat in local restaurants.

▲ Figure 2 Who benefits?

'Green' tourism

The use of 'Green' implies a holiday that is environmentally friendly. It may just be a sales gimmick. It may do no more than just distinguish between mass-market package tours to popular destinations, and small tours to more distant, environmentally interesting places. One person has described it as 'ordinary tourism dressed up in a politically correct manner' by sticking 'Green' in front of it.

What '**Green tourism**', or '**Eco-tourism**', really refers to is **sustainable tourism**. To describe it in simple terms, Green tourism not only places an emphasis upon protecting the environment, but also involves the local people in making decisions that affect their land and living. The role for the local people is what makes it so different from other types of tourism.

Since banning tourism is an impractical solution, the challenge is to find how it can be used for the benefit of both the environment and local people. For eco-tourism to be effective it needs to be run with the cooperation of the local inhabitants, who need to be able to gain from it.

The need for management and stewardship

The pressures from the growth of tourist numbers have increased the need for management everywhere. In most cases effective management only begins after tourism has begun and some damage has already occurred. However, there is one exception – Antarctica. It offers tourists magnificent scenery, icebergs and nesting penguins by the million (**Figure 4**).

Figure 4 Antarctica, an attractive but different tourist location.

Until recently its remoteness had saved it from tourists. In the summer of 1995 tourist numbers passed 10 000 for the first time. Most arrive by cruise ship, and living on ship reduces the chances of damage to a fragile land environment. The cruise operators comply with the guidelines from the International Association of Antarctic Tour Operators (IAATO).

Visitors must NOT:
- disturb wildlife in any way
- go within 5 metres of penguins
- walk on the lichens
- leave litter or waste.

'Green' tourism in Kenya

Three-quarters of the wildlife in Kenya is found outside the game parks, much of it on land owned by the Masai (**Figure 3**). In colonial times the Masai were driven off the land to make way for wild animals in the parks. The Masai were seen as a nuisance. Now the vegetation is healthier and wildlife more plentiful outside the parks. Three tented camps, owned and run by Kenyans, have been set up in Kimana on an important migration corridor for wildlife between Amboseli and Tsavo National Parks. The Masai are paid a rent of about £1000 a year. The Masai are now seen as vital to the success of these smaller, less environmentally damaging tourist developments.

However, there are problems. Only a small amount of tourist money is trickling down to the Masai. Unable to read or understand leases, they are regularly cheated by tour operators. They need to carry on with their traditional way of life of planting crops and keeping cattle, activities which do not fit well with encouraging wildlife. Until they can be convinced of the benefits of tourism, the living space for the wildlife will continue to decline.

Figure 3 Masai tribesperson.

Hopefully by such stewardship Antarctica's natural beauty will be sustained despite the arrival of tourism.

Activity

The government of an LEDC wishes to increase the number of tourist visitors it receives.
a In what ways might it do this?
b What disadvantages might result?
c What should the government do to try to ensure the greatest benefits to the country and its people with the smallest amount of damage to the environment?

In each case answer the question and explain your answer.

Towards a cleaner planet

Industry
– be more energy-efficient
– switch from dirty fossil fuels (coal and oil) to cleaner natural gas.

Electricity companies
– clean up the gases before they are emitted
– rely more and more upon renewable energy sources such as water (HEP), wind and the sun (solar).

Homeowners
– reduce heat losses from roofs, walls and windows
– fit tiles that include solar cells inside them
– do not waste heat or hot water
– choose electrical appliances designed to use minimal electricity.

Drivers
– choose small, fuel-efficient cars instead of 'gas-guzzlers'
– look for cars that run partly on fuel cells or batteries
– switch to public transport when it is available.

▲ **Figure 1** How lifestyles need to change to reduce carbon dioxide emissions significantly.

Activity
Describe, with examples, how the following can reduce damage to the environment:
a governments
b companies
c ordinary people.

The Treaty from the Kyoto Summit does not cover the emissions from traffic in LEDCs such as Chile. The streets of its capital city, Santiago, are choked with traffic on every working day (Figure 2). The advertisement from the makers of orange juice on a hoarding along the same street shows that they feel their product is much purer than the air in Santiago (Figure 3)!

▲ **Figure 2** Normal traffic levels in one of Santiago's main streets.

▲ **Figure 3** Advertisement for orange juice above all the street traffic.

Much still needs to be done if planet Earth is not to be left for future generations in the state shown in the cartoon on page 190.

Chapter 13
Development and interdependence

Rush hour in a country's capital city. What do you think is this country's level of economic development? Is it a low-income, middle-income or high-income country?

Key Ideas

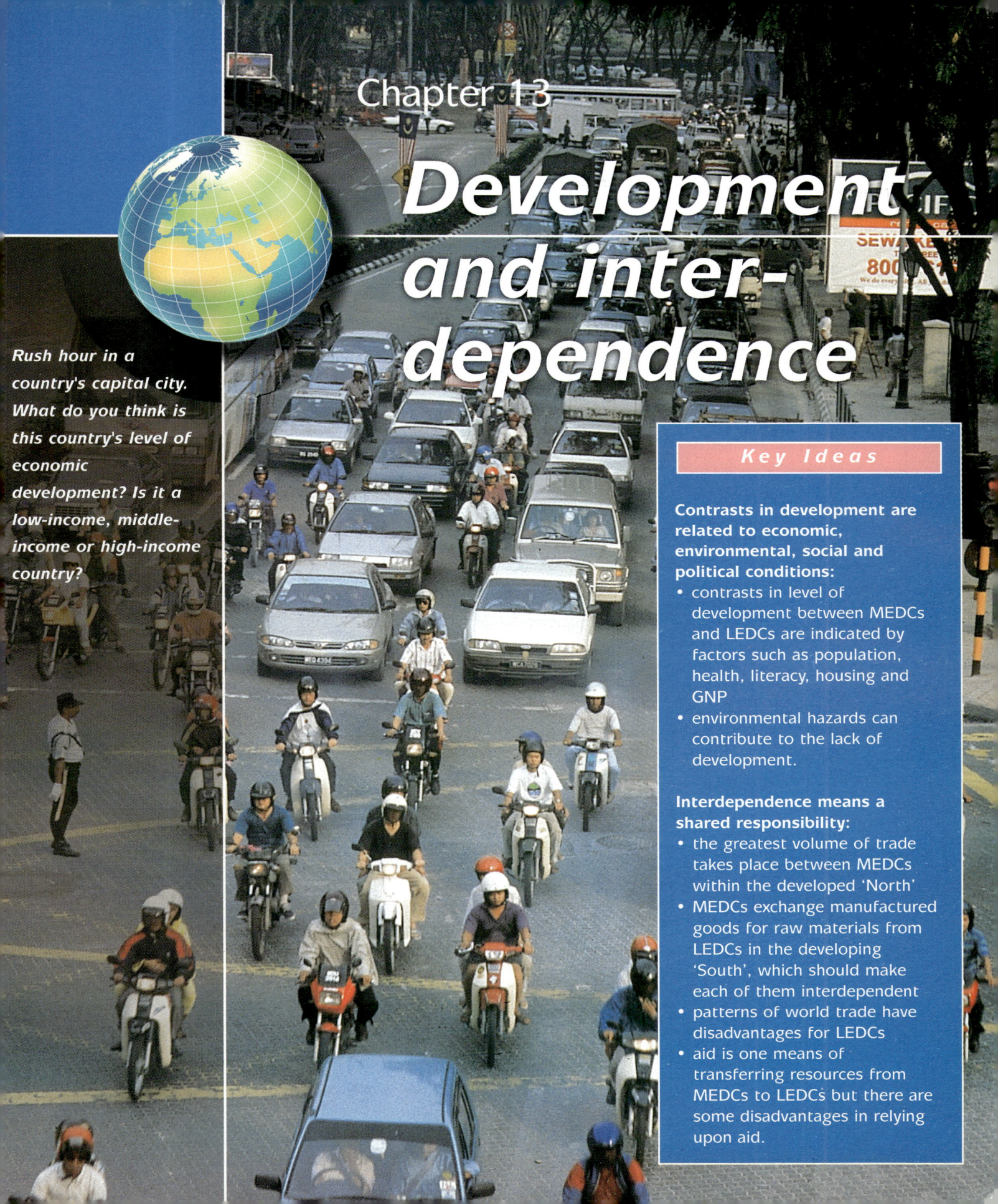

Contrasts in development are related to economic, environmental, social and political conditions:
- contrasts in level of development between MEDCs and LEDCs are indicated by factors such as population, health, literacy, housing and GNP
- environmental hazards can contribute to the lack of development.

Interdependence means a shared responsibility:
- the greatest volume of trade takes place between MEDCs within the developed 'North'
- MEDCs exchange manufactured goods for raw materials from LEDCs in the developing 'South', which should make each of them interdependent
- patterns of world trade have disadvantages for LEDCs
- aid is one means of transferring resources from MEDCs to LEDCs but there are some disadvantages in relying upon aid.

Contrasts in development

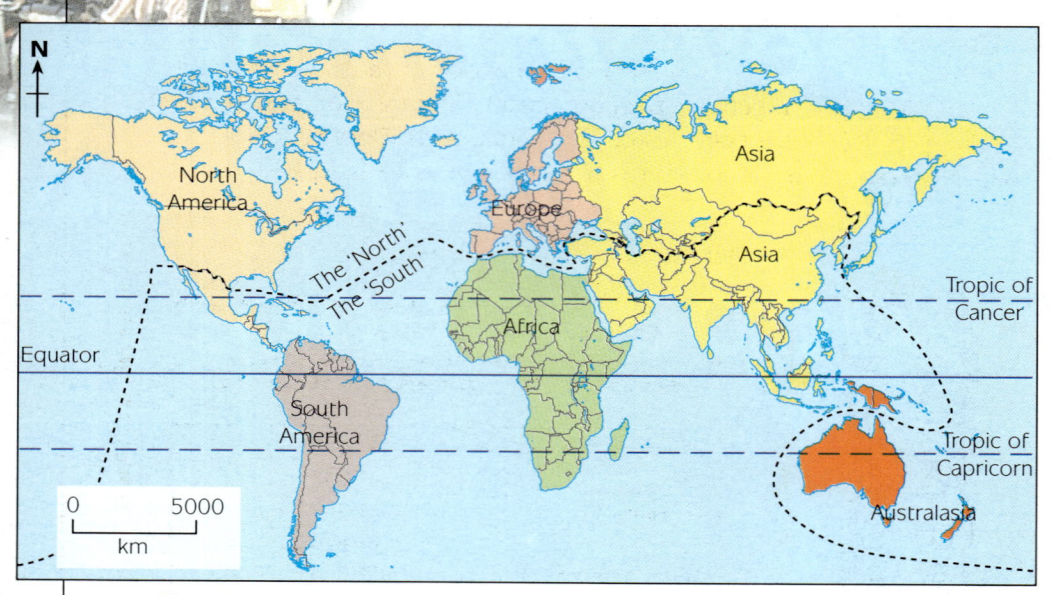

Figure 1 The world divided into more and less economically developed countries.

Throughout this book there have been repeated references to more economically developed countries (MEDCs) and less economically developed countries (LEDCs). These labels for countries are based upon a world split into two parts – an economically developed 'North' and an economically developing 'South'. The course of the dividing line between the two is shown on **Figure 1**.

Of course, any attempt to place about 175 different countries into one of only two categories of development must have exceptions. There are bound to be countries that do not fit into either category in a satisfactory way. Also, the fortunes of countries change with time and sometimes there are major political changes (as in the former USSR) which affect development, but the dividing line between MEDCs and LEDCs remains in the same position as the one originally fixed in 1980. In addition there are significant variations in levels of economic development and prosperity between different regions within most countries. The UK has its divide between the 'North' and 'South' which is perhaps both real and imagined (**Figure 2**). In LEDCs the more likely divide is between rural and urban areas or between the capital city and the rest of the country. It is best to rely upon national averages as the basis for determining whether a country is classified as more or less economically developed, no matter how misleading these might be.

One example of a clear-cut divide between 'North' and 'South' is where the line follows the USA–Mexico border. Mexico has achieved higher levels of development than most of the other LEDCs, but it is dwarfed by the size and wealth of the USA. Some of the differences are summarized in **Figure 3**. The wealth per head in the USA is more than six times greater; this means that Americans have more money to spend on consumer goods such as televisions and cars. Health provision is greater so that there is a much lower chance of a child dying in the first year of life, when infants are at their most vulnerable. Many Mexicans are farmers; more Americans are employed in manufacturing industry and services, sectors which generate more wealth than farming. With such a large difference in level of development on each side of the border, it is not surprising that illegal immigration by Mexicans is a major problem for immigration authorities in the USA. Some Mexicans earn the same in one hour in the United States as they would earn in one day in Mexico! Some people hope that the creation of NAFTA (the North American Free Trade Area) will lead to economic growth in Mexico and reduce the size of the development gap between the two countries.

The recession has hit the South badly …

But has hardly affected the North

Figure 2 Unemployment in the UK in the 1990s – real or imagined differences between North and South?

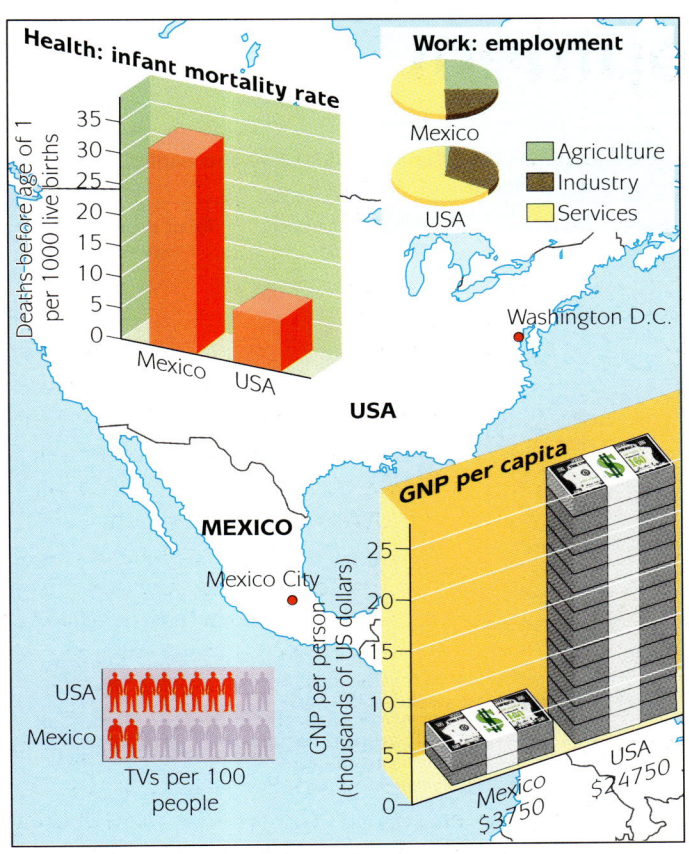

Figure 3 Contrasts between the USA and Mexico.

What is meant by 'development'?

'Development means almost the same as 'wealth'.

A developed country is a rich country. It may be endowed with natural resources that have been used to create wealth. Most developed countries are industrialized. Incomes are high. After fulfilling the everyday human needs for water, food, shelter and clothing, most people have money left over (disposable income) for buying consumer goods and luxuries for the home and for themselves, or for spending on entertainment, leisure and travel. A large, productive service sector develops.

A less developed country is a poor country. In many of these countries there is still a great dependence upon farming, which has not been modernized and from which output is low. Although industry is increasing in some countries, in others it still makes only a small contribution to the economy, while the service sector is dominated by the provision of small services for poor people. For all but the few people who are very rich, there is a constant struggle to achieve even the bare necessities of life. With insufficient food and without clean water, health suffers, particularly that of infants and children. Medical care is sparse. Access to education is limited as well, with resulting low levels of literacy, and the chances of a child improving upon the standard of living and quality of life of its parents are not good. Living in dirty, cramped conditions is the lot of many millions of people in South America, Africa and Asia.

Wealth is an economic factor, but variations in wealth affect quality of life, health, literacy and housing, which are examples of social conditions. Both economic and social measures of development are used.

Activities

1 The table below shows average income per head by continent.

Continent	Average income per head (US$)
Africa	660
Asia	1 980
Australasia	13 540
Europe	11 870
North America	24 340
South America	3 040

a Show these values on an outline world map using the shading (choropleth) method.
b Add the dividing line separating 'North' from 'South'.
c How effective is this line for showing world differences in wealth?

Figure 4 A: A village in Peru. B: A village in Malaysia.

2 a Describe the features of each village shown in **Figure 4**.
b Explain the evidence from the photographs which suggests that:
  (i) there is a lower level of development in the village in A
  (ii) natural resources are better in the area where the village in B is located.

Measures of development

The most widely used indicator of a country's level of development is its **GNP (Gross National Product)** per head. The GNP is calculated by adding up the values for all the goods and services produced in that country during the year; the total is then divided by its population to give the GNP per head. The result is given in US dollars for easy comparisons between countries. This is an *economic* indicator.

The GNP value is more reliable for MEDCs for two reasons:

1 The statistics for working it out are likely to be more readily available and more accurate.

2 Only the values of products sold are included in its calculation. Food produced for subsistence purposes by farmers (to feed themselves and their families) does not have a recorded money value. In many LEDCs farming remains the main occupation so it is likely that the GNP represents an undervaluation for poor countries.

When the GNP for individual countries is plotted on a world map (**Figure 2**), some indication is given of the world distribution of wealth and of the global pattern of high and low levels of economic development. (Note that the map is not complete. For some countries, events such as wars or government secrecy make it impossible for a value even to be estimated. Other countries are omitted because their total population is so low – generally below one million – that the GNP value has limited meaning.)

Highest GNP per head (above US$20 000 and minimum population 1 million)

Rank	Country	GNP per head (US$)	Total population (millions)
1	Switzerland	36 410	7
2	Japan	31 450	125
3	Denmark	26 510	5.2
4	Norway	26 340	4.3
5	Sweden	24 380	8.9
6	USA	24 750	264
7	Germany	23 560	82
8	Kuwait	23 350	1.5
9	Austria	23 120	8
10	United Arab Emirates	22 470	1.9
11	France	22 360	58
12	Belgium	21 210	10
13	The Netherlands	20 710	16
14	Canada	20 670	30

Lowest GNP per head (below US$200)

Country	Total population (millions)
Mozambique	17.4
Tanzania	28.5
Ethiopia	56.0
Sierra Leone	4.5
Nepal	22.6
Bhutan	0.8
Vietnam	75.0
Burundi	6.4
Uganda	21.3
Rwanda	7.8

Source: Population Concern, *1995 World Population Sheet*

▲ **Figure 1** GNP per head – the world's highest and lowest in the mid-1990s.

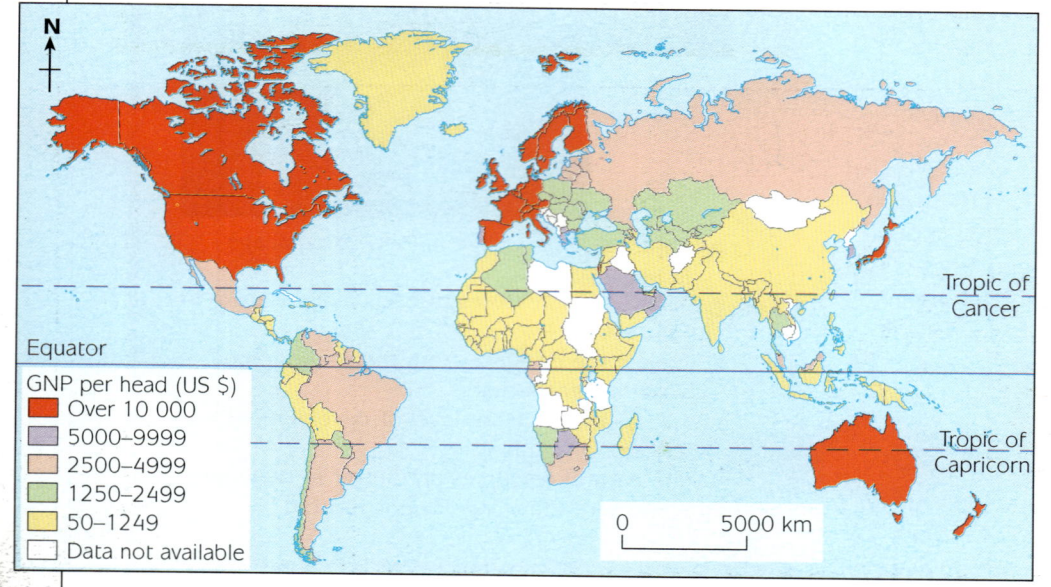

◀ **Figure 2** GNP per head in the mid-1990s.

- To what extent does plotting the data for GNP in **Figure 2** support division of the world into two parts as shown in Figure 1 on page 210?
- Can the position of the dividing line be justified by the economic data shown?
- How large are the variations in levels of economic development between those countries classified as LEDCs?
- Some prefer a three-way split of countries into high income, middle income and low income. Is there support for these three groups in **Figure 2**?

GNP per head (US $)
- Over 10 000
- 5000–9999
- 2500–4999
- 1250–2499
- 50–1249
- Data not available

Chapter 13 Development and interdependence

Before other ways of measuring development are studied, two questions need to be asked about the statistics used for their calculation. How reliable are they? Think of the difficulties of trying to get 175 countries to collect the same data in the same way. Imagine the data-collecting problems in some of the world's remote regions. How up-to-date are they? Census data, for example, are only collected every ten years in most countries and take years to be processed. If data less than five years old can be obtained, that is a real bonus.

In Chapter 8, **population** differences between MEDCs and LEDCs were identified and explained. These are summarized in **Figure 3** below.

These population characteristics are examples of *social* indicators of development. A fall in a country's birth rate usually accompanies an increase in national and personal wealth. The national government has more funds with which to promote birth control campaigns and to set up family planning clinics. With greater personal wealth, attitudes towards having children change. No longer are children looked upon as economic assets for old age; instead they are seen as an economic cost that reduces the amount of money left for purchasing consumer goods and services. As birth rates decline the proportion of young people under 15 goes down. Closing the gap between birth and death rates brings down the rate of natural increase; in this way a country progresses from stage 2 to stage 3, which, if continued, will allow transition into stage 4 of the DTM (Demographic Transition Model) (Figure 4, page 107). All these changes go hand in hand with increased economic development, which is why population characteristics, such as those used in **Figure 3**, can be regarded as reliable indicators of a country's level of development.

Indicator	MEDCs	LEDCs
Birth rate (per 1000 per year)	High	Low
Typical values	20–45	10–16
Natural increase (% per year)	Low	High
Typical value	Below 1%	2.0–3.5% (or more)
People below the age of 15 (%)	Small	Large
Typical value	Below 25%	30–50%
Stage in the Demographic Transition Model	4	2 or 3

▲ **Figure 3** Population characteristics.

Activities

1. **a** On an outline world map, shade in and name the countries given in **Figure 1**, using different colours for those with high and low GNP.
   b Describe the differences in location between them.
   c Suggest why the economic importance of the USA, Japan and Germany is greater than that of the other countries named in **Figure 1**.

2. Try to answer the questions in the text next to **Figure 2** about GNP.

3. Draw labelled diagrams, graphs or sketches to illustrate the differences in population characteristics between MEDCs and LEDCs in **Figure 3**.

4. **a** Describe the differences between Europe and Africa shown on **Figure 4**.
   b Using information from Chapter 8, explain these differences.

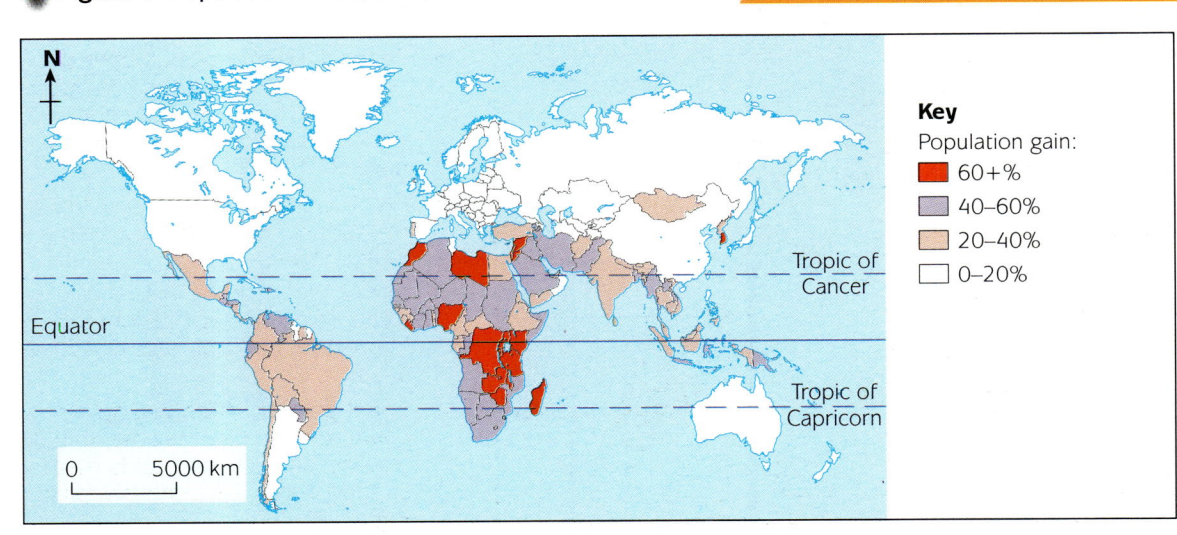

◀ **Figure 4** Population change, 1986–2000.

Key
Population gain:
- 60+%
- 40–60%
- 20–40%
- 0–20%

Other measures of development

Reliable statistics for comparing levels of development between countries are not easy to obtain. Therefore it is safer to try to use statistics for several different measures of development. If all of them reveal a similar picture and point in the same direction, more confidence can be placed in the variations highlighted by them. For example, some prefer to use what is called the 'Physical Quality of Life Index' which is an overall value (or index) based upon combining the separate values of three measures – life expectancy, infant mortality and literacy. These are just three of the many *social* measures which are used in the study of development (**Figure 1**).

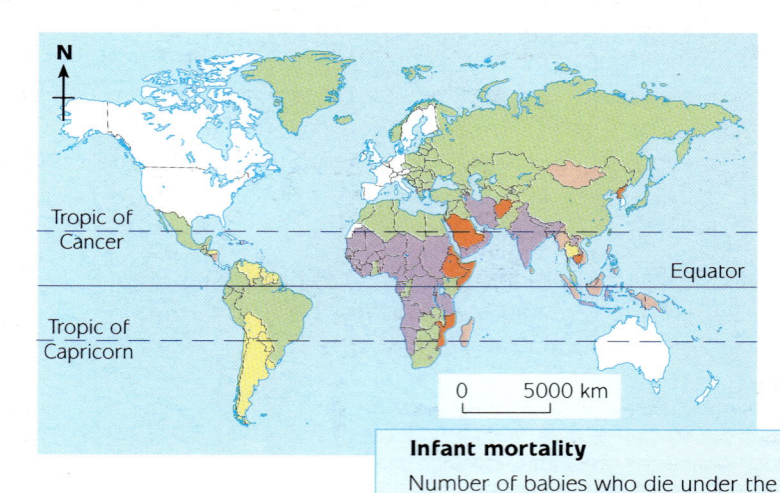

▼ **Figure 1** Social measures of development.

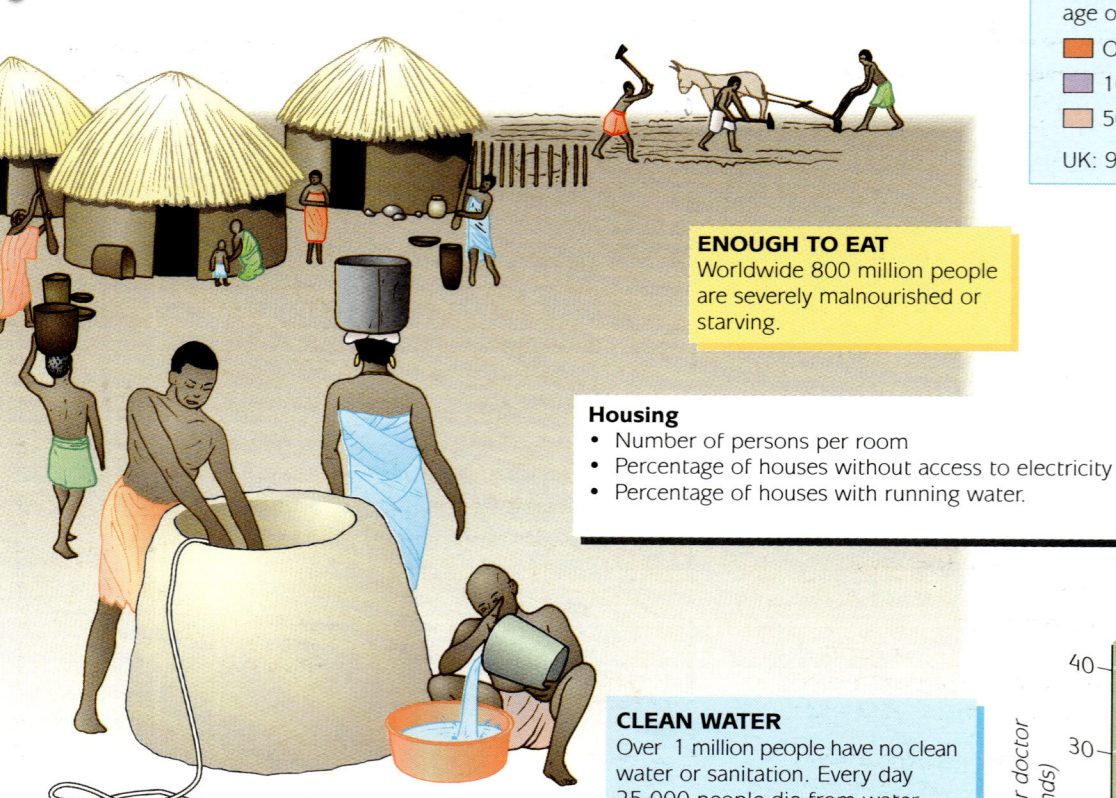

Infant mortality
Number of babies who die under the age of one, per 1000 births

- Over 150
- 100–149
- 50–99
- 20–49
- 10–19
- 0–10

UK: 9 deaths per 1000

ENOUGH TO EAT
Worldwide 800 million people are severely malnourished or starving.

Housing
- Number of persons per room
- Percentage of houses without access to electricity
- Percentage of houses with running water.

CLEAN WATER
Over 1 million people have no clean water or sanitation. Every day 25 000 people die from water-borne disease.

Health
- Infant mortality rate (the number of infants who die within their first year of life per 1000 live births)
- Under-five survival rates
- Life expectancy at birth
- Number of people per doctor
- Number of people per hospital bed
- Percentage of population without access to health services
- Percentage of population without access to safe water
- Average calorie intake per person per day.

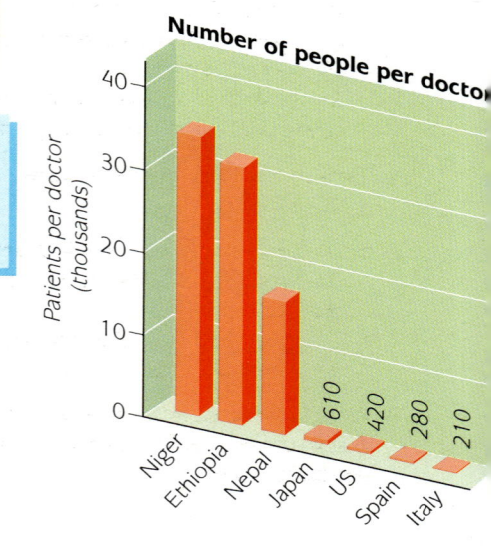

Number of people per doctor

Patients per doctor (thousands)

- Niger
- Ethiopia
- Nepal
- Japan: 610
- US: 420
- Spain: 280
- Italy: 210

EDUCATION
Nearly one-third of adults in the Third World cannot read or write. Over 125 million children were not attending school in 1991; two-thirds of these were girls.

[...]racy
[...]dult literacy rate (proportion of the adult [po]pulation who can read and write)
[av]erage number of years at school per child
[pr]oportion of children who attend secondary [sc]hool.

Children who do not finish primary school
(6–11-year-olds not at school (%)) — 1980, 1990, 2000 (projected), 2015 (projected) across LEDCs, Sub-Saharan Africa, Latin America and the Caribbean, East Asia, South Asia.

Clearly, many of the different measures are inter-related in their effects upon people. Children become an infant mortality statistic by not reaching their first birthday because nearby clinics and hospitals do not exist or are too expensive. Many diseases, such as dysentery and typhoid, are spread by unsafe water supplies and poor sanitation, to which young children have least immunity. The limited availability of food means that both mother and child are less able to fight off diseases. With better parental education and with clean running water to the houses, fewer children would die. It is estimated that some 35 000 children are still dying every day from preventable diseases in less economically developed countries because of poverty. Many are in the poverty cycle trap (**Figure 2**).

The measures of development in **Figure 1** are labelled *social* measures because they are measuring either personal details or factors which directly affect people's lives. However, it is clear that it is difficult to separate the social from the economic, which is why some measures in **Figure 1** can also be described as *socio-economic*. Other measures of development that are more clearly economic have already been referred to, such as employment structure (Figure 3 page 211) and GNP (Figure 1 page 212), but they have strong social effects.

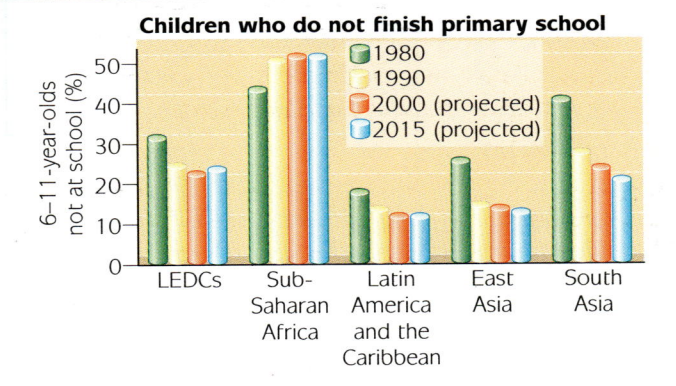

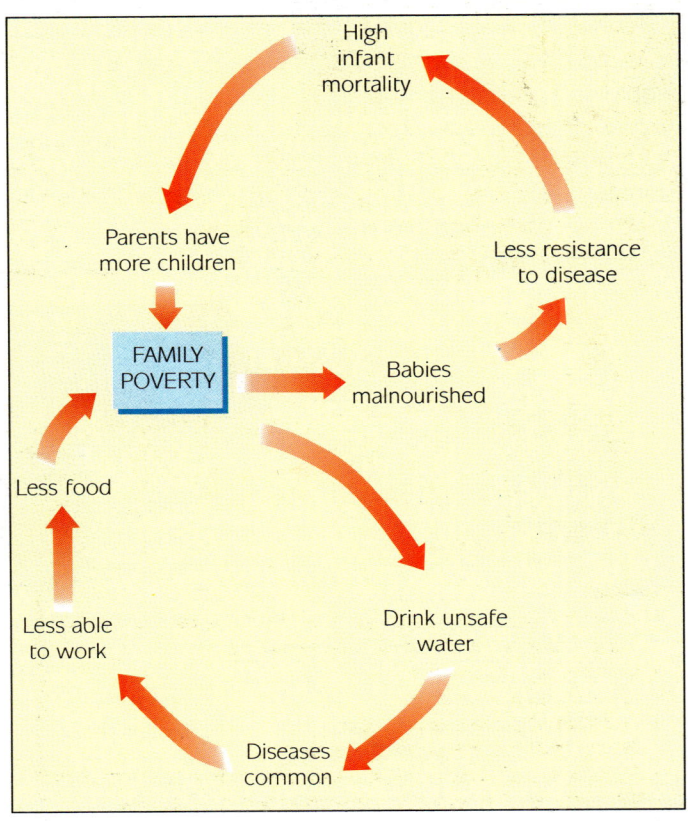

Test questions

1. **a** Give definitions for each of the following measures of development:
   (i) GNP (ii) infant mortality
   (iii) adult literacy rate. (3 marks)
   b State one advantage and one disadvantage of using GNP to show development. (2 marks)

2. Explain how lack of clean water supplies leads to family poverty. (3 marks)

3. **a** Describe two ways in which schooling in sub-Saharan Africa is shown to be different from that in South Asia. (2 marks)
   b Suggest how lack of schooling may contribute to family poverty. (3 marks)

4. Describe and suggest reasons for the world distribution of areas with low and high infant mortality rates. (7 marks)

▲ **Figure 2** Poverty cycles.

Poverty cycle: FAMILY POVERTY → Babies malnourished → Drink unsafe water → Diseases common → Less able to work → Less food → (back to FAMILY POVERTY); also FAMILY POVERTY → High infant mortality → Less resistance to disease; Parents have more children → FAMILY POVERTY.

Causes of the lack of development – environmental hazards

Although measures of development allow LEDCs to be identified, they do not explain why little economic development has occurred. We need to look elsewhere for reasons why these countries are concentrated in the continents of South America, Africa and Asia. Why is it that more than one billion people, mainly in Asia and Africa, live in absolute poverty?

Location may be a factor. LEDCs lie further south than MEDCs and many are within the tropics. This difference in location suggests that *environmental* reasons are responsible for, or at least contribute towards, their present low levels of development. How important are environmental factors?

Environmental (natural) hazards

A natural **hazard** is likely to cause damage to people and property. Natural disasters resulting from environmental hazards such as drought, tropical storms, earthquakes, floods and volcanoes cause considerable loss of life. **Figure 1** shows percentage loss of life from these during the 25-year period beginning in 1969. Some hazards, such as earthquakes and tropical storms, have an immediate impact with a dramatic effect upon people and property in the areas affected. For others, such as drought, the effects act more slowly but are much greater overall as famine takes its toll. The continued existence of drought, particularly for people in the African continent, has meant that its cumulative effects have been great.

Are natural hazards more likely in tropical countries?

- *Tropical storms*, with their hurricane-force winds, are responsible for about one-fifth of the deaths. Whole settlements can be destroyed and plantation crops wiped out. LEDCs are most affected; the only area in the developed world regularly at risk from tropical storms is the south-east corner of the USA.

- *Floods* occur when rivers break their banks, and have more widespread effects. There is also coastal flooding due to tropical storms or high tidal surges which follow earthquakes. Bangladesh, with its low-lying coastal location on the Ganges delta, is an example of a tropical country with a high flood risk. The risk comes both from the River Ganges, which is swollen by monsoon rains from June to October, and from tropical cyclones, which are driven onshore into Bangladesh after crossing the Bay of Bengal.

- *Earthquakes and volcanoes* are mainly restricted to certain zones, many outside the tropics (**Figure 2**). The earthquake risk is high in wealthy California and throughout highly industrialized Japan. However, when they do strike, it is the poor in LEDCs who are hit harder (**Figure 3**). The energy released by an earthquake creates the hazard, but whether or not a house falls down has much to do with the way it was built. Many buildings in Kobe withstood a 7.2 magnitude earthquake in 1995 because of the Japanese rules for building. Many buildings in

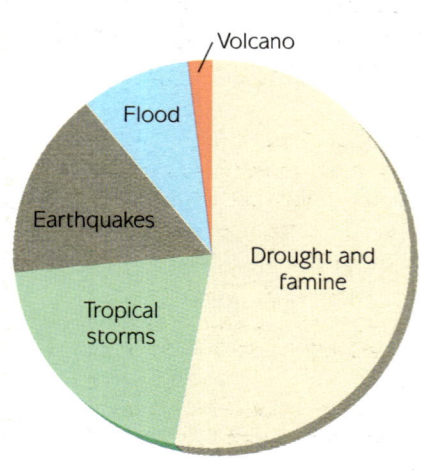

▲ **Figure 1** Percentage loss of life from natural hazards, 1969–1993.

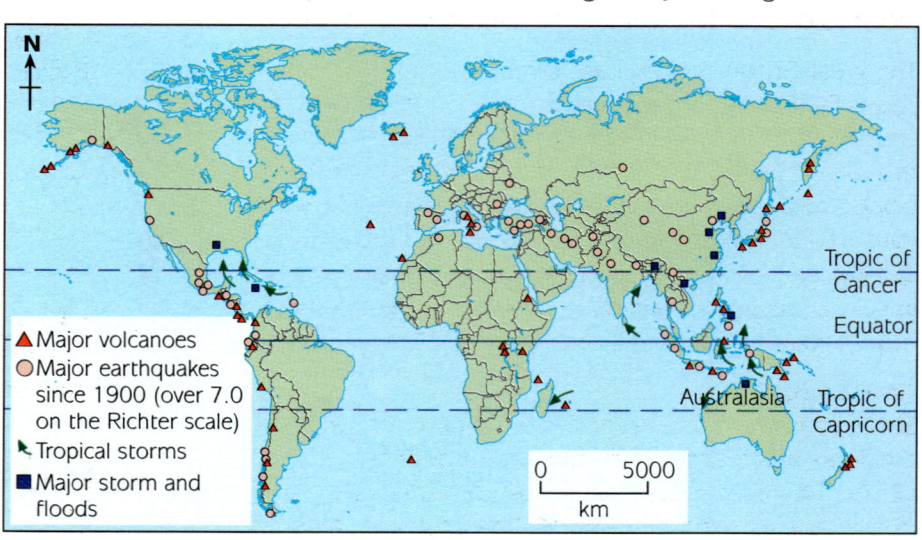

▲ **Figure 2** Areas at risk from some of the world's natural hazards.

Year	Place	Magnitude on Richter scale	Number killed
1993	Maharashtra, India	6.4	22 000
1995	Kobe, Japan	7.2	5 400

▲ **Figure 3** Two earthquakes compared.

Maharashtra in India fell down in 1993 because that kind of disaster was not expected, and people could not afford stronger buildings. Yet the energy released in the Indian earthquake was only one-thousandth of that in the Kobe earthquake.

- *Drought* occurs when the rainfall in an area is significantly lower than the average amount expected there. Drought does not mean that no rain falls, although in extreme cases there may be no rain for months, or even years, in a particular region. It means that crop yields and grass growth are reduced by the lower rainfall, which can trigger off famine, especially in rural, subsistence communities. The longer the rainfall remains below average, the greater the risk of famine and the more people affected. In parts of the Sahel the drought has been almost unbroken for 25 years (page 228).

Many of the deaths from drought-created famine over the past 30 years have been in the Sahel region in Africa. The drought in Ethiopia in the 1980s eventually received great media attention which led to massive food aid. Less publicized was the severe seasonal drought which affected countries such as Zimbabwe, Mozambique and South Africa in 1992. Rural food supplies were reduced, leading in some cases to malnutrition and death, and fewer crops were available for export, affecting the incomes of both farmers and the national economies.

The great British drought was referred to in Chapter 6 pages 86–87 but it was no more than an inconvenience and a cost to a few people. Droughts in LEDCs affect millions of people each year. High temperatures in the tropics mean high rates of evaporation, so that if the rains fail or arrive late the ground dries up much more quickly than it would in temperate lands. Thus the impact of drought is always likely to be greater in the tropics where most of the LEDCs are located.

Conclusion

Some natural hazards occur more frequently in tropical countries and contribute to the lack of development in LEDCs. However, hazards alone cannot explain the size of the development gap between LEDCs and MEDCs.

Activities

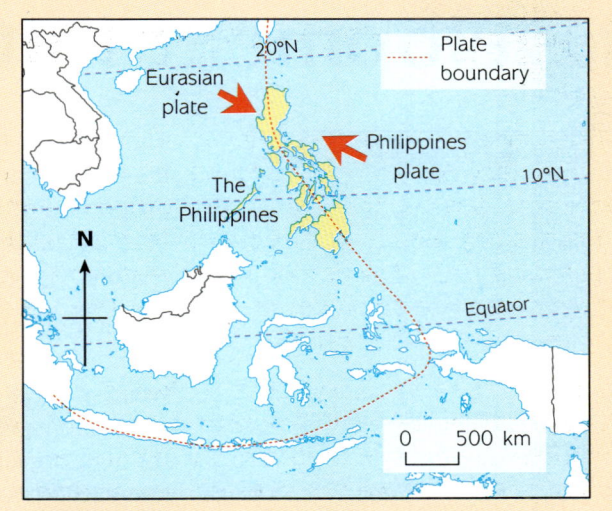

▲ **Figure 4**

Use information from earlier chapters to help you answer the following questions.

1 Look at **Figure 4** and Chapter 1.
   a Name the type of plate boundary which passes through the Philippines.
   b Describe what happens along this boundary.
   c Explain why:
      (i) there is a risk of earthquakes in the Philippines
      (ii) violent volcanic eruptions occur, such as that of Mount Pinatubo in 1991.

2 Look at **Figure 1** and Chapter 1.
   a Show the information in **Figure 1** using a different type of diagram. Add a key.
   b (i) State the difference between the percentages killed by earthquakes and volcanoes.
      (ii) Describe two reasons why more people are killed by earthquakes than volcanoes.
   c Explain why (i) earthquakes and (ii) volcanoes can lead to greater loss of life in LEDCs than in MEDCs.

3 Look at **Figure 4** and Chapter 6.
   a (i) Describe the main features of a tropical storm such as a hurricane.
      (ii) Explain how these features can lead to great loss of life.
   b From **Figure 4**, explain how (i) the latitude and (ii) the country's nature and layout mean that the Philippines will be at risk from tropical storms.
   c Why is a tropical storm in the Philippines likely to lead to greater loss of life than a hurricane in Florida?

Health hazards affecting development in tropical countries

The hot, wet tropical climate has one major disadvantage for human health – it is the climate in which insects and bacteria thrive and multiply best. A large proportion of the diseases that make people sick and too weak to work, or that kill children and infants, are associated in some way with water (**Figure 1**).

Sudan in north-east Africa has the world's highest rate of Guinea worm infection. One-third of the world's cases are recorded in southern Sudan, where people in almost every village are affected. Poor and remote rural populations are the most vulnerable because Guinea worm is transmitted through drinking unclean water. The worm grows below a person's skin and may reach over 60cm long. Every wet season in southern Sudan, which is when the planting season begins, the worms break through the skin searching for water in which to release their larvae. This begins a new life-cycle for a parasite that causes great pain and suffering.

Too much water

As with Guinea worm, the risk of catching these diseases increases during the wet season. For example, the many areas of warm, stagnant water standing on the surface make ideal breeding grounds for mosquitoes. This risk is multiplied many times during floods when there is water everywhere. Also, the water flows over the surface and picks up human excrement, carrying it elsewhere and mixing it with the water used for drinking.

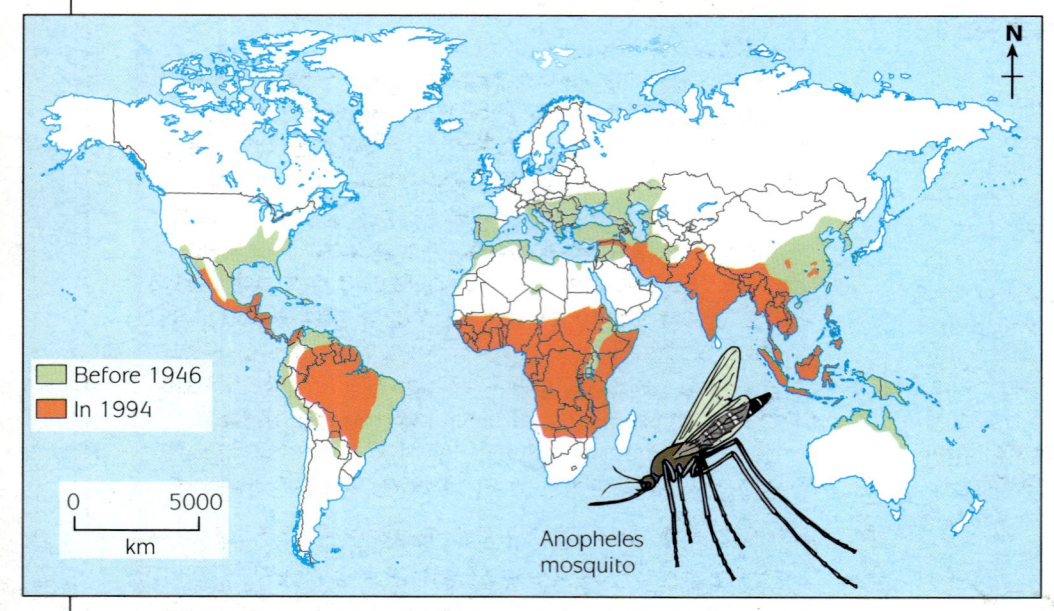

The wet season is the busiest time of the year for farmers. Without the rains their crops will not grow. Because this is also the time of the year when insect pests are present in greatest numbers, farmers are not always at their fittest for work. Many other pests, which have a disastrous effect on the amount of food available to people, thrive in the hot and wet conditions as well. Tsetse flies in Africa and cattle ticks in tropical regions in other continents spread disease to herds of cattle. Fields full of healthy crops may be eaten off by a swarm of locusts passing through. Termites, rats and mice take their shares of the harvested crops in store.

A Water-borne diseases – diseases spread by drinking or by washing food in contaminated water:
  Diarrhoea
  Dysentery
  Cholera
  Typhoid
  Hepatitis

B Water-related insect-borne diseases – diseases spread by insects that breed in water:
  Malaria – carried by mosquitoes
  Sleeping sickness – carried by tsetse flies

C Water-based diseases – carriers of the disease live in water:
  Bilharzia – carried by water snails
  Guinea worm – worms release larvae into water

▲ **Figure 1** Diseases in tropical regions associated with water.

▲ **Figure 2** Malaria – still a killer disease in tropical countries.

- threatens 40 per cent of the world's population in over 90 countries
- kills four children every minute
- puts 20 million Western tourists at risk every year
- was widespread in the Mediterranean until 1960
- is most prevalent in Africa south of the Sahara – 90 per cent of all cases
- cases in 1992: over 1 million in the Americas; over 3 million in south-east Asia.

Life-cycle of the Guinea worm

7. In two weeks the larvae reach a stage where they can infect humans.
6. Water fleas consume worm larvae.
5. On contact with water, the emerging worm releases larvae into a pond or shallow well. Larvae can survive only three days without a host.
1. Person drinks water contaminated with fleas carrying Guinea worm larvae.
2. The larvae are digested and they grow and mate in the intestines.
3. Female worms migrate to different parts of the body, usually the legs (male worms die soon after mating).
4. A year after infection the worm begins to emerge through the skin causing a painful blister.

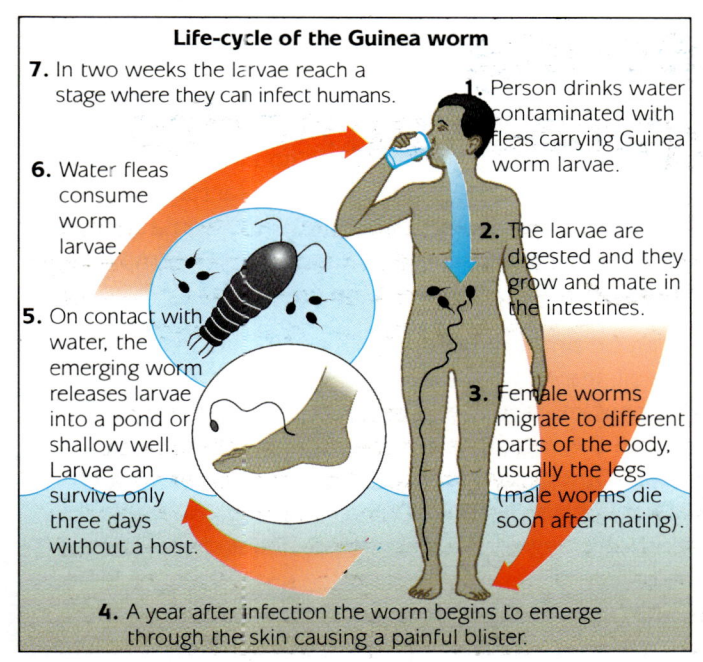

▲ **Figure 3** The Guinea worm in Sudan.

Insufficient clean and safe water

In rural areas in LEDCs it is the exception for a person to live in a house that has a tap with safe water. In areas where water is plentiful it is often taken directly from the streams without any treatment. In poorly watered areas people from the village, usually women and children, have to walk a kilometre or more for all their water supplies; even then it may be taken from a river or mudhole from which animals drink as well. Many illnesses stem from:

- the absence of clean, safe drinking water
- the absence of proper sanitation facilities
- the failure to treat human excrement and keep it separate from water used for other purposes.

Conclusion

Tropical heat and the presence of water provide ideal conditions for the origins and spread of numerous

Activities

1 Choose one water-related tropical disease for a case study. Give information about it using headings such as:
   - Areas affected
   - Causes
   - Consequences
   - Prevention.
   Illustrate with diagrams or otherwise where appropriate.

2 Explain why sanitation facilities should be installed at the same time as clean drinking water is supplied.

Childrens' health and mortality rates

Every day 25 000 children in the world die from diseases caused by unsafe water. Repeated stomach upsets caused by bacteria and viruses in their drinking water mean that children become malnourished. Eventually they become so weak that they can die of starvation.

If mothers make up dried milk with dirty water to feed their babies, they can unknowingly make their babies ill. In many places there is clean water below the ground, but how to reach it and keep it clean is the problem. Wells can be dug by hand in order to locate fresh water. Once the bottom of the well fills with clean water it can be pumped to the surface. But the source has to be protected. Potentially harmful water has to be kept away so that there is no contamination. This means that simple basic sanitation has to be installed at the same time.

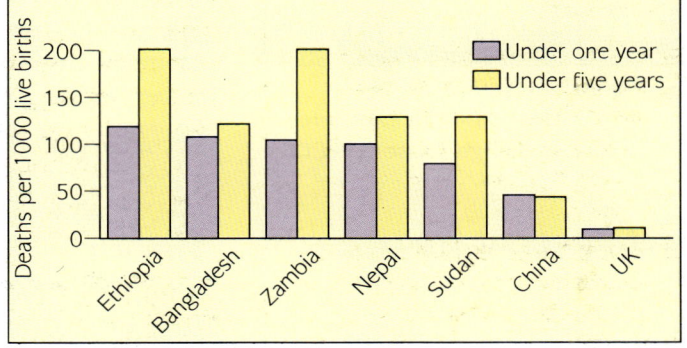

▲ **Figure 4** Children's health and mortality rates.

diseases in many LEDCs. Most medical research is undertaken in MEDCs. Research into methods of prevention and cures for tropical diseases has never been generously funded.

Too little water

In some tropical areas drought is a greater problem than water-related diseases. The wetter than average years in the Sahel in the 1950s and early 1960s (**Figure 2**, page 228) encouraged an extension of cropland, allowed more animals to be kept and led to population growth because more people could be fed. Attempts to keep feeding the same number of people in the drought years led to environmental damage and **desertification**. This is the destruction of the land so that fewer trees, bushes, grasses and crops can grow on it. In the end desert-like conditions may result. Once the rains return, in the worst affected areas it is not possible to use the land for farming because the soil structure has been destroyed.

Symptoms of desertification

- Reduction in, or disappearance of, the vegetation cover
- Soil erosion
- Lowering of ground water levels
- Sand dune formation on land formerly farmed.

An introduction to world trade

Figure 1 Hotel resort in the tropics. Tourism is a vital source of foreign exchange for some LEDCs.

Trade is the exchange of goods and services between countries. It is called **visible** trade if goods (raw materials, foodstuffs and manufactured goods) are exchanged, because they can be counted, weighed and given a value. It is called **invisible** trade if services are exchanged. Tourism is one example; earnings from workers overseas and foreign aid are two more.

The goods exchanged may be **primary products**. These include *raw materials*, such as crude oil, iron ore, cotton or natural rubber, from which other products can be manufactured. They may also be *foodstuffs*. A country may not be able to grow all the food that it needs to keep its population well fed, so it engages in trade. Other countries import foods they cannot grow themselves due to unsuitable physical conditions. The UK diet would be less varied without the import of oranges, bananas, tea, coffee and chocolate.

Secondary products are *manufactured goods*, which may need to be imported into that country because they are not made there. Among MEDCs, however, the same types of goods are traded across borders, such as cars, reflecting freedom of choice and wealth rather than need.

Volume of world trade

More than half the world's trade takes place between the top seven trading nations – USA, Germany, Japan, France, UK, Italy and Canada. These are known as the G7 countries and include the most industrialized countries in the world. They need large quantities of raw materials and fuels and produce a wide variety of manufactured goods.

Relatively little trade takes place between LEDCs. Countries in South America and Africa do not always have goods a neighbouring country wants to buy. They produce a narrow range of commodities, which are often the same as their neighbours'. Their economies and transport links are organized towards exporting to the industrialized countries. They are likely to compete with surrounding countries for overseas markets. When there is the desire to increase trade with neighbouring countries, factors such as lack of money, poor land communications and customs red tape limit opportunities for exchange of goods.

Figure 2 shows the dominance of the G7 countries and countries in free trade areas in world trade. Japan is Asia's industrial giant but has few natural resources of its own for manufacturing industry. Trade is vital for importing the raw materials and fossil fuels needed. Japanese companies have sought out markets in every continent for their manufactured goods. The relative importance of the rest of Asia in world trade has been increasing because there are several newly industrializing countries (NICs) such as Taiwan, South Korea and Malaysia. The largest export commodity from countries in the Middle East and from some African countries such as Nigeria and Algeria is crude oil.

Trade and economic groupings

The aim of these groupings is to increase trade, leading to increases in wealth for the member countries. Cross-border restrictions on trade within the grouping, such as tariffs and quotas, are lightened. While they create a

---

ℹ Usefulness of trade

1 A country can sell its surplus products.

2 A country can specialize in what it does best.

3 People in a country can eat food or use goods which are not grown or made there.

4 Trade may make a country richer and better developed.

ℹ Factors encouraging trade between countries

1 Wealthy countries – they can afford to exchange goods

2 Highly industrialized countries – they need to import raw materials and energy and to sell manufactured goods to pay for them

3 Good transport and communications – for the easy and cheap movement of goods

4 Member of a common market or free trade area – to allow goods to move between countries without restrictions such as tariffs and quotas.

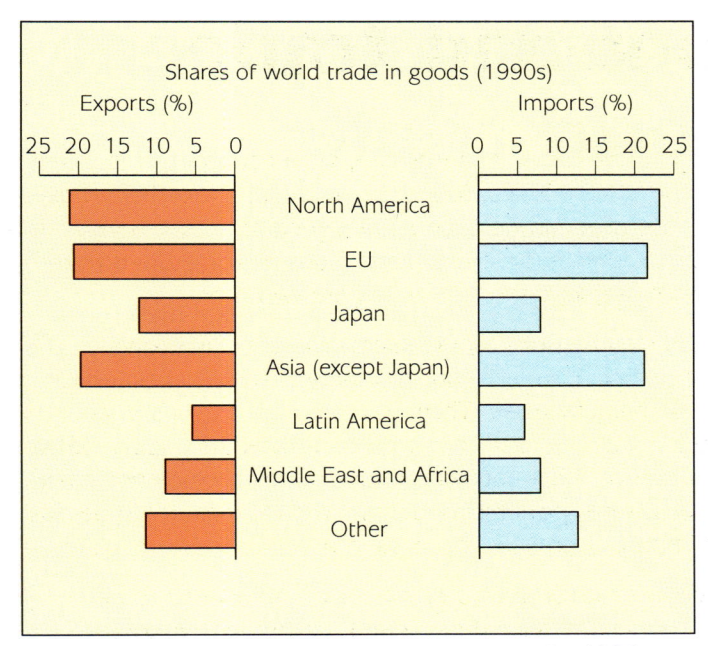

Figure 2 Shares of the world trade in goods, 1990s.

common market within the grouping, tariffs and quotas are set up for goods from countries outside, which means that the creation of these groupings does not necessarily help free trade worldwide.

1 EU (European Union)

What began as a common market of six countries in 1957 had developed into the EU with fifteen members by 1998. Customs controls for goods and people have virtually disappeared between member countries. There is a free market in goods, so that someone buying a new car in the UK has little idea in which countries the parts were made or assembled. The European Commission has always been keen to encourage cross-border transport links to allow free movement of goods. There is the network of 'E' (European) roads, most of them motorways. High-speed trains run from France into Belgium, and the UK has been integrated into the European railway system by the Channel Tunnel. The EU has undoubtedly led to increased trade since 93 per cent of the international trade of EU countries is with other EU countries. This, of course, only leaves 7 per cent of trade with the rest of the world. LEDCs complain that they have limited access into the EU market. The policy of self-sufficiency has also reduced trading opportunities for LEDCs.

2 Mercosur

The name stands for 'The Common Market of the South', and refers to South America. This was first proposed in 1986 and tariffs between the four member countries began to fall from 1991. The full Customs Union began in 1995. By 1995 about 90 per cent of the trade between the countries was tariff-free; tariffs on the remaining 10 per cent will continue to fall until they reach zero by 2000. Trade has increased in all areas, with noticeable increases in the export of industrial goods from Brazil to Argentina and of raw materials and temperate agricultural produce, such as cereals, apples and wine, from Argentina to Brazil. The increased traffic has highlighted some barriers to movement which will take some time to overcome: lack of good roads, the funnelling of most of the trade between Brazil and Argentina across just one bridge, and slow, poorly trained customs officials.

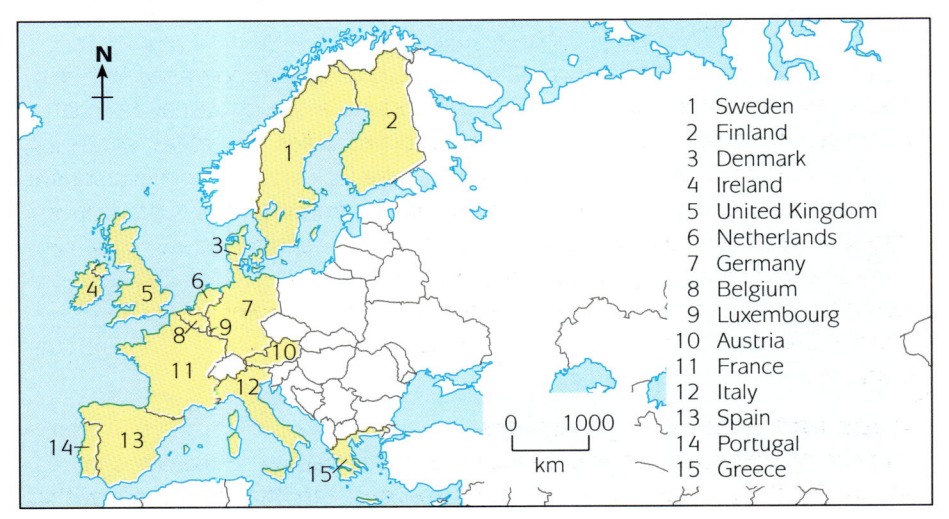

Figure 3 Member countries of the EU in 1998.

1 Sweden
2 Finland
3 Denmark
4 Ireland
5 United Kingdom
6 Netherlands
7 Germany
8 Belgium
9 Luxembourg
10 Austria
11 France
12 Italy
13 Spain
14 Portugal
15 Greece

Figure 4 Location and trade.

Causes of the lack of development – the pattern of world trade

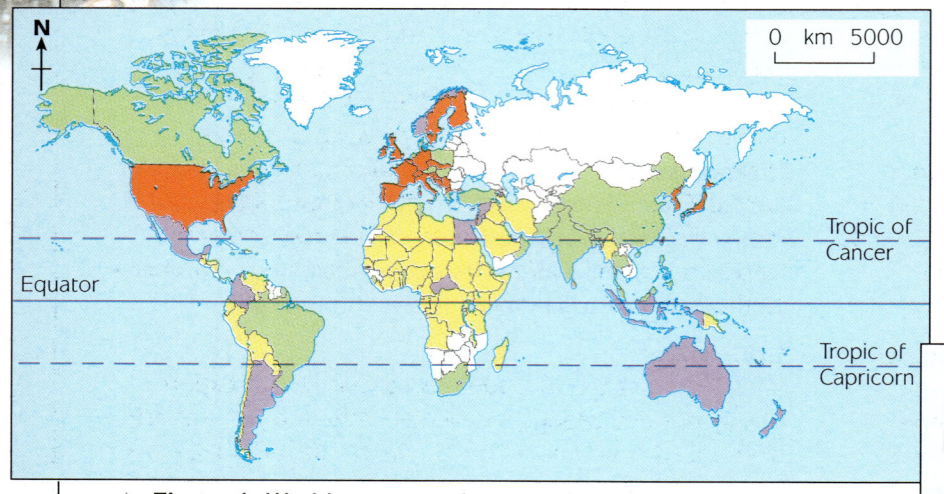

Trade between MEDCs and LEDCs forms only a small percentage of total world trade.

MEDCs need raw materials and fuels found in LEDCs to keep their factories working. The largest deposits of metals such as bauxite (for making aluminium) and iron ore (for making steel), are found in tropical countries. The world's greatest concentration of oil and gas reserves is in the Middle East. **Figure 1**

Figure 1 World export trade.

Percentage of total exports
- Primary products: Over 75, 50–75
- Manufactured products: Over 75, 50–75
- Data not available

illustrates a typical pattern of raw material movement between LEDCs and MEDCs. Some raw materials come from plants which only grow in tropical climates, such as rubber and cotton. Without such imports MEDCs could not have industrialized.

LEDCs need to import manufactured goods, such as cars and computers, and the machinery, technology and knowledge to help them develop economically. With the foreign currency earned from selling their raw materials and foodstuffs, LEDCs should be able to buy what they need from MEDCs; MEDCs will benefit by having a market for their manufactured goods and services. Many LEDCs depend upon the export of a small number of commodities. In Africa, for example, at least 25 countries depend upon just one or two commodities for their export earnings (**Figure 2**).

There is **interdependence** between LEDCs and MEDCs because each group of countries offers what the other group wants, and there is a clear need for such trade. Since one depends upon the other, the trade between them should be in balance. However, there is a trade surplus for the MEDCs and the LEDCs are in debt.

One-commodity dependency

- More than 90%: Oil and gas – Algeria, Congo (Brazzaville), Nigeria, Libya, Gabon; Bauxite – Guinea
- More than 80%: Coffee – Burundi; Copper – Zambia; Uranium – Niger
- More than 70%: Live animals – Somalia
- More than 60%: Coffee – Ethiopia; Cocoa – Ghana; Iron ore – Liberia
- More than 50%: Cotton – Mali; Gold and diamonds – South Africa

Two-commodity dependency

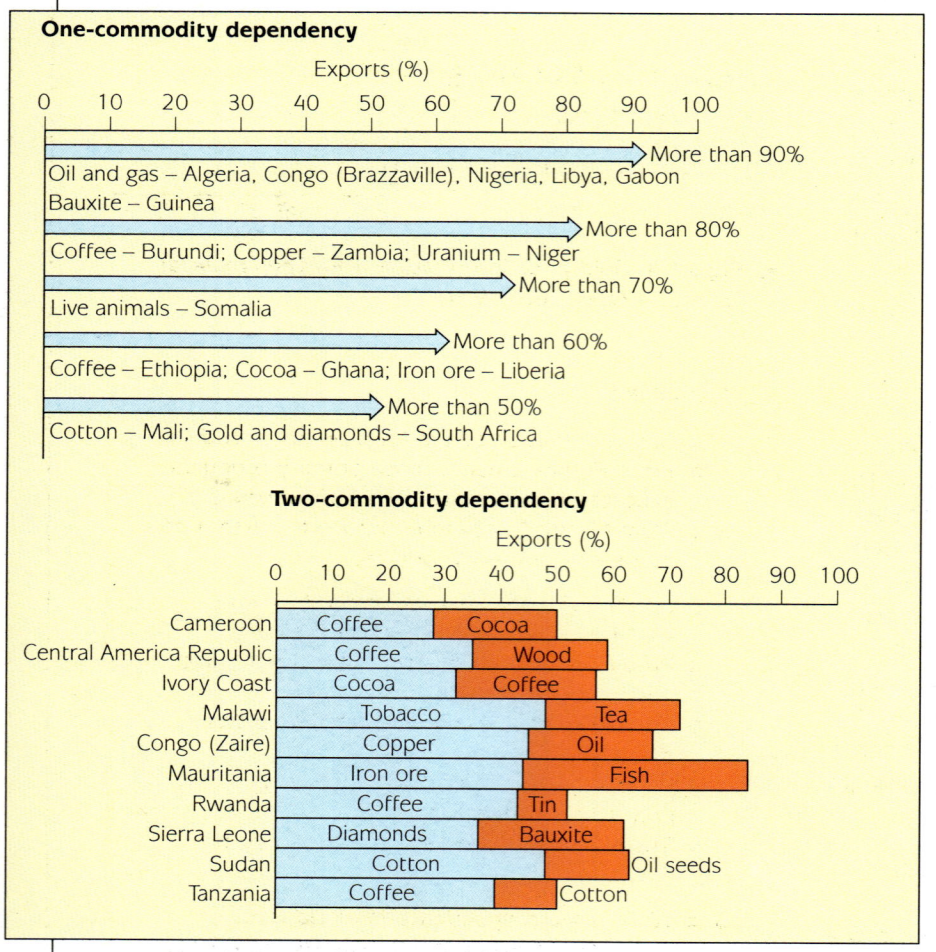

Country	Commodity 1	Commodity 2
Cameroon	Coffee	Cocoa
Central America Republic	Coffee	Wood
Ivory Coast	Cocoa	Coffee
Malawi	Tobacco	Tea
Congo (Zaire)	Copper	Oil
Mauritania	Iron ore	Fish
Rwanda	Coffee	Tin
Sierra Leone	Diamonds	Bauxite
Sudan	Cotton	Oil seeds
Tanzania	Coffee	Cotton

Figure 2 Dependence upon a limited range of exports by countries of Africa.

- 33% Wholesale and retail
- 35% Storage and shipping costs
- 2% Farm workers in producing country
- 20% Ripening, importer's costs and advertising
- 10% Farmer's profit, fertilizer and transport costs

▲ **Figure 3** Rich pickings – but for whom?

The pattern of world trade favours MEDCs

Primary products upon which LEDCs depend are *low in price*. Look at **Figure 3**. When you spend £1 on bananas in your local shop, how much goes to the banana worker? How much goes to the producing country?

Primary products *go up and down in price*. There are world prices for metals, minerals and commodities which are determined by markets in financial centres such as New York and London and over which the producing countries have no control. When there is an economic recession in industrialized countries, the price and demand for raw materials goes down. Goods from LEDCs are sold at world market prices. Oil is used in every country and is in high demand, but even its price fluctuates (**Figure 1**, page 190). Its world price today is much lower than it was in the 1970s and 1980s, which is bad news for the six African countries whose exports are dominated by oil and gas (**Figure 2**). Reduced gold prices in November 1997 was not good news for the economy of South Africa.

Overdependence upon just one or two export commodities is dangerous but is a normal situation for many LEDCs (**Figure 2**). As people in the MEDCs become more environmentally aware, more aluminium cans are being recycled, reducing the world demand for bauxite. Which African countries may be affected? Half the rubber used in the world does not come from trees in the tropics any more; instead it is a synthetic product made from crude oil. On Caribbean islands hurricanes have destroyed banana plantations. Health scares in Europe and North America may reduce the demand for sugar or coffee from South American and African countries. Many countries attempt to diversify, but some do not have the natural resources for easy development of alternatives.

Manufactured goods, which LEDCs need to buy from MEDCs, sell at high prices. As raw materials are processed, value is added at each stage. When you buy a jar of coffee, about 10 per cent of the price pays for the coffee beans. Unlike raw materials, the price of manufactured goods, most of which are made in MEDCs, tends to move upwards. To import the same number of tractors or cars as it did ten years ago, an LEDC will need twice the number of raw material exports.

When LEDCs do begin to process and manufacture their own raw materials, the next obstacle is *trade barriers*. Local raw materials and lower wage rates give many LEDCs a price advantage over MEDCs. However, MEDCs protect their own manufacturing industries against cheaper imports by high tariffs and quotas. The WTO (World Trade Organization) promotes free trade and the removal of import duties. International meetings are held but progress is slow because of the vested interests of the powerful G8 countries.

Conclusion

The pattern of world trade means that LEDCs export mainly primary products which are low in price. Imports from MEDCs are high in price. The result for LEDCs is a trading loss and debt.

Gold price below $300 for first time in 12 years

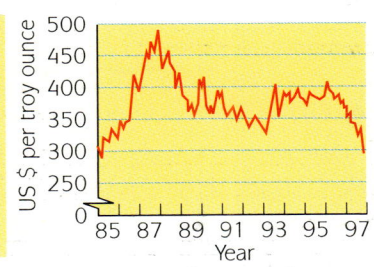

▲ **Figure 4** Gold price information from *The Financial Times*, 27 November 1997.

Activities

1. a Give a definition of the term *primary product*.
   b From **Figure 2** name those primary products exported by more than one African country.
   c From **Figure 1**, describe the world pattern of exports of primary products.

2. State the evidence for each of the following, using labelled illustrations where helpful.
   a Producers of primary products do not make much money.
   b The prices of primary products go up and down.
   c Dependence upon one or two primary products is dangerous.
   d There is little trade between countries in Africa.

3. a What is interdependence in world trade?
   b Why does it not exist and why should it exist?

Can poor countries develop economically?

The prospects for most countries are not good. The cartoon below suggests that the *interdependence* between less and more economically developed countries is not a reality.

Figure 1 Does interdependence between rich and poor countries exist?

However, it is wrong to think that the interests of all the LEDCs are the same. Back to bananas! The World Trade Organization, continuing its drive towards free trade, says that the favoured treatment given by the EU to banana imports from producers on Caribbean islands is illegal. The small farmers in the Caribbean know that they cannot hope to compete with bananas grown on plantations in Central and South America (called 'dollar' bananas) (**Figure 2**). Without the favoured EU treatment the Caribbean producers will go out of business and there are few obvious alternatives.

Figure 2 Caribbean versus 'dollar' bananas.

This pattern of world trade, whereby LEDCs in South America, Africa and Asia export raw materials to be used in industries in Europe, is well established. It had its origins in colonial times. One of the main reasons why Britain set up colonies was to obtain supplies of raw materials not available in the home country. Additionally, markets for Britain's manufactured goods were opened up overseas. Colonies were intended to be an economic asset to the mother country. It is difficult to break a pattern of trade once it is established, especially in Africa where many countries have had less than 50 years of independence (**Figure 3**).

A few of the old colonies, notably Australia and Canada, have become MEDCs. They have great riches in mineral resources, shared among small total populations for the size of their land area. Others making some progress with economic development include a large and populous country like Brazil and smaller countries in south-east Asia such as Singapore and Malaysia. **Figure 4** shows the changes in Malaysian exports over a 25-year period. Can you explain how they show that economic development has occurred? Judged by its GNP, Malaysia is one of the middle-income countries. The photograph on page 209 shows a scene in Kuala Lumpur, its capital city. Too many people have private forms of a transport for it to be a low-income country. In high-income countries most people replace motorbikes with cars as soon as they can afford to do so.

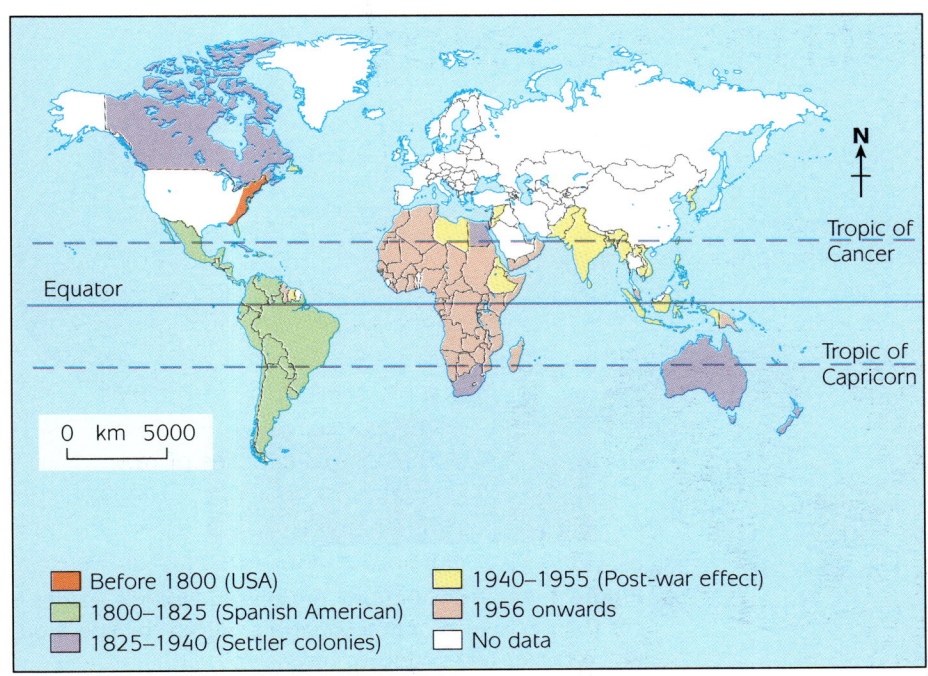

Figure 3 Decolonization: independence for countries that were once colonized (mainly by European countries).

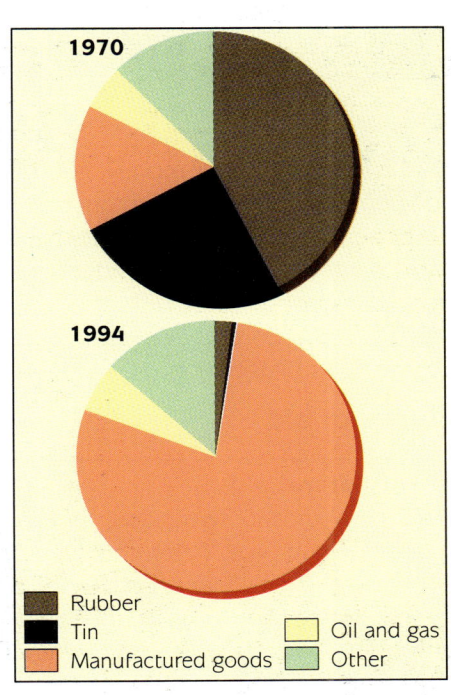

Legend:
- Before 1800 (USA)
- 1800–1825 (Spanish American)
- 1825–1940 (Settler colonies)
- 1940–1955 (Post-war effect)
- 1956 onwards
- No data

Figure 4 Exports from Malaysia in 1970 and 1994.

Legend: Rubber, Tin, Manufactured goods, Oil and gas, Other

For most LEDCs the trade gap, or the 'trade trap' as it is sometimes called, remains a reality and has led to debt. Money borrowed has to be paid back with interest. Interest rates have risen (due to economic conditions in the industrialized world). Raw material prices have fallen. The debt has increased without any more money being borrowed. In some countries the size of the debt is more than the annual value of the country's exports. The only option open to some countries is to accept **aid** (Figure 5), which is a last-hope solution.

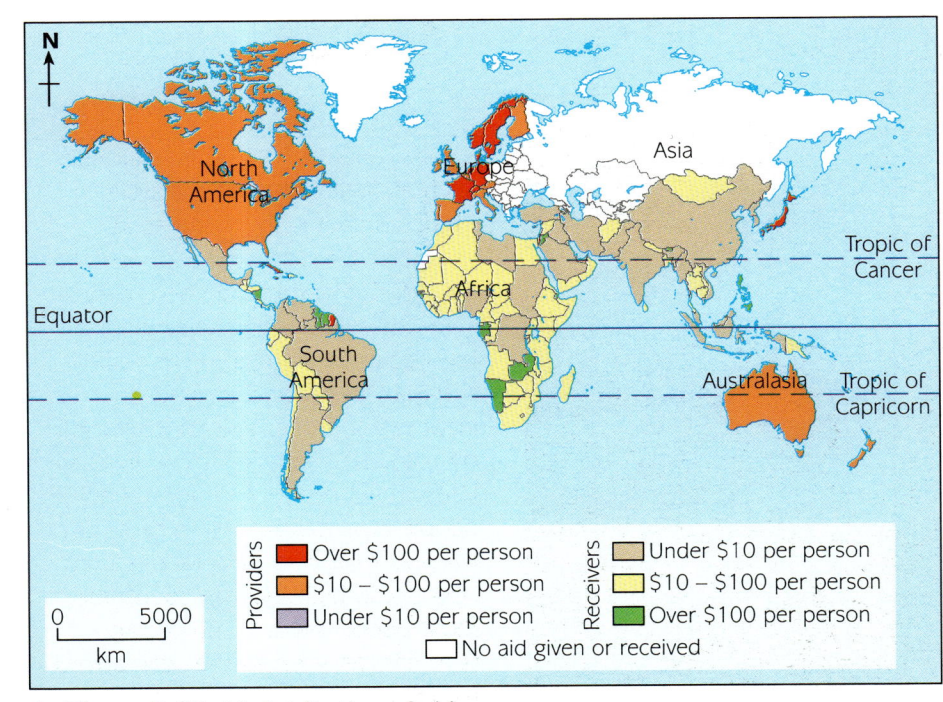

Figure 5 World distribution of aid.

Legend:
- Providers: Over $100 per person / $10 – $100 per person / Under $10 per person
- Receivers: Under $10 per person / $10 – $100 per person / Over $100 per person
- No aid given or received

Activities

1. Explain what **Figure 1** suggests about interdependence in world trade.

2. Write down the arguments against free trade in bananas that producers in the Caribbean would use to gain support for their cause.

3. Use **Figure 4**.
   a. List the 1994 exports of Malaysia in order of importance.
   b. Explain how the changes between 1970 and 1994 show that:
      (i) primary industries have declined in importance
      (ii) secondary industries have increased in importance.
   c. Why do the export data suggest that economic development has occurred?

Aid

Aid is the transfer of money, goods and expertise from one country (the *donor*) to another (the *recipient*). Aid may be given freely, but sometimes low rates of interest are charged on loans or conditions are attached to the goods supplied. Three different types of aid can be recognized according to how it is funded and who controls its distribution.

Types of aid

1 Bilateral aid

Bilateral means 'two-sided'; in this case both sides are governments. Often this type of aid is *tied aid* because the recipient has to use the aid to buy goods and services from the donor country. It may be little more than trade promotion – finding an overseas market for the donor country's manufactured products and funding the trade with credits or low-cost loans.

The political nature of this aid raises several problems. The goods may not be best suited to the real development needs of the country and its people. Many bilateral deals focus upon large-scale projects such as dams and power stations, which rank high in prestige but low in value to ordinary people. A second problem is that the choice of donor country is made for political reasons rather than on the basis of need. The UK and France give most bilateral aid to their former colonies. Israel is the single largest beneficiary of aid from the USA.

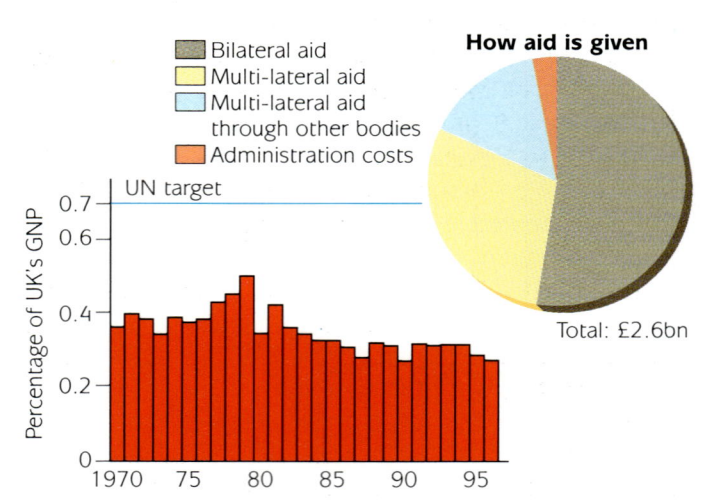

Figure 1 Aid from the UK. The United Nations' target is for 0.7 per cent of a rich country's GNP to be spent on aid, a target few countries reach.

3 Non-governmental organizations (NGOs)

These are mainly *charities*. Most are based and funded in industrialized countries. Money is raised through public appeals, regular voluntary donations and charity shops. They also receive grants from governments, some of which now realize that the NGOs are better able to run projects which are more likely to reach the people in greatest need. Some, such as Oxfam and Christian Aid, have developed a vast international network of operations, but they do work closely with community-based organizations. This allows aid to be more closely targeted on local need, which makes it more effective.

2 Multi-lateral aid

Governments give money to international agencies which decide how the money is spent. Many of these agencies operate under the United Nations. Each one has a particular area of interest. WHO is the World Health Organization while UNICEF focuses upon helping children, UNESCO upon education and the World Bank upon funding development projects. Although these pay more attention to development needs, as large organizations they are often slow to change and do not always target the real needs of people in poor countries.

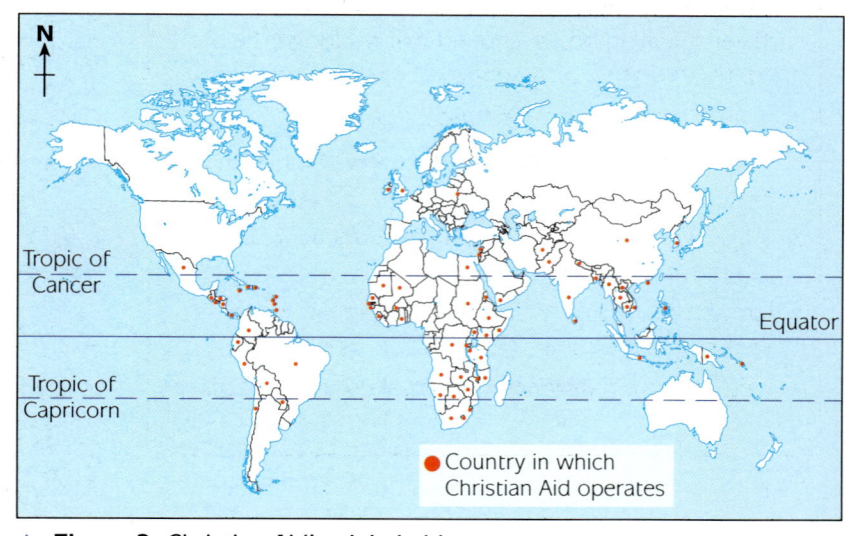

Figure 2 Christian Aid's global aid programme.

Short-term (relief) aid

This is needed to deal with an emergency situation. It is a lifeline. Often the emergency is caused by a natural disaster such as drought, flood or earthquake, but it may be the consequence of a human disaster such as war. It is hard for people in the Western world to ignore television pictures beamed by satellite showing the suffering. Food, medical help, clothing, blankets and tents are supplied to help survivors and to relieve the human misery of refugees (hence the name 'relief'). These are only supplied for as long as the emergency exists; once something approaching normal life is resumed they are withdrawn (hence 'short-term').

Figure 3 Short-term emergency aid in Shindhapalkchock district, Nepal

Long-term (development) aid

The purpose of this type of aid is to increase a country's level of development for the future by improving the standards of living and quality of life of its people. This is the type of aid upon which aid agencies prefer to spend their funds. Work for improved health care, much of it done through UN agencies, includes:

- immunization programmes against TB (tuberculosis), polio, measles and diphtheria
- health education programmes in rural areas
- family planning clinics
- clean water supplies and sanitation facilities
- funding research in MEDCs to develop new vaccines against tropical diseases.

Figure 4 A Bangladeshi woman draws safe, clean water from the village hand-pump at a time of severe flooding. The water pumps are an example of practical long-term aid, useful and appropriate to the local community.

Most of the practical improvements are funded and organized by NGOs, which work through local partners. Their first task is to identify the real needs of the people. The next is to provide practical help. The overall aim is to make changes which are sustainable by the local community so that self-sufficiency will increase and aid will no longer be needed. The types of help given to farmers include:

- agricultural support and technical training
- provision of good-quality seeds suitable for local conditions
- digging ponds and irrigation systems using low (appropriate) technology
- community projects for providing loans for tools and business credit
- setting up organizations for marketing surpluses.

Activities

1. Make a full-page copy of the table below. Complete it as fully as you can.

Type of aid	Main features	Advantages	Disadvantages
A Bilateral			
B Multi-lateral			
C NGOs			
D Short-term			
E Long-term			

2. For the UK's aid, from **Figure 1**:
   a give details of the amount of aid
   b state the approximate percentage of bilateral aid.

3. Give reasons why:
   a governments usually prefer to give bilateral aid
   b charities prefer to spend their money upon development aid rather than emergency aid.

4. Put together information for 'A case study of an aid organization'. Refer to Christian Aid, or find out about the work of another organization, such as Oxfam or Save the Children Fund.

Case Study – Aid to Ethiopia

Ethiopia in the 1980s and 1990s

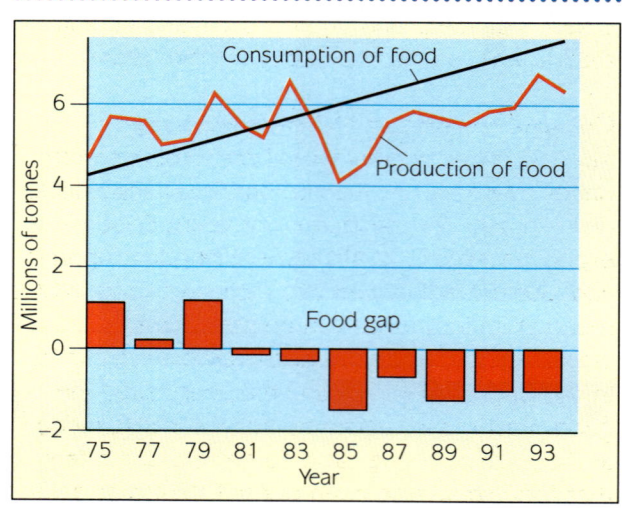

Figure 1 Food production and consumption trends in Ethiopia.

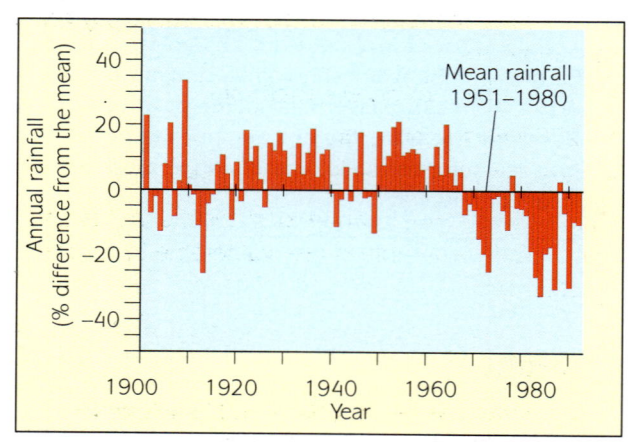

Figure 2 Variations in annual rainfall in the Sahel region, 1900–1992.

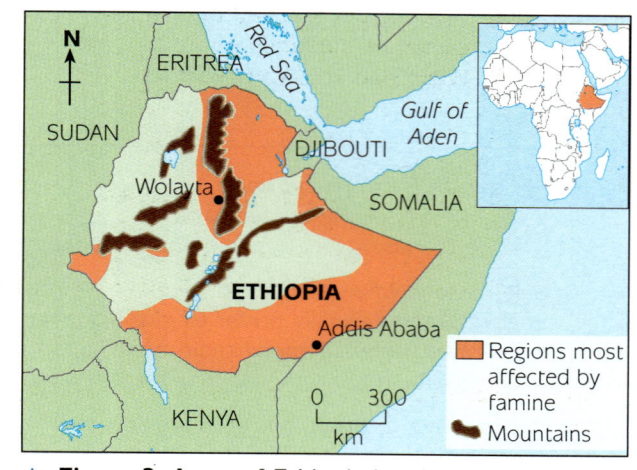

Figure 3 Areas of Ethiopia in which people were most badly affected by famine in 1984.

The 1980s – the need for relief aid

The last year in which Ethiopia was able to feed itself was 1982 (**Figure 1**). The famine was at its greatest in 1984. The natural cause was drought – after years of lower than average annual rainfall, the rains failed again in 1983/84 (**Figure 2**). Human factors worsened the impact of the drought. The military government was engaged in a civil war and spent one-third of Ethiopia's budget on the armed forces. There were food surpluses in some parts of the country, but food could not be moved to areas of need because transport, organization and security were lacking. An estimated 500 000 people died in 1984. People living near the borders in the north and south were most badly affected (**Figure 3**). Some of the first TV pictures seen in the West were of Korem in northern Ethiopia, towards which thousands of people trekked for days in search of food.

Nearly £15 million was raised in 1994 in Britain alone by the UK Disasters Emergency Committee consisting of Christian Aid, Oxfam, Save the Children and Cafod. Nearly all the relief aid was food aid, some transported from overseas and some bought locally with overseas funds. Some food aid was taken by the Ethiopian government for its troops, but most reached the affected areas. Many more people died than was necessary because the military government of Ethiopia concealed news of the famine, which delayed the start of the food aid operation. From 1984 to 1992 the Ethiopian Famine Relief Fund, consisting of Band Aid and Live Aid, raised £110 million. Ethiopia received a massive amount of short-term aid in the 1980s.

The 1990s – continued need for relief aid

The problem of drought has not gone away, but the military government has. It was overthrown in 1991, which has given Ethiopia a chance to start again. However, birth rates remain high and there were two million more mouths to feed in 1994 than in 1984. Half the population still live in poverty and there are malnutrition and severe food shortages in some areas. Many people remain vulnerable if the rains fail or arrive late.

In the first half of 1994 it was estimated that some 5000 people died in Wolayta, southern Ethiopia. There was a bumper harvest in 1992 and so the aid agencies scaled back the levels of food aid. A delay in the rains in 1994 meant that the people's own food stores were used up. The poor road links limited the speed with which the aid agencies could react to the emergency. **Figure 4** shows how villagers in Wollo can just about exist without food aid in a year of normal rains, but are still very vulnerable when rainfall is below average. Soil erosion and environmental destruction continue to be real threats.

Attempts are being made to develop an early-warning system for famines. Save the Children Fund and the Food and Agriculture Organization (FAO) are building up a database of information about local human and physical conditions. They will use this to draw up maps and charts of likely hunger levels in different regions of the country.

Switching towards development aid

Some NGOs are setting long-term targets to increase the amount of food produced in a sustainable way. The Catholic agency Cafod, a British NGO, is working through local partners to promote integrated agricultural development, helping farmers to identify their own needs. Cafod provides practical help such as:

- finding high-quality seeds which mature even if the rains are poor
- planting drought-resistant trees
- digging ponds and wells
- marketing the surplus produce
- providing loans for buying tools and setting up businesses.

The plain outside Korem is no longer the bare place that it was in 1984. Better drought-resistant varieties of seeds and improved irrigation are giving the local people more security for the future.

Comments about aid dependency

More aid organizations would like to concentrate on long-term aid with its emphasis on sustainable development for the local community. Food aid is expensive. People can become dependent upon it and lose the will to produce their own food. NGOs feel that limited funds can be used more effectively to try to prevent the problem recurring. In the rush to deal with an emergency situation, good practices in aid-giving, such as consultation at the local level, are easily forgotten. Some feel that food should be given out in Ethiopia as a wage instead of a ration. In a typical drought year in Ethiopia one million tonnes of food aid are given out. It has been estimated that this could pay for the labour for:

- 167 000km of access road, or
- 2700 earth dams, or
- over 400 000km of irrigation channels.

Each of these would bring long-term benefits and make local communities less vulnerable in future emergencies.

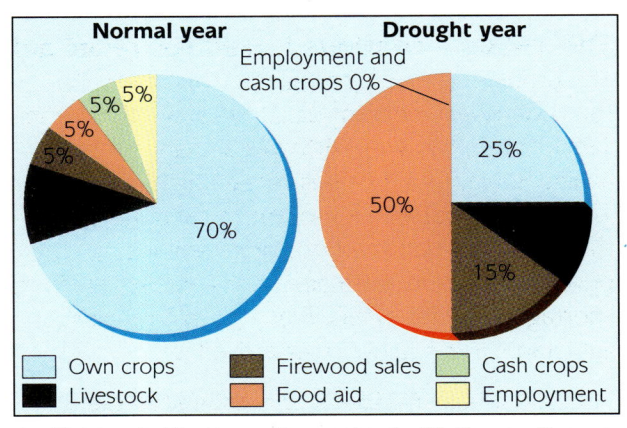

Figure 4 How people survive in Wollo, northern Ethiopia.

Activity

1 Under the heading 'Aid in Ethiopia', write out the answers to the following.
   a In the 1980s:
      (i) Name the type(s) of aid received.
      (ii) Give the physical and the human causes of the famine.
      (iii) Which was the worst year for famine?
      (iv) Where was aid most needed?
   b In the 1990s:
      (i) Name the type(s) of aid received.
      (ii) Give the physical and the human reasons why aid was still needed.
      (iii) Do you think Ethiopia will need aid by the end of the 1990s? Explain your views.

Case Study – Bangladesh

Country on a delta

	Bangladesh	UK (for comparison)
GNP per head (US$)	220	17 970
Birth rate (per 1000)	36	12
Death rate (per 1000)	12	11
Infant mortality rate (per 1000 live births)	108	7
Life expectancy	55	76

▲ **Figure 1** Development indicators.

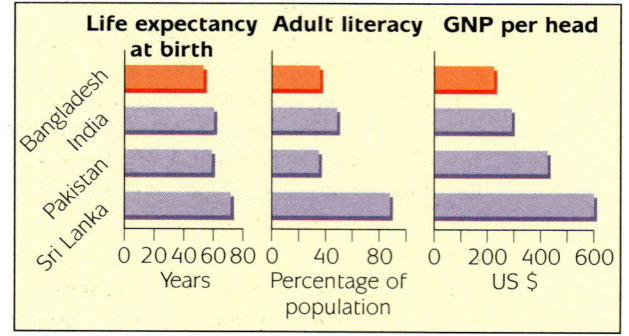

▲ **Figure 2** Level of development compared with other countries in South Asia.

Bangladesh is one of the world's most densely populated countries, with almost 800 people per square kilometre. Its 120 million people are crowded onto the delta formed by the Ganges and Brahmaputra rivers. It is also one of the world's poorest countries. Bangladeshis have to live with natural disasters – floods and cyclones (tropical storms). Overseas aid is a vital source of income to the country. Now, more of the aid is being channelled into local community projects in the villages, in which almost 80 per cent of the population still live.

	US$ (millions)
Value of goods exported	2600
garments (clothes) 52%	
fresh fish (shrimps) 14%	
jute 10%	
leather 8%	
Value of goods imported	4300
Money sent back by Bangladeshis working overseas	944
Aid inflows	1675

▲ **Figure 3** Bangladesh's trade in the mid-1990s.

Physical features

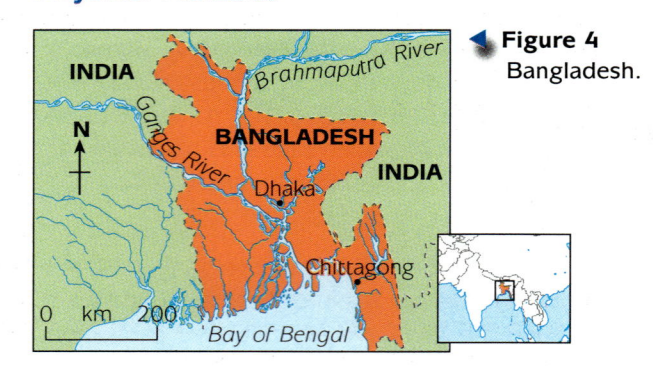

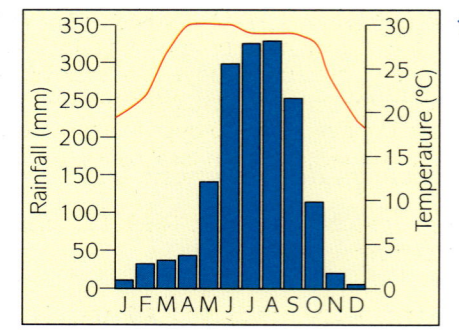

◀ **Figure 4** Bangladesh.

◀ **Figure 5** Climate of Dhaka.

Advantages
- Hot climate allows all-year crop growth.
- There is plenty of water from monsoon rains and large rivers.
- Great thicknesses of alluvial materials (silt) are very fertile.
- Rivers flood one-third of country's cropland every year and renew the silt.
- Watery environment is ideal for the two main crops – rice for food and jute for export.
- Farmers regard normal flooding as beneficial for soils and crops.
- Fisheries along the rivers are another natural resource.

Disadvantages
- Cyclones bring hurricane-force winds and storm surges which cause coastal flooding.
- Heavy monsoon rains cause river floods.
- Flat and low-lying land (most below 10m) means that almost all the country has a flood risk.
- Cyclones (e.g. 1991) and floods (e.g. 1994) have destroyed crops, killed thousands and left millions homeless.
- Drinking water supplies are contaminated and outbreaks of typhoid and cholera occur.

Aid from overseas

Most of this is either bilateral or multi-lateral. It can be described as 'project' aid because it is mainly used to fund power stations, bridges and roads which Bangladesh cannot afford to provide itself. However, there are several disadvantages associated with this type of aid (see pp226–27).

1. The majority of people, who are poor and rural, feel little benefit.
2. Much of the funding is in the form of loans, which may be at a low interest rate but still have to be paid back.
3. It leads to widespread corruption, because the control of aid projects gives great power to politicians, and fortunes can be made by suppliers and contractors.

More funding is now going to NGOs working in the villages, although it remains a small proportion of the total. NGO staff meet the entire community and ask for their views. Such surveys reveal the need for better health care; education for the children; local job opportunities for the landless; better credit facilities from local banks; flood protection.

Only after village consultations do the NGO staff analyse the problems and prepare a plan of action.

A community-based NGO with Oxfam support – Manab Mukti

The community of Manab Mukti, which has about 5000 households, lives on a *char* in the Brahmaputra river. *Chars* are low-lying islands which can be farmed by poor families on a seasonal basis. To help them cope with the regular flooding of the Brahmaputra they were trained in disaster preparedness. They were helped to:

- raise their homesteads above regular flood levels
- make platforms on which to keep their livestock
- build latrines
- install extra piping to raise the community tubewells above flood levels to ensure the availability of clean drinking water during floods.

To enable people to survive extreme floods, two community shelters were built which also had tubewells and latrines. These measures greatly reduce the risk of many water-related diseases.

Measures were also taken to help community development. Agricultural training was given, accompanied by a credit scheme to allow families to take loans for agricultural purposes, especially for growing flood-resistant crops.

Although the people remain poor, Manab Mukti is now a healthier, happier and more prosperous community. This example shows how a small investment of funds in the right place at the right time can have a great effect on people's lives.

Activities

1. *Physical background and human settlement*.
   a. Describe the main features of the climate (see page 77 for instructions about what to refer to).
   b. (i) Describe the evidence from **Figure 2** that Bangladesh occupies a delta.
      (ii) Explain the formation of a delta such as this (see Chapter 3).
   c. Explain why living in a delta is both a blessing and a curse for the Bangladeshis.

2. *Natural disasters*
   a. Name the two natural disasters which affect Bangladesh.
   b. For one of these natural disasters:
      (i) explain why it affects Bangladesh
      (ii) describe the damage it causes
      (iii) show how aid can help people prepare for it.

3. *Trade*
   a. (i) Draw two vertical bar graphs to show the value of goods imported and exported.
      (ii) Work out the size of the trade gap.
      (iii) Draw a pie graph to show the types of goods exported.
      (iv) What is the total value of invisible income (see page 220)?
      (v) Explain why the earnings from invisibles are so important.
   b. Some LEDCs earn a lot of invisible income from tourism, but Bangladesh is not one of them. Suggest reasons why few tourists visit the country.

4. *Development*
   a. Describe the evidence which shows that Bangladesh is one of the world's least developed countries.
   b. Explain how the evidence indicates this.

5. *Aid*
   a. Give three reasons why aid is important to Bangladesh.
   b. (i) For what is bilateral aid used?
      (ii) Name and explain two disadvantages of bilateral aid.
   c. (i) Describe how NGOs operate in Bangladesh.
      (ii) For one village, give details of the ways in which the lives of villagers have been improved by aid.

Chapter 14

Examination technique

The questions
Each geography GCSE examination question can be broken down into at least two parts:

1. the command words – i.e. what you are being told to do
2. the question theme – i.e. what the question is about.

Some questions specify a location or world region for the question and have a third part:

3. where – the area or areas of the world.

Example of a two-part question:

Name two volcanoes.
(command words) (question theme)

Example of a question with three parts:

State two problems in inner city areas of cities
(command words) (question theme)
in more economically developed countries (MEDCs).
(where)

Command words

A • Name • Give • State • List

Name one country in which ...

Give two reasons for ...

These are simple and clear command words and need no further comment.

B • Define the term ... • What is meant by ...?
• Give the meaning of ...

These command words are asking for definitions. You are likely to be asked to define terms used in the syllabus. Many of these have been highlighted in bold type in the earlier chapters because of their importance. Look at the number of marks – this is vital with this type of question.

Question What is meant by *intensive farming*? (3 marks)

Answer from Candidate 1 Getting a lot from the land. A lot is grown and sold by the farmer. *(same point made)*

Examiner comment 'The candidate has only attempted to make two points in a three-mark question, and can't gain more than two marks. The answer is only worth one mark because the two statements are making the same point – high inputs.'

Answer from Candidate 2 Intensive means producing as much as possible from the land. To gain a high output, large inputs are needed and the land is carefully farmed.' *(same point made)*

Examiner comment This candidate also begins the answer by making the same point twice, but then extends the answer, making two other valid points. There is just sufficient for the candidate to be given all three marks.

Note that the examiner said *just sufficient* for full marks. If you know and understand the topic and want a high grade, give a little bit more information than you think is needed for full marks, in case part of your answer does not match what is in the mark scheme. Candidate 2's answer could have been extended to say: large inputs, such as using a lot of labour and fertilizers.

C Describe

Describe the features of a delta.

Describe what Figure 1 shows.

(Figure 1 may be a graph, diagram, map or photograph.)

Describe is one of the most commonly used command words in geography examinations. 'Describe' commands you to write about what is there, or its appearance, or what is shown on a graph. You are **not** being asked to explain. The amount of detail expected in the answer is suggested by the number of marks for the question.

Let us take one example. Describing landscapes and landforms is an important part of physical geography. When asked to *describe* a landform (volcano, corrie, etc.), you are really being asked to *say what it looks like*.

- Write about its shape, size and what it is made of.
- Be generous with your use of adjectives, such as wide/narrow, steep/gentle/flat, straight/curved, etc.

Question
Describe the physical features of the landform in the photo.

Approach to the answer	Possible answers
• Name the landform first	volcano (or even composite volcano)
• Describe its shape	cone-shaped
• Describe other features	lava flows on its sides
• Give a more detailed description	steep slopes on the snow-covered top of the cone
	slightly more gentle slopes lower down
	bare rock (lava) on the lower slopes

D
- Explain the formation of ...
- Explain why ...
- Give reasons for ...
- Why have ...?
- Why does ..?

To answer these questions you need geographical knowledge and understanding. You are being asked to account for the appearance or occurrence of physical and human features of the Earth's surface. These command words do not usually cause problems. What causes problems is giving enough precise information.

Question Why is population growth high in LEDCs?
(4 marks)

Answer Because birth rates are high and death rates are low.

Examiner comment This is the basic answer, which has only reached the first level of explanation. It is a one-mark answer. Explanations why birth rates are high and why death rates are low are also needed.

Question Explain the formation of spits along some coasts.
(5 marks)

Answer A spit forms after longshore drift moves sand along the coast. I have drawn a diagram below to show how it does this.

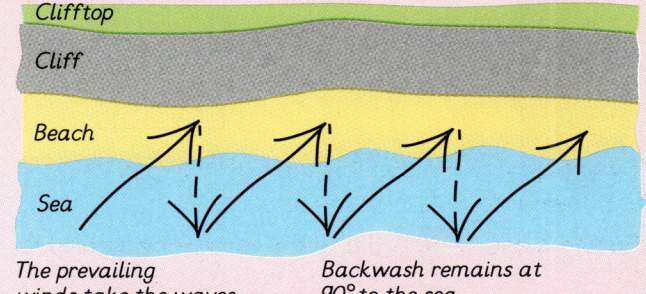

Clifftop
Cliff
Beach
Sea

The prevailing winds take the waves on to the beach at an angle

Backwash remains at 90° to the sea resulting in transportation of material in a zig zag fashion

▲ Longshore drift.

Examiner comment Everything is correct and longshore drift does play a part in the formation of a spit. The question does not ask for a diagram, but relevant points accurately made on the diagram will be credited. But there is only partial explanation here. How and why the spit actually forms after the longshore drift has transported sand is not explained. This answer is only worth two of the five marks.

Questions based on source materials

The source materials used in geography examinations are many and various. However, you will be familiar with:

- the type of source itself, because those most used in examinations will include maps, graphs, diagrams, photographs, tables of data or cartoons.
- the geographical topic covered, because this is part of the syllabus.

There is only a small chance that you will have seen the data before, or the photograph, or the chosen OS map extract. This is why most questions begin with short questions looking at the source materials. **Figure 1** takes you through a question based on pie charts.

Although most questions follow this style, in some you must use knowledge and understanding from the beginning. This makes these questions more difficult and they are likely to be used later in the examination. **Figure 2** is a question of this type, based upon photograph interpretation.

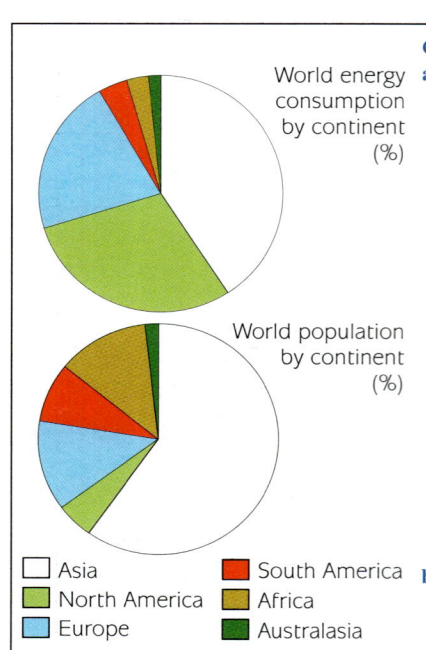

Figure 1

Question
a Study the pie charts.
  (i) Name the continent in which least energy is consumed. (1 mark)
  (ii) Place the names of the six continents under the appropriate heading in the table below. (2 marks)

Continents with energy consumption greater than their share of population	Continents with share of world population greater than their energy consumption
1	1
2	2
3	3

  (iii) State one difference between the continents in the two columns of the table. (1 mark)
b Suggest reasons why a person living in North America consumes more energy per year on average than a person living in South America. (6 marks)

Pie charts: World energy consumption by continent (%) and World population by continent (%). Key: Asia, North America, Europe, South America, Africa, Australasia.

Annotations:
- The starter question to give you the chance to look at the data: simple command word and one clear answer
- The data need to be studied more carefully and all the data used. Only the data from the source are needed for the answers.
- Understanding of the difference between continents with MEDCs and those with LEDCs is now needed.
- Knowledge and understanding are now needed. You are being asked to explain the differences. 'Suggest reasons' have been used as the command words instead of 'explain' because the syllabus does not specify study of North and South America. However, you should have learned that rich countries consume more energy resources per head than poor countries and you can be expected to give reasons for this.

▲ **Figure 1**

You need to make a careful study of the photograph before answering part **a** and you should understand what is meant by an urban zone. Do not rush into the answer; take a careful look at the photograph and think the answer through. When answering part **b** use evidence from the photo to justify your choice. Do not just describe everything that you see.

Question
Study the photograph taken in a city in a more economically developed country.
a Name the urban zone in which the photograph was most likely to have been taken. (1 mark)
b Describe the evidence from the photograph which supports your choice of zone. (4 marks)

▲ **Figure 2**

Questions based upon maps

Many candidates find questions which include the words *distribution* or *pattern* awkward to answer. Remember that in *describing a distribution* you should concentrate upon saying where things are found, but you can also mention where they are not found. Do the same when *describing a pattern*; say where there are many and where there are few. It is important to end with a comment summarizing the main feature of the pattern.

Approach the answer like this:

- Identify the command word – 'describe'. This is telling you to write about what the map shows.
- Identify the question theme – 'rates of illiteracy above 50 per cent'. Study the key to see how they are shown on the map.
- Study the map.

1 Look first for the locations of countries with above 50 per cent rates of illiteracy. Possible answers would be:
  (i) Most are in Africa.
  (ii) Almost all the countries except for a few countries in the centre and south of Africa are above 50 per cent.
  (iii) A band of very high values above 75 per cent runs from the west coast across to the Red Sea.
  (iv) Some are above 50 per cent in the Middle East and south Asia.

Question
Study the world map (page 235), which shows rates of illiteracy in the world. From the figure, describe the distribution of countries with high rates of illiteracy (above 50 per cent). (5 marks)

Chapter 14 Examination technique   235

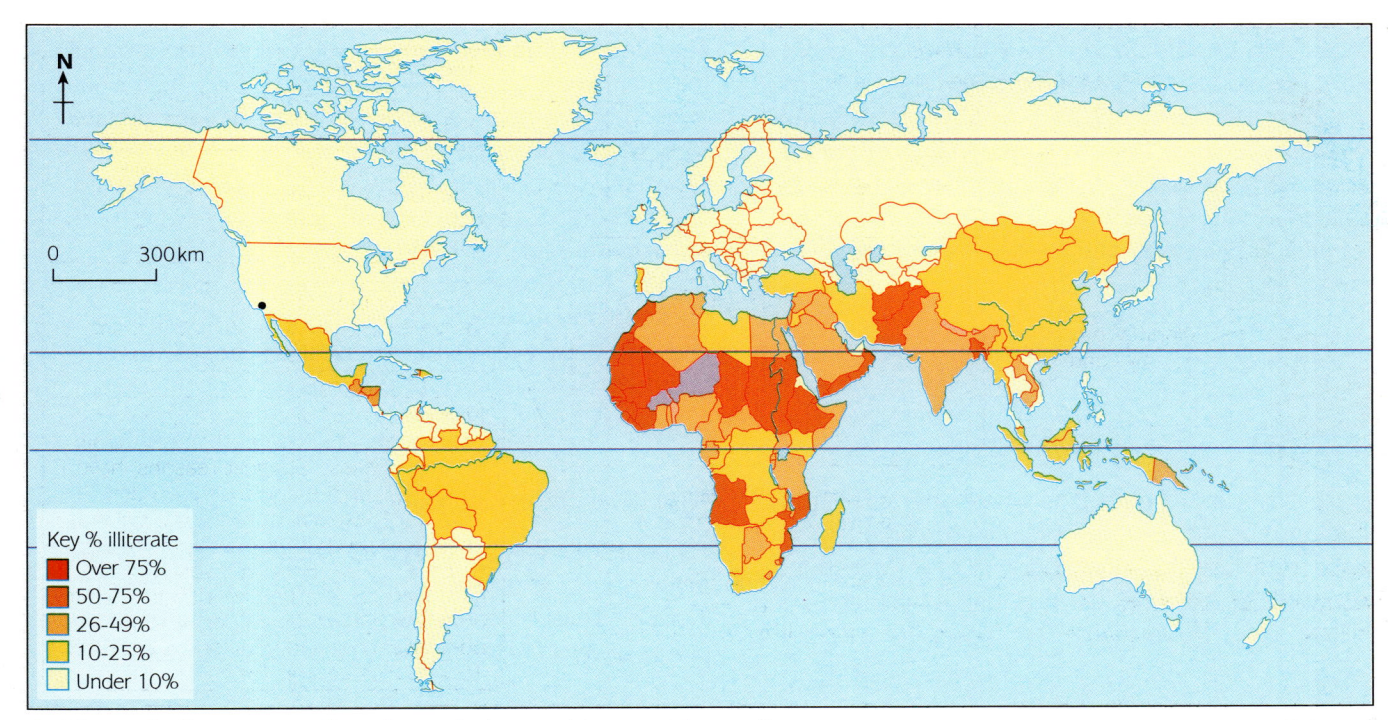

Figure 3 Percentage of total population unable to read or write.

2   Next look for the location of countries with rates of illiteracy below 50%. Possible brief answers would be:
   (i) In the rest of Asia and in South America illiteracy is lower (mainly 10–50 per cent).
   (ii) Lowest rates, below 10 per cent, are in North America and Europe.
   (iii) These lowest rates are in MEDCs.

Note the following points about these answers:
- They are taken from what can be seen on the map.
- Percentage values are used from time to time.
- The names of continents are used for effective description (think of the world map).
- More than five points are described to try to ensure full marks.

Using case studies

Sometimes the wording of the question makes it clear that you are expected to use your *case study* information. However, the term 'case study' is not normally used in the question. You must look for other wording that suggests that a case study is needed. Examples include:

With reference to an example you have studied ...
Using an example ...   For one farming system in the UK ...
For one industrial area in an LEDC ...

In these questions you have little chance of gaining more than half marks unless you include some case study information in your answer. Look at these examination answers from two candidates.

Question
For one named area with many footloose industries, give the reasons why these industries have been attracted to the area.
(7 marks)

Answer from Candidate 1   There are many footloose industries along the sides of the M4 between London and Bristol. One area is on the industrial estate next to the M4 in Reading where there are food-processing and high-tech industries because it is near a motorway junction. High-tech industries need skilled workers, who are produced in nearby universities such as Oxford and Reading. Rail and road links are very good. I have already said that the footloose industries are along the sides of the M4 motorway, which gives fast road links to London, the biggest market in the country. The M4 also passes Heathrow Airport for markets overseas. High-speed trains run along the rail line between Bristol and London.

Examiner comment   This candidate begins in the best possible way by naming an area. The rest of the answer clearly refers to this chosen area. Some precise information, such as the source of the skilled workers, is used and the significance of some of the points made is stated, such as Heathrow Airport for overseas markets. This answer reaches the highest mark band called Level 3 and is worth six marks. With a little extra detail, or if another reason for location had been referred to in a similarly precise way, the answer would have been worth all seven marks.

Answer from Candidate 2 There are lots of workers who are needed in footloose industries. There are good roads. The railway lines are also good. There are some high-tech industries. These are making lots of money because everyone is now buying computers. High-tech industries are footloose industries. There are lots of these near London near the M4 because of good markets.

Examiner comment Only at the end of the answer is there a named area for footloose industries. This is just 'tagged on' without the other information being related to it. Most of the rest of the answer is very vague with too many 'good's in it. Such general statements could apply to the location of any industry in any place. Although the answer tells us something about the nature of footloose industries, this is not relevant in a question about reasons for their growth. It is a weak and very basic answer to the question, only of Level 1 standard, worth one or at the most two of the seven

These are examples of questions where your case study information must be used to obtain high marks. However, try to use this information in other questions where it fits. For example, the question might be:

What disadvantages can tourism bring to an LEDC?

This question can be answered solely by making general points, but if you have studied Kenya or another LEDC, include relevant information. Specific information about places always enhances the quality of an answer.

Activity – Answers that have gone wrong

What is wrong with these answers? Give your own correct versions.

1. Name a country which has suffered from drought and been given much food aid. (1 mark)
   Answer Africa.

2. With reference to an area you have studied in a Less Economically Developed Country (LEDC), explain the disadvantages tourism can bring. (6 marks)
   Answer Costa del Sol in southern Spain. A line of villas owned by rich Europeans continues for 50 kilometres along the Mediterranean coastline. This has brought wealth to a region which 50 years ago was one of the poorest in Europe. There are many jobs in service industries and young people are attracted from all parts of Spain by the prospects of work.

3. a Measure the distance along the railway line between stations A and B on **Figure 1**. (1 mark)

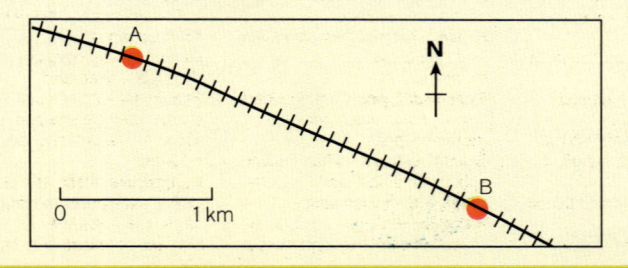

   Answer 2.5

   b In what direction would you be travelling if you took the train from station B to station A? (1 mark)
   Answer Eastwards.

4. Study **Figure 2** which shows part of the coastline of north-east England. Describe the coastal features shown. (4 mark)

   Answer The main features of this coastal area allow us to see where the sea crashes against these rocks. It also allows us to see that the rocks have been severely beaten by the sea in one particular place. Abrasion is one way in which the sea batters rocks. The rocks have obviously been eroded away in one place. This has weakened the rocks themselves making them more vulnerable to more erosion by the sea.

▲ Figure 2

◀ Figure 1

Glossary

Chapter 1
Core the centre of the earth
Mantle the molten rock surrounding the earth's core
Crust the thin layer at the earth's surface
Plates sections of the earth's crust
Convection currents changes in the flow and pressure of the earth's mantle affecting Plate movement
Compressional plate boundary (margin) where two plates are moving together (destructive)
Subduction zone where a plate is sinking and melting
Geosynclines a depression between two plates
Sedimentary rocks rocks forms from sediments laid down under water
Anticlines an upfold, like an arch
Synclines a downfold
Nappes a severe form of folding where the rocks have moved along a fracture
Lava the name given to molten magma when it errupts at the surface
Acid lava thick, viscous lava with a high silica content, flows short distances
Basic lava thin 'runny' lava, low silica content, flows long distances
Vent the opening through which the lava flows in a volcano
Tensional plate boundary (margin) where two plates are moving apart (constructive)
Seismograph measures and records the intensity of an earthquake
Richter scale measures the strength of an earthquake
Focus the point on the earth's surface directly above the epicentre
Epicentre the point within the earth's crust where the earthquake occurred
Primary effects (of an earthquake) The direct effects of an earthquake e.g. buildings collapsing
Secondary effects (of an earthquake) the indirect effects e.g. fire, tidal waves, disease
Fire example of a secondary effect of an earthquake (see above)
Tsunamis huge tidal waves caused by submarine earthquakes
Landslides rapid movement of rocks and soil under the influence of gravity
Disease illness often caused by a natural disaster

Chapter 2
Igneous rocks rocks which began as magma in the interior of the earth
Sedimentary rocks rocks which began as sediments usually on the sea bed
Metamorphic rocks rocks whose shape or form have been changed by heat and pressure
Tors blocks of rock outcropping on top of granite plateaus such as Dartmoor
Limestone pavements flat surfaces of white bare rock broken up into separate blocks
Clints flat surfaces of the block of rock in a limestone pavement
Grykes vertical gaps between blocks of rock in a limestone pavement
Sink holes places where there are joints or cracks in limestone rock through which water from a surface stream disappears underground
Swallow holes funnel shaped holes down which surface streams disappear underground through limestone
Caverns underground chambers in limestone larger than caves
Stalactites columns of lime hanging down from the roof in limestone caves or caverns
Stalagmites columns of lime built up from the floor in caves or caverns
Pillar (of limestone) a column of lime from floor to roof in a limestone cave or cavern
Gorge steep sided rocky valley with a stream flowing at the bottom
Karst scenery area in which several landforms of Carboniferous limestone are found
Limestone solution process of chemical weathering which dissolves limestone rock
Chalk escarpment landform with both a steep scarp slope and a gentle dip slope
Dip slope the gentle slope on a chalk escarpment
Scarp slope the steep slope on a chalk escarpment
Dry valleys V shaped valleys but without any streams flowing in the bottoms
Bournes streams which only flow for part of the year in chalk areas
Clay vale large area of low land (larger than a valley) which tends to be a wet area because of the impermeable clay
Springs points where water from underground reaches the ground surface
Aquifers underground stores of water in permeable or porous rocks
Weathering the breakdown of surface rock by weather without any movement
Physical weathering break up of the rock by processes such as freeze-thaw without any changes in the minerals which form the rock
Chemical weathering break up of the rock by processes such as solution by changes in the minerals which form the rock
Freeze-thaw break up of rocks by alternate freezing and melting of water trapped in joints in the rock
Scree pieces of rock with sharp edges below rock outcrops
Exfoliation a type of physical weathering common in deserts which results in the outer layers of rock being peeled off

Chapter 3
Source the starting point of a river
Mouth where a river enters the sea or a lake
Tributaries smaller rivers which flow into a larger river
Confluence where two rivers meet
Drainage basin the area of land drained by a single river
Watershed the imaginary line which surrounds a drainage basin
Hydrological cycle the cycle of water between the air, land and sea
Channel the feature in which the river flows
Hydraulic power a process of coastal and river erosion caused by the force of the water
Corrasion a process of river erosion where the leads rubs against rocks
Corrosion a process of erosion caused by the solution of minerals e.g. salt
Attrition a process of erosion whereby the load rubs against itself
V-shaped valley a river valley in the upper course, steep sided and narrow
Interlocking spurs spurs of highland which overlap in the upper course of a valley
Gorge of recession steep sided narrow valley created by waterfall/river retreat
Meander bend in the middle and lower course of a river
River cliff - the steep river bank on the outside bend of a meander
Slip-off slope the gentle slope on the inside bend of a meander
Traction boulders rolling along the riverbed
Saltation small particles 'jumping' along the river bed
Suspension small particles of clay, silt carried along the river bed
Solution a form of chemical weathering
Alluvium river deposited material (sand and silt)
Ox-bow lake semi-circular lake formed by sealing off a meander bend
Meander scar a dried up ox-bow lake
Delta often triangular shaped flat land jutting out into the sea at the mouth of a river
Estuary a drowned river mouth in a lowland area
Distributaries small channels on a delta where the main channel has dried up Whinstone - a hard resistant igneous rock
Discharge the amount of water flowing in a river per second
Velocity the speed of a river's flow
Volume the capacity of a river
Flood hydrograph graph showing how a river responds to different rainfall levels
Rising limb (hydrograph) part of the graph showing the rivers rising discharge
Falling limb (hydrograph) part of the graph showing how after a storm the discharge falls
Lag time the difference in time between the peak of rainfall and the peak of discharge in a river

Chapter 4
Glacier moving mass of ice
Valley glacier a moving mass of ice confined within a valley
Ice sheet a moving mass of ice which covers all the land surface over a wide area
Abrasion (glacial) a process of erosion in which rocks carried in the bottom of the ice wear away the surface rock
Plucking a process of erosion in which blocks of rock are torn away from the bed rock as the ice moves away
Striations deep groves in rock outcrops made by abrasion as the ice flowed over them
Pleistocene Ice Age when most of the British Isles was covered by ice about 20,000 year ago
Snow line above this point the land is covered by snow
Corrie a circular rock hollow high on a mountain side surrounded by steep and rocky walls
Cirque another name for the circular hollow of a corrie Tarn circular lake which fills the bottom of a corrie after the ice has melted
Neves snow fields such as the ones which fill corries with snow and ice
Arete sharp edged two sided ridge on the top of a mountain
Pyramidal peak three sided slab of rock which forms a mountain peak
Glacial trough a flat floored and steep sided valley usually called a U shaped valley
Hanging valleys a tributary valley left hanging high above the main valley floor with a waterfall
High level bench flatter area high on the valley sides above the steep sides of the U shaped valley
Misfit streams small streams in large glaciated valleys
Ribbon lakes long and narrow lakes on the floors of glaciated valleys
Terminal moraines ridges of boulder clay dumped by the glacier where it was melting
Truncated spurs higher areas on the straight rocky sides of a glaciated valley
Waterfalls (glacial) falls of water down the sides of the U shaped valley where there are hanging valleys
Rock basin hollow on the valley floor eroded by glacial abrasion and plucking
Rock bar outcrop of hard rock between rock basins made of softer rocks
Erratic large boulder dropped by a glacier, of a different type of rock to the rock below
Moraine all materials deposited after having been transported by ice
Lateral moraines lines of glacial deposits along the sides of valleys
Medial moraines lines of glacial deposits down the middle of valleys
Boulder clay all materials deposited by ice, usually it is clay with boulders of different sizes within it
Glacial till another term for boulder clay, especially for sandy glacial deposits
Ground moraine boulder clay deposited by glaciers which gives a hummocky surface
Drumlin an egg shaped hills made of boulder clay
Snout the furthest point reached by the glacier where all the ice is melting

Chapter 5
Destructive waves high waves, with strong backwashes, which break frequently causing erosion
Fetch the length of water over which the wind has blown which affects the size and strength of waves
Wave cut platform a gently sloping area of flat rocks exposed at low tide
Cave an area which has been hollowed out by the waves at the bottom of a cliff
Arch a rocky opening through a headland
Stack a piece of rock surrounded by sea and left standing away from the coastline
Longshore drift the current which transports materials along the coastline
Swash forward movement

of water as the wave breaks on the coast
Backwash backward movement of water down the beach after the wave has broken
Spit a long ridge of sand and shingle, attached to the land, but which ends in the open sea
Coastal management attempts by people to maintain or alter the natural features of the coast to their own advantage

Chapter 6
Temperate maritime climate the warm wet climate of the UK
Climate the average weather conditions of a place over many years
Latitude distance from the Equator which affects the temperature of a place
Insolation heating of the earth's surface from the sun's rays, greatest in the tropics
Distance from sea factor which affects the temperature of a place
Prevailing winds direction of winds which blow most frequently at a place
Altitude height of the land which affects temperature and precipitation
Precipitation all types of moisture from the atmosphere such as rain, snow, hail and fog
Convectional rainfall heavy rain formed by the cooling of moist air which has risen from heated surfaces
Relief rainfall rain formed by the cooling of moist air as it is forced to rise over mountains
Frontal rainfall rain formed by the cooling of moist air forced to rise along a warm or cold front
Urban heat island when the temperature in a city is higher than that in the surrounding rural areas
Leaching minerals washed out of the soil by high rainfall to make the soil less fertile
Weather day to day conditions of temperature, precipitation, cloud, sunshine and wind
Low pressure a depression in which the air is rising leaving low air pressure at the surface
Front dividing line between air masses with different temperatures; air is rising giving rain
Warm front the warm air behind the front is rising up above the cold air ahead of the front
Cold front the cold air behind the front is pushing up the warm air ahead of the front
High pressure an anticyclone in which the air is sinking giving high air pressure at the surface
Gentle pressure gradient slow change in pressure between places leading to light winds or calm conditions
Hurricanes tropical storms which affect the Caribbean (West Indies) and Florida

Chapter 7
Ecosystem the living community of plants and animals and the physical factors upon which they depend such as climate and soil
Podsol soil type under coniferous woodland
A horizon the top layer in the soil profile
B horizon the second layer in the soil profile, found in soils where the minerals have been washed down from the layer above
C horizon the third layer in the soil profile, made of materials weathered from the rock below
Soil profile the layers of soil between the ground surface and the solid rock below
Hard pan soil layer in which minerals washed out from higher up the profile, such as iron, have been compressed together
Biodiversity great numbers of plants and animals in one ecosystem, greatest in tropical rain forests
Latosol the red and yellowish-red soil which forms under tropical rain forests
Sustainable preserved and able to be used for many years into the future
Sustainable management of forests the forests will not be destroyed so that the forest resources and products can be used by people for many years into the future

Chapter 8
Densely (populated) high numbers of people per unit area
Dot map a map which uses dots to represent numbers of people, cows etc.
Choropleth map a map using a shading technique to show density
Sparsely (populated) low numbers of people per unit area
Physical factors factors such as relief, soils, climate and drainage
Natural increase the increase (or decrease) in a population found by the birth rate minus the death rate and normally expressed as a percentage
Zero population growth when birth rates equal death rates, sometimes called the replacement rate. The population neither grows nor declines
Census a questionnaire usually every 10 years to find out the population characteristic of a country
Population pyramid a graph to show the population structure or age-sex composition
Dependency ratio the number of children (under 15) and the number of older people (over 65) expressed as a ratio of the number of adults between 15 and 64
Life expectancy the average number of years at birth that a person is expected to live
Polders an area of land reclaimed from the sea as in the Netherlands
Overgrazing too many animals allowed to graze an area so the carrying capacity is exceeded
Overcultivation crop growing too intensive for the land causing loss of fertility
Salinized when soils are made salty
Desertification land turning into desert
Age- and sex-selective migration often involves younger males in LEDCs which is both age and sex selective
Periphery the edge ñ often poorer regions in a country
Core the heart ñ often the richer, most successful region in the country
Transmigration policy used in Indonesia, a government policy to encourage people to migrate from the core
Migration the movement of people
Emigrated when people leave a country
Migration balance the difference between the numbers of immigrants and emigrants
Forced migration people forced to move e.g. as a result of natural disasters, war
Refugees persons forced to move from one country to another, often as a result of war or famine
Voluntary migration people choose to move to a new place
Push and pull factors factors which force a person away from and attract them to a particular place
Internally displaced migration within a country usually forced by civil war or persecution
Rural to urban migration movement from the countryside to the towns
Urban depopulation the movement of people out of the towns and cities
Counter-urbanization the opposite to urbanization where people move back into the countryside from the towns
Perception a person's view

Chapter 9
Site the physical land on which a settlement is built
Situation the settlement in relation to its surrounding area
Wet-point sites the site of a settlement close to a water supply such as a spring line settlement on a chalk escarpment
Dry-point sites the site of a settlement which avoids land prone to flooding such as a gravel mound or the valley side.
Bridging points a settlement located where a river is forded or bridged
Route focus where communications focus i.e. roads and railways converge
Catchment area the area that a school, shop or settlement serves
Hinterland the area surrounding a settlement, port etc
Convenience goods goods which are cheap and bought frequently e.g. papers, food
Comparison goods goods which are expensive and bought less frequently e.g. furniture
Commuter or dormitory villages villages on the outskirts of a town city
Millionaire cities cities with over 1 million people where people live but travel to wok in the city
Megacities cities with over 5 million people
Informal sector in LEDCs many people work in the informal sector as shoeshine boys, servants etc
Urban land uses the use of the land in towns and cities
Zones areas of land with similar uses
Central Business District (CBD) the heart of a city where the financial and business interests are
Morphology the arrangement of land uses in an urban area. Different land uses tend to be in dstinct zones rather than jumbled up
Burgess' model a model of urban structure
Hoyt's model a model of urban structure
Inner city the urban zone outside of the CBD in MEDCs
Suburbs a mainly residential area outside of the inner city in MEDCs
Rural-urban fringe on the outskirts of an urban area beyond the suburbs where there is a mixture of rural land uses and urban land uses
Recreational facilities sports fields, clubs and leisure comlexes
Industrial estates zones of light industry often on the fringes of towns
Core of the CBD the heart of the CBD where the large department stores are located
Frame of the CBD the outer area of the CBD with smaller shops and offices
Decentralization the outward movement of shops and offices from the CBD to the suburbs
Hobby farming small pockets of land in the rural urban fringe owned by townspeople and used for market gardening
Horsiculture the increasing ownership of horses by towns people
Self-help schemes in LEDCs people who live in shanty towns often improve their homes by building them
Periferia a housing zone in San Paulo where shanties have been upgraded
Green belt an area of land around a large town or city protected from development in an attempt to halt the expansion of towns into the countryside

Chapter 10
Inputs physical and human raw material which goes into a system of farming or industry
Processes the activities carried out to turn the inputs into outputs
Outputs the end products of a system
Arable the growing of crops e.g. wheat, barley
Pastoral the rearing of animals
Mixed (farms) the growing of crops and rearing of animals on a single farm
Subsistence farming in which the production is for the farmer and his family
Commercial the sale of farm products for profit
Intensive a farm system usually practised on small areas of land with high inputs and high outputs per hectare
Yields the amount produced by the growing of crops or rearing of animals
Sedentary where people are settled permanently in a location
Nomadic the movement of people e.g. with their animals to find good grazing land
Relief the height and shape of the land
Soils the thin layers of weathered material and organic matter on the earth' surface
Climate the average weather of an area
Cash crops crops grown to be sold for profit
Agribusiness farms operated by large companies such as Findus, Birdseye
Agrochemicals fertilizers, pesticides use din farming
Self-sufficient where enough of the foodstuff is grown to satisfy demand

Glossary

Soil erosion the loss of topsoil by wind and water
Eutrophication the loss of oxygen in streams and lakes caused by chemical polution
Open fell the upland moors in the UK where sheep graze, the land is not fenced
Intake fields bounded by stone walls on the lower slopes in upland areas
Inbye the flatter land close to the farm in the valley floor in hill sheep areas
Biodiversity a rich range of plants and animals
High-tech (farming) using modern machinery methods to farm
Machetes primative hand held axes used by tribes in Amazon Basin
Chagras a clearing in the Amazon Basin
Monoculture the growing of a single crop as on a rubber plantation
Multinational or transnational corporations (TNCs) large businesses who often have their HQ in a MEDC but have facilities all over the world
Jengka Triangle Project a scheme to grow more oil and rubber in Malaysia
Soil conservation the techniques to maintain soil fertility and to reduce leaching and erosion
Staple crop the main crop grown e.g. rice in Bangladesh
Monsoon the heavy rains in countries such as India and Bangladesh
Irrigation the artificial watering of the land by sprinklers, canals, spraying etc
High-yielding varieties crops such as IR8 rice which produce higher yields than ordinary seeds
Double or multiple cropping where two or more crops are produced from the same plant of land in a year
Tube wells modern wells used to provide water for irrigation
Wells a means of extracting water from the level of the water table
Inundation canals a network of channels used to flood the land next to a river for crop growing
Appropriate technology technology appropriate to the needs, skills, knowledge and wealth of the people

Chapter 11

Raw materials used for making goods in the factory
Primary industries those which extract raw materials from land and sea such as mining, forestry, farming and fishing
Secondary industries manufacturing industries which process raw materials into other products
Tertiary industries these provide services to people and other industries
Quaternary industries high technology research based industries involved in designing and assembling products such as micro-electronics for computers
Footloose industries light or hi-tech industries which have considerable freedom in location
Fuel supplies coal, oil or natural gas used as energy sources for making goods
Transport movement of raw materials to the factory, or goods from the factory to market, by means of transport such as road, rail and sea
Markets places where the goods made are sold
Labour the workers
Sunrise industries new growth industries such as hi-tech industries
Light industries industries producing small sized goods mainly for people (consumers) to buy, not needing bulky raw materials
Newly industrializing countries less economically developed countries in which manufacturing industries have grown leading to economic development
Global companies multi-national companies operating in many different countries of the world
Brownfield sites urban areas cleared of their old industry or housing, now available for new developments
Greenfield sites rural open land, not previously built on, in an out of town location
Industrial estates areas in which several manufacturing companies have their factories, often located on the edges of urban areas
Business parks attractive areas, often located on the edges of urban areas, for offices, research establishments and light industries
Science parks attractive areas, pleasantly laid out, for research establishments linked up to a University

Chapter 12

Renewable a resource which is naturally replaced after use so that it never runs out
Sustainable - activities and economic growth with a good future because the environment upon which they depend is not being destroyed
Industrial Revolution period of great industrial growth and change
Coal fossil fuel made from trees and plants
Consumer society when people are wealthy enough to buy many different goods for themselves and their homes
Reserves fuel supplies already discovered which can be used in the future
Primary energy obtained from fossil fuels which give off heat and energy when they are burnt
Secondary energy this is electricity which needs to be generated from another source such as coal, oil, water or wind
Alternative (energy source) that which can be used instead of fossil fuels, usually new and renewable sources such as wind and solar power
Nuclear power energy released from using uranium and plutonium
Recycling recovery of waste products converting them into materials which can be used again
Resource substitution using a different product such as aluminium instead of tin and steel for making a can
Energy efficiency measures to reduce heat loss or the amount of energy needed to complete a task
National Park an area of beautiful scenery and relatively wild countryside which is managed for conservation of its beauty and for visitor recreation
UK England, Northern Ireland, Scotland and Wales
World-wide (tourism) long distance holidays including some new destinations in less economically developed countries
Honeypots places which attract large numbers of visitors and feel visitor pressures
Benefits economic or social advantages for people
Eco-tourism tourism in which the protection of the environment and the way of life of the local people is considered to be very important (the same as Green tourism)
Green tourism tourism in which the protection of the environment and the way of life of the local people is considered to be very important (the same as Eco-tourism)
Sustainable tourism tourist activities and tourist locations with a good future because neither the environment nor the way of life of the local people are being destroyed

Chapter 13

Gross National Product (GNP) total value of all the goods and services produced by people and companies from a country in one year
Desertification - turning an area into a desert by reducing the amount of vegetation and the fertility of the soil
Trade exchange of goods and services between countries
Visible (trade) exchange of goods which can be counted, measured or weighed
Invisible (trade) exchange of services and transfers of money including aid and foreign exchange from tourists
Primary products those obtained from the land or sea without being processed or made into another product, such as food, minerals and wood
Secondary products manufactured goods
Interdependence when two or more countries have a shared need to exchange one another's goods
Aid transfer of money, goods and expertise from one country to another either free or at low cost

Index

agriculture see farming
aid 225, 226–9, 231
Alps 9–10
Amazon Basin 96–7, 105, 158–9
anticyclones 75, 84–5

Bangladesh 227, 230–1
Brazil 96–7, 105, 142–3, 158–9
business parks 165, 182

Central Business District 132–3
China 112, 193
cities see settlement; urbanization
climate 76–8, 80–1, 148
coasts
    deposition 66–7, 71
    erosion 61, 62–3, 71, 72
    landforms 64–5, 67, 70, 74
    longshore drift 66–7
    management 68–9, 72–3
    Yorkshire case study 70–3
delta 38, 39, 230
depressions 82–3
deserts, hot 90, 91
development 210–11
    hazards affecting 216–19
    measurement 212–15
    trade and 222–3
drought 86–7, 217

earthquakes 8, 16–17, 216–17
earth's structure 6
ecosystems 89–100
    global distribution 90–1
Egypt 115, 143–4
energy resources 188–9, 196–7
    alternative sources 11, 190–2, 193
    conservation 194–5
environments, management 60, 201–2, 205, 206–7
Ethiopia 228–9

farming
    arable 145, 148, 150–3
    diversification 155, 156
    factors and types 146–7, 150–3
    intensive rice 162–3
    livestock 148, 149
    market gardening 148, 157
    plantations 160–1
    shifting cultivation 158–9
    uplands 10, 41, 58, 154–6
floods 44–7, 216
    hydrograph 45
    protection 43, 44, 46–7
fog 64, 75, 85
fold mountains 8–9, 11
forests 58
    coniferous 11, 90, 92–3, 100
    human use 96–7, 100, 159
    management 98–9
    tropical rain 89, 90, 94–7
France 39

Germany 176–7

glaciers and ice sheets 49–51
    deposition 56–7
    erosion 50–1, 52–3, 56
    landforms 51, 52–3, 54–7
Green Revolution 163, 164
gross national product (GNP) 212

health 214, 218–19
hurricanes 88, 216

Indonesia 114
industry 28–9, 41
    developing countries 178–81
    footloose 169, 174
    heavy 172–3, 183
    high-tech 174–5, 182
    light 174
    location 170–1, 182–4
    Rhine-Ruhr region 176–7
    as a system 168–9
    types 166–7, 174–5
inner city areas 134–5
interdependence 209, 222–3, 224
irrigation 115, 163
Italy 18

Japan 17

Kenya 203–5, 207

land reclamation 110–11
land use
    coasts 68–9
    glaciated areas 58–9
    mountains 10–11
    river basins 40–3
    landscapes 19–30
    chalk and clay 26–7
    granite 22–3
    limestone 19, 24–5, 29
latitude 78, 79
LEDCs
    cities 128, 130, 140–4
    farming 158
    industry 178–81
    population problems 109, 112–15
    tourism 203–5
    trade 222–3, 224, 225

Malaysia 161
MEDCs
    cities 128, 130
    population problems 109, 110–11
    trade 222–3, 224
Middle East 119
migration 114, 116–17, 120–2
Mississippi River, floods 46–7
Montserrat 5, 14–15

National Parks 19, 29, 198, 200–2
natural hazards 216–17
Netherlands 111, 157

pollution, reduction 194–5, 208

population
    demographic transition 107
    distribution 102–3, 104, 105
    growth 106–7, 112–13, 188
    migration 114, 116–17, 120–2
    problems 109, 110–15, 118–19
pyramids 108
    structure 108–9
precipitation 77, 79, 81

quarrying 28–9

rainfall see precipitation
refugees 118–19
resources
    conservation 185, 194–5
    energy 188–9, 190–2, 196–7
    types 186–7
    use 188–9
rivers
    basins 32–3, 40–3
    channel 34, 36, 37
    deposition 36, 37–8, 39
    erosion 34, 36
    landforms 34, 37, 38
    lower course 37–8, 42–3
    middle course 36, 48
    regimes 44–8
    upper course 34–5, 40–1, 48
rocks
    economic uses 22, 25, 27, 28–9
    types 20–1
rural-urban fringe 138–9

settlement 27, 41
    growth 124–5, 128–9, 140–4
    hierarchy 126–7
    site and situation 124–5
    urban zones 123, 130–7
shanty towns 140–1, 142
soils 93, 95

technology, appropriate 164
tectonic activity 5–18
    plate movements 6–7
Tees, River 40–3, 172–3
temperature 77, 78–9, 80–1
tourism 198–9
    impact 206–7
    LEDCs 203–5
    UK and Europe 10, 29, 41, 59, 201–2
trade 220–3

UK
    climate and weather 75, 80–1, 82–7
    farming 148–9, 150–3, 154–6
    industry 182–4
    population 104, 121
urban zones 130–7
urbanization 128–9, 140–4

volcanoes 7,
    eruptions 5, 14–15, 18
    formation 12–13

water supply 41, 86, 219
waterfalls 31, 35, 55
weather 75, 82–7
weathering 30, 53